'This is a deeply impressive work, a truly global history of cricket, that draws on a wide range of sources and is itself elegantly written. This is both sports history and social history, as Heller and Oborne analyse the influence of class, gender, race and empire on how cricket has been played in different times and different places. The book is celebratory when required, yet does not shirk from drawing attention to the darker side of cricket (and of some well-known cricketers). Full Circle deserves, and shall surely get, a wide readership among cricket fans all across the globe.'
Ramachandra Guha, author of *The Commonwealth of Cricket*

'A proper, meaty history, independent in perspective, global in its sweep and trenchant in its judgments.'
Gideon Haigh, journalist and author

'A remarkable account of cricket's fascinating journey from its origins, capturing all major events which have shaped the game and its governance, to the present day.'
Ehsan Mani, former President of the ICC

'This encyclopaedic journey through the history of the game confirms the romanticism of cricket's self-anointed purists as completely delusional, if not outright dishonest.'
Fazeer Mohammed, cricket commentator and journalist

'Original, informed and beautifully concise, this most readable general history moves beyond tired colonial tropes and conventions to help us understand the dynamic changes the global game has experienced in the past 100 years.'
Professor André Odendaal, author of *The Story of an African Game* **and project co-ordinator of The History of South African Cricket Retold, 1795–2025 series**

FULL CIRCLE

A HISTORY OF CRICKET

RICHARD HELLER &
PETER OBORNE

Elliott&Thompson

First published 2026 by
Elliott and Thompson Limited
2 John Street
London WC1N 2ES
www.eandtbooks.com

Represented by:
Authorised Rep Compliance Ltd
Ground Floor, 71 Lower Baggot Street
Dublin, D02 P593
Ireland
www.arccompliance.com

ISBN (hardback): 978-1-78396-944-9
ISBN (trade paperback): 978-1-78396-845-9

Copyright © Richard Heller and Peter Oborne 2026

The Authors have asserted their rights under the Copyright, Designs and Patents Act, 1988, to be identified as Authors of this Work.

All rights reserved. No part of this publication may be reproduced, stored in or introduced into a retrieval system, or transmitted, in any form, or by any means (electronic, mechanical, photocopying, recording or otherwise) without the prior written permission of the publisher. Any person who does any unauthorised act in relation to this publication may be liable to criminal prosecution and civil claims for damages.

9 8 7 6 5 4 3 2 1

A catalogue record for this book is available from the British Library.

Typesetting by Marie Doherty

Printed by CPI Group (UK) Ltd, Croydon, CR0 4YY

To all my family, especially all those who discovered how to straight drive when I bowled at them. To my cat Theo, who occasionally left his favourite sleeping place on my computer to allow me to work on the manuscript. To all the cricketers worldwide who taught me, an American intruder, to love cricket, even the early ones on the school playground who said 'Oh no, it's your turn to have him' when teams were selected.

Richard Heller

To all those teachers at Eagle House School who taught me to play and love cricket, including the maths teacher Mr Murray, the Latin teacher Mr Mitchell and Paul Wootton, headmaster. Without them, I would never have written this book.

Peter Oborne

CONTENTS

Note on Naming Conventions		xi
Introduction		xiii

PART ONE • ORIGINS

1	Born in Obscurity	3
2	The Rise of the Leisure Class	11
3	Technical Change	21
4	A Struggle for Power	25
5	The Impact of Grace	37
6	Women (Re-)Enter the Narrative	45
7	The Challenge of Association Football	53
8	The First Golden Age	65

PART TWO • CRICKET AND EMPIRE

	Introduction to Part Two	72
9	Australia: Birth of a Cricket Superpower	75
10	New Zealand: Cricket's Farthest Realm	93
11	South Africa: Cricket's Original Sin	99
12	Cricket Reaches the Indian Subcontinent	111
13	West Indies: Destined for Glory	117
14	North America: Cricket's Failed State	123
15	South American Odyssey	131
16	The Uniqueness of Irish Cricket	139

PART THREE • THE IMPACT OF WAR

17	The First World War and Its Aftermath	151

18	The First Women's Test Matches	161
19	Bradman, Bodyline and Empire	165
20	The Expansion of Test Cricket	185
21	The Second World War and Its Aftermath	191
22	After the War	203

PART FOUR • THE EMPIRE STRIKES BACK

23	The West Indies Emerge as a Major Power	219
24	Independence and Separation	233
25	The Battle Against Apartheid	239

PART FIVE • THE SECOND GOLDEN AGE

26	Cricket Reinvents Itself	251
27	Test Cricket Widens and Deepens	269
28	Features of the Second Golden Age	285

PART SIX • CRICKET'S UNDERSIDE

| 29 | Corruption and Scandal Stain Cricket | 295 |
| 30 | The Return of Racism | 307 |

PART SEVEN • WAITING FOR THE BARBARIANS

31	Permanent Revolution	319
32	The ICC Expands Cricket Globally	329
33	Cricket Comes Full Circle	347
34	Cricket Reborn	357
35	Does Cricket Make Money to Exist or Exist to Make Money?	371

Acknowledgements	383
Endnotes	388
Index	417

There can be no summer in this land without cricket.
　　　　　　　　NEVILLE CARDUS

*I tend to think that cricket is the greatest
thing that God created on earth.*
　　　　　　　HAROLD PINTER

*In the soft grey silence he could hear the bump of the balls:
and from here and from there through the quiet air the
sound of the cricket bats: pick, pack, pock, puck: like drops of
water in a fountain falling softly in the brimming bowl.*
JAMES JOYCE, *A Portrait of the Artist as a Young Man*

NOTE ON NAMING CONVENTIONS

We have not been consistent in naming cricketers. This is deliberate. Conventions change over time. Modern players tend to be known by their first names (Harry Brook, Denis Compton). In the Victorian era, initials were favoured (W. G. Grace, C. B. Fry). M. C. Cowdrey, also remembered as Colin, was (characteristically) ambiguous. We have chosen in each case whatever usage seemed to us most familiar and natural.

Roughly the same applies to cricket statistics. Garry Sobers hit six sixes in one over off the bowling of Malcolm Nash against Glamorgan in August 1968. However he claimed 6-21 for the Rest of the World in the Lord's Test 1970. We have chosen whatever form looks most natural to the reader.

INTRODUCTION

Two matches played on a single day, 6 April 2024, encapsulate almost all of cricket's history.

One was the opening fixture of the English County Championship at Lord's between Middlesex and Glamorgan. For about a century, such matches were a great day in the cricket calendar, not just for England but for the world of cricket. At their peak, they attracted more than 15,000 live spectators.[1] But that calendar has been progressively elongated, and so this first-class County Championship was being played at a time that would previously have been thought outlandish, forced back into the chill of early April to accommodate a fixture list crammed with other competitions that were more commercially attractive, especially to television.

The prime viewing month of August was given over to a short-form tournament called the Hundred, confected to create new and sellable cricketing assets. The season's Test matches – traditionally at the apex of the English cricket season – were shunted around the calendar to accommodate the upstart tournament. The Lord's Test match against the West Indies, steeped in history since their famous victory in 1950, began on a Wednesday in June during the school term, making the weekend – the peak viewing days for live spectators, especially families – the fourth and fifth days, thus automatically robbing them of excitement and quality. As it happened, a weak West Indies team lost in three days, so all those who had planned for a special day on the weekend at the 'home of cricket' did not see any play at all.

The few hundred who braved a chilly Lord's on 6 April 2024 saw something memorable. Sam Northeast, the Glamorgan captain, recorded the highest individual score at the ground: 335 not out. Another 20,000 or so watched at least some of the innings on the YouTube streaming channels of the two counties concerned. About 24,000 watched highlights online provided by the England and Wales Cricket Board and the MCC.

In times past, Northeast's achievement would have dominated the sports pages of national newspapers and perhaps been mentioned on the BBC's main news bulletin. He might have been offered opportunities for endorsements and his value as a cigarette-card hero for swaps would have risen exponentially. In 2024, the coverage was spotty, terse and generally local. After a brief round of interviews, he went back to the day job, leading players whose total wage bill was estimated at about £1.75 million, at the lower end of the permitted range of £1.5 million to £2.5 million.[2] Glamorgan's highest paid player (more likely its overseas star Marnus Labuschagne of Australia than Northeast) earned just short of £60,000.[3] He and his Glamorgan team were sponsored by a Cardiff printer.[4]

That same day, 4,000 miles away from the self-anointed 'Home of Cricket', another English batter, Jos Buttler, was drawing considerably more attention than Sam Northeast by playing in the Indian Premier League. All in, thirteen English players missed the start of the home summer to take part in the IPL. Seven of them would play no first-class cricket in the County Championship in 2024 and only one, Sam Curran of Surrey, played in more than half of his county's fixtures. Lancashire alone lost four of its brightest lights. Buttler, who has played sixteen T20s and no other cricket for the county since the start of 2020, could be considered to be closer to a club ambassador than a member of the playing staff.

Yet here he was, a Rajasthan *regular*, putting bowlers to the sword. Every Buttler smash was greeted with roars of approval from the 20,000 spectators[5,*] crowded into the Sawai Mansingh Stadium.

---

* There are no official figures, but the average home attendance at Jaipur is said to be 22,119.

The stands were decked out in Rajasthani pink; thousands of Royals-branded flags fluttered in the sky.

The Royals 'represented' Rajasthan in only the loosest sense. Owner Manoj Badale – born in Maharashtra but raised in West London – had assembled a gang of globetrotting mercenaries: coaches from Sri Lanka, Zimbabwe and New Zealand; players from England, New South Wales and the West Indies.[6] Their sole Rajasthani player, Kunal Singh Rathore, remained on the bench all season.[7]

Nonetheless, the noise was deafening, whereas for much of Northeast's innings, you could hear a pin drop. The IPL is beamed into living rooms in every corner of the earth – in India alone, five years' worth of TV and streaming rights sold for $6.02 billion.[8] The County Championship has long since abandoned its quest for commercial broadcast partners.

The most salient difference was in player pay. Buttler received about £900,000 for IPL 2024.[9] Across the season, he faced 255 balls – far fewer than Northeast batted away in the Championship's opening match. Still, by IPL standards, he might be considered a bargain: Australia's Mitchell Starc was paid £2.35 million for his services,[10] well in excess of Glamorgan's salary total for their entire squad.

In this book we peer into cricket's prehistory in a family of stick-and-ball games with a multitude of local variations, flirting with the idea that it was not invented in England, as maintained by cricket historians from H. S. Altham onwards. By the late sixteenth century it had acquired enough basic identity to be referenced in the English language and in legal proceedings, and later in the political and religious battles of the early Stuart era.

After the Restoration, it became organised as a commercial entertainment, to attract spectators into public houses and induce them to buy food and drink. It developed its first symbiotic relationships with media, promoted by local newspapers and helping to sell them. Although still played with countless local variations in rural communities it also became a more organised leisure pursuit for aristocrats, providing a pretext for entertainment, the display of property and wealth – and above all for gambling. It acquired its first Laws to settle bets.

By the early nineteenth century, cricket had acquired enough popularity to be exported by Englishmen away from its rural heartlands in the south-east into London and the new urban centres created by the Industrial Revolution, and overseas by conquest and commerce and settlement. It had also generated enough revenues to become a minor industry that sold books and merchandise and provided a largely itinerant profession for the best players. It had also acquired the semblance of national governance through the Marylebone Cricket Club or MCC, a preserve for the landed upper class leavened grudgingly by the admission of new money and entrepreneurship, and later granted a layer of moral authority by the rise of a class of teachers at public schools of whom Altham was an outstanding manifestation. For all these advances, cricket remained 'only a game' – a leisure pursuit with enough following to give it some commercial salience.

In the Victorian era, however, cricket evolved from a game into an ideology. It came to teach the values that were thought necessary to build an empire: grit, determination, self-sacrifice, restraint. It tried (without complete success) to purge itself from betting, corruption and dissipation. Victorian cricket also became an agency for patriarchy, social hierarchy and, as it expanded into British Dominions, racism.

Most sports embody a creative but unstable conflict between the individual and the team. English cricket, like a regiment, put the team first. 'Team player' was one of many cricketing metaphors, along with 'straight bat', that entered the English language and came to embody the British approach to government. The grand viziers who controlled cricket created structures that rewarded these values, above all the long-form county game and Test matches. Three days minimum became the marker of first-class status. These structures also suited the leisure hours of the English upper classes both at home and when they exported themselves to their imperial possessions and their commercial empire.

The system was challenged, at first by itinerant professional teams, and later by Saturday leagues based in the thriving cities of the industrial north. These leagues pioneered short-form structures much closer to association football than cricket, and anticipated the dominant form of the game as it is played today. They were more successful commercially, but subverted the control of cricket by the ruling classes, and as a result had to be beaten back. Only by recruiting the greatest paid cricketer of the age and pretending that he was one of them did the amateur controllers manage to do so.

The long ('first-class') form of the game originally established in England was exported across the Empire. Over time, the Dominions (Australia, South Africa, New Zealand) and the colonies (India, West Indies, Ceylon – as Sri Lanka was known while under British rule) would copy the structures, and internalise the values, of the English game. By the 1930s these values were starting to break down. Douglas Jardine, England's captain in the Bodyline series, used 'unsportsmanlike behaviour' – the ultimate crime – to win a Test series (see chapter 19). Political and commercial pressures at the highest level were needed to preserve cricket as an imperial bond.

The Second World War democratised British society and extinguished the Empire. Nevertheless control of cricket by the British ruling classes continued as if nothing had happened. They eventually yielded control reluctantly in the face of national and global political, social and commercial forces too strong to resist. The past twenty-five years have seen revolutionary change. The structures of English cricket, and the assumptions that lay behind it, are being washed away. Test match cricket has been consigned to near irrelevance and the English cricket establishment is now set on the destruction of the traditional county game. The changes have been driven by money, reflecting a power shift to media owners and the men who finance them. India has replaced Britain as cricket's hegemon.

In the process, cricket has come full circle. T20, the dominant short form of the sport, has more in common with the Georgian game. Now as then it is dependent on wealthy benefactors, with Bollywood stars and industrialists replacing landed English gentry as patrons of teams and employers. As in the Georgian era, betting and corruption have become a major feature. The links to communities, and even to the nation state, have been wiped out by franchise tournaments. Although commercial forces in world cricket are inescapable, we will argue that these ill-effects are not inevitable.

Part One
ORIGINS

Village cricket spread fast through the land. In those days before it became scientific, cricket was the best game in the world to watch, with its rapid sequence of amusing incidents, each ball a potential crisis!

G. M. TREVELYAN, *English Social History*, 1942

Of all the inventions that ever worked a revolution in cricket, nothing had more effect than the heavy roller and the mowing machine.

R. H. LYTTELTON, 1892

Once in my heyday of cricket,
One day I shall ever recall!
I captured that glorious wicket,
The greatest, the grandest of all.

ARTHUR CONAN DOYLE
(on dismissing W. G. Grace), 1922

Chapter 1

BORN IN OBSCURITY

Most of cricket's history can be found behind a small shopfront in a quiet suburban street in Surrey, forty minutes on the commuter train service from London Waterloo. John McKenzie, England's premier cricket bookseller, has been in the business for over fifty years. On our visit, he claimed ruefully that he was overwhelmed by his ever-expanding stock of cricket books and memorabilia across two floors and eight rooms. But we were certain that he could put his hand to any one of the 10,000 or more volumes on his shelves, each numbered and catalogued. Sure enough, like a conjuror, he pulled out two of his treasures.

The first was an edition of Britcher's Scores – a precursor of Wisden. Its full title is *A Complete List of All the Grand Matches of Cricket That Have Been Played in the Year 1799*. At this stage, bowling was still underarm; pitches, even at Mr Lord's first ground in London, were rough and ready – 10 was a fine individual score and 50 a respectable one for a whole team. Scoring was still done by notches and sticks, and Mr Britcher must have gone to pains to reconstruct the match details.

The other treasure was an 1804 edition of T. Boxall's *Rules & Instructions for Playing at the Game of Cricket*, the first English cricket manual. It included instructions for measuring the pitch as 22 yards, running up and holding the ball and from where the bowler might deliver it, and the latest Laws (from 1800) including the limit on bat width (4¼ inches) to frustrate the ingenious Mr White who played with one as wide as the stumps.

Quietly, McKenzie dropped his most startling fact. 'At that time, only I think about four hundred books were published each year.' The appearance of Britcher's and Boxall's titles therefore showed that a market for cricket had already developed in Georgian England, when the game had no organisational structure and was barely codified.

If an obscure medieval reference can be trusted, English cricket was first recorded in 1299–1300, when King Edward I paid £6 to one Lord John of Leek for helping his teenage son, Prince Edward, play games with his friends.[1] The only game mentioned by name is 'creag'. Major Rowland Bowen, the eccentric scholar who produced a comprehensive and radical history of cricket, wrote magisterially: 'No one, scholar or other, has ever come up with any other explanation than that "creag" was cricket.'

It would be nice to believe this, for it would make Lord John the earliest recorded cricket coach.[2] He was hugely well-paid by today's standards. Six pounds in 1300 would have bought him seven horses or thirteen cows, and represented 600 days' wages for a skilled tradesman.[3]

There are glimpses of bat-and-ball games that *might be* cricket in Church sources even before the mysterious 'creag'. These references date from what might be called the pre-history of the game. A stained-glass window at Canterbury Cathedral around 1180 showed a 'Boy/Man with curved stick and ball' as part of the Six Ages of Man. In 1344, Flemish artist Jehan de Grise illustrated the *Romance of Alexander*. He produced the first image of something that looks like an organised game of cricket. Now in the Bodleian Library at Oxford, it shows a nun about to throw a ball at close quarters to a left-handed monk swinging a bat. Her delivery looks easy to hit but there is a quartet of monks and nuns waiting for a nick in the slips.[4]

It is striking how many women are playing this game, but they disappeared from any published narrative or illustration of cricket or any game like it for the next 400 years.[5]

In 1369, Edward III banned something called 'pila baculorea' because it was interfering with archery, the foundation of his military effort in the wars against France. It is usually translated as 'club-ball' but there is no description of the game concerned and the term could refer to any number of local games in which people hit a ball with a stick.[6]

The earliest history of cricket is therefore almost totally speculative. It relies on interpreting terms such as 'creag', or 'pila baculorea', including 'wicket' and 'bail', which of course survive into cricket today, in documents scattered across many places and long distances.

According to Bowen, the first reference to 'cricket' comes from present-day France. In 1478, a letter to King Louis XI from a traveller to Thérouanne, a town in the Pas-de-Calais, complained about a disagreeable encounter with some locals playing a game called 'criquet'. This ended in a riot, which resulted in the first cricket-induced death. It was little use complaining to the French king since the cricketers were subjects of the independent Duke of Burgundy.[7] This is the source of the claim that the French invented cricket.[8]

There are also representations from the Netherlands, Belgium and Ireland,[9] and from present-day Asian countries, especially Iran, Pakistan and India. The latter claims the surviving game of *gilli-danda* is the origin of all games in which a ball is hit with a stick, asserting that this concept reached Europe in the tenth century CE through gypsies and traders.[10] This theory gains some plausibility from the fact that no ancient Greek or Roman game looks anything like an ancestor of cricket.

All of these theories are entertaining studies not only in sport but in chauvinism, but they each founder on imprecision. At this distance we do not know what games people played with stick and ball, and whether they can be regarded as proto-cricket, proto-rounders, proto-hockey or proto-golf. The one certainty is that specific references to cricket first appear in England in the Elizabethan period and with a growing frequency unmatched in any other country. The references are thickest in the south and east of England, especially around the Weald of Sussex, Surrey and Kent. In London young Prince Edward played 'creag' and other games under Lord John of Leek in 1300.

The first formal record of cricket, in a court case of 1598, identifies it as a game played at the Free School in Guildford around 1550. The following year, Signor Florio mentioned cricket in his English–Italian dictionary in terms that suggest a shrill game played by chirping boys.[11] Oliver Cromwell was reputed (on admittedly slender evidence) to have played cricket at school and then at Sidney Sussex College, Cambridge.[12] John Churchill, 1st Duke of Marlborough, may have played it at St Paul's School.[13]

Intriguingly, the boys of Stonyhurst College, founded in 1593 as a Jesuit school for exiled English Catholic families at Saint-Omer in northern France, played a distinctive version of cricket there; single-wicket, one batter at a time rather than a pair. This survived the school's relocation to England into the age of photography. The boys may have taken this form with them from England, but it is equally likely that they absorbed it from the local French population. It feels significant that Saint-Omer is fewer than ten miles north of Thérouanne, scene of the riot in 1478.[14]

Both Rowland Bowen and Derek Birley, the social historian of English cricket, make a suggestive negative inference about the status of early English cricket. They note that other monarchs followed Edward III in proclamations banning sports and pastimes for a variety of reasons, especially public order, policing the Sabbath day, striking at privileged pre-Reformation clergy, and the protection of archery. England's longbow- and arrow-makers were as skilful in lobbying as modern military contractors long after their contribution to national defence had faded. They had particular influence on Henry VIII. Conversely, in 1616 James I courted popularity among sports lovers resisting Puritanism by allowing a list of sports to be played on Sunday so long as they did not interfere with divine worship. Cricket does not appear in any of the lists of banned or permitted sports. That would make sense if cricket was considered unimportant, as a children's game or a sporadic local entertainment.[15]

In this context, it is significant that there is no reference to cricket in the entire works of Shakespeare – although he uses images from fifty other sports and pastimes, including football, real tennis, hunting, hawking, cards, chess, dice, bear-baiting and many childhood games.[16,*] One can only assume that a cricketing image would have meant little to Shakespeare's adult audiences, whether royal, noble or lower-class 'groundlings'.

The start of organised cricket

The early Stuart period sees the first evidence of English cricket as an adult entertainment in organised matches between villages. A 1640 court case records a match at Chevening in Kent about thirty years earlier.[17] The first recorded on-field death was recorded in 1624 at Horsted Keynes in Sussex. The dead man was a fielder, Jasper Vinall, hit on the head by a cricket bat. The batter was making a then lawful attempt to prevent a catch by striking the ball a second time.[18] A generation later, in 1647 another fielder, Henry Brand, met a similar fate, though the exact circumstances are not clear.. A further hundred years would pass until the Laws of Cricket outlawed the lethal practice of hitting the ball twice.[19]

Some records show cricket being drawn into religious conflict. Chichester, in Sussex, seems to have been a hotbed. In 1611 in the nearby village of Sidlesham, two cricketers were prosecuted for not going to church. Eleven years later in the nearby village of Boxgrove, six men were prosecuted for playing cricket in the churchyard – traditionally a place of rural recreation but during this period a religious battleground. At East Lavant in 1628, ten cricketers were not only fined the standard shilling (roughly a day's wages for a skilled tradesman) for missing church but also forced to make a public confession of their sin.[20]

---

* In *The Two Noble Kinsmen*, Shakespeare's last play, a collaboration with John Fletcher, there is a reference to stoolball, which has been described as a cousin of cricket and baseball.

A case in Kent the following year is interesting because the defendant was a curate. In the first recorded case of social elitism in the game, Henry Cuffen, of Ruckinge, on the edge of Romney Marsh, justified his rush to 'go and play at Cricketts' immediately after evening prayers because the game was played by gentlemen of 'repute and fashion'.[21] In 1646, a match in Coxheath, Kent, ended up in court in a dispute over betting. The stakes involved were modest enough by later standards.[22] Nevertheless it was an augury of the future of cricket.

Sport in this period was local. An early stagecoach managed at best 5 mph, without suspension on rutted unmade roads.[23] Any long journey carried the risk of foul weather, robbery or plague. Villages played their neighbours and agreed conditions and umpires without any central body of laws and regulations. But Rowland Bowen, based on scattered evidence and inference from the impact of later changes, identified some common features of the games known as cricket at the time. In particular he asserts that the basic game was double-wicket (that is, a pair of batters[24,*]). The ball was bowled all along the ground and a batter had to defend a wide low wicket of two stumps with a curved bat. There were three main modes of dismissal – bowled, run out and caught (the ball often popped on rough surfaces) – and, as noted in the cases of Vinall and (possibly) Brand, a batter could frustrate an attempted catch by hitting the ball twice.[25]

Both Bowen and Birley have argued that cricket may have been a beneficiary of the English Civil War.[26] The victorious Parliamentarians cracked down on almost all amusements in London and other large towns. Some Royalist landowners suffered confiscation but most were allowed to sit out the Interregnum on their estates. With no conventional courtly amusements they might have turned to cricket, already the pastime of their tenants.

---

* We use the term 'batters' because women may have taken part in early village matches although no one saw fit to record them.

Cromwell's repressive measures against popular entertainments ceased with the Restoration. These did, however, leave two lasting legacies that favoured cricket above competing attractions. One was the Puritan hostility to bear-baiting and other pastimes that involved cruelty to animals. The other was Cromwell's linkage of sports with public order.[27] As we shall see, eighteenth-century matches would produce occasional brawls and riots, but cricket was easier to control than cockfighting, bare-knuckle boxing or wrestling (a property that would later favour its take-up by English public schools). Partly for this reason, cricket did not recede after the Restoration ended the crackdown on established pastimes and introduced some new or revitalised ones (yachting, ice skating and horse racing).

Cricket began to develop its long-standing connection with alcohol. Sir John Major, in his superbly researched history of cricket's early years, shines a light on a court case in Maidstone in 1668 where the judge refused to give excise men (local treasury officials) the right to extract taxes from brewers who sold beer at cricket matches.[28]

In 1676 came the first known export of cricket to, of all places, Aleppo in Syria, then part of the Ottoman Empire, by English sailors. The game would take more lasting root in India, where it was first planted by sailors of the East India Company in the early eighteenth century.[29] It's important to realise that the English were not the sole exporters of cricket: the French exported a version of their own to their West Indian colony of St Lucia and the Dutch may have introduced a version years before 1676 to New Amsterdam, later New York. English colonists and visitors are recorded as playing cricket in the American colonies, but not till 1709.[30]

In 1677, the first aristocrat entered cricket's history as a spectator: the Earl of Sussex, married to Lady Anne Fitzroy, one of Charles II's bastards, watched a match at the Dicker ground near his estate in Herstmonceux.[31] By now cricket was embarking on a period of dynamic growth based on three forces that influence it to this day: drink, media and, most eye-catching of all during this period, gambling.

Chapter 2

THE RISE OF THE LEISURE CLASS

In 1710, Zacharias von Uffenbach, a visiting German, watched a cockfight. He noted with concern: 'The people, gentle and simple, they sit with no distinction of place, act like madmen and go on raising the odds to 20 gns [guineas] or more.'[1] Twenty guineas in 1710 was more than a year's wages for a farm labourer.

Uffenbach had witnessed the new frenzy for gambling in late Stuart England: part of a cult of masculine fortitude to make enormous wagers, not only at cards but also on crazy events, and to accept huge losses with equanimity. The politician Charles James Fox lost £140,000 at cards in three years and calmly read Herodotus after each loss. The biological sex of the transexual Chevalier d'Éon attracted bets of £120,000 and a court case, unresolved because the Chevalier refused to provide the evidence. Massive wagers also included pointless feats of physical daring and immense bouts of drinking.[2]

Cricket might have been invented for this new culture. A noted patron, the Earl of Tankerville, gambled £100 that his gardener 'Lumpy' Stevens could land the ball, underarm, on a feather placed on a good length. Tankerville won the bet. Lord March in 1758 bet that he could not post a letter over a certain distance within a set time. He won by having the letter sewn into a cricket ball, which was then thrown by relays of players.[3]

Early cricket, like modern versions, offered multiple contests: early gamblers would bet not just on the result but on the outcome of a single delivery or stroke, leading to practices today known as spot-fixing.[4] In the first half of the eighteenth century, single-wicket challenge matches were popular: two men bowling and batting against each other with a limited number of fielders and no runs scored behind the wicket. But these matches did not give so many opportunities for skilful, informed gambling, and crucially were more vulnerable to fixing.[5] Moreover (like world heavyweight boxing contests), they often required protracted negotiations between the challengers about match conditions. In the next century a match between two champions, Fuller Pilch and Thomas Marsden, took five years to set up.[6] These factors helped convince gentlemen players and gamblers to favour a team version of cricket with preset rules.

In 1697 came the first newspaper report. *The Foreign Post*, a beneficiary of the end of newspaper censorship, covered a 'great match' in Sussex of eleven a side. Significantly, it gave no details of the play, only of the stakes – 50 guineas a side. (It would be characteristic of early newspapers to focus on the stakes and any eminent spectators.) In 1718 a cheating controversy ended up in court after a match at London's White Conduit Fields between eleven 'gamesters' (the name is meaningful) of London and eleven of Kent. The latter were accused of walking out of the match to save the loss of half a guinea per man; the Kent men rejoined with an accusation of forgery. The dispute gave rise to £200 in legal costs, without resolution.[7]

However, shortly afterwards, such stakes became petty as aristocrats promoted 'great matches' as gambling vehicles. The first serious patron was Charles Lennox, Duke of Richmond, grandson of Charles II. In the 1720s, he began regular matches. One of these, in Surrey in 1727 against a Mr Brodrick, was significant for two reasons. The captains agreed a set of rules *in advance*, including conditions for the selection of players, specifically to pre-empt disputes over bets.

Later the duke also selected a local all-rounder, Thomas Waymark, and paid him nominally as a groom but in reality as a cricketer. Waymark became one of the very first professional cricketers (or perhaps even the first 'shamateur'). When Waymark established an independent cricket career, the duke hired a talented replacement,

Richard Newland, a member of one of England's leading cricketing families. His two brothers were outstanding cricketers, but Newland is especially important for coaching his nephew, Richard Nyren, a leading light of the future Hambledon Club and the first cricketer among many to be celebrated in nostalgic literature.[8]

Another landmark in cricket history was the match staged at the Artillery Ground in Finsbury, where 'At the request of two gentlemen *who have laid a very great sum of money* [our emphasis] the ground is to be staked where all gentlemen are desired to keep to the outside of the rope which will be round the ground.'[9]

An even more exalted patron than the Duke of Richmond now entered the scene: Frederick, Prince of Wales, heir to King George II. 'Poor Fred', as he was called in a celebrated obituary poem, was a mediocrity whose driving force was the well-reciprocated loathing of his father. Fred tried to position himself politically and culturally as a patriotic Briton against his Hanoverian father. His adoption of cricket may have been part of this; if so, it is significant that cricket should already have become a marker of English identity. With a base at Kennington, site of the future Oval, which he owned as Duke of Cornwall, he led star-studded teams in two matches against Kent sides led by the sons of the Duke of Dorset for the colossal stake of £1,000 (about £150,000 in today's money) a side. He lost them both but recouped 500 guineas by beating a team led by the Duke of Marlborough. Poor Fred died in 1751 before inheriting the throne – according to some accounts as the delayed result of a blow from a cricket ball.[10]

He and his brother, the Duke of Cumberland, attended 'the greatest match ever known' at the new Artillery Ground in 1744 between Kent (led by Lord Sackville's gardener) and 'all-England', led by Newland.*

---

* It was celebrated in 'Cricket, An Heroic Poem' by James Love, a poet and actor. The poem opens with a long panegyric on cricket as a glorious manly British game, the start of an enduring cultural archetype. The poem is written

That year saw the publication of the first set of Laws intended to govern *all* cricket matches. These laid down a 22-yard pitch, a low set of two stumps, a ball of 5 to 6 ounces, and no limit on bat size. There was no leg before wicket (LBW) law – this was long before pads, even underarm bowling along the ground could be painful and this was thought a sufficient deterrent. The Laws were drawn up by a committee of 'noblemen and gentlemen' in the Star and Garter club, an informal meeting place in Pall Mall. This took place at roughly the same time as a similar effort for horseracing by the more formally constituted Jockey Club. The description as Laws rather than rules is significant.[11] The most important Law of 1744 provided for umpires to be given jurisdiction over disputes. A feature that survives in cricket to this day, uniquely in major sport, is that the umpires give decisions only on appeal from a player.

The 1744 Laws did not last long, being revised in 1774 and 1788. The revisions reflected a search for a game that could be played anywhere, by any group of people, without having to reinvent it each time. All the versions of the Laws were impelled to allow the settling of wagers, but they also had to accommodate a remarkable period of innovation in playing techniques – and to frustrate methods that threatened the game with extinction.

English cricket in the late eighteenth century continued to rely heavily on aristocratic patronage. The death or insanity of some of these patrons, especially Frederick, Prince of Wales, the Duke of Richmond and Lord John Sackville, therefore produced a temporary eclipse and a retreat of cricket to rural parishes. One newspaper suggested in 1767 that cricket would be replaced as a fashionable pastime by golf, another in 1771 spoke of cricket's 'expiring fame'.[12]

But new aristocratic players and gamblers revived 'great' matches. Two deserve special attention. One was the Earl of Winchilsea, for his role in the formation of the MCC with its private ground created

---

self-consciously in the 'mock-heroic' tradition of Pope, Swift and Gay where some (perhaps not all) of the 'manly' narrative is *deliberately* overblown.

by Thomas Lord. The other was the Duke of Dorset, son of the keen cricketer Lord John Sackville. Not only was he a better player than Winchilsea, he was more progressive. He brought distinction to the first overseas excursions. The first, in 1786, produced an exhibition match in the Champs Élysées. The *Daily Universal Register*, soon to be renamed *The Times*, reported this in chauvinistic terms, which would become characteristic of British sports coverage: the French 'cannot imitate us in such vigorous exertions of the body'.[13] The second tour was more formal. Dorset, as ambassador to France, secured the foreign secretary's approval for a goodwill tour to cement the Peace of Paris of 1783. This was aborted by the French Revolution, and England forfeited the chance to absorb France into its cricket system, as it later lost the USA.[14]

This period saw the rise of independent cricket promoters and professionals. Two especially important examples were the Artillery Ground and the White Conduit Club, just beyond the fringes of contemporary London. The White Conduit Club had a rule that 'only gentlemen may play', although they were allowed to hire professionals, especially as practice bowlers. But there were no practice batters: an early example of a long-running division in English cricket, exported overseas, especially to hot countries. Upper-class amateurs preferred to bat and left it to the professionals to bowl and assume the more toilsome or dangerous positions in the field.* The Artillery Ground, run by George Smith, landlord of the Pyd Horse Inn, charged 2d to spectators at matches and gave them the chance to drink his specially brewed ales all day and to bet. Unruly elements prompted a short-lived hike to 6d, abandoned when crowds fell from 7,000 to 200.[15]

---

* This tradition was still prevalent in the late twentieth century at the MCC. Members could drop into Lord's and ask for a ground staff member to bowl at them. Some would have encountered Ian Botham in this role in the early 1970s: they are probably still giving imaginary accounts of their performances against him to their grandchildren. Parliament's team, the Lords and Commons, founded in the 1840s, was run in much the same way until a Labour takeover in the 1990s: MPs and peers tended to bat and field close, staff and other 'hired help' tended to bowl and work in the outfield.

One can trace the beginnings of a recurrent motif in the efforts of the amateur patrons to make use of the essential talents of the promoters and professional cricketers without yielding any of their own control over the game. Despite some eras of weakness and near-oblivion their chosen instrument, the MCC, would dominate the administration of both domestic and later international cricket for 200 years until its abrupt decline at the end of the twentieth century.

The Hambledon Club in Hampshire has been mythologised as the cradle of English cricket. This myth-making was acerbically challenged by Rowland Bowen.[16] But Hambledon *was* significant. First, it was an especially successful example of a cricket promotion: the game was championed there by its leading player, Richard Nyren, to entice trade to his inn, renamed the Bat & Ball Inn instead of the Hut. Second, it gave its leading players a good income from match fees, attracting fine players from further afield and enabling them to work as independent cricketers. The club competed for £30,000 (broadly equivalent to £3.5 million today) in stake money between 1770 and 1790, of which the hired players won over £22,000.[17] Third, these concentrated talents produced dramatic innovations in batting and bowling, which fed off each other, generated new Laws to keep up with them and made the game better to play and watch.

These players were the first to generate a recurring myth of a past golden age. This was the result of the prodigiously successful memoirs of John Nyren, Richard's son (brilliantly assisted by a professional writer, Charles Cowden Clarke), first published in serial form in 1832, long after the club's demise. With Mary Russell Mitford's *Our Village* (which also contained cricket scenes, more accurate than Nyren's book) it promoted a wave of rural nostalgia in an England that was becoming increasingly urban and industrial.

Major talents launched by or associated with Hambledon included David Harris, Tom Walker and 'Lumpy' Stevens. Instead of rolling the ball along the ground, they 'pitched' the ball underarm in the air (one description of Walker's action suggests that he might have discovered round-arm, which was still unlawful).[18] These techniques imparted to all subsequent bowlers the virtues of line and length, while opening up the weapons of flight, spin and swerve. Cricket balls developed by the firm of Dukes in Penshurst, from layered cork and yarn encased in leather with six seams, gave new opportunities to bowlers. Bowen notes that red is 'the opposite end of the spectrum from green' and thus the 'perfect colour' for cricket balls. Dukes' early success indicates demand for a specialised ball for an organised game: the firm would expand greatly in the railway age.[19]

The new bowling techniques inspired a permanent change in bat design. Hambledon's John Small, removed the curve at the bottom, thus creating a flat surface with square shoulders. Small was the first recorded batter to discover the virtue of a straight bat, presented in line with the ball rather than across it, and became renowned as unbowlable. This reputation was assisted by the two-stump wicket. In one match a series of deliveries from Stevens passed harmlessly through the middle and inspired the addition of a middle stump. The first major match with three stump wickets took place on the Duke of Dorset's home ground in 1778.[20]

Thomas White of Reigate went too far in 1773 by using a bat as big as the wicket, prompting a sequence of limitations on bat size.[21] Other important revisions of the Laws included provisions for rolling, watering and mowing the pitch with the consent of both captains, tossing a coin for innings, and in 1811 the provision of penalty runs for wides. All these changes were designed to make the game more attractive to players, spectators and gamblers, especially the last after a match that became becalmed when bowlers bowled deliberate wides, which the batters refused to hit. These revisions were all made by the new MCC, which, with great speed, established itself as the vehicle for regulation of the game.

Romantic accounts of early cricket hail its supposed breakdown of class barriers. The Whig historian G. M. Trevelyan conjured the spectacle of the local squires playing in the same team as their tenants.

If only the French aristocracy had done the same, mused Trevelyan, the French Revolution might never have happened. In fact, English nobility lived in constant fear of the mob and any outbreak of popular feeling was likely to send them scuttling away from any sort of open public gathering into their private homes and clubs, and other places they could fortify. When the Duke of Richmond was manhandled by a crowd in 1731 at one of his great matches (out of disappointment primarily induced by gambling), he concentrated on building a team in the orderly village of Slindon, near his estate at Goodwood.[22]

This fear, which deepened after the French Revolution, was a factor in the demise of Hambledon, which was too open and isolated for nervous aristocrats. Hambledon may have acquired a radical reputation, as is suggested by an unusual visitor to one of its final matches – Tom Paine, defying a conviction for treason that carried a death sentence.[23] Paine may have been the most left-wing cricket lover in England until H. M. Hyndman, a hard-hitting batter for Sussex, who claimed that he became a leading Marxist theorist in disappointment at not getting his cricket blue at Cambridge. Paine and Hyndman started a tradition that stretches through the great post-war Labour prime minister Clem Attlee to the playwright Harold Pinter.

The export of cricket

By the end of the eighteenth century, cricket was established in some form in almost every county in England, except in the far north and west. Fraser Simm, historian of Scottish cricket, dates the first recorded match near Alloa in 1783. Cricket may have been exported to Scotland by English soldiers in the occupying Hanoverian army and later by English workers in Scotland's textile, paper and iron works during the Industrial Revolution.[24]

Historian Dr Andrew Hignell gave us the first reference to cricket in Wales in 1771: a complaint about boys and youths swearing while playing cricket on a Sunday. Until the mid nineteenth century, cricket in South Wales was primarily rural: landowners organised frequent 'country house' matches. Railways and British soldiers en route to Ireland gave cricket a stimulus, as did the arrival of the steel industry in the early nineteenth century.[25]

The first recorded match in Ireland was played in 1792, when Dublin Garrison beat All-Ireland by an innings. Arthur Wellesley, future Duke of Wellington, was one of the players.[26] British commerce exported the game to the Netherlands, Denmark, Portugal (through the port wine trade in Lisbon and Oporto*) and Naples: although played mainly by expatriates it was strong enough in Europe to continue when contact with England was lost during the Napoleonic conquests. Seamen of the East India Company played cricket in Calcutta, Bombay and Seringapatam.† Surviving versions of cricket in France had been exported to its West Indian colony of St Lucia and later to its colonies in Quebec.[27] From the end of the eighteenth century, cricket was recorded at British bases and among British garrisons in the West Indies, the Cape (taken from the Dutch in 1796) and the first British settlers in Australia.[28]

British settlers planted the game in their American colonies. Always tenuous because of distance and communications, contact between American and English cricket was weakened after independence and the new United States missed most of the great innovations in techniques and Laws mentioned above.[29]

The game was regularly reported in newspapers, and the early emphasis on betting and titled patrons was beginning to yield to reporting of events on the field.[30] Significantly, the old system of scoring, by making notches in sticks, was being supplemented by detailed pencil and paper accounts with details of individual events and performances.[31] At the very end of the century, a market developed for books of scores of leading matches, especially Samuel Britcher's

---

* The Oporto Lawn Tennis and Cricket Club still thrives, but the cricket is dominated by English expatriates.
† Now known as Kolkata, Mumbai and Srirangapatna respectively.

sixteen-year series.[32] Cricket's insatiable appetite for statistics was under way.

The year 1801 saw the first instructional book about cricket, by successful professional Thomas Boxall.[33] Many of Boxall's readers were probably upper-class boys at independent schools. The boys organised matches themselves in defiance of authority, which often generated anarchic and alcoholic revelry, punished by mass floggings.[34] A notable example was Byron's Eton v Harrow match at Lord's in 1805.[35] But public schoolboys would continue to play cricket more responsibly at university and in later careers as landowners, officials, parsons, army officers and colonial administrators. They would be an extra force for codification of the game (to allow them to challenge each other and form teams after school). Dr Thackeray, headmaster of Harrow from 1746 to 1760 and an ancestor of the novelist, foreshadowed the Victorians by encouraging cricket as a civilising force.[36]

At this point English cricket fell victim to a multiple squeeze. The French wars drained away manpower into militias and regiments or the press-ganged navy. Aristocratic patrons were removed from the game to act as officers or enter public service (although the Duke of Richmond, as a general, was famous for playing cricket with his men, including a game on the eve of Quatre Bras). The upper classes were impoverished by wartime taxation, including Mr Pitt's shocking and supposedly temporary introduction of income tax at 2d in the pound. Fear of the mob and sedition not only inspired fierce legislation[37] but also accelerated the aristocracy's retreat into private recreation.

Agricultural enclosures accelerated and removed recreational land. Modern manufacturing destroyed cottage industries, sucked labour from the countryside and truncated leisure hours, since expensive new machinery could not be left idle.

Cricket itself became less attractive to players, spectators and gamblers as the result of gamesmanship and betting scandals. The result was years of stasis, unblocked eventually by the next great invention, round-arm bowling, and galvanised by railways and public schools.

Chapter 3

TECHNICAL CHANGE

The Eton–Harrow match was revived at Lord's in 1818 (it had been suspended after Byron's post-match revelries in 1805) and became an annual commercial success after 1822. Harrow produced a crop of fearsome early fast bowlers who went on (perhaps in atonement) to become clergymen. The future Reverend W. Marcon smashed one opponent's bat and wicket with his first ball, and broke another batter's unpadded leg.[1]

Marcon and his Etonian colleague Harvey Fellows had a wicketkeeper standing well back and three long stops behind him. In official history, they bowled underarm. It seems impossible for them to have created such terror with pure underarm pitching, and it is likely that they experimented, like other bowlers, with the possibilities of a raised arm, assisted by a clumsily drafted MCC Law and the compliance of umpires.

Round-arm bowling differs from underarm in being delivered at shoulder height. It allows a much faster and fuller arm motion, and gets more advantage from a run-up. For those who could control its direction, it allowed not only more speed and bounce but brought swing into play (curving the ball in the air as late as possible). In modern times, its dynamic possibilities were revived by the self-taught Sri Lankan Lasith Malinga, much imitated by young players in defiance of coaches. In the nineteenth century, with uneven pitches and unprotected batters and wicketkeepers, it was lethal.

After the professional Tom Walker's early experimentation with round-arm, which earned him an outright ban at Hambledon, the next major experiment was by the Kentish amateur John Willes. There is an enduring legend that he learned round-arm in imitation of his sister, Christiana, who could not bowl underarm because of her hooped skirts. This has been much debunked, since hooped or otherwise-voluminous skirts were unfashionable in Christiana's time. The debunkers do not allow for the possibility that she might have discovered round-arm independently without such prompting.

For the next decade or so a characteristic battle broke out between cricket's old guard of administrators and players, and innovatory bowlers and their followers. As with modern battles, it was fought out in sporting media as well on the field and in committee rooms. In the media the main supporters of the old guard were William Denison, cricket correspondent of the *Sporting Magazine*, and John Nyren (and his ghostwriter). The innovators were two Sussex players, William Lillywhite (the 'Nonpareil') and James Broadbridge. They were supported by a Kentish bowler who was also an unusually forward-looking member of the MCC, G. T. Knight.

Knight arranged some 'experimental' matches allowing the use of round-arm, which provoked a rebellion by traditionalists (yet more precursors of later times). The MCC clung to its unworkable 'hand-below-the-elbow' Law. Lillywhite and Broadbridge and a host of local imitators exploited this to use their own methods, and the MCC eventually capitulated. A momentous revision of the Laws legitimised round-arm using Knight's formula: the ball was to be bowled, not thrown or jerked, with a straight arm at or below shoulder height.[2]

Three early superstars

An examination of scorecards in this period shows how hard it was to score rapidly or even at all on uneven pitches and rough, barely cropped outfields. It was common to see four completed innings of fewer than 100. Ten was a good score for an individual batter. The advent of round-arm bowling slowed matters still further. Study of the batting averages of the three greatest players of the age – Fuller Pilch

(18.61); Nicholas Wanostrocht, known as 'Felix' (18.15); and Alfred Mynn (13.42) – shows the difficulty of scoring runs.

Round-arm gave rise to a technical revolution in the invention and use of protective gear by batters and wicketkeepers. This was stimulated by a terrible injury to Mynn in a major match in 1836. He characteristically ignored the battering of his unprotected leg by the new round-arm deliveries to score his only first-class century, then collapsed in pain, was carried away and narrowly escaped amputation.[3]

In underarm days, Robert Robinson had experimented with boards of wood strapped to his legs. The derisive laughter when these were hit led him to abandon them. Wicketkeepers and even long stops experimented with sacks of straw and thick leggings in the 1820s. Round-arm saw an immediate revival of pads, initially concealed under trousers for fear of looking unmanly. In the 1840s they were advertised extensively, generally made from cork, although Felix recommended them in the form of longitudinal rubber strips within stockings. He also promoted his own invention of gloves with finger stalls but gave the patent away before he made much money from it. The 1850s saw specialised wicketkeeping gauntlets and the earliest advertisements for 'boxes' to protect the genitals, the first described as a 'cross-bar India rubber guard', the second as 'Palmer's Patent Groin Protector'.[4,*]

Round-arm had a permanent influence on bat technology. English willow became the preferred wood, yielding the right balance of strength and lightness, and separate cane handles were spliced into bats to absorb the shock of the new fast bowling.[5]

No new technology changed cricket more than the lawn mower. In 1830, Edwin Budding of Stroud invented a cylindrical push mower,

---

* One invention that failed was Mr Emanuel's inflatable gloves, although in the 1930s the eccentric cricket patron Sir Julien Cahn used pads inflated by his butler for fielding.

and soon after gave a manufacturing licence for it to the firm of Ransome's of Ipswich. In 1854, Mr Shanks found a way of getting the machine pulled by a horse (giving rise to the expression Shanks's pony) and in 1859, Thomas Green improved mower design still further by incorporating a rake.[6]

Rollers were widely used from the round-arm era onwards, drawn by horses. Horse boots then had to be invented to stop them from cutting up the pitch.[7] By the 1860s, rollers, horse boots and mowers were being advertised extensively.[8] The resulting improvements in pitches hugely benefited batters, especially Grace, rewarding footwork and placement.

Characteristically the MCC resisted the new technology and pitches at Lord's remained terrible, under the care of scythes and sheep. When James Dark, its owner, borrowed one of the new mowing machines, a reactionary committee member, Robert Grimston, enlisted a gang of navvies to smash it.[9,*] But Lord's eventually caught up with the new science of pitch preparation and appointed its first full-time groundsman in 1865.[10] A generation later the noted all-round sportsman R. H. Lyttelton wrote in the 1892 *Wisden*: 'Of all the inventions that ever worked a revolution in cricket, nothing had more effect than the heavy roller and the mowing machine.'[11]

---

* Grimston, an old Harrovian, coached many boys at the school in the same spirit. In fairness to him, the *Dictionary of National Biography* dwells on his work as a pioneer of the electric telegraph.

Chapter 4

A STRUGGLE FOR POWER

By the start of the Victorian epoch, Britain was changing at incredible speed from a slow-moving agrarian society to an industrial powerhouse. New cities and towns were springing up, while the railways had developed as the first external technology to transform cricket. The old class divide between a landowning class and subordinate village labourers and craftspeople for the time being survived. But an increasingly prosperous middle class was on the rise and, with it, an avid market for entertainment, especially in towns.

To grasp the nature of the conflict within cricket at this pivotal moment, it helps to recall that similar arguments convulsed other areas of public life. The middle class demanded political representation, and achieved it through the Reform acts of 1832 and 1867. At Westminster, the Conservative Party split over a battle between the landowners, championed by Benjamin Disraeli, who demanded protective tariffs against imports of foreign wheat, and manufacturers who demanded cheaper food, marshalled by Robert Peel. That momentous argument was ultimately won by the free traders.

In cricket, the leader of the rebels was a portly, one-eyed bricklayer who supplemented his income by playing professional cricket in Nottingham. After marrying Mary Chapman, owner of the Trent Bridge Inn, William Clarke enclosed the field behind the pub, and established the Nottingham Club for paying spectators. Clarke would enjoy a proud place in cricket history as the founder of one of England's premier Test match grounds if he achieved nothing else. However, in the mid 1840s, he could not make Trent Bridge compete with the free cricket available elsewhere in Nottingham, so he delegated the venture to his stepson and sought employment as a ground bowler for the MCC.

There Clarke, already forty-seven, showed his playing conservatism by continuing to bowl underarm although the new round-arm action had been legal and usual for ten years.[1] However, in one respect Clarke was an insurrectionist. His often unplayable on-field lobs were accompanied by a volley of loaded comments and his off-field behaviour, especially in business matters, was abrasive.

Through the MCC, Clarke met leading players, including Alfred Mynn, Felix and Fuller Pilch. This was his eureka moment. He hit on the idea of combining all of England's major cricketers, including himself, into one permanent touring eleven. The one-eyed bricklayer had spotted a new market. Like Kerry Packer more than a century later, he exploited the fact that professional cricketers were underpaid and could be enticed away from their existing employers.

Even when in work at Lord's or the Oval, ground staff rarely, if ever, earned in a week the £4 that Clarke offered his players per match. That sum represented nearly a month's wages for a skilled tradesman. The players, initially, did not object to Clarke collecting a guaranteed £70 a match himself, and often a good share of receipts and sponsorship income on top.

Clarke took his team away from London and the south-east to British industrial centres. In 1847, the team's venues were Leicester, York, Manchester, Birmingham, Sheffield, Leeds, Newcastle-upon-Tyne, Stockton-on-Tees and Stourbridge, all hubs of new manufacturing wealth. In 1848, the touring itinerary expanded to include Derby, Bradford, Coventry, Sunderland, Darlington, Chelmsford and Southampton.

On the playing side, Clarke enlisted established stars such as Felix (like Mynn, a nominal amateur but glad of Clarke's match fees as 'travelling expenses'), William Lillywhite (in his fifties still the 'Nonpareil' of round-arm bowling), the grandly named but depressive Julius Caesar and England's best wicketkeeper-batter, Tom Box.

Clarke also introduced new talents, including the fast-scoring George Parr and John Wisden, a devastating bowler who would later become more famous for other reasons.

The team were received by civic dignitaries on arrival and given banquets at the end of their matches, where Clarke liked to devour an entire goose after confining himself to a cigar and a glass of soda water during play.[2] They played against local talents who were often ready to pay for the privilege. Their matches attracted crowds of thousands (in which local newspapers regularly noted the presence of fashionable women), providing great opportunities for local caterers and bookmakers who had been driven out of Lord's and other amateur-controlled centres in the 1820s. One match in Manchester attracted more than £40,000 in betting turnover.

Clarke's success was built upon Britain's new railway network. He realised that with meticulous planning, trains (some reaching the incredible speed of 50 miles an hour) could take his team to many more matches in new cricket centres than had ever been possible before. Clarke's son, Alfred, was in his eleven; although not much good as a player, he was a master of railway timetables and fare deals, and therefore the organiser of its tours.[3] To Clarke senior belongs the disgrace of the first recorded act of sporting hooliganism on a train, in 1846. It was narrated by a later famous Victorian cricketer, Richard Daft. Asked by a porter to stop smoking his cigar in a non-smoking compartment, Clarke extinguished it on the porter's hand. It is an unpleasant story, made worse by Daft's treatment of it as a jolly joke.[4,*]

Railways are a golden thread in the history of cricket, making national competition possible in every current Test-playing nation (with the exception of the West Indies and Afghanistan). In later years, we will see railway workers as exporters of cricket to Scotland and Wales and beyond to Britain's formal and informal commercial

---

* To balance the many stories of his greed and boorishness, it is fair to note that Clarke donated substantial sums to local charities and old players' testimonials.

empires. We will see enduring railway-based teams, including in Pakistan the winners of cricket's most comprehensive first-class victory. We will see more examples of railway hooliganism, especially by white cricket tourists against local people. We will see railways used to reinforce class distinctions in cricket: in India, visitors travelled first-class and local players third-class. We will see a great cricketer nearly murdered on a train.

The introduction of the penny post, which travelled by rail, galvanised the organisation of cricket fixtures by providing for the first time a reliable national service, paid by the sender.[5] It hugely increased the power of cricketers and spectators to share their experience with others. The railways also enabled the second ingredient that facilitated Clarke's tours: the rise of the national sporting press. As we have seen, cricket was occasionally reported in eighteenth-century papers, but almost invariably in the context of fashionable spectators or betting rather than the cricket itself. By the 1840s a specialist press had become the main source of information about forthcoming fixtures and new club formation. Classified advertisements in cricket-related media were the main labour exchange for professional cricketers, coaches and ground staff.

Bell's Life was the major source of cricket reporting in this period, and it grew thicker and more vivid. In 1838, it covered 130 matches over five weeks. In 1843, the total rose to 230 over a longer period; in 1848, 400 and by the 1860s about 500, by which time it was facing much greater local competition. There was also a spate of cricket statistical reference books: Haygarth's *Scores and Biographies*, Bat's *The Cricketer's Manual*, Denison's *The Cricketer's Companion*, *The Young Cricketer's Guide* by Fred Lillywhite (William's son), and finally Wisden's first *Almanack* itself, in 1864 (padded out with non-cricketing information, including astronomical events and historic anniversaries).[6] With the betting market for cricket in sharp decline, these books were bought for pleasure rather than as a form guide. The period also saw a wave of instructional books, most famously Felix's eponymous study *Felix on the Bat*. Clarke produced one of his own:

almost his last act was to give a copy to the mother of a very young spectator – W. G. Grace.[7]

Cricket and Victorian morality

Clarke's peak season was 1851. By this stage he was running a highly successful commercial cricket enterprise under professional leadership. That year his team played thirty-four matches, mostly in the north. These contests were a response to the hunger for entertainment generated by the commercial exuberance of early Victorian Britain.

Suppose that at this juncture a time-travelling Kerry Packer could have surveyed English cricket. He would probably have concluded that Clarke's tours foreshadowed a future for the sport based in the urban centres where most people lived, a sport moreover adapted to their leisure hours. Clarke's vision could have reshaped Victorian cricket completely and displaced its amateur organisers, as would later happen with association football. So why did this not happen with cricket?

In 1852, Clarke's star bowler, John Wisden, walked out on him and formed a rival team with its own circuit: the United All-England Eleven. In 1854, Clarke lost another key player, the all-rounder Billy Caffyn. Clarke himself died in 1856, having taken a wicket with his last delivery in first-class cricket.[8] Yet these setbacks were not in themselves the reason for the failure of the project to commercialise cricket. More profound forces explain why the landowning establishment, against all the odds, would emerge as unlikely victors.

At the start of the nineteenth century cricket was governed, insofar as it was governed at all, by the more sporting elements of the Georgian aristocracy. They viewed cricket as a vehicle for betting and needed an even playing field to avoid disputes. They entertained no generous view of the larger interests of the game.

This landowning aristocracy were in retreat socially and politically even before Victoria became queen. The rising middle class were determined to wipe out what it viewed as the 'old corruption'. But reformers did not look to entrepreneurs such as William Clarke as the means. They were intent on keeping his commercial values out of cricket. While it is true that Clarke was the first to professionalise the game, he can also be understood as the last gasp of the publican promoters who sponsored cricket in the Georgian era.

As the political philosopher David Marquand brilliantly set out in his masterly *Decline of the Public*, the early Victorians invented what he calls the 'public domain'. Writing in the 1990s of this 'gift of history, and of fairly recent history at that', he argued:

> It is literally a priceless gift. The good of the public domain cannot be valued by market criteria, but they are no less precious for that. They include fair trials, welcoming public spaces, free public libraries, subsidised opera, mutual building societies, safe food, the broadcasters of the BBC World Service, the lobbying of Amnesty International, clean water, impartial public administration, disinterested scholarship, blood donors, magistrates, the minimum wage, the Pennine Way and the rulings of the Health and Safety executive.[9]

Most of these things did not yet exist in the 1840s, but it is fair to say that this was the decade that cricket became public property. Marquand notes that 'in the public domain, market power is overridden, and private clientelism forbidden'. That is exactly what happened to cricket. Aristocratic power was defeated, but free market capitalism kept at bay. The game became part of what H. C. G. Matthew, biographer of the standard-bearer of Victorian morality William Gladstone, refers to as part of a 'vast network of voluntary organisations' animated by active citizens, involved in local affairs and in charitable organisations of all sorts. Cricket became part of Britain's public space and very quickly part of its language. This improbable outcome would shape not just the sport but also the British sensibility for more than a century.

The rise of the public schools

In the 1820s and 1830s, numbers at England's boarding schools, including the so-called seven 'great schools', had gone into sharp decline, a reaction to appalling living conditions and discipline that veered from anarchy to sadism. Their narrow syllabus provided a smattering of classical learning to the sons of landed aristocracy who would never expect to use it, and who taught themselves more, in their own time, about drinking, gambling and abusive sex.[10]

These schools were particularly unappealing to families with new wealth. They wanted their sons to learn useful skills for business or public administration, and they did not wish them to be brutalised and starved (although some schools then and later were skilled at suggesting that these things were good for character-building).

From the 1840s the decline dramatically reversed itself. Moribund schools revived and expanded. They were joined by dozens of new foundations and by conversions of former private proprietary schools (owned by their headmasters) into independent schools where the head teacher was a manager appointed by independent governors. (This mirrored the contemporary creation of limited liability companies, managed by servants of their shareholders.) These institutions were major beneficiaries of railways, which made it far safer and cheaper than the stagecoach for families to send away their children to board. Shrewsbury was almost the only significant exception: it lost its former competitive advantage from its location on the old stagecoach route to North Wales and Ireland.[11]

Of course it was not enough to be near a railway station. Boarding schools improved their curriculums and teaching methods, but even more importantly they changed their discipline and ethos. In this they relied to a remarkable extent on organised games and, within these, cricket was assigned almost mystical powers to shape character and inculcate morality.

This shift is commonly attributed to Thomas Arnold at Rugby, even though he was uninterested in cricket. Before Arnold, headmasters at the traditional schools of Eton, Harrow, Winchester and Charterhouse discovered the attractions of organised cricket matches between houses as a safe means of channelling energy and aggression, and forestalling the regular riots of the previous century.

It kept boys on school property, and away from pubs and bookmakers, over a long period on summer days. (Apart from boys playing, it also required the attendance of boys scoring, umpiring or retrieving lost balls, and headmasters were quick to discover the advantages of compulsory spectatorship.) Arnold did not like games, but he saw these advantages and recognised astutely that boys themselves would establish hierarchy and codes of behaviour through organised competitive team sports if they were allowed to make the major decisions themselves, especially the selection of teams and the award of colours in different degrees with different scales of privilege.

Arnold's influence was indeed paramount in establishing cricket as a moral engine, partly because he trained so many disciples but even more because Thomas Hughes' idealised view of him in *Tom Brown's Schooldays* was a runaway success, selling 11,000 copies in its year of publication, 1857.

Hughes had many successors. Some 70 per cent of all cricket fiction titles before 1979 were written for children and the great majority of these were about boys at public schools. This takes no account of such stories published only in children's magazines. These works had a huge following beyond public schoolboys, and in the Empire, as attested by C. L. R. James in *Beyond a Boundary*. They projected a stereotype of the best sort of cricketer and the best sort of leader, in which individual ability was less important than playing the game honourably and supporting one's teammates. Such chaps always volunteered for extra responsibilities and even personal danger without thought of reward.[12]

Arnold's more fervid followers created a remarkable cult of sport and physical fitness in the idea of 'muscular Christianity'. The term's inventor, Charles Kingsley, regarded a robust body as essential for the harmony of body, mind and soul: both he and Herbert Spencer considered physical training more important than intellectual. They and other muscular Christians endorsed physical strength as good and godly if not used against the weak, and identified all frailty as a sign of unnatural vice, to be overcome by prayer, discipline and exercise.[13]

Cricket success at school was thought to be a sign of moral as well as physical health. Many schools gave their capped cricketers the privilege of walking arm in arm and, informally, the privilege of 'taking up' younger boys, acting as their heroes and mentors.[14] A notable fictional example is E. F. Benson's successful school novel *David Blaize*. Two boys some years apart in age have an intensely romantic relationship but they are both fine cricketers, so there is no suggestion of 'beastliness'.*

Under the influence of Anglican muscular Christianity, Non-Conformist clergy abandoned their general opposition to sport dating back to the Puritans. They began to promote it instead, through their own teams and cycling clubs, and the delightfully named Pleasant Sunday Afternoon Societies. In the 1880s, the evangelical minister Thomas Waugh published *The Cricket Field of The Christian Life*, in which godly Christians bat against cheating Satanic bowlers (incidentally reinforcing cricket's informal hierarchy of batters over bowlers).[15]

Some Victorian headmasters fretted about the strength of the cult, especially Edward Thring at Uppingham and George Cotton at Marlborough (a disciple of Arnold who appears as the 'young master' in *Tom Brown's Schooldays* and takes part in the extraordinary schoolboy conversation defining cricket as a national institution akin to habeas corpus). But none could resist the demand for cricket from pupils and their parents, or the temptation to use it for marketing.† Some schools went to extraordinary lengths to promote their cricket. At Harrow, a housemaster was given three days' special leave

---

* Benson's novel was published in 1916, which suggests the durability of such idealised relationships.

† This continues very strongly to the present day.

to compose a song in honour of the cricket achievements of a pupil, F. S. Jackson.[16]

Schools competed intensely to secure the services of England's leading players as coaches. School seasons began earlier and earlier to offer them short-term engagements before their professional commitments began. Caffyn coached at Brighton, Cheltenham, Clifton, Haileybury, Wellington and Winchester, while James Lillywhite (senior) worked at both Marlborough and Cheltenham. Some former players had long relationships with a single school, for instance the fierce H. H. Stephenson, captain of the first England touring party to Australia, at Uppingham.[17]

Notwithstanding their experience and proficiency, the professional coaches were kept aware of their inferior status to staff and pupils. They were expected to support and endorse the doctrine that public schools were the nursery of all that was best in the game, that prowess in public-school cricket was a marker of good character and that leadership in it was a preparation for leadership in later life. Indeed, they were expected to look down on their own calling as professional sportsmen and accept that people who were not paid to play (perhaps for not being good enough) were better representatives of the spirit of the game.

The public schools transmitted this view of cricket – and themselves – deep into the British establishment when their alumni went on to Oxford or Cambridge, and then entered domestic or imperial government service, the Church of England, the law and other professions, or took up their responsibilities as landowners. Public-school values were nourished still further by a spate of private cricket clubs founded in the mid nineteenth century to allow old boys to continue playing each other, notably I Zingari, the Free Foresters and the Harlequins (whose red, yellow and blue cap was felt by enraged Australians to be a calculated insult when worn by Douglas Jardine in the Bodyline series).

Against such a nexus of authority, the professionals had little power of resistance when their own cricket enterprises faded in the

1860s. They were glad to accept employment from the public schools, either directly as coaches and ground staff, or indirectly when public-school alumni created and subsidised county clubs.

Even with these formidable advantages, the public-school amateurs might not have wrested back control of the game without suborning the greatest and most influential cricketer of them all.

Chapter 5

THE IMPACT OF GRACE

No athlete in history has done so much to change the course of a sport as W. G. Grace. His achievements were on such a spectacular scale, and he became so overpowering a national figure, that it is instructive to compare him to Benjamin Disraeli. Both men reached national pre-eminence in the late 1860s: Disraeli when he succeeded Lord Derby as Tory leader; Grace when he burst onto the scene as a sportsman of unsurpassed brilliance. Both used their own astonishing gifts, bordering on genius, to rescue moribund British institutions.

The Tory Party was facing the prospect of slow extinction when Disraeli became leader. It found it hard to attract any audience beyond the shires and seemed doomed to irrelevance till Disraeli made it a national party with an appeal not just to landed gentry but also the middle classes and even to working men. Grace achieved something similar with cricket, expanding the constricted amateur interpretation of the sport for the benefit of the wider nation.

Both cases are paradoxical. Disraeli and Grace were outsiders. Disraeli was urban, with Jewish heritage, literary, brilliant – everything the Tory Party wasn't and much that it despised. His natural home was probably as a mid-Victorian radical. The same applied to Grace, whose grandparents were domestic servants. He did not belong to the amateur elite, and it always regarded him with suspicion and resentment.

His talent was so staggering, and generated such a following, that he was able to set his own terms for participation. He elected to join England's cricket establishment, thereby saving it – and preserving its ideology that amateurs were the highest exponents of the game and its natural leaders. In exchange, the establishment allowed him to make staggering sums for playing cricket without any of the social stigma attached to being a professional sportsman. In so doing, he also embedded hypocrisy at the heart of the game, where it remains to this day. Disraeli struck the same sort of deal with the Conservative Party.

Statistics show how Grace towered over his contemporaries. One is the longevity of his first-class career, with an unmatched span of forty-four years. Four English batters stand ahead of his total of runs: Jack Hobbs, Frank Woolley, Patsy Hendren and Phil Mead. All were from a later generation and played most of their innings on better pitches. Only Woolley was a bowler as well. It is easy to forget Grace the bowler (initially brisk round-arm medium, later guileful slows) but only nine bowlers have taken more career wickets and just two, Wilfred Rhodes and J. T. Hearne, had any overlap with him, both in the later part of his career. Of any contemporary, Rhodes alone approaches Grace's total of catches, second only to Woolley's.

Grace was eighteen when he scored his first century (a double, undefeated one) for MCC against Surrey. He was excused from appearing on the last day to run – and win – a national athletics trophy for the 400-yard hurdles. Five years later, he was the first batter to score 2,000 first-class runs in an English season, with an average of 78. The next average (of the highly regarded Richard Daft) was 37.[1]

By 1875, aged twenty-seven, he had scored his fiftieth first-class century. No other batter had approached this, and none would reach it younger until Walter Hammond, by seven weeks, in 1930. While Grace was making his fifty hundreds, his contemporaries managed a total of 109 (the nearest competitor, hard-drinking Harry Jupp of Surrey, assembled twelve). Grace scored nearly a third of all the centuries made in his first decade of first-class cricket. Not even Don Bradman, who completed a century in over a third of his first-class innings, ever achieved that superiority over his contemporaries.[2]

There is endless testimony, especially from the leading bowlers of the time, to his stamina, technique and shot selection, especially his ability to play equally well off front or back foot, on any pitch against all types of bowling.[3,*] He benefited from another innovation in cricket technology: the light cane-handled bat. His father and maternal uncle gave him one and taught him to play straight with it, rather than hit across the line with the club used by his elder brother, E. M.[4] Aided by his height (at 6 foot 2 inches, about nine inches taller than the average for a late Victorian male[†]), his magnificent physique and, of course, the black beard that was his gift to artists, he carried an aura to the wicket that would later be attributed to Bradman, Garfield Sobers and Ben Stokes.

Grace on his own was enough to sustain and animate a team. The greatest beneficiaries were the Gentlemen in their regular contests against the Players. Their last twenty matches before Grace produced nineteen defeats and one draw. In Grace's first decade, the Players won only three times, five matches were drawn and eighteen won by the Gentlemen, and he had made the fixture England's prime cricket attraction.[5] H. S. Altham hailed his impact on it as the most remarkable feature of his 'monumental history'.[6]

Grace was not the first sportsman to become a nationally recognised figure: the boxers Tom Cribb, Jack Broughton and Tom Sayers preceded him. But he was certainly the first cricketer, and his longevity and international performances made him a representative of English character and, in the long Victorian peace, helped sport to replace war as an indicator of English superiority over foreigners. At the outset, the queen's long seclusion following the death of Prince Albert made him almost a substitute monarch.[7]

---

* Grace finally retired just after the invention of the googly in the 1900s and faced it only in a club game from the South African maestro, A. E. Vogler, one of a quartet who bamboozled England. He survived it and passed on the advice to watch it off the pitch.

† The commonest cited contemporary figure for Grace's height is 6 foot 2 inches. The *Memorial Biography* of him by Lord Hawke, Lord Harris and others adds another half-inch.

Newspapers made it easier to read about him; railways made it easier to see him than any previous idol. Indeed, Grace's domestic career was made possible by railways, which enabled him to combine first-class engagements as a nominal amateur with lucrative non-first-class personal appearances. In his busy 1873 English season, he played twenty first-class games: twelve in London, the others in Kent, Gloucestershire, Hove and Sheffield. He also played twenty-three non-first-class matches, but only four in London. The others took him to Gloucestershire, Kent, Hertford, Oxford, Darlington, Salford, Northampton, Lincoln and Scotland. He finished his match in Lincoln on 6 September and promptly took off by train for Inverness.[8]

Grace was the first sportsman to be used regularly to sell newspapers and magazines. He also pioneered the sale of non-sports goods. In the 1890s, an image of him stepping out from a pavilion was captioned 'Colman's Mustard Like Grace Heads the Field'.[9,*] His image was still used after his death, appropriately to promote the Stamina brand of self-supporting trousers in the 1920s.[10]

Grace was the first English sports performer of international repute. This enabled him to extract the staggering sum of £1,500 as 'expenses' for his first tour of Australia in 1873–74, a sum which represented over twenty years' wages for a skilled tradesman. Grace also managed to secure a free first-class honeymoon for his wife, Agnes. The professionals on the tour received a basic £150 and £20 spending money. For his second tour, in 1891–92, his expenses were doubled and two of their children – Bessie, aged thirteen, and Charles, aged nine – joined him and Agnes.[11]

Just as railways had enabled his domestic career, the steamship and the Suez Canal facilitated his international appearances. En route to his second tour of Australia, he became the first great cricketer to

---

[*] Colman's was a notably welfare-minded firm who invested heavily in sports facilities for their workforce in Norwich. Its head, Sir Jeremiah Colman, was a cricket lover who created a decent cricket library and became President of Surrey CCC.

play in Malta and then in Ceylon, on a stopover in Colombo. After a cameo, he for once agreed with the umpire that he was out and went to rest in the shade.[12]

The privileges of amateurism

Grace's paternal grandparents were both in domestic service. His grandfather had figured as a sinister butler worthy of Victorian melodrama in a celebrated fraud trial. Grace's widowed grandmother had escaped the resulting stigma by opening a school. Their son achieved respectability by becoming a doctor. Grace's mother, Martha Grace, was the daughter of an eccentric private-school proprietor who experimented with kite-powered carriages, published radical pamphlets and quarrelled with the local leaders of his Methodist faith.[13]

Both of Grace's parents had a huge influence over their four sons. It was unthinkable for them to compromise their hard-won social ascent by becoming professional sportsmen.*

At this distance, it is hard to understand the intensity of the Victorian taboo against being a professional sportsman, or even training and practising like one. It was in part a hangover from the Georgian era in which sportsmen were part of the domestic household of their aristocratic patrons (typically cricketers as gardeners, pugilists as bodyguards, and jockeys as stable lads and coachmen). As noted already, it also had an overlay of the new public-school ethics, which exalted playing sport in the right spirit above the pursuit of victory and reward. The 1850s onward were a great era for forming sports clubs, and most of these went to extraordinary lengths to define

---

* Grace's medical skills have been unfairly disparaged. Notwithstanding his frequent absences, he treated many poor people personally and without charge. After a terrifying accident at a county match, he gave prompt aid to his colleague A. C. M. Croome, who forever credited him with saving his life, although there is also evidence that Grace's role was exaggerated to form part of his legend. Grace was certainly no worse than many celebrated contemporary practitioners, such as Sir Morell MacKenzie, the eminent laryngologist who fatally misdiagnosed Emperor Frederick III of Germany, Queen Victoria's son-in-law.

who was eligible for membership as an amateur and a gentleman. Britain's rowers needed three separate organisations, for gentlemen, tradesmen and professional watermen respectively.[14]

Grace was never a full member of the cricketing or any other establishment. In spite of his role in the revival of the Gentlemen, he was not appointed captain until there was no alternative: he was also a delayed choice as captain of England.[15] Although he played frequently against I Zingari, he was never asked to represent them or to join any other elite wandering club.[16] He was often the object of snobbery and mocking comments on his West Country accent or dirty neck.[17,*] Although he was the saviour of the MCC, the club never offered him any influential position (only eventually the status of life membership). He never received any official honour, although Asquith included him in 1911 among the 500 or so men proposed as peers to force through the Parliament Bill and Lloyd George's radical People's Budget.[18] Grace, a lifelong Conservative, was a curious choice: perhaps he was put there to reassure the new king, George V, who had reluctantly agreed to the mass creation.

Grace did not go to public school or Oxbridge. But even that might not have guaranteed passage into the cricket establishment. Many gifted amateurs from public school and Oxford or Cambridge never achieved this either, including C. B. Fry, Archie MacLaren, Gilbert Jessop, Percy Fender and later Trevor Bailey.[19] All of these picked up some undefined black mark. Grace's public behaviours gave the establishment ample grounds for his exclusion.

One was his appetite for money. His career earnings as an official amateur were estimated at £120,000.[20] Applying that sum to his final first-class year, 1908, it has a present-day purchasing power of about £18.4 million.[21] In 1879, some committee members of his county, Gloucestershire, which was virtually a family fiefdom, nerved

---

* Grace himself admitted cheerfully that he was not fond of bathing. On his first Australian tour, he waved aside the apologies of a hotel keeper for his lack of bathrooms, saying 'We Graces ain't no bloody water spaniels.'

themselves to attempt to cut his expenses and those of his brothers. They were rebuffed. In the same year, *John Lillywhite's Cricketers' Companion* (an early competitor to *Wisden Cricketers' Almanack*) accused him of making more profit from cricket than any professional. The MCC, which had connived in his amateur status, denied the charge with a blustering lack of conviction and gave him a testimonial that raised £1,458 and some silver artefacts. Its present purchasing power would be about £230,000.[22] A second testimonial in 1895 (his late annus mirabilis) raised a further £9,000, including contributions from the Queen and the Prince of Wales.[23]

It is instructive to compare these figures to the benefits* obtained by leading professionals in Grace's time. Counties had no obligation to give them, and some set difficult qualifying conditions or refused them altogether. The biggest benefit before the First World War went to George Hirst of Yorkshire: £3,703 in 1904. The batter Grace admired most (apart from himself), Arthur Shrewsbury, got £900 in two benefits. The bowler who dismissed him more often than any other, Alfred Shaw, had a disastrous benefit of just £130 in 1892 (to his credit, Grace topped it up with the proceeds of one of his own second testimonial matches).[24,†]

As an official amateur, Grace got away with conduct for which a professional would have been severely punished. Incidents were either hushed up (as with his potentially criminal assault on a teenage boy[25]) or weaved into a suitable part of his legend (larger than life character ... endearing rogue ... monarch of the game ... hearty, natural Englishman ...). His regular gamesmanship, intimidation of umpires, exploitations of his personal authority and earning power were all excused in such ways.[26] They caused no concern to the young Clement Attlee, who told the Cricket Society towards the end of his

---

* In another example of social stratification, cricket professionals received benefits and amateurs, testimonials.

† Shrewsbury and Shaw suffered for their temerity in leading a pay protest at their county, Nottinghamshire, in 1880.

life that 'for him and his schoolfellows cricket was a religion and W. G. stood next to the Deity'.

The Labour leader and prime minister might have added that had W. G. Grace chosen a different path, and remained loyal to the social class from which he emerged, he could have revolutionised the game. In the process, he would not simply have made a fortune for himself, but improved the economic circumstances of his fellow cricketers, too. Although he could be personally generous with his immense wealth, he chose not to do this. W. G. Grace's cricketing achievement was prodigious. It was also selfish. He turned cricket into a Tory sport and his spirit lives on today.

Without Grace's decision to claim amateur status, one can conceive of an alternative direction for cricket – one in which league cricket would have come to dominate the English game using the same model as football. Long-form cricket might not have come into being at all, nor become recognised as the game's supreme form. Short-form competitive cricket would have been the version exported to the Empire – and thus used for international matches.

With no reward or reverence for the amateur, talented players would have found less stigma in joining the professional ranks. Cricket could have had a very different influence on the English class system as a whole, rewarding entrepreneurship and achievement, rather than inherited status and social shibboleths.

Chapter 6

WOMEN (RE-)ENTER THE NARRATIVE

Barring one medieval illustration of monks and nuns playing a game that appears to be cricket in 1344, women are invisible in the records and representations of the game's early history.

It is likely that over the next four centuries women joined in cricket-like sports not only in England but other countries. But there is no record of them playing cricket till the women of two Surrey parishes, Bramley and Hambledon (not the famous Hambledon in Hampshire), became the first in history to have played a match on 26 July 1745.

The date of this match makes sense. From the early Tudor period till the end of the seventeenth century, Britain had endured what the social historian Lawrence Stone defined as an era of 'reinforced patriarchy and discipline'. This was a function of the Puritan movement, which grew in influence from the Reformation and was driven by a blind determination to remove Catholicism from British life.

Puritanism, described by the American satirist H. L. Mencken as the 'haunting fear that someone, somewhere, may be happy', was opposed to public enjoyment. This explains why so many records of the sport from the early Stuart period involve prosecutions of cricketers. If men could be punished for playing cricket, it was altogether out of the question for women.

The situation began to improve after the death of Oliver Cromwell and the return of monarchy. An early sign was the emergence of female actors. As patriarchy relaxed, women stepped forward to play roles in other spheres. There were women boxers in the Bear Garden in London in the 1720s – and some legendary female smugglers and even pirates. Women writers and artists appeared. New wealth brought demand for leisure. Horse racing and cricket were two beneficiaries. It would not last for long. History does not move in a straight line. Puritanism would return in the shape of evangelism and Methodism at the start of the nineteenth century, holding back the growth of men's cricket and putting paid to the women's game for a generation.

The next recorded women's match, in 1747, was somewhat grander and sponsored by George Smith, the proprietor of the Artillery Ground in Islington. He paid the expenses of two teams of Sussex village ladies to perform there. Like the important men's matches he staged there it was intended as a vehicle for betting (although punters can have had little guide to the form) and he evidently thought it would attract spectators even at his highest admission charge of sixpence. In this he was wrong, because the game had to be halted following crowd protests at his prices.[1]

Local newspapers then began to record more and more village matches in the south of England involving women. Often staged as Married v Single, these games attracted gambling. Unlike contemporary men's matches they were rarely played for large money stakes, but they often had prizes in kind of considerable value at the time. One example was the regular Married v Single Women of Upham, Hampshire in the 1760s, when the winners carried away a plum cake, a barrel of ale and a 'regale' (choice sample) of tea.[2] These matches were played by lower-class women. One notable aristocratic exception is recorded, staged in 1777 by the Countess of Derby at her rural retreat at the Oaks in Surrey. The star performer was Miss Elizabeth Anne Burrell, sister of Lord Gwydir, the best batter at the elite men's White Conduit Club. Her batting certainly attracted the attention of one of the spectators – her future husband the Duke of Hamilton. Another spectator, the Duke of Dorset, was reportedly inspired to a ringing tribute: 'What is life but a game of cricket? And if so, why should not the ladies play it as well as we? . . . Let your sex go on and assert their right to every pursuit that does not debase the mind.'[3]

A major milestone came in 1811 with the first county match between women's teams: Hampshire v Surrey. It was cruelly caricatured by Thomas Rowlandson at the time, but twenty years later all the players' names were recorded in the *Book of Sports* of Pierce Egan, the father of British sports reporting.[4]

In 1833, the women cricketers of Sileby, near Loughborough, got too drunk to play. The male reporter said that they had shamed their menfolk.[5] In view of the behaviour of male cricketers then and since, the incident could be viewed as an early mark of equality.

From the 1840s onwards, women of all classes almost disappeared from the narrative of English cricket for a whole generation. The already few leisure opportunities for labouring women contracted even further with longer working hours and the unpaid demands of households and children.

Upper-class women were denied opportunities for serious cricket by Victorian expectations of their role as supporters and admirers of their husbands in both their occupations and their leisure activities. They were occasionally allowed to provide an amusing diversion – and romantic opportunity – in country-house cricket. They would play matches at odds against men compelled to play left-handed (a social taboo made natural left-handers unusual among gentlemen cricketers) and use broomsticks for bats.

Victorian patriarchy was reinforced by medical advice about the delicacy of women and the dangers of stress or injury. Of course, the most famous cricketing doctor had to weigh in. W. G. Grace wrote magisterially: 'Cricket is not a game for women, and although the fair sex occasionally join in a picnic game, they are not constitutionally adapted for the sport.'[6]

Girls' public schools and their revival of cricket

Girls and women from affluent families were delivered from cricketing exile by a succession of girls' public schools over the second half of the nineteenth century. Often caricatured in fiction and (later) film, these schools and their founders and early teachers should be credited as pioneers. They offered their pupils a chance to experience life outside home, and a better and wider education than they could obtain from governesses. The best of them resisted the assumptions that girls were naturally weak and passive.

Roedean, Wycombe Abbey, Clifton Ladies and Royal High Bath were early adopters of cricket for girls, as were the Chantry School in Frome, Abbots Bromley in Staffordshire, Moira House in Surrey and St Leonards in Scotland, which became a special powerhouse of cricket. By 1897, Roedean had formed eight teams from barely a hundred pupils. As early as the 1870s, former public schoolgirl cricketers had asserted their right to play 'serious' cricket and form clubs of their own. The most celebrated was the White Heather Club, launched in 1887, whose seven founders, mostly from the Brassey and Neville families, were tired of the derisory games they were offered by men at their country houses.

Cricketing talent (allied to connections and marriages that gave them access to excellent pitches and facilities) made membership an attractive prospect. The batting of one early star, Lucy Ridsdale, won an admirer and a husband, a wealthy ironmaster called Stanley Baldwin, later a long-serving prime minister. She supported the club, and cricket generally, for the rest of her life. During the General Strike of 1926, she held a committee meeting of the club in the Cabinet Room. Another club member, Lady Marie Brassey, married a Sussex amateur cricketer called Freeman Thomas. As Lord Willingdon, he would become Viceroy of India in the 1930s, where she helped him exercise a baleful influence on Indian cricket.[7]

Other notable women's clubs, playing serious cricket, were the Derbyshire Ladies, or 'Dragonflies', Severn Valley and Clifton Ladies, who benefited from the big hitting of Bessie Grace, the most talented of W. G.'s children. Tragically, she would die before him. In 1887, another Miss Grace, no relation, scored the first recorded double century by a woman, at Burton Joyce in Nottinghamshire. In 1901, Miss Mabel Bryant* made 224 not out in Eastbourne for the Visitors against the Residents in 135 minutes, and then took ten Resident wickets and smashed a stump.[8]

The thriving women's scene attracted the notice of the veteran cricketer Richard Daft. He suggested astutely that their performance might benefit from lighter bats and balls (instead of borrowing from their brothers or other men) and a shorter pitch. The leading sports goods retailer, Gamages, commissioned Readers to produce a lighter ball for the new women's market in 1897. Unfortunately, they thought women would appreciate a pretty colour and chose light blue, which was not ideal for use under a clear summer sky. A lighter red ball (at the now official weight of 5 ounces against the men's 5½) was not introduced until 1929 and lighter adult bats had to wait for another thirty years or so.[9]

New sports for New Woman

In 1895, *Cricket* (by then the most authoritative journal of the game under the editorship of the ubiquitous Charles Alcock, of whom much more in the next chapter) remarked astutely that 'The New Woman is taking up cricket, evidently with the same energy which has characterised her in other and more important spheres of life.'[10] New Woman was a term recently coined by the bestselling American novelist Sarah Grand for advocates of votes, higher education and rational dress for women, and the end of sexual double standards. By extension, it came to apply to any young woman making or seeking any independent personal choice. In cricket, the most dramatic

---

* Bryant went on to play top-class cricket into her fifties, and also excelled at hockey, lacrosse and swimming.

example was Helen Archdale, a leading suffragette, imprisoned for throwing stones through the windows of the National Liberal Club, stones supplied to her by her young daughter, Betty, a future captain of England.[11]

In the late nineteenth century, a number of developments identified with New Woman gave a lift to women's cricket. One was the Rational Dress Society. It urged women out of thick voluminous dresses and constricting (and dangerous) corsets. Under its influence, women cricketers adopted lighter and freer clothing. Those at Cambridge women's colleges adapted a new invention – the tunic – for cricket.[12]

Martina Bergman-Österberg was a pioneer for physical education for women and as a profession for women. She set up a series of training colleges in and around London, which included cricket in their curriculum. Her trainees at Dartford were coached by a male professional, Mr Ballard. Many of her graduates would take their love and expertise for cricket to girls' schools and inspired the next generation of women cricketers, including Marjorie Pollard.[13] (Discreet romantic crushes on the young games mistress would become a staple of girls' school fiction.)

Bergman-Österberg, a eugenicist, argued forcefully against the male fiction that sport was a danger to female reproduction: on the contrary, she held that it created healthier, stronger women whose children would raise the stock of humanity.[14]

Apart from inspiration, Bergman-Österberg gave women cricketers a new profession. More than a third of the women who represented England before the Second World War were physical training teachers. Middle- and upper-class women cricketers were the main beneficiaries of her work: sadly most girls in state elementary schools were confined to gymnastics, netball and rounders.[15]

Finally, the growth in admissions of women to higher education kept female cricketers together and gave them a motive to continue playing the game. This happened in women's colleges in Cambridge and London before the First World War, but not in those at Oxford, which, in a display of obscurantist conservatism, banned cricket for being too masculine. Hitchin College (later Girton), Cambridge was an early adopter of cricket, first playing informal matches on its hockey pitch, then, on the eve of the First World War and playing in long tunics, progressing to organised matches against other colleges and universities and engaging a professional coach.[16]

By 1914, English women had pushed their way back into the record of English cricket. However, they were heavily concentrated in well-to-do families who gave their daughters an independent education. Women's participation in cricket would broaden during both world wars and in the interwar period, but amateur control of England women's cricket would persist even longer than for men's, and women of all classes remained heavily dependent on men to secure access to cricket.

Chapter 7

THE CHALLENGE OF ASSOCIATION FOOTBALL

The amateur establishment had captured Grace and seen off the professional competition. But the fundamental problem remained: the ramshackle structure of the amateur game with its curious, otherworldly mix of university teams, social clubs and a fixture list whose highlights were the Gentleman v Players matches and annual Eton v Harrow social fixtures at Lord's.

Association football offers an alternative history by which to consider the course cricket might have taken. Both football and cricket emerged fairly recently from obscurity to become national sports. In each case their early history is almost totally obscure, although we can surmise that there were countless different variations in numberless towns and villages up and down Britain. As late as the 1840s annual football matches were often a pretext for general mayhem and violence, aggravated by protest at attempts to ban them. Conditions were not much better in the versions played at public schools, where massed scrimmages and legitimate personal assault often caused lasting casualties. Public-school football did not acquire the moral ideology of public-school cricket.

Organised football in Britain began along the same lines as cricket: an attempt by amateurs to seize control. In 1863 a group of former public schoolboys met at Cambridge to agree a set of rules to govern the wide variations in forms of football played at different schools. They were seen off. Enduring snobbish rivalries between schools gave them little force and the attempt by 'gentlemen' to shape the future of the sport failed.[1]

Football only took off when people of a different class – especially from urban centres such as Sheffield, Manchester and Glasgow – demonstrated a better way to play it and run it. Predominantly working-class players from these cities produced a fluid, mobile game based on passing: predominantly middle-class entrepreneurs recognised its attractions, and organised matches and competitions that spectators were willing to pay for.[2]

Association football began its life with natural advantages over county cricket. Matches were much shorter: football promoters could guarantee working-class spectators a completed result on the Saturday half-day that was becoming normal after successive legislative restrictions on working hours. Football clubs put down strong local roots in cities, unlike county cricket clubs, which tended to wander all over their counties. Matches required less expensive specialised space in cities. The game itself was easier to understand and to play. It was simpler for spectators of all ages to become authorities on the game and for the youngest ones to imagine that they might follow their heroes. As an invented, syncretic game, association football had far fewer moral and ideological associations than cricket.

Amateurism nevertheless continued in football, especially in the control of early internationals and selection for them. School teams with such demotic names as Old Etonians and Old Carthusians were successful in the first decade of the FA Cup. But the nature of the sport militated against the cult of the amateur. Matches were always focused on the achievement of a result within a short period, win, lose or draw.

The professionals played the new passing game much better than amateurs still wedded to dribbling and charging.[3] It quickly became wholly implausible for amateurs to claim leadership in football based on skill. Unlike a cricket team, football teams could not carry a single weak player in any position. There was no room for amateur captains with the right social background and supposed gifts of character and leadership who could not actually play.

In sharp contrast there was no such gulf in talent between professional and amateur in cricket before the First World War. The greatest cricketer of the age, W. G. Grace, was a nominal amateur, and many of his crowd-pleasing successors, including C. B. Fry, K. S. Ranjitsinhji, Gilbert Jessop, F. S. Jackson, Archie MacLaren, Lionel Palairet and Kenneth Hutchings (killed in the First World War), were nominal or even real amateurs.

Football has kept these comparative advantages over cricket in every country that plays both, despite the almost concurrent development of simpler forms of cricket, and more and more complex football analysis. By the last quarter of the nineteenth century, English cricket for the first time faced a serious competitor as a codified team sport with a popular and media following. In the long run, cricket's incapacity or reluctance to fight back would cause it to lose its status as England's national game.

The double life of Charles Alcock

By a significant coincidence one man loomed large in both sports during this formative period. Charles Alcock, one of the greatest and most far-sighted sports administrators of all time, was secretary simultaneously of the Football Association and of Surrey County Cricket Club. His formula in administering both sports could be described as controlled professionalism: good pay and conditions for the sportsmen needed to attract gate money, and the tightest feasible controls on their influence over their sport and their ability to move within it and bargain with their employers. As we shall see, Alcock would be a firm but deft handler of a very rare cricketers' strike.

Yet in every other way, Alcock's approach to cricket and football was different. He was painfully aware that cricket needed to look for revenues outside the sport. This led him to convert Surrey's ground, the Oval, into the first British multisports centre. It staged not only England's first international cricket match but also athletics, cycling, lacrosse, skating, baseball and the new-fangled sport of lawn tennis.

England's rugby union internationals (amateur) also began officially at the Oval, but Alcock's biggest successes as a promoter were the first international association football match and the first Football Association Cup. The first FA Cup final (1872) was hosted at Surrey's Kennington Oval headquarters. Alcock wrote letters to himself as secretary of the FA from himself as Surrey secretary.[4]

An attempt at a knockout competition was tried and failed under MCC stewardship at Lord's the following year. Had it taken place under Alcock's keen and capable entrepreneurial eye at the Oval, history might have taken a different course and cricket would not have needed to wait a further ninety years for its first significant knockout competition, the Gillette Cup. It's hard to overstate the importance of the FA Cup in spreading the popularity of football.

In temperament and methods, Alcock had more in common with the new owners of professional football clubs than with the amateur patrons and controllers of county cricket teams. Under his guidance, amateurs quickly yielded leadership in football administration to club owners.

In cricket it was the other way around. As secretary of the Football Association, Alcock could shape directly the future of football, whereas at Surrey he was a junior partner compared to the potentates who dominated the sport from its MCC headquarters. However, he did acquire influence as founder-editor of a successful magazine, *Cricket*, and he made history as the promoter of England's first home Test match against Australia in 1880.[5]

The birth of the County Championship

Alcock and other football entrepreneurs magnified their advantage by staging meaningful matches, in cups and internationals, with something at stake in the result. The nearest cricket could offer to a structure was the county game. The county system has its origins in the post-Waterloo economic depression. Dire finances squeezed the ability of individual patrons to recruit and maintain a private team. This prompted landowners to become a collective and form clubs based on their counties to organise matches between themselves.

The biggest problem was that county cricket meant little in the absence of formal competition. Counties played whatever matches they chose. They could recruit players from anywhere without birth or residence qualification. There was no system to determine the champion, a status that newspapers started to bestow in the 1860s on different criteria.[6] The MCC, even more useless during this period than normal, did little to promote county cricket, still less organise it. In these chaotic circumstances it is no surprise that some early counties foundered financially. During the 1850s, when the threat from William Clarke's professional touring teams was most dangerous, the entire county system became moribund and almost died.

From the 1860s onwards, the results of the heavy public-school investment started to show up in county cricket, aided by a much more relaxed admissions policy by Oxford and Cambridge (a system that persisted well into the twentieth century, accounting for Colin Cowdrey's otherwise inexplicable presence at Brasenose College in the 1950s). Prominent public-school and Oxbridge amateurs included several sets of brothers, the Walkers, the Steels, the Studds and the three Lyttletons, all of whom were Honourables and one also a Reverend. Old clubs were revived and new ones founded, largely by merger or, in effect, hostile takeover of established clubs. Kent, for example, first played under that name as early as 1709 and became a mighty power under its patrons until the Victorian era. It dissolved into two pieces in 1859 under financial pressure and was revived and reconnected by the Harris family in 1870.[7]

The family's young heir, later the fourth Lord Harris, not only became its captain but the nearest approach to a supreme dictator in English cricket.* He went on to establish a model in which amateurs ran counties with professionals as employees. He wanted them decently paid and provided for in winter and in retirement, so long as they knew their place.[8] The MCC, lacklustre on other issues, came to the aid of Lord Harris's neo-feudal project with the introduction of qualification rules. This reduced the bargaining power of the best professionals and was a key step in Harris's plan to make them all employees rather than itinerant freelancers.[9]

Sussex (formed in 1839 and today the oldest county club with an unbroken history) and Surrey had survived from the earlier era. Nottinghamshire re-emerged in 1860. Its players were nearly all professionals and were generally reckoned the hardest to beat.[10] Middlesex, Hampshire and Yorkshire formed or reconstituted their county clubs in the 1860s followed by Lancashire, Worcestershire, Warwickshire and Gloucestershire. The last was virtually a Grace family property: W. G.'s father its main founder, his brother E. M. its secretary, his eldest brother on its committee and W. G. himself as captain and chief selector. Derbyshire was formed in 1870.[11]

Northern counties enjoyed more patronage from industry and trade than the agrarian south and were generally far better administered. A north–south divide was thus built into English cricket.[12] The leading names in Lancashire and Derbyshire demonstrate a sometimes uneasy alliance between landowners and new urban industrialists, merchants and professional classes. Lancashire's first club secretaries were cotton manufacturers and its first captain a solicitor. Its dominant family were the Hornbys, paternalist industrialists who supplied a long-serving captain, immortalised in Francis Thompson's evocative poem 'At Lord's' with his opening partner, Barlow.

---

* Lord Harris (fourth baron) 1851–1932: amateur captain of Kent and England, Conservative politician and junior minister, governor of Bombay, president of MCC and many influential roles there for over fifty years, largely self-appointed regulator of English first-class cricket, co-founder and leading figure in Imperial Cricket Conference. Born in Trinidad where his father was serving as governor.

Derbyshire's inaugural meeting united the local lace-making concern of Boden and Black with a wine and spirit merchant, a tailor and a surgeon. Like all counties, they sought an aristocratic patron and secured first the Earl of Chesterfield, then Lord Belper and in due course the uncle of Lord Harris, a local landowner.[13,*]

Public pressure eventually forced even the MCC to produce some clarity. In 1890 a County Championship was established with eight contenders: Gloucestershire, Kent, Lancashire, Middlesex, Nottinghamshire, Surrey, Sussex and Yorkshire. A year later, Somerset (a county with good railway connections) was admitted.[14] These nine counties were recognised as 'first-class'.

This status was made formal when the MCC met their secretaries in 1894. Apart from championship matches, this meeting agreed that certain other matches and teams would have first-class status, including the MCC, Oxford and Cambridge Universities (but no others), Gentlemen v Players, North v South, touring sides from Australia and South Africa as of right and other visitors by concession, along with a few elite teams such as Free Foresters and those raised by grandees such as C. I. Thornton (founder of the Scarborough Festival). Remarkably the MCC and the counties left open the number per side and the minimum number of days, although they did exclude (by convention rather than agreement) one-day and one-innings matches. These matters were not finally resolved until the Imperial Cricket Conference of 1947, which settled on eleven-a-side matches only of three days' minimum.

Before the 1894 meeting there had been no attempt to define and codify 'first-class status'. The term was used by promoters and media alongside 'great' or 'important' or 'major'. From this point the concept of first-class cricket becomes seminal to cricket's history and ideology. It is a key identifier of the best players and the

---

[*] Typically, the Graces went two degrees higher with their patron, the Duke of Beaufort.

most important matches. As international contests became the biggest source of cricketers' earnings and reputation, performances in 'first-class' cricket became the sole gateway for selection. Establishing the status of 'first-class' was therefore vital not only commercially, but also socially and ideologically: it enabled the controllers of the game in each country to enhance their status as guardians of its standards, and to exclude entire categories of players from its highest levels on grounds of race, gender, nationality and class.[15] The concept of first-class was extended to women's matches only in 2021, retroactively, by the ICC.

The challenge from league cricket

There was no qualification for membership of the County Championship except the agreement of six other counties to play home and away matches against the newcomer. This meant that certain new 'first-class' counties were makeweights with no realistic chance of winning the Championship, and able to influence it only by the occasional shock result or rain-affected draw. Below the Championship were about twenty English and Welsh counties competing in the sub-first-class Minor Counties Championship, reinforced by the second elevens of the first-class ones.[16] Joining the mix were Oxford and Cambridge Universities, about a hundred wandering social teams – some with first-class status such as Free Foresters, most of them not – a few lingering professional 'circuses', works and business teams, teams representing towns and villages, service teams (generally excluded from local cricket), and boys' public-school teams and those of their old boys. These were virtually autonomous, choosing their own fixture lists.

The price of such autonomy was to play matches with nothing at stake. For grand viziers of cricket, such as Lord Harris, playing for 'honour' was all that any cricketer should want. However, many clubs and players sought something more competitive, especially after the success of the competitive football matches promoted by Alcock.

In association football, the biggest step was the league system. It stemmed from a logical proposal by William McGregor, a director of the recently formed Aston Villa. Five cancelled fixtures proved to him that knockout competitions alone could not give clubs a guarantee of meaningful matches after they were knocked out. As a remedy, he proposed an organised league, with a set number of fixtures between all members. This was generally known as 'the American system' – an early sign that American sports management was overtaking British – although McGregor claimed cheekily to have been inspired by county cricket, which was an open shambles. In 1888, his proposal took shape in the Football League.[17]

Its early success inspired a host of imitators in cricket. Birmingham and District (the geographic home of Aston Villa, one of the founders of the Football League) were the first, followed by Bristol and District.[18] The North East Lancashire League, renamed the plain Lancashire League, would become the mightiest of them all. Cricket leagues multiplied in Scotland, significantly a pioneer of association football. Scottish clubs searched English cricket and advertised regular vacancies for its professionals. Gala, based in Galashiels, did especially well with its signing, a nineteen-year-old called Wilfred Rhodes.[19]

Football leagues and other forms of competition also reached southern suburbs and rural areas. They attracted some amateur resistance amid snobbish fears about importing supposed bad behaviours of northern football players and spectators. But many of these initiatives had influential support from the cricketing establishment. The London and Suburban Association set up its league at a meeting chaired by Henry Perkins, the MCC secretary. In 1896, Surrey's president, Lord Alverstone, created the Surrey Cup for local teams in the county. A traditionalist cricketing parson, the Reverend A. W. Leach, gave his approval and noted the higher interest in cricket produced by the cup. The first winners, Cranleigh, received a standing ovation. The first winners of the Lancashire League, Nelson CC, did even better – a civic reception with a brass band.[20]

Keeping control of the professionals

The MCC and the amateur controllers of county cricket saw off the challenge of professional league clubs. This was primarily due to the one aspect of cricket that they had managed coherently: terms and conditions for professionals.

At county level, professionals were limited to playing for the county of their birth or one in which they had lived for at least two years. Characteristically, amateurs were given an extra option. 'A cricketer may elect to play for the county in which his family home is, so long as it remains open to him and an occasional residence.' In 1882, Alcock explained the purpose of this rule explicitly in *Cricket*: 'to thoroughly encourage county cricket by allowing the admission of amateurs under a third qualification distinct from either birth or residence.' This special provision was abolished in 1900, but not before the Indian genius K. S. Ranjitsinhji was allowed to join Sussex in 1895 on the strength of a bare promise to go and live in Eastbourne.[21]

For professional cricketers, the one-county-per-season rule and the two-year residence requirements ended their previous status as free agents. Since most county professionals were on one-season contracts, committees held great power over them by the threat of non-renewal. A further weapon for committees was the promise of a benefit match and the selection of opponents for it. Under the influence of the paternalistic Lord Hawke (who had seen many ruined ex-professionals) the counties in 1889 committed themselves to invest players' benefit proceeds on their behalf. This system continued well into the next century. Len Hutton was not allowed to touch his benefit money in the 1950s and the Yorkshire committee invested it badly for him.[22]

An important sanction against professionals was non-selection for MCC matches, whether the Players against the Gentlemen, overseas tours, or the increasingly frequent matches against visiting overseas sides (whether or not they were given the newly coined name of Test matches).

Most importantly, counties kept their pay rates ahead of the new league clubs. Surrey were the most generous, and their stars before the First World War could count on £245 a season, an additional £45 in winter and discretionary 'performance bonuses'. At that time a skilled manual worker in London earned up to £100 a year and an agricultural labourer about £40. Lancashire paid rather less, but at around £200 a year their professionals were well ahead of those in the Lancashire League, on £65 for twenty weeks of cricket.[23]

County cricket pitches were usually better. For those at the end of their careers, county cricket offered more contact with patrons who could get them a job as a school coach or a groundsman (which at this stage was becoming a specialist occupation).[24] A recurring theme in English cricket history, and indeed in other walks of life, is the degree to which skilled professionals were willing to accept the superior status of other players and managers from the traditional ruling class. There were episodes of resentment against amateurs assuming this status by pretending to be unpaid, but protest and even criticism of the genuine amateur gentlemen players and administrators was unusual. The late nineteenth century saw a general rise in labour militancy – but not among professional cricketers. There were two major threatened strikes in this period. The first was in 1881 by the leading Nottinghamshire professionals, including the two best-regarded players other than W. G. Grace, Arthur Shrewsbury and Alfred Shaw. The second, in 1896, involved five major players selected for England's Oval Test match. The first failed completely; the second achieved its major objective (a match fee of £20) only after delay to the team selection and a public climbdown. In both cases, the counties and the MCC, shrewdly guided by Alcock in 1896, acted like an employers' cartel. They succeeded in dividing the strike leaders and deterring other professionals from joining them.[25]

A further advantage for the county clubs over the league clubs was national media attention. In 1892 the MCC and the counties finally determined a coherent points system that generated an uncontestable champion county. This gave a new importance to results and individual performances, and secured them priority in newspaper reporting. The 1890s saw a general expansion in their coverage of sport, especially in the popular newcomer, the *Daily Mail*, where it soon rose to 12 per cent, dominated by cricket in the summer.[26] Players could aspire to national stardom only through success as a county professional.

The major leagues, including Lancashire and Birmingham, further reduced their competitive power for professional services by limiting their clubs to one professional.[27] In general the new clubs had to make do with unremarkable players from English counties. One league professional stood out as an exception to the journeymen: Sydney Barnes, still the most common choice for greatest bowler of all time. Barnes' talent and ego made him impervious to the pressures that the counties could apply to lesser players. He did not need a first-class county to be chosen for England and acquire a national following. League and minor county cricket gave him an adequate living and the time to pursue his lifelong occupation as a calligrapher and inscriber of legal documents.[28,*]

Without major stars in their ranks the new league clubs could never replace county clubs at the apex of English cricket, or compete for national attention. They remained locally significant and commercially successful. Over time, they would make a huge contribution not just to English but also to overseas cricket in developing new players and showcasing stars. But they never threatened the supremacy of county cricket or the control of English cricket by amateurs and gentlemen, who were about to enter their heyday.

---

[*] Barnes' achievements as a bowler and in his other working life both required exceptional skill and control with his right hand.

Chapter 8

THE FIRST GOLDEN AGE

From 1890 until the First World War, English cricket lovers enjoyed an extraordinary outburst of talent and achievement. In 1895, W. G. Grace, aged forty-six, scored 1,000 runs in May and then completed his hundredth first-class century, both unprecedented feats. In the same year, Archie MacLaren made the first quadruple century in first-class cricket. In 1899, Ranjitsinhji scored more than 3,000 runs in an English season, also unprecedented, with strokes of his own invention. Two years later his friend C. B. Fry hit six consecutive first-class centuries. Then came Jessop's match at the Oval: with England in desperate straits, he scored 104 in seventy-seven minutes (still the fastest Ashes century in terms of time)[*] to make it possible for the last-wicket pair of George Hirst and Wilfred Rhodes to accumulate 15 to win one of the most exciting Tests ever played. In 1906, a summer of heatwaves, Hirst completed a 'double double' of 2,000 first-class runs and 200 first-class wickets. The rise of the short-form game means that we can be certain that feat will never be equalled. His search for the 200th wicket was a daily story in the national press.

There was a succession of notable slow-left-arm bowlers: Rhodes, Bobby Peel, Johnny Briggs and Colin Blythe. At the end of the period, Jack Hobbs and Frank Woolley would establish themselves. In Australia in 1911–12 Woolley scored the first century by an England left-hander in thirty-four years of Test matches.[1]

---

[*] This is still the case after Travis Head's match-winning century in Perth in November 2025. Given the pace of play in the twenty-first century, there's no chance it will be beaten.

All of these players and dozens more became national figures through county cricket under amateur control. The County Championship doubled in size, from eight to sixteen, before the First World War. One minor county – Staffordshire – was conspicuously stronger than most first-class counties. It was fed by a high-quality local league and fielded Sydney Barnes, when he could be induced to overlook the toil and, to him, servitude of first-class county cricket.

Batters everywhere were helped by better pitch preparation, especially at first-class level. This became a recognised profession, backed by science, as specialist groundsmen replaced unskilled labourers. This was the era when the 'square' became sacred, part of the ground roped off and policed.

Batters were also rewarded by a change in the Laws. Six was given for a hit that cleared the boundary: previously it had to clear the ground. This period saw two major bowling innovations. The first was the use of a delivery that acquired mystic associations: the googly. It was and is a wrist-spun delivery that, with no visible change of action, deviates sharply and unexpectedly into a right-handed batter rather than away.* No one knows the precise origins of the term, which quickly passed into metaphor to designate any kind of unfair surprise. The professional batter Arthur Shrewsbury pronounced googly-bowling immoral.

Astute self-promotion and a self-deprecating literary style allowed a Middlesex amateur, Bernard Bosanquet, to claim to be its inventor. In Australia it was named the Bosie in his honour, after he dismissed the national hero, Victor Trumper. The name Bosie fell out of use, possibly because of the risk of attribution to Oscar Wilde's lover. Many Victorian bowlers may well have used the googly earlier, but Bosanquet was certainly the first to deploy it as a major weapon in first-class and Test cricket.

---

* Left-arm wrist-spinners, a rare breed, can produce them as well with the opposite effect.

The second discovery was swerve, a term later superseded by swing. Both refer to the ability to make a ball deviate at pace through the air: swerve was a little slower but the deviation was typically sharper and later. Its most popular exponent was George Hirst, but the formidable American Bart King was at least his equal, as English spectators could judge when he toured England with the fine Philadelphian side in 1908 and topped the English first-class bowling averages.[2]

Australian visitors included Trumper, colossal in ability and delightful in personality. Two other legends, Clem Hill and Charlie Macartney (a right-handed bat), followed Woolley's trajectory as a left-arm spinner who became even more famous as an attacking batter. A hitherto unsung Australian, Frank Tarrant, was a great success at Middlesex and would become influential in Indian cricket as an import for several maharajahs. A left-handed all-rounder, C. B. Llewellyn, forced to leave his native South Africa, became a mainstay of Hampshire.

Such was the success of overseas imports[3] that in 1906 *The Times* campaigned against them,[4] foreshadowing agitations in the 1960s about overseas players in county cricket, and indeed about immigration in general. At this stage, any subject of the British sovereign, wherever born, had an unrestricted right to visit, settle and work in the UK. The counties narrowly failed to agree on a proposal to extend the qualifying period for overseas professionals to five years, which almost certainly would have choked them off entirely.

This dynamic era in English and global cricket came to an abrupt and tragic conclusion with the outbreak of the First World War. The nostalgia that this later induced found expression when the *Manchester Guardian* journalist Neville Cardus began to write after the war. Cardus created a new form of cricket writing, turning the players into heroes of epic and poetry. Of Jessop's innings at the Oval in 1902, he wrote 'The vision, the undying chivalry of it, belong not only to cricket, but to the unwritten saga of the English people; less worthy themes have served the bardic strain.'[5]

He called Reggie Spooner 'the Herrick of cricket', recalling the sixteenth-century poet famous for his carpe diem poem 'To the

Virgins, to Make Much of Time' with the first line 'Gather ye rosebuds while ye may'. He described his hero Archie MacLaren as 'magnificent in his ambition and reckless in his sovereignty'.[6] Other writers would add to Cardus's myth-making. J. B. Priestley later wrote: 'I will admit I am very much a *Golden Age* man . . . My own is roughly from 1910 to 1914 when I joined the army and began to lose so many friends, when I entered another sort of world, which could never again be trusted . . . There never seemed to be much money about from 1910 to 1914, but then you didn't need much money and if you were young you could have a lively night out on a shilling.'[7]

Cardus's greatest flights were induced by the amateur players of his Golden Age. His professional heroes tended to be typecast as functional auxiliaries: Sancho Panzas rather than Don Quixotes. For northern players, he had the unfortunate habit of inventing blunt colourful dialogue. At least one of them, Arthur Mitchell of Yorkshire, took him to task for his treatment.[8]

Cardus's myth-making thereby consolidated, perhaps helped to ossify, the ideology that identified the glories of the Golden Age with the amateur spirit. The highest compliment that could be given to any *professional* batter was to say that he batted like an amateur. This trope persisted. In 1970, even the radical, iconoclastic Rowland Bowen could endorse Plum Warner's view of Jack Hobbs as 'a young professional who played just like an amateur'.[9]

A lot of this was bogus. Many leading amateurs earned a good living from playing cricket. Considerable efforts were made to disguise this, to enable them to continue as custodians of the amateur spirit. They caused resentment among professionals and were a factor in the two players' strikes mentioned earlier. The term 'shamateur' came into use at this time and was applied to Fry, MacLaren, A. E. Stoddart and many lesser lights. They earned money from journalism (their own or ghosted), from product endorsements, from specially created sinecure jobs (especially as 'secretaries' to rich patrons), or simply from gifts and expense payments. These earnings were contingent on them playing cricket.[10]

The biggest shamateur was Ranjitsinhji. His public image made him an archetype*: the fabulously wealthy Indian prince who plays cricket for joy with effortless magic. Almost every part of this was false. He was not wealthy at all, especially not after providing for an entourage of spongers such as MacLaren. He regularly dodged creditors. He was not a prince. He played cricket to win the favour of Indian and British patrons who might make him a prince. Assisted by Fry, he turned cricket into a source of income through highly paid journalism, culminating in his bestselling *Jubilee Book of Cricket*. This delivered technical instruction, extolled cricket at public schools and analysed past great players (mostly amateur) with photographs. Above all, it extolled cricket as a marker of English identity, a unifier of the British Empire, and the highest form of mental and physical training.[11] His cricket was magical but certainly not effortless. He trained and practised rigorously, especially in his first year at Cambridge, when he hired a professional to teach him to play like one and tethered his back foot to improve his technique against fast bowling.

Apart from his cricketing skills, the most authentic aspects of his public personality were his loyalty to Britain's Empire and its upper classes, despite the racial barriers they forbade him to cross.† Historian Mihir Bose has brutally noted that Ranjitsinhji 'has no place in Indian cricket history'.[12] He never played there, except in occasional social matches.

---

* There is an instantly recognisable derivative of him, the Nabob of Bhanipur, in the hugely popular Billy Bunter stories of Frank Richards. The Nabob is depicted as courageous, intelligent and very good at cricket, though his nickname Inky and comic language would now be unacceptable.

† These were most evident in cricket when he was denied selection against white South Africa at the latter's behest and in his personal life when he was denied any hope of a relationship with the English women he loved. The best account of the real Ranjitsinhji, especially his political and financial problems, is *Ranji: A Genius Rich and Strange* by Simon Wilde.

He was nevertheless a gorgeous manifestation of the British Empire as it reached its late nineteenth-century apotheosis. In the next section, we examine the expansion of cricket across the globe, and its indelible connection with British imperialism.

Part Two

CRICKET AND EMPIRE

> *In Affectionate Remembrance of English cricket,
> which died at the Oval . . . Deeply lamented by a large
> circle of sorrowing friends and acquaintances.
> R.I.P.
> N.B. – The body will be cremated
> and the ashes taken to Australia.*
> Sporting Times, 1882

> *An emergent, enfranchised black middle class in
> Southern Africa . . . were among the pioneers of the game
> in South Africa and the broader colonial world.*
> ANDRÉ ODENDAAL, KRISH REDDY, CHRISTOPHER MERRETT
> AND JONTY WINCH, *Cricket & Conquest*, 2016

> *I haven't the slightest doubt that the clash of race, caste and
> class did not retard but stimulated West Indian cricket.*
> C. L. R. JAMES, *Beyond A Boundary*, 1963

We began this history with an account of what H. S. Altham called the 'archaeology' of the game. We then showed how wealthy landowners took command with the imposition of rules ('Laws'). In the mid-Victorian era the County Championship, organised around the agrarian categories of pre-industrial Britain, took shape.

By this time cricket was expanding rapidly overseas. As far as the British cricket player was concerned, this was hardly noticeable. The domestic cricket programme continued to be shaped by clashes between counties, schools, regiments or academic institutions. Gentlemen v Players, a contest based on class distinctions, loomed largest of all.

Yet the surge of population growth set in motion by the Industrial Revolution was provoking a great movement of peoples. The highland clearances caused countless Scots to seek fresh lives in America. Over a million Irish people crossed the Atlantic to escape the great famine of 1850. At the end of the eighteenth century the British government addressed the mother country's 'crime problem' (often caused by conditions of desperate poverty) by transporting convicts to penal colonies in Tasmania and the south-eastern coast of Australia.

They were encouraged to settle once they had served their term. Soon many Britons, like Dickens' Wilkins Micawber, were travelling of their own choice. Don Bradman's grandfather, Charles Bradman, made the long sea journey down under in 1852. This process led to the creation of British Dominions – self-governing colonies owing allegiance to the Crown – in Australia, New Zealand, Canada, South Africa, Newfoundland and for a brief time the Irish Free State.

Britain also developed her colonies – dependencies under the Crown. In 1876 Disraeli elevated Queen Victoria to Empress of India as the British state took direct control in the wake of the first Indian War of Independence in 1857. The opening of the Suez Canal twelve years later secured easy trading and military access to India, opened up East Africa and thus helped set in motion the scramble for African possessions which dominated European politics in the decades before 1914.

This distinction between 'colonies' and Dominions is essential to an understanding of the development of international cricket during the first half of twentieth century and beyond. In the Dominions (especially Australia, South Africa and New Zealand) cricket quickly emerged as a game played by white settlers who had brought cricket with them from the metropole. Indigenous peoples were almost completely excluded, just as they were excluded from society as a whole. This racial segregation was especially blatant in South Africa and Australia.

It was a different story in the colonies. A strong indigenous cricketing culture emerged in India, the West Indies and more slowly Ceylon (today's Sri Lanka). Even before the First World War India had emerged as a serious, though not yet world-beating, cricketing nation. Its team was purely composed of Indian players. It feels counter-intuitive that local people should have played cricket with relative ease in the colonies, which were run directly from Whitehall, while they were prevented from doing so in the Dominions. The paradox is easy to unravel. Whatever the many faults of their system of colonial rule in India, the British did not seek to displace the local population. In South Africa and Australia, in sharp contrast, the white settlers had come to stay.

It is misleading, however, to draw the dividing line too abruptly between cricket in the Dominions and the colonies. In South Africa, even under formal apartheid, a brilliant cricketing culture would emerge parallel to the white cricket establishment. In Australia, a handful of indigenous players managed to break through into the first-class game. The most complex case is the West Indies, where a white-settler presence persisted alongside colonial rule from Whitehall. This could have been, and sometimes became, a toxic combination. It also produced some of the most exhilarating cricketers to have played the game and inspired the finest book written about the sport, *Beyond a Boundary* by C. L. R. James, a dissident Marxist from Trinidad.

Chapter 9

AUSTRALIA: BIRTH OF A CRICKET SUPERPOWER

By area, Australia is far and away the largest single major cricket-playing entity in the world. It has the greatest distance between two Test match centres: Brisbane and Perth are 2,700 miles apart. Distance is a central theme of Australian cricket. It was played in its earliest white settlements scattered across its coastline, linked to each other only by uncomfortable and perilous transport by sea or by horse. As the settlers pushed into the country's interior and took cricket with them, it meant a hard journey, before rail, to get from one settlement to another. Having made such a journey, cricketers did not want to play an inconsequential match. For this reason Australian cricket never evolved the purely recreational cricket that emerged in nineteenth-century England, a compact space with far more reliable transport links, full of affluent people with leisure time.

Immigration from the British Isles was the other early and enduring influence on Australian cricket. This remained the largest source of arrivals into Australia until the twenty-first century, when it was overtaken by China.[1] As recently as 1945, 98 per cent of Australians had their family origins in Great Britain or Ireland.[2] This is a very different immigration history to that of the USA. It ensured that once established on the Australian subcontinent as the pre-eminent summer game, cricket faced no challenge on demographic grounds from new arrivals. There was no market for baseball and Australian cricket saw off its challenge in the late nineteenth century. During the 1930s a fissure opened between Anglo-Saxon Protestants (led by Don Bradman) and Irish-origin Roman Catholics (led by Bill O'Reilly), but this did not affect the status of Australian cricket as an Anglo-Irish monopoly.

Other ethnic groups were excluded or marginalised, especially its original inhabitants. Australia's Aboriginal and Torres Strait Island population is estimated to have fallen by 84 per cent from the arrival of the British in 1788 to 1900,[3] victims of disease, conflict against enemies with superior arms, loss of habitat and food supply, and the cultural and emotional effect of displacement.[4]

In the mid nineteenth century, there was a brief attempt to draw 'civilised' Aboriginal players into cricket and one such group was the first Australian team to tour England. But they were treated as much as entertainers as cricketers, and the tour was a money-making venture by a white promoter. Controls on the movement and financial freedom of Aboriginal and Torres Strait people made it virtually impossible for them to reach the highest levels of Australian cricket. They never had the means to form cricket clubs of their own, as South Africa's black population did even in the worst days of apartheid.

Cricket made no effort to recruit the substantial Chinese population Australia acquired after the Gold Rush of the 1850s nor the Pacific islanders it enlisted as indentured labour. On the contrary, these groups were vilified as a threat to Australia's white identity. The drive to exclude them by a national immigration policy was a prime motive for the intercolonial federation in 1901. A few years previously, on England's Australia tour of 1897–98, Ranjitsinhji almost became a victim of the White Australia policy: a late official intervention spared him the payment of the £100 'deterrent tax' against the entry of non-white* visitors.[5]

As in England, Australian cricket became respectable. Publicans were gradually excluded as promoters of cricket and there were

---

* We hate using this white-created and white-defined term, but it is the most straightforward way to denote all cricketers of other ethnic groups.

crackdowns on drinking and betting. Clubs were taken over by professional people and members of the local establishment. But Australian cricket never acquired the rigid class structure of English cricket, nor the cult of the gentleman amateur who alone could be trusted to play in the right style and spirit. Although Australia produced many batters of notable elegance, it never valued them above those who scored duller runs and won matches. Australia never acquired the English bias against left-handed batsmen and hitting the ball to leg. Clem Hill, the first batter to make 1,000 runs in Test cricket, illustrates the point.

Cricket was the first team sport in which Australians gained international success – a full generation before there was a Commonwealth of Australia to represent. Australia's early cricket victories were regularly extolled as proof of the survival and strength of the British race in tough conditions far from home. But they were also presented as triumphs for Australian qualities – especially stamina, dedication, practice, mateship and a gritty sense of being the underdog.

The first record of cricket being played in Australia is in Sydney in 1803, just fifteen years after the arrival of the First Fleet.[6] The earliest matches were played between naval crews and garrison regiments, but civilians gradually took over, especially as free settlers and locally born people replaced convicts. Hyde Park became the setting for club matches in the 1820s. The Australian Club established in 1826 was locally pre-eminent in the 1830s and 1840s, and inspired several others to provide competition. A co-founder, mechanic Ned Gregory, was the patriarch of the first of Australia's great cricketing dynasties, producing six first-class players, including two Test captains and a pioneer of Australian women's cricket.[7] In these very early days, cricket was played in an enclave in and around Sydney, within an enormous colony called New South Wales, which encompassed not only the present states of Queensland, Victoria and South Australia but also present-day New Zealand.

English influence was overwhelming. Clubs adopted English names, including Mary-le-bone, and copied English club constitutions word-for-word. Some planted English trees. The chief sporting competitors to cricket were horse racing and boxing: cricket got a head start of some thirty years as a team game.[8]

Tasmania, known as Van Diemen's Land until 1855, was the second part of Australia to be settled by the British. Cricket developed in two widely separated settlements, Launceston (led by English cricketing expatriate John Marshall) and Hobart. In 1851 Launceston hosted the initial intercolonial match against the new colony of Victoria; it was later designated first-class. Tasmania gained a surprising victory, principally by bowling underarm. This was a sign of the island's isolation, brought about by poor internal and sea communications. Although it continued to play some first-class matches, Tasmania did not take part in Australia's organised domestic structure, the Sheffield Shield, until 1977. Tasmanian-born players, including Ted McDonald and Max Walker, were forced to move to the mainland to gain recognition.[9]

Cricket started later in what became Victoria than in and around Sydney, and was more formal and better financed. Melbourne was founded in 1835 and soon overtook Sydney as the financial, administrative and social centre of the still-giant colony of New South Wales. The Melbourne Cricket Club began in 1838 when the future city was still a muddy village, founded by five Englishmen with landowning antecedents in the old country, which included a connection with Hambledon. After two enforced moves (as with Lord's), it developed the finest ground in Australia. In consequence, the MCC (it prided itself on its shared initials) became the dominant single influence not only on Victorian but all Australian cricket until the twentieth century. Victoria separated from New South Wales in 1851. After an initial two fixtures against Van Diemen's Land, Victoria began to play intercolonial matches against New South Wales, which became, for over a century, the biggest rivalry in Australian cricket.[10]

South Australia was another early adopter of cricket. It was formed as a new colony in 1837 on a different model from its predecessors, consisting entirely of free settlers. Within two years, the new town of Adelaide had a cricket club as its intended centrepiece. An expatriate British cricketer, John Cocker, purchased a hotel in the town and used cricket to promote it. By the 1850s there were nearly a hundred clubs in the surrounding countryside, but they found it hard to travel to play each other and had to resort to internal fixtures such as Shopkeepers v Farmers and even Whiskers v Clean-Shaven. South Australia could not break into the intercolonial first-class duopoly of New South Wales and Victoria, and the first English tours of the 1860s did not travel there.

Queensland and Western Australia fared even worse in the early period, not only through distance but also, in Queensland's case, by climate, since January and February matches were often washed out by tropical storms. Queensland did not play in the competitive first-class Sheffield Shield until 1926; Western Australia had to wait until 1947 and did not get a full programme until 1956. Players from both colonies, later states, complained that they were regularly overlooked by national selectors.[11]

In 1860, the white population of Australia was about 1.2 million, of whom nearly a million lived in the three colonies of New South Wales, Victoria and South Australia. Australian cricket was stagnant and very much second to horse racing as an outlet for recreation. But in the next period it overtook horse racing, and by 1875 participation and spectatorship in cricket had risen from negligible to about a third of the white population. The prime reason for this was a series of visiting English tours.[12]

The first of these was by a professional team in 1862 led by H. H. Stephenson of Surrey. According to some accounts, the visit was a replacement for Charles Dickens, who had cancelled a lecture tour. Stephenson's team was by no means the best in England, but it was far too good for a series of local fifteens, eighteens and twenty-twos. It attracted big crowds, copious newspaper coverage and made the Melbourne-based promoters a substantial profit.[13] This tour saw the first use of the term 'Test match' by a journalist, William Hammersley, to describe some of the fixtures, all against odds.[14]

A second tour, led by George Parr and including W. G. Grace's elder brother E. M. (the Coroner), was marred by accusations of commercial greed against the English professionals, but was still a notable commercial success. Both tours drove up playing standards in Australia, and this was sustained because two English players stayed on as coaches: Charles Lawrence from the first tour and Billy Caffyn from the second. Caffyn coached Australia's first Test match winning performers Charles Bannerman and Fred Spofforth. The English tours also improved Australian pitch care.[15]

The first return visit by Australians came from an unexpected source – a team of Aborigines. Their English tour in 1868 was a brief exception to their exclusion from Australian cricket. It owed much to the work of Thomas Wentworth Wills, an early hero of Australian sport, who has lately become a contentious figure.

His background is undisputed. He was the grandson of an English highway robber who was transported to Australia. After being pardoned, he became a prosperous merchant. His son, Horatio, continued the upward trajectory as a pastoralist, newspaper editor and politician. Based in western Victoria, he was on good terms with Aborigines and employed many of them as agricultural workers. Horatio's son, Thomas, played with their children, before being sent away to Rugby School in England. He excelled in all sports, including the school's unique version of football, but especially cricket. He captained the Eleven and once took twelve wickets at Lord's with fast round-arm bowling. He went on to play for Cambridge University, Kent and Ireland as an amateur.

Returning to Victoria in 1856, aged twenty, he carried all before him as a bowler, although he was frequently no-balled by umpires not used to the latest English versions of fast bowling. He was irked by the lack of fitness of many of his colleagues. Inspired by rugby and perhaps also by the Aboriginal ball game of Marn Grook, he and a group of fellow enthusiasts invented Australian football as a winter pursuit for cricketers.

Then in 1861 came a traumatic episode that became the subject of controversy.

Horatio took Thomas on an expedition to the Queensland outback to establish another property. Horatio expected the local Aboriginal population to be as friendly as that in Victoria. They were in fact fighting a fierce war to keep their lands, and massacred Horatio and nineteen other Europeans. Tom and a young friend had been sent away on an errand: they returned to see the graves of his father and the others.

According to the mainstream narrative of Wills as a national hero, 'Retribution was swift and severe with some accounts suggesting three times as many Aborigines were killed as a result. *Wills, however, refused to participate* [our emphasis].'[16] Instead, according to his 2008 biographer Dr Greg de Moore, Wills combatted what would now be recognised as post-traumatic stress disorder by coaching Aborigines in cricket.[17]

This account has been challenged by the investigative journalist Russell Jackson,[18] earning him fierce attacks for besmirching a legend, but also enough expert support to generate a cautious addition to Wills' entry in the *Australian Dictionary of Biography*: 'In 2021, suggestions arose that Wills had admitted to participating in violent reprisals related to his father's death, drawing on an anonymous 1895 report in the *Chicago Tribune*.'[19] The doyen of the Wills family, Mr Terry Wills Cooke OAM, remains adamant that Wills was *not* present at any stage of the reprisals, on the basis of contemporary records.[20]

Returning to undisputed fact, Wills did indeed coach Victorian Aboriginal players. With a local promoter, William Hayman, he formed an Aboriginal team that played at the Melbourne Cricket Club on Boxing Day 1866 in front of 10,000 spectators in the ground and with another 3,000 outside. Despite Wills' captaincy they were well beaten but their performance led to many other local fixtures, where crowds also appreciated Aboriginal displays of throwing the boomerang and other athletic events.

That in turn led Hayman to organise an English tour for them, with himself as manager. Charles Lawrence, the English professional then coaching in Australia, replaced Wills as captain. The Aborigines were given new names. Their best player, Unaarrimin, became Johnny Mullagh; the brothers Yellenach and Grougarrong became Johnny and Jimmy Couzens. Other were given more condescending names, including Bullocky, Dick-a-Dick and even Jim Crow. On their arrival in England, *Sporting Life* assured readers that they were all 'perfectly civilised, having been brought up in the bush to agricultural pursuits as assistants to Europeans'.[21]

Their six-month tour, in unfamiliar climate and conditions, was arduous. They played forty-seven matches, winning fourteen, against good amateur sides, including an MCC team where they took a first-innings lead, and were also expected to entertain crowds with boomerang and spear throwing, as well as athletic and circus feats. 'King Cole' died on the tour, while 'Sundown' and 'Jim Crow' had to be sent home ill. Mullagh, Johnny Couzens and Lawrence were the dominant players, especially Mullagh, who took 245 wickets at an average of 10 and scored 1,698 runs.

They attracted good crowds and receipts (creamed off by the white management), but met racism in both English and Australian media, the latter angry that Aboriginal Australians not whites should be the first side to represent Australia in 'the home country'.[22]

On their return to Australia, Johnny Couzens died of dysentery. 'Twopenny' got one match for New South Wales against Victoria, before reverting, like most of the other survivors, to agricultural labour. Mullagh alone had a cricket career of any note afterwards, as a professional at Melbourne Cricket Club, where he played for Victoria against the English tourists of 1878–79 and top-scored in the second innings. Mullagh refused to accept racism either in England or Australia. He would not take his meals separately on the tour and preferred to live in a primitive shack on waste ground than on the Aboriginal reservation. He died aged fifty. Over a hundred years passed before he was recognised as an Australian sporting hero. His name was given to several trophies, including the Mullagh Medal for the best performer at Australia's Boxing Day men's Test matches. The second winner was the fast-medium bowler Scott Boland, the second man with Aboriginal ancestry to play Test cricket for Australia.

The official response by the Victorian government to the returning tourists was a ban on Aboriginal Australians from leaving the colony without ministerial permission. The official reasons were fears 'that a sharp change in climate might injure the health of the players and that they might fall into dissolute habits or be exploited commercially'. The first and third fears were well-founded but they were nonetheless pretexts for eliminating the opportunity for Aboriginal players to represent Victoria in away matches in other colonies.[23] Elsewhere Aboriginal Australians were controlled even more tightly. Queensland's rules were still in force in 1971, shocking the visiting English cricket reporter Scyld Berry.[24]

Two Aboriginal players had meteoric careers as fast bowlers at state level, Jack Marsh[25] and Eddie Gilbert.[26] They were victims of umpires rather than legal restrictions and no-balled out of the game. Marsh dismissed the leading Australian batters of his time, including Victor Trumper; Gilbert memorably worked over Don Bradman before clean-bowling him in three balls, described by Bradman later as the fastest he had ever faced. Marsh's fate may have been influenced by two visiting English captains, Archie MacLaren and Plum Warner, to keep him out of the Australia team, and both he and Gilbert might have been victims of commercial pressure. There was simply no market for Aboriginal bowlers who dismissed Australia's star white batters – especially Bradman, the financial saviour of Australian cricket in the depths of economic depression.

Reciprocal tours became more frequent in the 1870s and 1880s. The Suez Canal, opened in 1869, cut the journey time by several weeks and greatly reduced the danger of a rough passage. Those in Australia were all sponsored by the Melbourne Cricket Club.

In 1873–74 it paid an astronomical sum to secure an English tour led by W. G. Grace, including a free honeymoon.* Grace and the amateur players under him were less popular personally than the professionals, whom the Australians found more gentlemanly on and off the field, above all the courteous veteran James Lillywhite. He bonded with the Victorian player and promoter John Conway and they arranged an all-professional English tour under Lillywhite in 1876–77. Improved Australian performances led Conway to press for a match on equal terms. To general astonishment, the combined colonial team won, by 45 runs, with a match-winning undefeated century by Charles Bannerman. Retrospectively, this became the first international Test match. More than 2,500 Tests have been played since, but Bannerman's performance still holds a record as the highest proportion of a team's runs in a completed innings.

The contest, entirely a private arrangement between Conway and Lillywhite and disavowed by the cricket associations of Victoria and New South Wales,[27] did not involve the best eleven players of either England or Australia. It induced demand for an instant replay. This second retrospective Test match was won by England (prompting suspicions of match-fixing in the first) but it led Lillywhite to suggest a reciprocal tour by white colonials. This happened in 1878 and was marked by an astonishing victory within a single day by the visitors over a powerful MCC side including W. G. Grace – dismissed twice in the match in four balls for a total of four runs. Both sides were considerably better than those in the first so-called Test match, but the 1878 match has not received Test status.

The victory was gained by two bowlers, Harry Boyle and Fred Spofforth, who gave England the first demonstration of the full pace and bounce available from overarm bowling. That in turn generated in both countries improved batting techniques, better bats and pitch preparation. Lord Hawke, the amateur captain of Yorkshire and

---

* Grace's tour was the first to use the Suez Canal.

panjandrum of English cricket, called this match 'the commencement of the modern era of cricket'.

The English press noticed that the Australians had overtaken their players in fielding. They returned the ball full pitch to the wicket-keeper or bowler rather than on the bounce and the wicketkeeper, the superlative Jack Blackham, stood up to the fastest bowlers and dispensed with a long stop.[28] This position faded out of English cricket, except in boys' schools to hide the duffers.

These early tours and Tests were unofficial, commercial enterprises, which only gained their status later as national contests. The first England–Australia Test match in England in 1880 was organised at short notice by the always astute Charles Alcock of Surrey, not by the MCC, and followed by some years the successful association and rugby football internationals he had already staged at the Oval. It had never been planned as part of the visitors' programme and Alcock arranged a generous payment of £100 to Sussex for cancelling their intended fixture. Appropriately, W. G. Grace scored England's first Test century: a matching effort by the urbane Australian captain Billy Murdoch was not enough to save them from defeat.

An ambitious all-professional English tour followed in 1881–82, which took in the USA and New Zealand, as well as Australia: the English lost two and drew two representative matches. 'The colonists' returned to England in the following summer and played a lone representative match, which remains one of the most exciting in Test history. Enraged by a piece of gamesmanship from Grace, Spofforth bowled Australia to an unlikely victory by seven runs. One spectator dropped dead from excitement, another bit through his umbrella handle. This match inspired the celebrated obituary notice in *Sporting Times*: 'In Affectionate Remembrance of English cricket, which died at the Oval.' The key sentence was an addendum: 'NB — the body will be cremated and the ashes [sic] taken to Australia.'[29]

This is usually taken as a jolly joke by a jobbing journalist, Reginald Shirley Brooks. It was actually a political statement. Brooks was a leading campaigner for the legalisation of cremation. By nearly 150 years,

Brooks anticipated Extinction Rebellion's use of cricket matches for political propaganda.[30],[*]

Whether joke or propaganda, no one expected Brooks' reference to survive. But it was revived by two visiting English captains in Australia, Ivo Bligh and Pelham Warner, to generate public interest and bolster their credentials. The great Australian all-rounder George Giffen gave the term two chapters in a book in 1899, but it did not receive the imprimatur of *Wisden* until 1905.

Bligh 'won back' the Ashes by two 'Test' victories to one. A fourth match was added and won by the Australians but Bligh said that it did not count and Australians of that time still deferred to English amateurs.[31] A group of Melbourne ladies reportedly burned a bail and presented Bligh with the real resulting ashes in a small urn; he came back to marry one of them, Florence Murphy. For years afterwards the urn stayed with the Blighs (later Earl and Countess of Darnley) at their stately home, Cobham Hall. By the time Bligh died, Warner and other captains and media figures had made the Ashes famous (and upper-case). Florence gave the urn to Lord's, where, with short exceptions, it has stayed ever since, whichever country wins a Test series. It is not at all certain that the ashes inside are those of the original stump. In this way a historic sporting contest of great commercial value is still being played for an almost totally mythical trophy.[32]

In the era of private enterprise, from 1876 to 1899, England and Australian cricketers met each other in twenty tours and played fifty-six Test matches. England used thirteen different captains and Australia ten. There were no formal rules on player qualification: five early Australian players also played for England.[33] Certain recurring themes in Anglo-Australian cricket relations established themselves in this early period. The English tourists complained of uncouth

---

[*] The connection is unconsciously maintained in the idiosyncratic alphabetical cataloguing system of the London Library, which places cricket books next to cremation.

and violent spectators, and poor local umpiring, which allowed Australians to get away with no-balls. Australians found the English amateurs snobbish and imperious, and prided themselves on their own togetherness. Writing in Alcock's *Cricket* magazine, the visiting Australian umpire Jim Phillips attributed much early success to the Australian habit of sharing the same dressing room, where the captain could get guidance and advice from his colleagues and avoid making bad decisions on his own.[34] In contrast Lord Hawke, for the English, expressed surprise that Australians did not understand that 'our professionals prefer to be on their own off the field rather than to be in the same hotel as the amateurs. Indeed, I know that some of our professionals would prefer to have second-class passages on board ship rather than having to dress for dinner.'[35]

At different times, each country accused their visitors of being financially grasping. Australians in England were nominally amateurs (and referred to as Mr on scorecards and in *Wisden Cricketers' Almanack*) but the profits they made on tour aroused resentment: a factor in the England players' strike of 1896.[36] Australian players controlled their early tours, and their early captains needed to be exceptional man-managers (Billy Murdoch) or disciplinarians (Joe Darling) to keep order. Weaker personalities such as Blackham might see their tours disintegrate into factional fighting, drunkenness and brawls.[37] A long struggle began between players and administrators over selection and discipline. The Australasian Cricket Council (it endeavoured to include New Zealand too), formed to keep order in 1892, was almost totally ignored not only by the players but also by the still-powerful Melbourne Cricket Club.[38]

International matches had more benign effects. They encouraged participation in Australian cricket by South Australia and Queensland (Tasmania was still a backwater and Western Australia cut off by distance). Above all, they created a demand for structure in Australian cricket and a means of identifying the better players for development and promotion rather than a patchwork of different clubs. This produced the great institution of district or grade cricket. Players advanced by performance in competitive matches through grade three to grade one teams into the colonial (later state) side. This system kept young players in regular contact with stars and helped them absorb their technical and mental techniques. It also encouraged local rivalries and the spread of cricket to country towns, where the cricket club became a community hub. The structure of Australian cricket was given more definition by Grace's second tour in 1891–92. Apart from paying Grace's massive expenses (which now included two children as well as a wife) the tour's patron, Lord Sheffield, arranged for a shield to be given to the winner of an organised intercolonial competition modelled on the English County Championship. Sheffield was open about his wider objective behind the shield: to promote a federated Australia as a trading and cultural partner in the British Empire.[39]

The integration of Australian cricket, and Australia itself, was promoted by the development of a railway network. By the time of the federation in 1901, all the mainland states and their principal towns had been linked by more than 12,000 miles of track. Western Australia again was the exception. Early journeys were dreary and uncomfortable and, because the colonies had adopted different gauges, interstate travel required a change of trains. The journey from Perth to Brisbane entailed six changes.[40] Once train journeys became more enjoyable in the 1920s, they promoted bonding for both state sides and visitors.

The Golden Age gave Australia a new international opponent it did not particularly want: South Africa. An invitation from South Africa was refused during the Anglo-Boer War of 1899–1902 (when Australians fought for the British) but eventually accepted afterwards and, unlike the English, the Australians sent their best team on their way back from triumph in England in 1902. They played three representative matches, which became retrospectively classified as Tests. Australia won two but were considerably extended, especially thanks to the all-round efforts of C. B. Llewellyn, the only mixed-race player to represent South Africa before the fall of apartheid.

South Africa pressed Australia for a return invitation. The new board deferred this continually because it would interfere with its preparations against England. This summed up Australia's attitude to South African cricket before the First World War: England was all that mattered and Australia had no need for the interloper. Eventually South Africa visited Australia in 1910–11, winning one Test but losing the other four. Victor Trumper filled his boots with 661 runs at an average of 94, and three other Australians averaged more than 50. The South Africans were not asked back until 1931 – when they ran into Don Bradman.[41]

A Golden Age of players – but not administrators

The coincidence of England's and Australia's Golden Ages produced some scintillating Test series and individual matches. The England tour of 1894–95, led by A. E. Stoddart, was the first in a decade to stage five Tests, a response to popular demand. England won the first Test by 10 runs after being made to follow on and chased a stiff target in the fifth to clinch the series 3–2. The contest attracted more than 95,000 spectators to Melbourne, some in special trains from Adelaide, Sydney and even the outback of Queensland.[42] In England, the series was followed avidly by telegraph: even Queen Victoria asked to be kept updated.[43]

In 1905 the defunct Australasian Cricket Council was replaced by a Board of Control for overseas tours. This followed the example of England in 1903–04, when Plum Warner's tour was selected and administered by the MCC, which had taken over selection for England at home to Australia in 1899.

The new board first showed its colours at home in the selections for England's visit in 1907–08. Australia won comfortably under Monty Noble against a weak English team (despite the first visit of Jack Hobbs) – and they were able to carry the board's curious choice as vice-captain, the veteran Victorian batter Peter McAlister, who came twelfth in the batting averages with a top score of 41.

McAlister was resented by his teammates as a board stooge and spy, and this intensified when he was reappointed for the 1909 tour of England with the additional role of treasurer. Noble organised a vote of confidence in himself as captain and no-confidence in McAlister as his deputy, but McAlister clung on and played in two more Tests, averaging 16, before disappearing to become one of the board's representatives on the newly formed Imperial Cricket Conference. The stress of fighting the board and McAlister drove Noble to quit Test cricket.

On Noble's retirement, the players' cause was taken up by Frank Laver, a strike bowler who had also been the players' choice of manager on the 1909 tour. He had not been on speaking terms with McAlister during the tour, and explained afterwards to the board that neither man had kept accounts of expenditure. He had simply assumed that McAlister would do it. Soured by economic depression, the atmosphere worsened still further in 1912 when the normally equable Clem Hill had a twenty-minute brawl with McAlister at a selection meeting.[44]

The top players continued to fight for Laver's appointment to manage the team in the Triangular Tournament in England in 1912. When this was refused, and the board set its own financial terms for the tour, six of them walked out of the team. Two – Warwick Armstrong and Hanson Carter, the wicketkeeper – came back after the First World War. The other four – Hill, Trumper, Tibby Cotter, the pace bowler, and Vernon Ransford, a prolific batter – did not. Trumper died of Bright's disease in 1915, while Cotter was killed in the war in 1917. In the tournament itself, a weakened team under the veteran Syd Gregory crushed South Africa but lost badly to England. The board's chosen manager, Mr Crouch, reported the players for brawling and drunkenness.[45]

The Golden Age of Australian cricket ended on this undignified note, but by the time of the First World War Australia was established as a cricket superpower with its own stars and style, a first-class structure fed by a well-organised club cricket system, and a strong national following by spectators and media. Players and administrators kept a sentimental fondness for England as 'the old country', but had lost any deference towards their English counterparts. Marginal regions had been drawn into cricket – but not marginal communities outside the Anglo-Celtic population. There were warning signs for the future in the clash between players and the board, and in the vulnerability of Australian cricket finance to economic depression.

Chapter 10

NEW ZEALAND: CRICKET'S FARTHEST REALM

Cricket arrived in New Zealand with its earliest British colonists, as in Australia. Early in its life, it had a distinguished spectator. Charles Darwin wrote in *The Voyage of the Beagle* of his experience in Waimate North in the Bay of Islands, in 1835. 'Several young men redeemed by the missionaries from slavery were employed on the farm. In the evening I saw a party of them at cricket.'[1]

Thereafter, a combination of factors prevented New Zealand cricket from taking off as its dominant sport. Two were basic: demography and communications.

In 1850 (eight years after the first recorded cricket match in New Zealand), the population of the colony was barely 100,000, of whom about two-thirds were still Māori, in spite of the impact of European diseases, European weapons (in the casualty rates of the so-called Musket Wars), and loss of lands and food supply. Despite the efforts of missionaries, New Zealand cricket had become a game for European men only, a population of about 15,000. Communications in New Zealand were even more rudimentary than in Australia. Internally they still relied heavily on canoes and walking, horses were few and horse transport moved slowly on barely cleared tracks.[2]

In Wellington, where the first cricket matches were staged, there were two early clubs, the Wellington for 'gentlemen' and the Albion for tradesmen and labourers. Wellington was an experiment in Edward Gibbon Wakefield's theory of 'systematic colonisation', which had also been tried in South Australia, where it ran into the same problems in establishing a price for land that would keep it out of reach of lower-income families and thus make them available as an agricultural labour force. When the experiment failed, Wellington cricket almost died with it. It was revived when the city became New Zealand's capital in 1865, followed fortuitously by a major earthquake that allowed the creation of the Basin Reserve cricket ground (to this day the world's windiest).

The northern city and port of Auckland was dominated by commercial and trading interests, mostly Australian. It had few people to form a leisured elite: early cricket there was democratic but frail, sustained by a small group of government officials. The Māori wars of the 1840s ensured the presence of a strong British garrison.[3] In spite of the later influence of the elite Grammar School, Auckland cricket kept a more fluid social character than elsewhere.

In the 1850s, Wakefield established a colony in South Island with the backing of English notables led by the Archbishop of Canterbury, after whom it was named. It aimed to model itself on rural England, with benevolent landowners and a contented labour force. Wakefield saw cricket clubs as a social hub in which gentlemen could meet and assert community leadership. 'I tell the boys in summer time to play cricket and play well,' he wrote, 'that those who are the best cricketers most likely will be the best readers and writers.'

Although Wakefield's company needed a bailout from its English backers, the colony established its leadership in New Zealand cricket for most of the remaining century, particularly in organising overseas tours and hosting visitors. Canterbury aligned New Zealand cricket strongly with the ideals of English amateurism. In its new town of Christchurch, 500 acres of land were set aside for a cricket ground called Hagley Park, after the Worcestershire seat of the Cobham family, who would have a major influence in both places for over a hundred years (and in South Africa).

Canterbury's first cricket club, established as early as 1851, was run by public figures, solicitors and politicians in preference to artisans, and the players included more white-collar workers than elsewhere in

New Zealand. Its expensive membership fees sustained the ground, a pavilion and a curator. It attracted alumni of English public schools, and Oxford and Cambridge universities (who understood English conditions and playing techniques).

English public-school influence was reinforced by the foundation of New Zealand's leading independent school, Christ's College. Its headmaster Charles Corfe placed sport, above all cricket, at the heart of the curriculum in the best Victorian manner. Christ's College became the leading nursery of early New Zealand cricketers and continues to produce them. Their Anglocentric ideals were also reinforced at Auckland Grammar School and even more so at Wellington College in the thirty-year reign of Joseph Firth, who modelled his school's cricket on Eton and Harrow, and employed English professionals to coach the boys.

As with Australia, contacts with English cricket were extremely important to early New Zealand cricket, not only technically but psychologically. By showing the English that they played cricket, New Zealanders demonstrated membership of the imperial family and pride that British strength and pluck were undiminished when exported far overseas. The English toured in 1864 under George Parr, in 1877 under James Lillywhite, and in 1882 under Lillywhite, Alfred Shaw and Arthur Shrewsbury as extensions of their tours to Australia. Unfortunately, unlike the Australians, the New Zealanders had very few performances to celebrate: even at heavy odds their early provincial teams were nearly always massively defeated.

Australia took over as the main visitors from the 1880s, and Australian sides would undertake fourteen tours of New Zealand until the First World War, providing the setting for two of the most dominant batting displays by Victor Trumper in his famous career. The early Australian captain Billy Murdoch hinted that a future Australian tour of England might include a New Zealander and in the late nineteenth century the integration of New Zealand cricket into Australian was promoted as a precursor to the integration of New Zealand itself into a federated Australia. But the New Zealanders spurned membership of the Australasian Cricket Council and retained their own cricketing and national relationships with Britain and its empire.[4]

New Zealand is proud of being the first country to give women the vote and of other early progressive women's rights legislation. But this attitude did not extend to cricket, and there are only scattered references to girls and women playing it before the First World War, often in the face of male mockery.

The biggest factors holding back early New Zealand cricket were climate and soil. These encouraged low-scoring matches on low-bouncing wickets where the ball would swerve and deviate without much effort by medium-paced bowlers. This pattern persisted for more than a hundred years and encouraged a succession of economical 'dibbly-dobblers'. Two latter-day examples, Gavin Larsen and Chris Harris, would earn New Zealand significant success in one-day cricket, especially at home. But before the First World War such pitches provided a dull spectacle for spectators and contributed to stagnant standards. Even more importantly, conditions favoured cricket's biggest competitor: rugby. Compared to Australia, New Zealand's climate allowed a longer playing season for rugby union and the state of its pitches meant far less fear of the injuries that had prompted Thomas Wentworth Wills and his friends to invent Australian football.

Cricket in the South Pacific

Apart from Australia and New Zealand, one other Pacific state played first-class cricket before the First World War: Fiji.

Briefly an independent kingdom, Fiji was reluctantly acquired as a British colony in 1874, on request of local chiefs, to escape their debts to the USA. Cricket was introduced the same year by the new colonial administration and twenty-one years later a Fijian team was playing matches of first-class status on a tour of New Zealand. They performed well, with four wins, two draws and two defeats. The team was mostly British: the captain was the new attorney general of Fiji,

J. S. Udal. He founded a cricketing dynasty: his great-grandson, Shaun Udal, played for Hampshire and England.

Several other British possessions in the Pacific also took to cricket before the First World War, but not to first-class standard, and indeed with scant regard to the Laws as cricket became subsumed in local ritual, politics and warfare.

The British shared New Guinea with the Germans and the Dutch before they handed over their portion to the new Commonwealth of Australia, which renamed it Papua. Cricket was introduced to it in 1880 by a muscular Christian Methodist missionary, Charles Abel, to wean boys away from head-hunting and sexual profligacy. Local people took to the new game without abandoning their old ones.[5]

In Tonga the game consisted simply of hurling the ball as fast as possible and then hitting it as hard as possible, both from static positions. Movement in the field was limited by the Tongans' predilection for size, and by the fact that ten separate matches were played at once on the same small ground.[6] Nevertheless, it became a national craze and the colonial authorities tried to limit play to one day a week.[7]

Nowhere was cricket more thoroughly appropriated by locals than in Samoa, where it was introduced by the British consul, William Churchward. He may have hoped to extend what is now called British 'soft power' in a volatile territory where Britain was vying for control with the USA and Imperial Germany. But almost nothing survived from conventional British cricket when the Samoans took to it. Bats became three-sided clubs, matches involved entire villages of hundreds of people (women and children as much as men), play included dancing, and both ritual and actual fighting, and was accompanied by feasting, drinking and gambling.* After a civil war the British abandoned their claims to the Americans and the Germans. But by then

---

* Most cricketing countries have tried to shorten the game: pre-war Samoa may be the only one to have sought to lengthen it.

the Samoan version of cricket had penetrated the entire territory to the vexation of the new imperial masters. The Germans took cricket matches as a pro-British demonstration. They were really an assertion of local identity and, above all, a pretext to avoid working and obeying official decrees.[8]

Chapter 11

SOUTH AFRICA: CRICKET'S ORIGINAL SIN

The history of cricket cannot be written outside the context of British imperialism, and the violence and racism that went with it. Nowhere was this more evident than South Africa, where the British presence involved campaigns against local peoples and two wars against the Boers, a rival white-settler community. After the second of these wars, the British and the Boers reached an accommodation, which was consolidated after 1910 by the Union of South Africa. This was essentially a delayed settlement by the two minority white races at the expense of all the others, whose subsequent exclusion from cricket mirrored the contraction of their rights to property, franchise and access to education and employment.

The story of South African cricket starts with the conquest of Cape Colony by the British in 1806. A visiting Dutchman, Dr Huibert Nahuys van Burgst, recalled: 'I twice a week played a game of ball-casting, called cricket by the English, on the level ground by the sea at the Lion's Tail.'[1] Van Burgst, an early example of the enduring cricketing friendship between Holland and England, was a Dutch lawyer who found himself in Cape Town after being captured on a 'confidential government mission' in Indonesia.[2] The Lion's Tail refers to Green Point, described by Rowland Bowen as 'probably the oldest surviving cricket ground but one outside the British Isles'.[3]

By the 1870s historians point to the emergence of several cricketing cultures besides the usual white British one: Christianised sons of African chiefs;[4] an assimilated Dutch colonial elite; 'Malays', though the term did not apply to people from Malaysia, but rather to Muslim descendants of slaves.[5] The category of 'coloured' cricketer remains difficult to describe and would not fully emerge until the white cricketing establishment imposed rigid classifications.[*,6]

White and black cricketers played each other with regularity and at a high level.[7] The turning point was the non-selection of William Henry 'Krom' Hendricks, who might well have been remembered as one of the finest fast bowlers of the era – had he been given the chance.

Hendricks, whose destiny was decided by obscure 'Malay connections',[8] was born in Bo-Kaap on the slopes of Signal Hill on the edge of Cape Town. On purely cricketing grounds, he would have been an automatic choice for South Africa's first touring side to England in 1894. Two years earlier, he'd played against a visiting English team whose captain, W. W. Read, compared Hendricks to Australia's terrifying pace bowler Fred 'The Demon' Spofforth, adding: 'If you send a team [to England] send Hendricks. He will be a draw card.'

Hendricks' nemesis was William Milton, a former English rugby international who ran Western Province Cricket Union. Milton also ran the prime minister's office. The prime minister in question, Cecil Rhodes, was set on the elimination of racial tolerance, whether in the ballot box or on the cricket field. 'We must adopt a system of despotism,' argued Rhodes, 'in our relations with the barbarism of South Africa.'[9]

Rhodes would not tolerate Hendricks. 'They wanted me to send a black fellow called Hendricks to England,' he told an audience of undergraduates at Oriel College, Oxford, including the future England captain Plum Warner. '[But] I would not have it.'[10] Rhodes explained: 'I suppose it is the instinct of self-preservation. In South

---

[*] For an explanation of the term 'coloured', see our discussion of Basil D'Oliveira's career on p. 243. A wider discussion of the problems faced by non-white people under the system of formal apartheid introduced by D. F. Malan's nationalist government in 1948, can be found in Peter Oborne's book *Basil D'Oliveira, Cricket and Conspiracy: The Untold Story*, 2004.

Africa we have perhaps a million or two whites, and many millions more of black people.'[11]

Hendricks' backers were led by Harry Cadwallader, a charismatic journalist, founding secretary of the South African Cricket Association and organiser of the tour of England. As a result of his support for Hendricks, Cadwallader was targeted by Milton, who dumped him as tour manager and secured his removal from other positions in South African sport. Cadwallader died three years later, a broken man and 'in such grievous need' that a public fund was set up to help his wife and children.[12]

Having destroyed Cadwallader, Milton put paid to Hendricks. In 1896, the Western Province Cricket Union passed Bye-law 10, which excluded non-white cricketers from playing 'championship' cricket in Western Province. In this way, Krom Hendricks became the first cricketer to be banned on grounds of colour.

His exclusion was part of a much wider attack on black people. The Union of South Africa (1910) was crucial. A year before it was enacted the South African Native and Coloured Delegation, a forerunner of the African National Congress, travelled to London to lobby the Asquith government against the colour clauses of the Act of Union. Intricate analysis by the historian André Odendaal has demonstrated how many of the delegates were intimately linked to South African cricket,[13] leaving no doubt that the estrangement of black cricket by the white establishment was part of a project to arrest black political and social development. There would be no going back till the collapse of apartheid seventy years later.

In the South African summer of 1888–89, the first English touring party arrived in South Africa. Many more would follow before the outbreak of the First World War twenty-five years later.

Taken at face value there's a cheerful British inconsequentiality about these journeys. The early tourists have something in common with Charters and Caldicott, the cricket obsessives caught up in an international crisis way beyond their comprehension when a Balkan war breaks out, as portrayed in Alfred Hitchcock's 1938 masterpiece *The Lady Vanishes*.

An Irish amateur, Emile McMaster, played in the second Test match. He was out first ball, did not bowl or take a catch. This was not just his sole Test, but his entire first-class career. Every club cricketer has known many Emile McMasters, the acquaintance recruited at the bar the night before a game who steps in to fill a vacancy, but McMaster is the only one to have gone on to play Test cricket for England. He is immortalised as England Test player number 67. The English manager, Major Warton, doubled up as umpire in the Tests. Aubrey Smith, the captain, was a fast-medium bowler for Sussex who went on to establish the Hollywood Cricket Club, which survives to this day.* However, Aubrey Smith's team was strengthened by several solid professionals, four of whom – Bobby Abel, Johnny Briggs, George Ulyett and Henry Wood – played in the Oval Test against the Australians the previous year.

Smith's team travelled 16,006 miles – 13,003 by steamer, 2,218 by rail and 785 by coach and cart. The tour lasted well over four months, including fifty-one days of cricket,[14] a vivid contrast to the effete environment of twenty-first-century international cricket, with identical five-star hotels and jet travel, diet experts, fitness gurus and twenty-four-hour immersion in a protective cocoon.

These early tours were more than plucky manifestations of English eccentricity. They were an essential part of the political and social engineering project that resulted from the discovery, in 1886, of vast deposits of gold in the Witwatersrand, known colloquially as the Rand, a 30-mile escarpment in the Transvaal. After a brief gold rush, a small group of European financiers gained control of the mining

---

* The actors who played for it include David Niven, Laurence Olivier, Leslie Howard and Boris Karloff. When the authors played against Hollywood CC on a tour of the USA thirty years ago, the James Bond star George Lazenby was one of our opponents.

industry, making unimaginable profits. The most famous of these so-called 'Randlords' remains Cecil Rhodes.

The Randlords needed cheap labour. This meant sending Africans down the mines on low wages. This they refused to do, or not in enough numbers. Chinese workers (derogatorily known as 'coolies') were used, with more success. But the only long-term solution was forcing Africans down the mines. That meant seizing their property, stripping them of rights and treating them as commodities rather than human beings. Indirectly, this excluded them from cricket, given that cricket was a badge of civilisation.

This project was alien to the official philosophy of the British Empire. Although, as with all empires, the British governed ultimately through violence, many imperialists maintained that their presence in foreign countries was benign and temporary, and their role was to educate and civilise native peoples in preparation for the moment they would be fit for self-government. The emphasis placed by British colonialists on education – from the native mission schools to the grander boarding schools for the elites – is hard to explain fully in any other way.

The Randlords destroyed this. The only way of forcing black labour down the mines was a united South Africa, embracing both white-settler minorities brought under the control of Britain. This involved persuading Britain to absorb South Africa on special terms, with local people stripped of their rights. White cricketers were the public-relations arm of the Randlord project. In the words of Denis Judd, historian of the Empire, 'Cricket also provided a vocabulary behind which acts of violence and brutality could be camouflaged.'[15]

English tourists played only one non-white team, the 'Malay' side containing Krom Hendricks described above, and did not face black opposition again til 1994. The match appalled the Randlords and was never repeated. Thereafter English tourists observed the racial parameters applied by their hosts. The cricket establishment in Britain became, in effect, an arm of South African mining capital, as illustrated by the career of Lord Harris, captain of England at the inaugural Test at the Oval in 1880 and remembered as a cricket-obsessed governor of Bombay in the first half of the 1890s. Harris, such a formative figure in cricket history, was chairman of Cecil Rhodes' great venture, Consolidated Gold Fields, for three decades, and helped design the cheap migrant policy when he visited South Africa in 1904.

Early cricket in Zimbabwe

In 1888, as England's first Test party was preparing to tour South Africa, Cecil Rhodes entered into a fraudulent treaty with Lobengula Khumalo, paramount chief of the Northern Ndebele people in what is today Zimbabwe. Falsely claiming to act with the knowledge (and authority) of Queen Victoria, Rhodes' emissary Leander Starr Jameson, a medical doctor, took advantage of the fact that he had once cured Lobengula of gout and persuaded the trusting chief to sign over mining rights.

On 11 July 1890, Rhodes dispatched his Pioneer Column, equipped with Maxim guns, Martini Henry rifles and field artillery across the Tuli river into Mashonaland. They then headed north-east into Shona territory where they hoisted the Union Jack flag in Fort Salisbury (modern-day Harare).

The settlers brought cricket equipment as well as guns. Rhodesia's first cricket match took place on 16 August at Fort Victoria (modern-day Masvingo). The standard was spectacular.[16] Monty Bowden, part of Aubrey Smith's 1888–89 team, was on that Pioneer Column, having stayed behind to join the Witwatersrand Gold Rush. He had fallen on hard times and took part in the adventure in an attempt to retrieve his fortunes. He died two years later after falling off a cart and being trampled underfoot by oxen. *Wisden* recorded that he was buried 'in a coffin made from whisky cases'.[17] A wicketkeeper-batter who played for Dulwich College and Surrey as well as England, Bowden remains on record as England's youngest ever Test cricket captain, at twenty-three. He was twenty-six when he died.

Rhodes hired Bowden and other pioneers by publishing recruitment notices in Kimberley. Each was offered 3,000 acres, as well as the right to mining claims.[18] Preference was given to wealthy applicants in the hope they were more likely than others to carry influence back in Britain.[19] When he realised he had been tricked, Lobengula sent messengers to Queen Victoria demanding justice. They were denied a fair hearing. Lobengula's warriors were destroyed when they attempted to confront Rhodes' British South Africa Company forces in 1893. Lobengula died from unknown causes a few months later.[20]

These were the high days of Empire. Take Major 'Bertie' Poore of the 7th Hussars, who was first dispatched to India, where he served as ADC to Lord Harris. In 1895, Poore was sent to South Africa, where he played for local teams against Lord Hawke's touring party with such success that he was invited to play in the Tests. After a period of indecision, Poore chose South Africa over England. Within weeks of the end of the third Test he was heading north with the Baden Powell expedition to crush the Ndebele and Shona rebellions. Poore destroyed Shona homesteads, forcing people to live in caves, then used dynamite to force them out. When not massacring tribespeople, Poore helped to build the Bulawayo cricket ground. Returning to England, he scored 1,399 runs at an average of 116.58 (only Wally Hammond can boast a higher average in a county season) before his 1899 season was truncated and Poore returned to fight in the Anglo-Boer War, where he was mentioned three times in despatches and secured a Distinguished Service Order or DSO.

'Of all the people in the history of the game,' wrote the military historian Leo Cooper,[21] 'he seems to stand for the Eccentric Ideal.' Others might place him in a tradition of imperial genocide that includes the German massacres of the Herero and Nama people in south-west Africa a decade later, and French settler atrocities in Algeria.

The first English touring team reached Bulawayo, Lobengula's old capital, in 1898–99. The team arrived by train after a three-day journey from Kimberley, Union Jack fluttering at the front of the engine. Lobengula's old parade ground was commandeered for the match. As Peter Hain and André Odendaal have written, 'Cricket arrived in Africa as part of the baggage of invading British military forces and accompanied the invading soldiers every step of the way through the subcontinent in a hundred-year process of systematic and violent conquest.'[22]

Anglo-Boer War stops play

There were no more visitors till Plum Warner led a team to South Africa in late 1905. By then new characters were on the scene. Rhodes had died from heart failure in March 1902, his dream of extending the Empire throughout Africa, South America and beyond under a British master race unfulfilled.

The first Test match, played at the Wanderers in January 1906, was one of the closest ever. South Africa deployed six debutants, including two practitioners of the googly. Aubrey Faulkner and Reggie Schwarz had perfected Bernard Bosanquet's weapon. The googly, one of the supreme cricketing skills, is hard to control, and Bosanquet never fully mastered line and length, a factor in his decision to abandon cricket at an early age. Like many inventors, therefore, he failed to profit fully from his invention.

Faulkner and Schwarz*,[23] exploited the mystery ball so effectively that it altered the balance of international cricket, and as a result helped to shape the history of South Africa. They performed their magic at the exact moment the Randlord sponsors of white South African cricket needed, for reasons of state, to establish their country as an autonomous force on the international cricket scene. Schwarz took 18 wickets and Faulkner 14 as South Africa defeated England 4–1 in a five-Test series.

---

* To ensure accuracy and control, Schwarz never bowled leg-breaks, concentrating on the googly.

In the first Test, Schwarz played mental games with a bewitched England top order, and the team struggled to 184. South Africa could only reply with 91 and when England set the South Africans a target of 284, the cause seemed hopeless. They scrambled home by one wicket thanks to a famous innings by Dave Nourse,* settling into a run of forty-five consecutive Test matches from 1902 to 1924.

The way was open for South Africa to gain full Test status. With Rhodes dead, Sir Abraham ('Abe') Bailey, one of the rainmakers of twentieth-century international cricket, took over as the senior figure driving the Randlords' political project. A good enough cricketer to play three first-class matches for Transvaal in the 1890s, Bailey made his fortune as a gold and diamond tycoon before fighting (with the British) in the Anglo-Boer War. Bailey was also the president of the South African Cricket Association, the body that would administer (white-only) cricket until the collapse of apartheid eighty years later. He embodied the triple alliance of politics, mining and cricket that created white South Africa. Echoing Rhodes, he said: 'If the coloured man thought himself equal to the whites there would be a bloody racial war in this country.'[24]

Just as Rhodes had worked hand in hand with William Milton, so Bailey discovered an astute collaborator in Reggie Schwarz who, as his private secretary, linked cricket directly to the Randlords. In November 1907, they approached the MCC with a proposal for a tripartite tournament to be held in England involving England, Australia and South Africa. This idea was rejected by Australia. However, the three countries agreed to meet at Lord's in 1909.[25]

At this meeting the Imperial Cricket Conference, governing body of world cricket, was created. It first convened on 15 June 1909. This time, Abe Bailey got his way and it was agreed that a triangular tournament would take place in 1912.

---

* His son, Dudley Nourse, would be one of the greatest South African batters of all time.

At a further meeting a few weeks later, rules for Test matches were agreed, establishing the structure that would shape international cricket for more than a half a century. The ICC defined Tests as matches between representative elevens from England, Australia and South Africa. Abe Bailey had secured for South Africa a place as one of three founder members of the governing body of world cricket.

There was one striking absentee from the ICC: the USA. Philadelphia alone could have raised a touring party of international standard, but the founders were determined to reserve cricket for the British Empire. This echoed Joseph Chamberlain's campaign for imperial preference, mutually agreed tariffs to turn the Empire into an economic zone protected from American (and German) competition. Two other contemporary casualties of cricketing imperialism were Argentina and the Netherlands.

After the First World War, India, New Zealand and the West Indies would join the ICC. But South Africa, as one of the three core members of the club, had double the voting powers of newcomers. Non-white nations had to accept as a condition of membership that South Africa would not play them. This arrangement (later duplicated in rugby and Cold War diplomacy) conferred a priceless institutional legitimacy on what was to become apartheid. Racism and the associated violence were embedded in the basic structure of international cricket from the start.

The status of early South African Test match cricket

According to the official record the first Test match between England and South Africa was played in March 1889. England, captained by Aubrey Smith, won by eight wickets. The South African team, made up of weekend cricketers, was probably of decent minor county standard. They did not know they were playing a Test match. Nor did anyone else.

England teams made four tours of South Africa before the outbreak of the Anglo-Boer War. Eight of these games were later designated Test matches. England won all eight, most by huge margins, with some improbable performances. Johnny Briggs, a left-arm spin bowler who played in the first tour, took 15 wickets for 28 runs in the second 'Test' match. It is telling that when Briggs died ten years later, his *Wisden* obituary did not mention his towering South African achievement. Likewise when McMaster died in 1929, his *Wisden* obituary ignored this Test match too.

How did these early contests obtain the status of Test matches, a term that at the time only applied to England–Australia contests? Record books are fragmentary and do not tell the full story. The decisive verdict came from F. S. Ashley-Cooper, the statistician responsible for *Wisden* records over the first three decades of the twentieth century. 'It was at Port Elizabeth on March 12th 1889,' determined Ashley-Cooper in the *Cricketer Annual* forty years later, shortly before his death in 1932, 'that the first match accepted as between England and South Africa was begun. There were two such games that season, and it is worthy of note that the term "Tests" was at the time applied to them.'

Ashley-Cooper was a frail, obsessive scholar. All tributes to him stressed his integrity and authority. Nevertheless, historian Richard Parry has established that Ashley-Cooper was mistaken to say that the term Test was used in 1889. It suited powerful interests – above all, Sir Abe Bailey and his allies at the MCC – to point to a long tradition of Anglo-South African Test cricket when none existed. As George Orwell later noted, those who control the past control the future.

These early 'Tests' were not on the official record. There is a discussion to be had whether they should today be returned to their original status.

Chapter 12

CRICKET REACHES THE INDIAN SUBCONTINENT

The first mention of cricket in India involves East India Company sailors in Cambay in 1721.[1] By contrast, we have no suggestion of cricket in Essex till 1724 and none in Norfolk till 1745.[2] Meanwhile the first mention of cricket in Boston, New England, is 1725. The sport was spreading from its southern base through Britain's maritime empire faster than the English counties.

Notwithstanding, cricket was slow to develop in India, mainly played in ports or barracks and other places frequented by the British. The East India Company's reluctance to impose English customs on Indians may help explain why cricket did not become a popular sport until the Crown took control following the First War of Independence (known to the British as the Indian Mutiny) in 1857.

The first Indian adopters were Parsis, fire-worshippers (Zoroastrians) who had fled Persia 1,000 years earlier. Despite having lived in India for a millennium, they regarded themselves as interlopers, acting as brokers between the British and wider society. They accepted much of the ideology of English cricketers and played an immense early role in cricket in the subcontinent. They did insist, however, that cricket was an adaptation of an ancient Persian game, *chowgan-gui*, a thesis expounded at length by late Victorian Parsi academics.[3]

Outside the Indian caste system, the Parsis wore Western dress and took jobs others didn't want. They often carry names that denote their occupations. For example, the Indian wicketkeeper-batter Farokh

Engineer is a Parsi, as is Nari Contractor, captain of India, whose career was ended by a blow to the skull from a ball bowled by Charlie Griffith on the 1962 Indian tour of West Indies.*

By 1848, the Parsis had founded their first cricket club, The Oriental. Its replacement, the Young Zoroastrian, still flourishes. According to Indian historian Ramachandra Guha, 'at least thirty Parsi clubs were formed in the 1850s and 1860s, named after Roman gods or British statesmen: Jupiter, Mars, Gladstone and Ripon for example.'[4] The first two informal cricket tours of England by Indian teams, in 1886 and 1888, were arranged by Parsis. In 1887–88, G. F. Vernon's touring party played only one local India team, the Parsis, who defeated them in a thrilling finish.

Indian cricket developed at first along communal lines. The Triangular – an annual competition between Parsis, Europeans (in reality British) and Hindus – began in 1907. Five years later the Muslims joined to create the Quadrangular. Muslims in India had been conflicted in their response to defeat and repression after 1857. Some favoured withdrawal from Western institutions into a purer form of Islam. Others, led by Sir Syed Ahmad Khan, sought to embrace Western science, technology and education. Muslim cricket was a victory for these modernisers.

One institution played an especially important role. Sir Syed's Muhammadan Anglo-Oriental School, in Aligarh, north India, was founded after the independence war as a 'British-style educational institution that would make adequate room for the religion of Islam'.[5] An outstanding schoolteacher, Thomas Beck, member of the Cambridge Apostles secret society, taught a muscular Islam that reconciled Muslims and cricket. Wazir Ali, one of the most celebrated Indian Test players of the interwar era, was educated at Aligarh as was his brother, Nazir. Jahangir Khan, uncle of Imran Khan, who famously

---

* Despite his name, Vijay Merchant, an outstanding batter whose best years were stolen from him by the Second World War, was not a Parsi.

killed a sparrow in flight when bowling for Cambridge University at Lord's in 1936,[6] is another Aligarh old boy.

Cricket reaches future Pakistan

Until well into the nineteenth century most of today's Pakistan was governed by independent rulers, who enjoyed cool relations with the British. There was little of the mingling of cultures, eased by trade, that developed in the southern centres of Bombay and Madras. When cricket finally found popular favour, it did so as the sporting wing of the independence movement. Its trajectory was therefore the opposite of pre-independence India, where cricket was a collaborationist activity opposed and often denounced by Gandhi's Congress Party.[7]

As the British moved north into Sindh (conquered in 1842) and the Punjab, they took cricket with them. In August 1843, the cricket correspondent of the *Bombay Times and Journal of Commerce* (precursor to the *Times of India*) reported the foundation of a cricket club in Karachi.[8] Reports of cricket in Lahore start in 1846, and by 1849 it was being played at the Khyber Pass and the garrison town of Rawalpindi, where a public noticeboard still marks a six struck there in 1852 by Lord Vansittart, a 'royal progeny'.* This would have been an enormous blow since, at this stage of the game's development, sixes were struck out of the ground altogether, not merely over the boundary as today's Laws require. The Pindi board also records that Prince Christian Victor, Queen Victoria's grandson, struck 205 for the King's Royal Rifles against the Devonshire Regiment.†

---

* This Vansittart was most likely Frederick, an officer in the 14th Hussars, whose regiment was based in Meerut in 1852. However, nobody called Vansittart was raised to the peerage till 1941, and there is no evidence of any royal connection.

† The prince was a fine cricketer who remains the only member of the British royal family to have played first-class cricket, for I Zingari against the Gentlemen of England in 1887. He had a serious military career, campaigning in the northwest frontier, the fourth Anglo-Ashanti war, with Kitchener in Omdurman and finally in the Anglo-Boer War where he succumbed to enteric fever.

As in India, some notables did take to the game. For instance, Donald Carr's MCC side after independence played against a team led by the Pir of Pagaro. As spiritual head of the Hur community of Sindh, the Pir is the most senior religious figure ever to play first-class cricket. This sometimes made him a dangerous opponent. The Pir was once felled in the nets by the Test match bowler Mohammad Munaf. The Pir's followers, who constantly accompanied him, assumed he had been attacked and pounced on the bowler, who was rescued in the nick of time by the Pir's secretary. Before independence, the British had hanged the Pir's father, Pir Sibghatullah Shah, for leading the Hur community rebellion.

However, unlike India, princely influence in the formation of Pakistan cricket was practically nil. Failure to appreciate this has led observers to overestimate the influence of Aitchison College, the public school situated in the heart of Lahore founded in 1886 to educate the 'young nobility of the Punjab'. Certainly some famous figures studied at Aitchison. Bhupinder Singh, the cricket-intoxicated Maharaja of Patiala, is one example, as was the Nawab of Pataudi, grandfather of Iftikhar Ali Khan Pataudi, who captained India on its tour of England in 1946. In modern times students have included Imran Khan, his cousin Majid Khan and Ramiz Raja.

For all that, Aitchison was virtually irrelevant to Pakistan cricket. Its early cricketing protégés tended to belong to the Indian aristocracy, which believed in British rule, rather than the Muslim League with its independence aspirations. These princely elements were detached from the cricket culture that emerged in middle-class schools in Lahore and Karachi after the First World War.

The most remarkable of these was Islamia College, just outside the Lahore city wall. Islamia produced the artists, journalists and intellectuals who gave purpose and moral inspiration to the Muslim League. Under the guidance of an outstanding headmaster, Professor Sheikh Mohammad Aslam, it also produced a candidate for the strongest school team of all time. These young men would guard Muhammad Ali Jinnah, the leader of the independence movement, during his frequent visits to Lahore. Later, they would form the basis of Pakistan's first Test teams: Gul Mahomed, Nazar Mohammad, Abdul Hafeez Kardar, Maqsood Ahmed, Imtiaz Ahmed, Shuja-ud-Din and Zulfiqar Ahmed. After independence, Professor Aslam served for many years as treasurer of the Board of Control for Cricket in Pakistan. As we will discover, he is part of the foundation story of Pakistan cricket and the country itself.

The beginnings of cricket in Sri Lanka

Ceylon, the name given by Britain to modern Sri Lanka, was (like South Africa) under Dutch control at the time of the French revolutionary wars of the 1790s. Fearful that the French would seize Ceylon as well as Holland, Britain dispatched an expeditionary force and deposed the Dutch.

The Dutch had controlled the coastal areas; Britain set about conquering the interior as well.[9] This meant subduing the Kandyan Sinhalese kings, who had cooperated with the British against the Dutch and soon had cause to regret it. By 1830 the British were in control of the entire island. Two years later the Colombo Cricket Club was formed. It hosted Sri Lanka's first recorded match in November 1832: a ten-wicket defeat at the hands of the Earl of Ulster's regiment.[10]

In South Africa, British colonisers had to deal with the self-contained and hostile Boers. In Ceylon, the British inherited the Burghers. They had started, like the Boers, as Dutch settlers, but unlike the Boers were multicultural, pragmatic and relaxed. The novelist Carl Muller, himself a Burgher, defined them in his *Jam Fruit Tree* trilogy as 'English-speaking, fair-skinned relicts of colonial trespass, eminently usable by the British'.[11]

In the early years the hard-drinking Burghers played a comparable role to the Parsis of India: mediator between coloniser and colonised. Ceylon's first significant cricketers were almost exclusively Burgher: the Kelaarts and de Sarams, the Van Geyzels and de Kretsers, Allen

Raffel, Russell Heyn and Cecil Horan. Clive Inman, who played county cricket for Leicestershire in England in the 1960s, was a Burgher.

Two schools in the Sri Lankan capital Colombo were pre-eminent. Royal College and St Thomas's (founded in 1835 and 1851 respectively) have been responsible for more than a hundred players in the national side.[12] Every long-term captain of Sri Lanka up to the great Arjuna Ranatunga was educated at these schools. To this day the annual contest between the two teams is attended by capacity crowds.

In 1872 the Malay Cricket Club was formed[13] and important Tamil and Sinhalese clubs were established by the end of the century.[14] C. E. Perera (known to history only by the initials on his scorecard) emerged as the world's first memorable Buddhist cricketer. He made his mark in 1901, when he played against Boer prisoners of war, who had been shipped to Ceylon in large numbers by the British, a rare instance of a South African team playing non-white cricketers.[15] Six years later he was dead of typhoid.[16]

For many decades Ceylonese cricket suffered from isolation. This ended when the opening of the Suez Canal in 1869 turned Colombo into a stop-off point between England and Australia. Ivo Bligh's English team, on a mission to 'recover those Ashes', paused there in 1882, pulverising the opposition.[17] Such tours opened new vistas. In 1899, Alfred Holsinger (another Burgher) became England's first non-white professional cricketer at Ryde in the Isle of Wight.[18] C. H. Gunasekara meanwhile was the first Ceylonese to capture the imagination of the English public, helping Plum Warner's Middlesex win the County Championship in 1920.[19]

Cricket in Ceylon followed a different trajectory to its northern neighbours, India and Pakistan. The presence of a small settler community, the Burghers, means that Ceylonese cricket can in some ways be more fruitfully compared with the West Indies, as we demonstrate in the next chapter.

Chapter 13

WEST INDIES: DESTINED FOR GLORY

According to Rowland Bowen, the first mention of cricket in the British Caribbean is from 1778[*,1] by a slave owner, Mr Thistlewood of Jamaica. It is peevish: he grumbled that two of his neighbours had the leisure to play it. Thistlewood was not affluent enough to plant sugar cane. He made his living raising other crops for wealthy planters and supplying them with the slaves they needed from those he had acquired as an overseer.

In this early era, there is simply no record of how many black slaves were allowed to take part in the white man's games and on what terms. Michael Manley, the former Jamaican prime minister, speculates in his history of West Indies cricket that they were used to weed and cut the pitches and roll the wickets (a demanding task in the heat with rough, uneven ground), and to chase and retrieve the ball when it was hit into the sugar cane. This gave them the chance to demonstrate their athleticism and throwing ability. From there, the white planters saw their value as outfielders and practice bowlers for themselves and their sons since bowling, even underarm in that era, was hotter work than batting.[2] If Manley is right, their trajectory into cricket is similar to that of the camp followers of the British army who were the earliest native cricketers in the Indian subcontinent.

---

[*] Characteristically, Major Bowen suggests that the French introduced their own version of cricket earlier to their colony in St Lucia.

Both groups passed into cricket through the enduring racial myth that non-white peoples are less sensitive to heat than white peoples.[3]

The present West Indies has never been a natural entity geographically, politically or culturally. Its present components were never administered as a single unit in colonial times. A West Indian Cricket Board was formed only in 1926. Before that, each colony administered its own cricket and pre-Test teams described as West Indies were selected by ad hoc committees of white administrators.[4] These teams evolved in the nineteenth century from contests between the three major colonies that were closest together and could reach each other in a single day's sea voyage: British Guiana (then called Demerara, now Guyana), Trinidad and Barbados. Jamaica took longer to become part of West Indies cricket, largely because of geography: Kingston, Jamaica, is 1,252 nautical miles from Bridgetown, Barbados, and 1,299 nautical miles from Port of Spain, Trinidad. But it may also have had political origins. The British always had more doubts about the loyalty of Jamaica to the Empire and policed it more heavily: they feared that its mountainous terrain offered more opportunities for resistance. The Morant Bay Rebellion of 1865 heightened these fears: it was fiercely repressed and led to direct British rule of the island as a Crown colony.[5]

This explains why Jamaican players did not join the West Indies team until 1928. The smaller Leeward and Windward islands took longer still to integrate. They did not produce a Test player until Alfie Roberts of St Vincent made his lone appearance in 1956, in a weakened team that gave New Zealand its first Test match victory.

The climate of each different island made a profound difference to playing styles. Guyana and Trinidad favoured the development of spin bowlers, Jamaica and Barbados pace. Still more important, the growing season for sugar cane occupied workers in the dry months, so that unusually in cricket environments, West Indies cricket was generally played in the wet ones, when rainfall was often violent and unpredictable. For batting sides, this set a premium on rapid scoring while pitches were dry and usable rather than (in general English fashion) long occupation of the crease. Climate, soil and economy made matting rather than grass the main surface in Trinidad and for most clubs below top level in the other colonies. The great spin bowler Sonny Ramadhin had never bowled on a turf wicket before his triumphant first English tour in 1950.

Each island in West Indies cricket was marked by strong hierarchies based on race, with white at the apex, then brown, then black; and within each race, class, which was also strongly identified with skin colour. The hierarchies pervaded the schools where each group of West Indians learned their cricket and even more so the clubs they played for after school. C. L. R. James vividly described the club hierarchies in Trinidad: Queen's Park at the apex (white wealthy 'bosses'), Shamrock (non-elite whites, especially Roman Catholics), Maple (brown middle-class), Shannon (black lower-middle class) and Stingo (blacks with no social status). Slightly outside the hierarchy were clubs founded by the Indian and Portuguese communities, and those of the police, railwaymen and other groups of employees. James had a long moral struggle between playing for Maple or Shannon, and came to regret his choice of the former, which cut off his contact with black players such as Learie Constantine.[6]

These club hierarchies were still potent as late as the 1950s. In Barbados they held back the careers of two all-time greats, Everton Weekes[7] and Garry Sobers.[8] Sobers eventually broke through only by gaining a place in the police team as a nominal bugler.[9] East Indians of any class or income group found it even harder to break into colonial or representative cricket.[*] Their first representative in the Test team did not arrive until 1950: Ramadhin.

*

---

[*] About the same time another prodigy, Mushtaq Mohammad, was employed as a twelve-year-old 'cement clerk' at the Pakistan Public Works Board by his family's patron, Mr Kalifuddin. Mushtaq told us years later that he had never lifted or even counted a bag of cement in his life.

Although interclub matches were hotly contested from the earliest times, there were limits to the excitement of the same small groups of white people in small islands, or the small coastal plain of British Guiana, in playing each other over and over again. They therefore sought opposition from other colonies, setting a pattern for top-class cricket in the West Indies. The first match designated first-class was played by a touring team from Demerara (British Guiana) on a very poor pitch in Bridgetown and was an all-white affair.[10] Three years later Trinidad began to play Demerara in matches designated first-class. The Trinidad players included Charles Warner, half-brother of Plum and Aucher Warner, key figures in early West Indian cricket. Another interesting name was Arthur Cipriani, whose son went on to become a political leader in Trinidad and whose biography was written by C. L. R. James.*

Attempts to organise a formal intercolonial tournament were sporadic and unsuccessful until 1893. Distance continued to exclude Jamaica, which was dependent for top-class cricket on British or American tours. Jamaica began to play other colonies in the 1890s but did not take part in the formal competition until after the First World War. Their best white players did manage to secure representation, with those of the other colonies, on the first West Indies overseas tour in 1884, to North America, where they overpowered Canadian opposition but lost to powerful Philadelphian teams.[11] The first tourists were Philadelphians on a return visit in 1888.

All these early ventures were led, managed and selected by the small white elite of English origin, in which two local families, the Warners and the Austins, were prominent. Black players' access to these matches was primarily as occasional net bowlers and fielders, but some became professionals at the leading white clubs. Their role was always on sufferance from the whites.

---

* C. L. R. James's *The Life of Captain Cipriani* was first published in 1932. An abridgement became his book, *The Case for West Indian Self-Government*, the following year.

Plum Warner would become an equivocal figure in English cricket history but in the West Indies he and his brother Aucher were a progressive force. Plum denounced white-only selection policies and lobbied for the inclusion of at least four or five black players in the first West Indian tour of England in 1900. He wrote in advance of the 1900 tour that they would be fine fielders but fretted that 'the black men will . . . suffer from the weather if the summer turns out cold and damp, as their muscles are extremely loose'. He claimed that most could throw the ball well over 100 yards. He compared the best black fast bowler, 'Float' Woods, with England's fastest bowlers – from a two-pace run-up that he preferred to make in bare feet.[12]

The best black player, Lebrun Constantine, father of Learie, could not afford to go. C. L. R. James tell us that his expenses were instantly met by public subscription and he was rushed onto a special launch to catch the departing tourists' ship.[13] He rewarded his followers with a century against the MCC at Lord's. Tommy Burton and Float Woods took many wickets as bowlers. The biggest success was Charles Ollivierre, from the small island of St Vincent, who topped the batting averages and was compared to Ranji.[14] His performances earned him a place with Derbyshire (as a nominal amateur) – the first black player to perform regularly in county cricket, where he became a popular favourite. Eye trouble ended his county career but Ollivierre continued as a professional in club cricket and as a coach in the Netherlands – testament to the power of cricket to transform the lives of black people in colonial West Indies.*

The black tourists of 1900 met with some mockery and outright racism in British media[15] as did their successors in 1906, whose matches were given first-class status. But in general, spectators were polite and appreciative towards the first black players they had ever

---

* One other West Indian of this era, Sydney Smith, would also have a successful county career, with Northamptonshire, and was a *Wisden* Cricketer of the Year in 1915, but he was white. Remarkably, Smith played representative but not Test cricket for three countries – West Indies, England and New Zealand – an illustration of the elasticity of qualifications before the First World War.

seen.[16] Before the First World War, West Indies cricket had developed a distinct character and distinct structures. Its leadership positions were all occupied by a white colonial elite, who selected its players, and its international commitments were approved and even administered by the MCC. But through both domestic cricket and tours, some black players had announced themselves as international class. Besides those mentioned, these included Wilton St Hill, also admired locally as an artist. George John and George Francis had begun a tradition of feared West Indian opening bowlers. As we shall see, the First World War severely stunted the advance of West Indian cricket.

Chapter 14

NORTH AMERICA: CRICKET'S FAILED STATE

Cricket was North America's dominant summer ball game throughout the colonial era until the Civil War. In 1737 William Stephens, a Georgia planter, recorded that 'Many of our townsmen, freeholders, inmates and servants were assembled in the principal square at cricket and other diverse sports.'[1] Newspapers show it played in New York, New England and in its future epicentre, Philadelphia. In 1751 a New York Eleven defeated a London Eleven (possibly tourists but more likely expatriate settlers) by 87 runs, a huge margin for the times. As in contemporary England, the local newspaper reported that the match was played 'for a considerable wager'. A match report in 1751 specifically refers to the 'London method'. As in England there were many local variations of cricket; colonial newspapers and diaries often mentioned one called 'wicket', which may or may not be an ancestor of baseball.[2]

During the Seven Years' War in North America the cricket-crazed British General Braddock took cricket equipment and even rollers with him in his attack on the French Fort Duquesne (in present-day Pittsburgh). Braddock was killed before he could use it, but he set an example to one of his officers, George Washington, who encouraged cricket in his Continental Army during the war of independence, especially to maintain morale after the retreat to Valley Forge. The diary of Lieutenant Eaton records that Washington joined in a game of 'wicket' with his platoon. On the other side, the British garrison in New York doubled in size to 60,000 and cricket expanded with it.

There were regular practice matches at its headquarters in present-day Brooklyn and formal club matches, between Brooklyn and New York teams.[3]

Cricket appeared in American art of the time, usually as an aristocratic pastime, as in Benjamin West's painting *The Cricketers*, where a group of well-dressed young men lounge with massive, curved bats in their hands. Engravings depict the game being played at Dartmouth and Yale.[4] Cricket remained popular in Baltimore and in the antebellum South as a suitable pursuit for plantation owners that was cheaper than horse racing or yachting. In the best style, the young men of Savannah Cricket Club abandoned the field in 1861 to enlist in the Oglethorpe Light Infantry in the Confederate Army.[5]

Independence did not check the growth of cricket in the USA, although it gave American players more latitude in devising their own Laws and variations. English settlers advanced American cricket steadily westwards, especially those from the English cricket centres of Nottingham and Sheffield.[6] Haverford College and Germantown, future nurseries of Philadelphia cricket, were founded in the early 1840s, but the pre-eminent club was New York, founded in 1838 and renamed St George by its Anglophile membership a year later. In 1840 it played the first international cricket match in unusual circumstances after being invited to Toronto by a hoaxer. Reciprocal visits in subsequent years would lead to the first matches between even sides represented as national teams: Canada beat the USA at New York in 1844, and again at Montreal in 1845. The fixture survived disputes over player selection and an on-field brawl to become cricket's longest-running international fixture, if allowance is made for the fifty-year suspension in 1912.[7]

In 1907 a special commission delivered its report on the origins of baseball. It was a triumph of professional myth-making. At the behest of Albert Spalding, the former player who had built a household-name business in the manufacture and supply of baseball equipment, the report overruled Henry Chadwick, a leading organiser and promoter of baseball for fifty years. Chadwick suggested that the game derived from the English game of rounders. The commission made it the invention of an American, Abner Doubleday of Cooperstown, New York, a future Northern general in the Civil War. In this way, baseball became not only an all-American sport but also one associated with the winners in the Civil War, as opposed to the cricket played by the slave-owning losers. The myth has been regularly debunked – but Cooperstown has housed baseball's Hall of Fame since 1939 and nourished a successful cottage industry around it.[8]

Spalding's myth-making aside, baseball ousted cricket in the USA for three main reasons. First, baseball games were far easier to play informally at short notice by the armies in the Civil War, and afterwards in the rough and scarce public spaces of America's congested cities. Second, other countries replaced Britain and Ireland as the main source of immigration into the USA. Baseball was far easier for their people to adopt in the process of assimilation than cricket. Third, baseball quickly benefited from professional and commercial administration and promotion, unlike American cricket. It also developed structures that allowed children (or, more accurately, white boys) early aspiration to athletic places at colleges and professional careers.

Against the professional and national competition from other American sports, above all baseball, American cricket remained localised, amateur – and English. It established itself in California during the Gold Rush and in Chicago after the Civil War, principally through new English immigration. Chicago CC was founded in 1876 and benefited from coaching from a former Yorkshire cricketer, Tom Armitage.

It survived in New York and Boston, centres of previous English settlement, despite the elitism of its principal clubs, especially St George, which inspired the foundation of a more inclusive club at Staten Island.

It thrived in Philadelphia, which had its own Golden Age for some thirty years before the First World War. Philadelphian teams attracted leading international visitors and played them in front of tens of thousands of spectators. Their crowd receipts funded lavishly appointed grounds. They toured overseas and acquitted themselves well against first-class opposition.

The first tour, jointly hosted with Canada, took place in 1859. The British visitors were a huge success in Philadelphia and New York, as recorded in cricket's first ever tour diary, by Fred Lillywhite.[9] In Philadelphia especially it generated a demand for coaching and instruction from English professionals.[10] The New York hosts, the St George's Club, boasted of the largest crowd for any American sporting occasion. Another England party came to the USA in 1868 under Edgar Willsher, credited with the invention of overarm bowling, and won all its matches easily but noted the rising standard of Philadelphia cricket. The next England party in 1872 included W. G. Grace, who drew crowds and newspaper coverage as in England. The organiser was R. A. Fitzgerald, the MCC secretary. His jocular tour report, *Wickets in the West*, established the USA and Philadelphia in particular as a popular destination for English amateur visitors and professionals looking for work in the winter season.[11]

In 1878 the Australians made a stopover on their way back from their first tour of England (before the Panama Canal was built they were compelled to cross the American continent): they drew crowds but were unpopular visitors for their complaints about the local umpiring. Four years later, another Australian team, with Fred 'The Demon' Spofforth, which had snatched victory over England and inspired the legend of the Ashes, played Philadelphia.[12]

During the 1880s and 1890s, Philadelphia received nine more touring teams from England and Ireland.* The visitors included Plum Warner and Ranjitsinhji, but in many ways more significant contacts were with early West Indian sides in reciprocal visits. Under G. H. S. Trott, the full Australian side made another visit in

---

* In fiction they also received a university tour including P. G. Wodehouse's cricketing hero, Mike Jackson, which forms the backdrop to *Psmith, Journalist*.

1896, playing matches for the first time on level terms. They won two but lost the last by an innings. This led to the Philadelphian tour of England in 1897: all the matches had first-class status, as they would in the next two tours of 1903 and 1908. Significantly, they played as the Philadelphians, not the USA, and acquitted themselves well. The star was the all-rounder Bart King, who had learned his deadly late-inswinging yorker, the angler, from baseball and wrote an instruction manual about it. King topped the English first-class averages in 1908 with an average of 11.01, unsurpassed for another fifty years.[13]

But Philadelphia cricket never broke out of its amateur, upper-class base to prevent the conquest of the American summer by the game's challengers – and even among the upper classes it lost ground, literally, to new competition from golf, polo and lawn tennis.[14]

As already noted, American cricket was deprived of international competition by the formation of the ICC. The decision was short-sighted but it is doubtful whether Test matches would have arrested the decline of American cricket, even if the USA had developed the structures to choose and maintain a Test team. Its summer competitors, especially baseball but also lawn tennis and golf, had already displaced it in the American leisure market: like American football, they did not need international competition to thrive, then or now.

It was never easy for black Americans to play cricket in the era following the Civil War. Some individual clubs were overtly racist, including Haverford, who in 1911 cancelled a match 'when it was learnt that some of their opponents might be . . . black Americans'.[15] When white clubs did play racially mixed matches, they often attracted fury in local media, as in 1869 when a Philadelphia newspaper fulminated against 'the proud Caucasian . . . fraternising with the despised n****** on terms of the utmost cordiality'.[16]

In broad terms, this expensive pursuit in time, money and land, played in genteel exclusive settings, was never likely to attract black

Americans compelled to work long hours for low wages. But it was at least open to them, unlike professional baseball until the breakthrough of Jackie Robinson in 1947. Black cricketers did play in Philadelphia after the Civil War, despite the local press, and in New Orleans and other cities. White officials occasionally intervened against racist behaviour in American cricket and integrated visiting teams, such as the British Navy in Portland, Oregon, were generally welcomed. George Wright, the promoter of racially segregated professional baseball, urged American cricketers to welcome West Indian teams with black players.[17]

West Indian immigrants were beneficiaries of this policy and would do much to renew American cricket in New York and Boston. A new wave of American immigration began in the 1880s with Caribbean workers moving on from the construction of the Panama Canal. They included the parents of the great West Indian batter George Headley, born in Panama.[18] In New York, West Indians set up their own cricket clubs in the 1890s.[19] The clubs were identified by their home islands. They included one for the Danish Virgin Islands. It is remarkable that Denmark, one of only two European countries to adopt cricket on any scale from the British, re-exported cricket to its West Indian colony before it was sold to the USA in 1917.[20]

Cricket has a long history in Canada. There are accounts of matches being played by British soldiers and sailors in Britain's Canadian colonies, although the first recorded match played by civilians took place in the French city of Montreal after its conquest in the Seven Years' War. Cricket's early strength was in the English provinces or Upper Canada. It benefited from pro-British so-called Empire Loyalists who migrated from the newly independent USA and from British soldiers who fought there in the war of 1812 and later served as a garrison against Native Canadian and French uprisings. One match between British sailors on Parry's expedition in 1822–23 in search of the North-West Passage was played on ice just below 70° North.

Unfortunately for the future of Canadian cricket, it did not catch on like ice hockey.[*,21]

As we have already seen, Canada took part in the first cricket match between two countries, defeating the USA in 1844, well ahead of the first official if retrospective Test match between England and Australia in 1877. Since it also anticipated the first international association and rugby football matches and the first modern Olympics, Canada has a good claim to be the first victorious international sports team.

In the second half of the nineteenth century, benefiting from improvements in transport, especially the transcontinental Canadian Pacific Railway, cricket broke out of its strongholds in Ontario and Quebec, and reached the Prairie provinces, British Columbia and all the eastern Maritime Provinces.[†,22] Canada had regular international fixtures against the USA, hosted major English and Australian teams, and sent out visiting teams itself, principally to its neighbour, the USA.

But Canadian cricket was weakened by distance and climate. It faced major challenges from competing sports: lacrosse, (ice) hockey, basketball, rowing and baseball. The first two were invented in Canada and codified there; basketball was invented by Canadian James Naismith but introduced and developed in the USA. All of these offered greater ease of preparation and participation in Canadian conditions than cricket, and were less dominated by wealthy elites.

---

[*] For many years this had the record of the farthest north cricket match. It has since been played at the North Pole, in the course of a naval exercise to show strength against Russia. Former New Zealand captain John Reid took part in a game at the South Pole in 1969.

[†] The province of Newfoundland and Labrador was not part of Canada at this time. The game was very popular in the capital, St John's, especially among its network of middle-class families at the end of the century, before succumbing to the same forces that put pressure on cricket in Canada.

For these reasons, Canadian cricket made little mark on any other country. The gulf between it and the major cricket nations was illustrated in 1913 when it hosted matches in a North American tour by an Australian team. The Canadian teams lost every match. Winnipeg were all out for 6 and Vancouver yielded the visitors 633 runs, still the highest total ever made in Canada.

Chapter 15

SOUTH AMERICAN ODYSSEY

The first cricket in Latin America was played in inglorious circumstances in 1806 by British captives of a bungled and unauthorised naval expedition to liberate the future Argentina from Britain's enemy, Spain. A few years later, Admiral Cochrane's more successful sailors played some onshore matches during the liberation of Chile. When Spain was finally ejected from all its mainland possessions, previously closed markets were opened to the British. They took cricket with them, and in a very short time began to play it among themselves, organise it and acquire exclusive land for it.

There is a pattern to cricket development in both Central and South America. One British community with a skill set was attracted to a Latin American resource and created a cricket-playing nexus, if not a formal club. As elsewhere, miners and railway workers were especially influential in spreading the game, particularly Cornish miners, which is intriguing because Cornwall was cut off, by geography and lack of railways, from the main centres of early nineteenth-century English cricket. Cornish miners played the first cricket in Mexico in the 1820s in the silver mining areas north of the capital. Their cricket legacy has disappeared but the area still serves wonderful Cornish pasties.[1] Cornish miners also exported cricket to the Brazilian gold mines in Minas Gerais in the 1830s: the miners' identities as cricketers helped to distinguish them from the slave labour that lingered lawfully in Brazil until the 1880s.*

---

* Its final legal abolition by the enlightened Emperor Pedro II was a major reason for his overthrow in 1889.

In the same period, British merchants, bankers and diplomats set up a formal Mexico City Cricket Club. Like later clubs in other great cities, it was intended as a symbol of Britishness, especially a manly commitment to exercise in a climate that had clearly enervated the previous colonists, the Spaniards, and the local population. Other such clubs often excluded locals, but Mexico City encouraged participation by well-connected upper-class Mexicans. One guest player was the imported Habsburg ruler, Emperor Maximilian, taking a break from preserving his flimsy throne from the exiled nationalist leader, Benito Juarez. He may well be the only ruling emperor to have played cricket, although his contemporary, Brazil's revered Emperor Pedro II, was a regular spectator at matches played by Rio Cricket Club in the palace grounds of his daughter Isabel, Princess Imperial.[2] The British also benefited from the patronage of several presidents. In Ecuador, the Guayaquil Sports Club, founded in 1899, had its ground weeded on the personal orders of President Alfaro.[3]

It is fair to say that the British did not evangelise cricket in Latin America or encourage local people to play it. In inhospitable locations where there were few of them, they allowed participation on their own terms out of necessity. In the accidental colony of British Honduras, now Belize, the Wanderers Club was founded for whites only, then admitted locals as net bowlers and, after further delay, as full members.[4] In Brazil, British railway workers played matches in front of curious local onlookers in São Paulo; they did not invite them to play and instead the Paulistas invented taco, their own version with local rules and materials, not unlike Pakistan's great invention of tapeball.[5]

Unlike in India, cricket was not ubiquitous in elite secondary schools, and the British sometimes grumbled at the consequences. Just after the First World War, the leading Argentinian cricketer Philip Foy wrote in Pelham Warner's *Cricketer*: 'The game is too slow for the Latin temperament to accept spontaneously *and there are no Argentine public schools where it could be taught*' [our italics]. He added: 'There is undoubtedly, however, a large element that would take to the game and play it well if facilities and education afforded.'

Cricket in Latin America had a strongly dynastic character. The same families recur in country narratives for two or more generations: the Leaches, Aylings, Dornings and Gibsons in Argentina, the Cunninghams of Brazil, the Jewells of Chile, the Vaughans of Nicaragua.* They learned their early cricket at exclusive local primary schools but were then turned into the finished article at English public schools. The same applied to the few elite Latin American cricketers with very distant British connections or none at all, such as the Colombians Julio Portocarrero O'Leary and Carlos Ordoñez. After the First World War, this pattern was repeated for the only England cricket captain born in Latin America, Freddie Brown, who learned his early cricket from his father at Lima Cricket and Football Club and St Peter's boarding prep school in Chile. They converted him from a left-hander to a right-hander, the sign of an enduring prejudice, before he was packed off to his English public school, The Leys in Cambridge.[6]

Cricket advances in Latin America

The deepest British penetration of Latin America was in Chile, Brazil, Uruguay and Argentina. These were therefore the countries that played most cricket, including the first international matches against each other.

In Chile, cricket was initially centred on the port of Valparaiso, whose club was founded in 1860, but was carried by British workers and managers all along the coastline and into the interior as the result of the country's double boom in nitrates and copper in the 1860s. A big force in Chilean cricket was the Nitrate King, John North, in modern terms a cricket groupie and proud of his friendship with

---

* One of us played with a scion of the Vaughan family at prep school in the 1960s. He was a very fine fast bowler.

W. G. Grace. His employees took cricket to the port of Iquique, originally part of Peru but lost to Chile in the terrible War of the Pacific of 1879–84. North's teams played those of the British-run copper mines in matches accompanied by lavish banquets. Another key figure was the British consul, Maurice Jewell, whose sons played for Worcestershire as amateurs after the First World War. One led the Gentlemen of Worcestershire on a tour of Nazi Germany.* Chile hosted an Argentine touring party in 1893, which had to make part of its journey over the Andes by mule. Both sides were heavily British in composition. The tour was an early exercise in cricket diplomacy, and helped to resolve disputes over water and frontiers.

A combination of traders and missionaries established a club in the deepest south of the country at Punta Arenas. Two of its members helped to rescue Ernest Shackleton's Antarctic explorers (including a well-known Scottish cricketer, R. S. Clark) trapped on the *Endurance*.[7]

In Brazil, 4,000 British railway workers were the core members of the São Paulo Cricket Club, founded in 1872. It was reformed in 1888 as the São Paulo Cricket and Athletic Club, a sign of challenge from other recreations, although cricket was still paramount. Its regular matches against Rio gradually expanded into provincial contests that represented the apex of Brazilian cricket.

The coffee boom drew the British – and cricket – to Santos. The Johnston family were pillars of the local club. After the First World War a young Brian Johnston had an unhappy apprenticeship in the family coffee plantation but was a good enough wicketkeeper to play for São Paulo, on his way to the BBC's *Test Match Special*.

Brazil's even more spectacular rubber boom took cricket deep into its interior at Manaus. British telegraph workers and sailors were the mainstay of cricket in Pernambuco, the first landfall for ships from Europe.[8]

The British took cricket to Uruguay in the 1840s. Established as a buffer state between Brazil and Argentina, its cricket benefited from

---

* A tour narrated brilliantly by Dan Waddell in *Field of Shadows*.

Britons fleeing the regular conflicts in both countries, although it was hit badly in the 1860s when Uruguay itself went to war with Argentina. Banking, a British-built waterworks and later a booming meat trade brought Britons – and cricketers – to Uruguay in numbers. Starting in 1868, Britons in Argentina played regular reciprocal matches against their counterparts in Uruguay. Not surprisingly, they won most of them. Next to Canada and the USA, this is the oldest international cricket series in the world.

Cricket's other failed state

The British gave cricket its greatest grip in Argentina. As already mentioned, the country attracted considerable British emigration. It was especially popular with adventurous public schoolboys.* In office jobs in the main cities, they had plenty of leisure time for cricket while the German clerks were said to do most of the work.

Despite British exclusivity, the game initially engaged enough Argentinians to make it worth putting out, in 1881, an instructional manual in Spanish, naturally written by an Englishman, J. W. Williams. There were also long accounts of matches in Spanish newspapers.[9] Argentina formed the first women's cricket club in the world, at Belgrano in 1865.

Argentina played three matches against the MCC before the First World War and called them Tests. They were not recognised as such but all were awarded first-class status. On the eve of the First World War, their best sides (all of British origins) were a match for many English counties. With recognition and encouragement, Argentina might well have ascended to Test status. Instead, a combination of war and association football made Argentina the world's second cricketing 'failed state'.

---

* One fictional example is Wyatt, the best friend of P. G. Wodehouse's schoolboy cricket hero Mike Jackson before he meets Psmith. Wyatt is delivered from a life of drudgery at a British bank (such as Wodehouse endured) by a job on an Argentinian estancia in which Mike's father has an interest.

As elsewhere, cricket in Argentina was shaped by waves of British immigration. The bankers and merchants in Buenos Aires were the first. They preserved good relations with Juan Manuel de Rosas, the early Argentine dictator and his successors, through whom they could preserve land for cricket. A later president, Domingo Faustino Sarmiento, developed a respect for cricket in the belief that it had enabled the British to stave off what they and he called the Indian Mutiny. This was useful in introducing cricket to Patagonia after Sarmiento's army conquered it from the Mapuche Indians with the help of new Remington rifles financed with British loans.

The Great Southern Railway allowed wealthy Britons and Anglo-Argentines to escape congested central Buenos Aires into salubrious suburbs, where they created new clubs. Their showpiece was Hurlingham (on the Pacific Railway and named after the English members' club) where the former professional from Nottinghamshire William Lacey created a ground and facilities of such magnificence that a town was created around them and it obtained its own railway station. Argentinian clubs in general demanded better and better grass wickets. When Argentina started to play Brazil, its regular victories were attributed by Brazilian captain Charles Miller (better known as the father of Brazilian football) to their superior experience of bowling and batting on grass, while Brazilian clubs were forced by climate to play mainly on matting.

Throughout Latin America, Argentina's cricketers were those most eager to tour overseas and to receive visiting tourists. Although gratified by their successes against neighbours Chile, Uruguay and Brazil, they wanted most of all to measure themselves against English teams. Their first approach was to Lord Hawke in 1898. Apart from his general love of touring and cricket evangelism, his Lordship had extensive business interests in Argentine railways. That approach foundered. So too did an approach to the MCC touring party in New Zealand in 1905–06 to visit the country on their return home. They were put off by the immense distance of the Pacific and the necessity of rounding Cape Horn.

Argentina's cricketers finally got their wish in the winter of 1911–12, when they received a touring party led by Hawke himself. It had a country-house quality about it (as did much of the cricket played) but the team did include an ageing and increasingly crotchety Archie MacLaren, and Rockley Wilson of Winchester, Yorkshire and later England. Argentina won the first match, lost the second badly and almost snatched the decider, which Lord Hawke's team, playing as MCC, won by just two wickets.

A few years later almost all the cricketers who had faced Lord Hawke went 'home' to Britain to enlist in the First World War. Other nationalities, with no navy ruling the waves, were cut off from their 'homelands' and remained in neutral Argentina – and continued to play the growing competitor sport of association football.

Latin American cricket would return after the First World War in its privileged British enclaves. Argentina would have more moments of amateur glory, and matches of first-class status, including its first tours of England. It would host distinguished amateur English tours including Plum Warner and a future British prime minister. However, cricket had lost whatever chance it had of becoming a dominant sport in Central and South America outside the West Indian outcrop of British Guiana.

Chapter 16

THE UNIQUENESS OF IRISH CRICKET[1]

In 1922 most of Ireland broke away from the UK and then, in progressive stages, it extinguished its formal links with the British Empire and Commonwealth, completing the process in 1949. But these great political changes had minimal impact on the status of Irish people and institutions within the UK. Whether from Northern Ireland or the Free State, later Republic, Irish people retained an unlimited right to settle and work in Britain, to serve in its armed forces and other public services, to vote in its elections and take political office. Irish institutions and qualifications were recognised as if nothing had happened.

In this sense most of Ireland was both independent and part of the English-dominated polity of the UK.

Irish cricket had the same sort of status for nearly 200 years. Flourishing and distinctive at a local level, it had no national autonomy or independent administration and was an informal part of the English and imperial cricket system. Its best players were automatically qualified for English counties and the national team (although few took up the opportunity). Some Irish teams and fixtures were given first-class status – by the MCC. Ireland attracted many distinguished cricket tourists, not just from England, and sometimes defeated them. Only in this century did Irish cricket achieve full independence – and even now its best players are automatically English if they choose to be, without having to complete any residential qualifications.

Ireland's cricket history is also deeply entwined with the island's internal politics and social history. Long before the anti-apartheid exclusion of South Africa, Ireland staged cricket's first politically motivated boycott. Because of its special character, we have followed the early story of Irish cricket past the First World War, our break point for other countries.

There is a contentious reference to a ban by Oliver Cromwell on 'krickett' in Ireland in 1656. It feeds into a general narrative of Cromwellian tyranny in Ireland and to the supposition that cricket was a well-established pastime on the island with deep Celtic roots.[2] However, Gerard Siggins, in his short but authoritative history of Irish cricket, suggests that the 'krickett' banned by Cromwell was far more likely to have been the Irish sport of hurling.[3]

Thereafter cricket remained a garrison sport. The British ruled Ireland and cricket generally remained confined to the army, some gentry, and members of the Viceregal or Chief Secretary's staff and household. This explains why the first officially recorded match in Ireland did not take place until 1792, between teams styled The Garrison and (misleadingly) All-Ireland, captained by the Secretary of War, Major Hobart. The former included the future Duke of Wellington, bowled for five runs by a delivery from the future Duke of Richmond. One thousand guineas were bet on the result. Stanley Bergin and Derek Scott note that 'such challenge matches were common enough then, but the Irish themselves appear not to have shown much interest in the game' until the 1820s.[4]

Cricket prospered in Ireland, and broadened its social base, after the Duke of Wellington's close-run victory (with the aid of Prussian substitutes) over Napoleon on a wet wicket at Waterloo. It was especially strong in the towns of Kilkenny and Meath,[5] and new clubs were established at Phoenix Park and Trinity College, Dublin. As in England, leading schools and railways were major contributors to the development of the game, while many historic landowning families supported it as a contributor to harmony with their tenants. However, Irish cricket had one distinct local contributor – a British garrison of up to 30,000.[6] In later years, cricket would suffer from being identified as a 'garrison' game played by an oppressive army of occupation.

The Irish potato famine reduced its population (of nearly nine million) by over a third. One million were lost to famine and disease, and two million to emigration.[7] The most important destinations were the USA, Australia and Great Britain. As noted elsewhere, Irish emigrants and their descendants made a major contribution to the development of Australian cricket, though it came at the cost of a recurring factional divide.[8] This was not true of American cricket. While some Irish continued to play in the USA and Canada, many factors discouraged early Irish-Americans from doing so. Low-wage jobs in American cities left them with little leisure time and open space. They were also the first wave of voluntary immigrants to attract racial and nativist prejudice.[9] They were targeted by America's first anti-immigrant political party, called the Know-Nothing Party (a name that might well be revived in the present day). All of these factors pushed Irish-Americans towards the new sport of baseball. It needed less space and expensive care, and it served to mark their assimilation into American society.

In Victorian times, three Irishmen played for England in early Tests, all as amateurs: the peppery baronet Sir Timothy O'Brien, the amiable Leland Hone and the legendary Emile McMaster, who as we have seen set an unsurpassable first-class record. In the twentieth century there was only one major professional English player of Irish descent: Patsy Hendren, of Middlesex and England, the third highest first-class run-scorer in history. Irish people in Britain never contributed to cricket the talent they offered to association football.

Meanwhile, in Ireland the game continued to prosper. It even inspired an annual, John Lawrence's *Handbook of Cricket in Ireland*, a year after the first slim *Wisden Cricketers' Almanack* for England.[10] The author was not related to Charles Lawrence, whom we have met as a leading player and promoter of cricket in four different countries.

Lawrence promoted home and away matches against leading contemporary sides, before being lost to Australia. Part of his legacy was the Gentlemen of Ireland, an amateur team whose matches were given first-class status at home and on tour.[11]

A new elite itinerant club, Na Shuler (a Gaelicisation of Wanderers), came into being in 1863. Modelled on England's contemporary I Zingari, it had the same founder, the future Earl of Bessborough. One of its leading members was Charles Stewart Parnell MP, Ireland's leading advocate of land reform and home rule. He was not a popular player because of his gamesmanship and finickity adherence to the Laws of Cricket (including some that he invented). This foreshadowed his reputation as an exploiter of parliamentary procedure.[12]

The harmony of Irish domestic cricket was broken by the rise of Irish nationalism, itself fuelled by resentment and, at times, violent protest of Irish tenants against absentee English landlords who were consolidating their estates, wiping out their smallholdings and raising rents for the survivors.

In 1884 the Gaelic Athletic Association came into being to promote traditional Gaelic sports such as hurling and Gaelic football. It organised the first politically motivated boycott of cricket, denounced as a foreign sport, which its members were forbidden to play or even watch. This ban lasted as long as 1971, drawing reinforcement when Eamon De Valera's Fianna Fáil government took power in the Free State, determined to demonstrate its political and cultural separation from Britain and its empire.* The ban had some comic effects, for example when Catholic and nationalist politicians including John Redmond, Cathal Brugha (the former Charles Burgess), John Hume and De Valera himself[13] were compelled to hide their interest in cricket. But it had a serious long-term impact in placing cricket on

---

* De Valera's promotion of the Irish language did no favours to Irish cricket either, and to this day there is no official translation of the Laws of Cricket (or *cruicéad*) as there is in Welsh, the A'r Gyfraithau Criced, published on the ICC website.

one side of Ireland's political and sectarian divide, and reducing the will and the opportunity for Irish children and young people to take part in it. Ed Joyce, who became the first of a wave of Irish players to break through into international cricket in the twenty-first century, hid his cricket kit as a boy travelling on trains in Dublin.[14,*]

Irish cricket after Partition

The Irish national struggle resulted eventually in a compromise Partition plan. Two civil wars had added more cricket casualties to those of the First World War; the second had claimed the life of Michael Collins, the great Irish leader who had done more than anyone to end the first.

Partition had the curious consequence of forming a single all-Ireland cricket union. As in rugby union, Ireland – North and the Free State – remained one cricket unit, unlike association football, where the working-class sectarian divide generated two separate teams. The new union had no executive power and confined itself to re-organising the fixtures of the Gentlemen of Ireland. Trinity College Dublin enjoyed first-class status in the 1920s, and Samuel Beckett played for them against Northamptonshire, thus becoming the only first-class cricketer to win a Nobel Prize for literature.

For the rest of the twentieth century the Irish team played exactly 100 first-class matches – the great majority against Scotland – and many other shorter matches against other international visitors as an adjunct to their tours of England. They had a few memorable results, especially a victory over the West Indies in 1969 after dismissing them for 25. Many sources still attribute this unfairly to the impact

---

* The boy's nervousness is the more striking because he came from a notable cricketing family. Two of his sisters played international cricket for Ireland; one, Isobel, routed a pioneering but weak Pakistan women's team in the only Test match Ireland's women have ever contested. The Pakistan team contained a debutante, Sajjida Shah, officially twelve years old and therefore the youngest person to appear in a Test.

of Irish pre-match hospitality rather than giving credit to two fine opening bowlers, Alec O'Riordan and Dougie Goodwin, exploiting a helpful wicket.

None of the first-class matches had any significance, except statistically. There were enough of them to ensure that Ireland's best bowler – the off-spinner Jimmy Boucher – several times topped the *English* season's bowling averages in a first-class cricket career that produced 168 first-class wickets in twenty-four years at an impressive average of under 15.[15] Boucher was good enough to have played professionally in England and in all probability at Test level. But he had to decline a tour of India, which might have led to such recognition. He could not afford to leave his clerical job on the Electricity Supply Board and was not willing to leave behind his widowed mother and unmarried sister.[16]

W. G. Grace visited Ireland several times in the nineteenth century (and advised their players to display more cunning) and they had some distinguished later visitors. Ranjitsinhji bought an Irish estate after his cricketing days were over, but his nephew K. S. Duleepsinhji came and delivered a scintillating all-round performance. Don Bradman skipped the Irish leg of the Australian English tour of 1938, leaving the captaincy to an Australian of Irish origin, Stan McCabe. The Irish also saw (and succumbed to) his Irish-origin contemporary Bill O'Reilly, and Richie Benaud's Australians came over in full strength in 1961. Garry Sobers toured as a new recruit in 1957 but never in his pomp. He missed the disaster in 1969 but the beaten West Indians included Basil Butcher, Clyde Walcott and Clive Lloyd.

After the Second World War, the Irish realised their appeal to high-quality amateur tourists and created a new club, the Leprechauns, specifically to attract more of them. The eclectic quality of Irish cricket is exemplified by its guiding spirit, Charles Bowlby, a misfit who might have stepped from a Graham Greene novel. He had narrowly escaped execution for treason, alongside William Joyce, 'Lord Haw-Haw', as a propagandist for Nazi Germany during the war.[17]

Between the Second World War and the 1990s, cricket almost vanished in the Republic outside Dublin and Cork. However, a small number of rural clubs survived; one was Mount Juliet with its scenic ground on the banks of the river Nore near Kilkenny, and a history dating back 200 years. Until 1970 their team consisted of the employees of a major equine centre where some of the great thoroughbreds of the twentieth century were bred. Ballyeighan, formed as a result of friendly cricket matches between fox hunts in the early 1970s, and Halverston, are farmers' teams that also flourished during a generally barren period for Irish cricket. When the ICC opened its doors to associate members in 1965, Ireland was not among them and it still had no central administration. These developments arrived only in 1993. Two years later they appointed their first national coach, former England pace bowler Mike Hendrick, a serious individual who resented the ingrained amateur ethos of his charges – as did his successor, Ken Rutherford of New Zealand.[18]

Associate membership allowed Ireland to compete for the first time in structured international competitions organised by the ICC, where victory had a purpose as well as an excuse for celebration. In 1980 the English had admitted Ireland to its best-known one-day competition, the Gillette Cup: it failed to win a single match in twenty years.

Better days for Irish cricket would owe more to the efforts of the ICC and individual Irish players, rather than their nearest neighbours.

Irish cricket in the twenty-first century

Irish cricket made an international breakthrough in the twenty-first century, from a combination of factors. Ed Joyce led several talented Irish players in seeking a professional career in England, including his county colleague Eoin Morgan, Boyd Rankin, Tim Murtagh, William Porterfield, Paul Stirling and the brothers Kevin and Niall O'Brien. Their success and experience would eventually return to Ireland as players or coaches. Ireland's cricket administration became much tauter and directed under an experienced CEO, Warren Deutrom.[19] The ICC handed out greater revenues to associates (although far below those of privileged full members), which coincided with a long boom in the Irish economy. Irish cricket became significantly richer and clubs could afford to offer professional contracts to experienced players and coaches. The ICC created a new competition – the Intercontinental Cup – to drive up first-class playing standards in the more advanced associate members (including Ireland and Scotland); its advocate, Bob Woolmer, was convinced that it would also drive up their one-day standards.[20] They expanded the entrants to the 2007 World Cup in the West Indies and gave Ireland a pathway to qualification for the first time.

Above all, Ireland started winning important matches and producing some fine individual performances even if they lost. They qualified for the Super Eights round of the 2007 World Cup after a thrilling tie with Zimbabwe and victories over Bangladesh and, most sensationally, Pakistan. At the next World Cup, in 2011, Ireland overcame England for the first time with a century off fifty balls by Kevin O'Brien. All these successes gave Irish cricket a popularity and media following it had never previously enjoyed. Deutrom cleverly exploited this by identifying it with the colours of Ireland's international soccer and rugby union teams.

For financial reasons alone, Deutrom was anxious to push Ireland further, into full member (or Test match) status. The move would secure not only a bigger share-out of ICC revenues but a far greater number of bilateral one-day contests against other full members. He secured his objective in 2018, when Ireland secured their first Test match – at home in Malahide – against Pakistan. Joyce was allowed to return to the fold for Ireland after his one-day career with England. Again Kevin O'Brien came to the fore, with a century that saved Ireland from a likely innings defeat. In their first Test match against England at Lord's, in 2019, Ireland led England on first innings, thanks to Murtagh, who had learned his trade there leading the Middlesex attack.

As of November 2025, Ireland had played twelve Test matches and won three of them – a decent record compared to the opening ten Test matches of most other cricket nations. But sadly, Ireland's Tests have been given inferior status: none has counted for the World Test Championship and most have been one-off matches rather than series, against lesser cricket powers. No domestic first-class matches were played in 2023 and just four in 2024, only one of these between two domestic Irish teams.

Since 2000, in addition to those twelve Test matches, the Irish men's team have played 210 one-day internationals and 178 T20 internationals.[21] In the same period Ireland's women have played a solitary Test match, 139 one-day internationals and 140 T20s.[22] Despite their recent successes, Ireland's men have yet to match the women's appearances in five World Cups. With even less official support than Ireland's male cricketers for most of their history, Ireland's women's cricket depended all the more on individual efforts by players and administrators. In 2001, after twenty years of independent life, the Irish Women's Cricket Union followed England's women in merging with their country's men's administration, on promise of more resources and attention.[23]

With long gaps and an irregular programme, many of Ireland's best players have understandably given priority to T20 franchise competitions. Ireland's first-class structure (created by Deutrom as a condition of Test match status) has disappeared. Ireland's example is likely to convince future nations that Test status is not worth the bother and expense, when T20 offers an easier pathway into international competition.

Part Three

THE IMPACT OF WAR

If I knew that I was going to die today, I think I should still want to hear the cricket scores.
G. H. HARDY

Pray God, no professional shall ever captain England.
LORD HAWKE, 1925

England has now begun the grim Test Match against Germany. We do not wish to win merely the Ashes of civilization. We want to win a lasting peace with honour and prosperity to us all.
SIR HOME GORDON, *The Cricketer*, 1939

Chapter 17

THE FIRST WORLD WAR AND ITS AFTERMATH

The 1914 season was reaching its climax when Britain declared war on Germany. At the Oval, Surrey was playing Nottinghamshire, whose captain Arthur Carr (later a mentor for Harold Larwood) received a telegram instructing him to join the 5th Lancers in Dublin. 'I'll have my innings first,' he remarked, scored 30, and left for Ireland.[1] The War Office requisitioned the Oval. Surrey moved its next match to Lord's. It was played against Kent, for whom Colin Blythe, killed three years later by a stray shell during the Battle of Passchendaele, took nine wickets in Surrey's first innings.

Two days later the MCC announced: 'No good purpose can be served at the present moment by cancelling matches.' By the end of the month, with the British Expeditionary Force taking heavy casualties, W. G. Grace wrote to *The Times*:

> The fighting on the Continent is very severe, and will probably be prolonged. I think the time has arrived when the county cricket season should be closed, for it is not fitting at a time like this that able-bodied men should be playing cricket by day and pleasure-seekers look on.[2]

In response the counties agreed to play a last round of matches and call it a day. Surrey was given dispensation to return to the Oval where, with the aid of Jack Hobbs' eleventh century of the season, the team beat Gloucestershire (a ten-man team because of wartime commitments) and secured the County Championship. No more county cricket was played till 1919.³ Grace died in 1915.

Hobbs, England's greatest batter, did not succumb to the jingoism of the early months of the war, arguing that he owed a duty to his wife and four children. He later infuriated Lord Hawke, heavily involved in wartime recruitment, by playing in the Bradford League along with Sydney Barnes.

Some 289 first-class cricketers died in the First World War.⁴ One of the first to fall was Captain A. E. J. Collins of the Royal Engineers, killed in action on 11 November during the First Battle of Ypres. Collins had achieved fame as a thirteen-year-old schoolboy at Clifton College when he compiled a world record 628 not out in a house match.

Wisden was the usual 800 pages in 1915, with match reports and scores. The following year it was less than half that size, with seventy-seven pages given over to obituaries. The 1917 *Almanack* is one of the hardest to obtain. Families of fallen cricketers bought *Wisden*, now dominated by their obituaries, as a memorial for their sons. Many had no known grave.⁵ Peter Wynne-Thomas has calculated that one in every eleven first-class cricketers between 1900 and 1914 was killed.⁶ *Wisden* recorded a total of 1,800 cricketing deaths.

This figure would have been much higher had the *Almanack* not (as ever) neglected league cricket. Among the 400 dead listed in the 1917 edition, just seven names can be identified as league cricketers. No one has compiled a full count of league club cricketers lost in the war. But many close-knit working-class communities were devastated by losses through the early system of 'pals battalions'. Accrington lost 630 pals from 720 in just two days on the Somme, while Burnley lost a total of 4,000 young men.⁷ Major (first name not military rank) Booth of Yorkshire and England died on the first day of the Somme in the arms of his Yorkshire teammate Abe Waddington.⁸

Wisden cites white casualties from the Indian army and Dominion and colonial forces but there is no count of non-white cricket players who were killed in the same forces, nor those who died as labourers or merchant seamen.

The Indian army sent over 1.5 million men to fight with the British Empire in all theatres.[9] Plenty of these will have been cricketers, but we can find no record of cricketing fatalities. India was one of the few countries where cricket continued to be played during the war, with the Quadrangular tournament carrying on unimpeded. Cricket ceased in Australia and South Africa, where Britain defended its colonies against a Boer revolt supported by Germany.

Upon returning home, some cricketers tried to resume their careers despite severe physical and mental wounds. Don Denton had made four unremarkable appearances for Northamptonshire before the war. In 1919 and 1920, he reappeared three times – with a prosthetic leg – and fielded only at point. Although not strictly entitled under the Laws, he asked for his brother to run for him during his innings on his return. The opposing captain replied, 'If any fellow has been to the war and has had his leg off and wants to play, he is good enough for me and can have twenty runners.' Denton scored 29 not out for his side.[10]

Arthur Jewell of the Chilean cricketing family returned to Worcestershire and scored three centuries in the two post-war seasons, despite the leg wound that killed him in 1922.[11] His teammate Fred Root was told that a chest wound had ended his own cricket career. He arranged a league contract while still in his hospital bed, became the mainstay of his county attack and played for England.[12] Frank Chester played with a hook fitted to his amputated right arm. He learned to hit and catch with his left hand only, and eventually became England's youngest first-class umpire and a legend in the role.[13] Harry Lee of Middlesex was given up for dead when he was shot in the leg and his femur shattered. He endured terrible conditions as a prisoner of war yet managed to have a long post-war career as an all-rounder for Middlesex, and (with one Test appearance) was England's second oldest player after Andrew Sandham at the time of his death in 1981.

Post-war cricket

The First World War had the surprise effect of improving the finances of most English counties because staff and outgoings were much reduced, and members loyally kept up their subscriptions even though there were no county matches to watch.[14] This effect may have demonstrated to some counties that they actually lost money by playing cricket. The MCC and other administrators were aware that they needed to attract more spectators in the first peacetime season. Their solution, as throughout the interwar period, was 'brighter cricket', naturally led by amateurs. They considered all manner of schemes to quicken its tempo, including penalties for maiden overs and even a ban on left-handed batters, which would have ended the career of England's greatest interwar crowd-pleaser, Frank Woolley.[15] In the end they adopted only one: two-day county matches, to take advantage of one of the war's permanent innovations, Daylight Saving Time in summer. It proved unpopular with players and spectators alike, and was abandoned after one year.[16]

The points-scoring system in the County Championship was amended eight times and there were intermittent new laws and regulations, generally in an attempt to discourage negative play and attritional scoring by batters.[17] One of these was noteworthy: the authorities ran trials allowing a batter to be given out LBW even if the ball had previously touched his bat.*

The boom in attendances proved short-lived. Yorkshire won the restored championship in 1919, followed by Middlesex in 1920 and 1921. The 1920 championship was secured under the captaincy of Plum Warner, aged forty-six. This was much celebrated in the media as a triumph for all that was best in amateur leadership, not least by Warner himself, who combined journalism with the roles of player, selector and administrator in a unique personal privilege. Thereafter

---

* The present Laws again reprieve batters who make an involuntary contact of bat on ball before being hit on the pads.

the championship moved north: Yorkshire won it eleven times, Lancashire five, Nottinghamshire and Derbyshire once each, the latter two primarily through superb fast bowlers recruited from local pits.[18] For most of the interwar years the counties were not obliged to play each other and the championship was settled on a percentage basis – the greatest points per game played. This made it hard for the public to follow and led to regular charges of gamesmanship or unfairness.[19]

Some batters from southern counties could still fill grounds – notably Woolley at Kent, Hobbs at Surrey (who was especially in demand for other players' benefit matches), Walter Hammond and, later, Charlie Barnett at Gloucestershire, Patsy Hendren of Middlesex and K. S. Duleepsinhji at Sussex. County finances were fitfully lifted by their performances or those of visitors (especially Don Bradman in the 1930s) or by long spells of fine weather. But there were no systematic plans to grow spectatorship and bold ideas for this were rejected, notably calls for a transfer system to promote an exchange of talent between counties and for a one-day knockout competition. This idea came into being only in 1963 after more decades of drift and decline.

Cricket could not retain its hold in the interwar leisure market, where association football gained an extra advantage through the introduction of football pools.[20] Cricket also had to compete with golf, tennis, cycling and fishing (as pre-war) and with two new sports: speedway and greyhound racing.* Other non-sporting recreations also helped to displace cricket: motoring, the cinema, dancing and 'listening in' to the radio, although commentary and match summaries on radio created a new form of spectatorship for international cricket.[21]

All but three counties were drifting into insolvency by 1937, as reported by the Findlay Committee.[22] Most begged more and more from their members or from rich patrons, such as the furniture

---

* The star greyhound, Mick the Miller, had a motion picture made about him, *Wild Boy*, in 1933.

magnate Sir Julien Cahn. Cricket and individual cricketers took Cahn's money eagerly while scorning him for being a vulgarian and a Jew.[23]

The short-lived post-war spectator boom encouraged the authorities to expand the Championship to seventeen* through the addition of Glamorgan in 1921, which found it hard to compete seriously and relied on amateurs of varied ages, talents and eagerness. For one match, against Leicestershire in 1922, Glamorgan enlisted a fifteen-year-old schoolboy, Royston Gabe-Jones of Blundell's School, who was the youngest to play in the Championship until Yorkshire's Matthew Fisher broke the record in 2013. Despite a creditable performance, he never played again.[24,†] The county slowly improved, mainly through imports from other counties although Glamorgan had three home-grown mainstays in Maurice Turnbull, John Clay and, at the end of the period, Wilf Wooller. Glamorgan became a proxy for a Welsh team and faced regular nationalist criticism for being part of English cricket, although they brought more money into Welsh cricket than Wales could ever have generated independently. There was also a short-lived unofficial Wales team, mainly representing North Wales, sponsored by a businessman, Mr Rowland of Denbighshire. Its greatest success was a victory over the touring West Indians in 1928, principally through the agency of a hitherto unknown Welshman, Sydney Barnes.[25,‡]

---

* Derbyshire, Essex, Glamorgan, Gloucestershire, Hampshire, Kent, Lancashire, Leicestershire, Middlesex, Northamptonshire, Nottinghamshire, Somerset, Surrey, Sussex, Warwickshire, Worcestershire and Yorkshire.

† Several Pakistani players are reliably believed to have played first-class cricket at twelve years old, including one, Aaqib Javed, as an opening pace bowler.

‡ Aged fifty-five, he took twelve wickets. The West Indians rated him the best bowler they had faced on tour.

League cricket between the wars

The professional leagues that flourished in the north and the Midlands were almost completely ignored by the national media, and until recently by historians as well. The cricket was hard, intense and, according to some informed observers, played at a higher level than much of the amateur-led county cricket that made newspaper headlines. Conditions in this version of the game were the same as league football clubs before and after the war: Saturday play, more professional management and close connections with local supporters. It was, as a result, more profitable. League cricket thus anticipated the move to one-day cricket, which the MCC was not to sanction till the 1960s. It also anticipated the employment of superstars from overseas, another defining ingredient of the contemporary one-day game. Although ignored and despised by the establishment, it is fair to say that the northern leagues were more progressive and farsighted than the dominant system of county cricket.

In 1922, the Lancashire mill town of Nelson, home to one of the best-run clubs, recruited Ted McDonald of Australia at an alleged astronomical salary of £16 a week. *Wisden* bristled at the spectacle of Australia's deadliest bowler, who had injured and unnerved a host of English batters, going off to play for a 'Pennine village team'. In 1929, Nelson secured the charismatic, crowd-pleasing and deeply ethical Learie Constantine of the West Indies.[26] He more than repaid the investment and had a measurable 'Constantine' effect on attendances for all league clubs. Throughout the 1920s, the Lancashire League was in a far healthier state financially and in terms of live spectatorship than almost all county clubs, including Lancashire itself, except when it hosted a Roses match against Yorkshire.[27]

League clubs signed more overseas stars in the wake of Constantine, including his fellow West Indians George Headley and the all-rounder Ellis Achong. India supplied its greatest early Test bowler Amar Singh, New Zealand Bill Merritt and South Africa

Jimmy Blanckenberg (who refused to socialise with Constantine and Headley).²⁸ Lionel Tennyson, an amateur captain of Hampshire and England with a private income, protested at the 'unwholesome trafficking' in foreign players.²⁹ The stars at league clubs were paid, pro rata, far better than the top county professionals. Even allowing for coaching duties, playing hours were shorter. There was far less arduous and dangerous travel (a major problem at Nottinghamshire whose team was driven by the heavy-drinking captain Arthur Carr).³⁰ They did not have to defer to amateur captains or rely on them for 'talent money': they earned extra performance money directly from collections in the crowd.

Lord Harris fretted about the league as 'a serious competitor' to county cricket.³¹ This worry was misplaced. County cricket remained at the apex of English cricket between the wars and for very much the same reasons as before 1914: the social and political conservatism of professional cricketers and their willingness to serve under the right sort of chap regardless of ability. Major Arthur Lupton was especially popular as captain of Yorkshire in his forties, with a career batting average of 10, boosted by non-competitive matches.³² Yorkshire's playing fortunes improved sharply however when Brian Sellers, a player of far greater ability and a distinctly 'professional' approach to captaincy, took over.³³

The counties still controlled passage into the most lucrative fixtures – especially Ashes Tests, which were becoming more valuable than before to those selected. The Kent wicketkeeper Les Ames was able to buy a house from his earnings from the successful Ashes tour of 1928–29.³⁴ Benefits (at the discretion of county committees) were worth more to players after an unexpected decision in the House of Lords made them tax-free.³⁵

Above all, league cricket, despite the influx of new stars, was ignored by national media, including the vital new innovation of radio. The most successful cricket fiction was either written for and about public schoolboys or extolled cricket as a southern rural idyll, as in Hugh de Selincourt's *The Cricket Match* or A. G. Macdonell's whimsical and mannered *England, Their England.** H. S. Altham devoted barely two pages of his magisterial history of English cricket up to the First World War to the leagues. Plum Warner ignored the leagues when he published *Cricket Between Two Wars* in 1942. Neville Cardus, who came from Lancashire and ought to have known better, shared the establishment's indifference to league cricket. In his rhapsody to pre-war and 1920s cricket, *Days in the Sun,* he does not mention the leagues at all and mourns that 'the average professional cricketer, despite his superb and honourable skill, too frequently tells in his play a sad tale of some struggle for existence, of a life led in grey streets or in empty villages which only the townsman can see romantically nowadays'.[36]

Wisden ignored the leagues until its 1960 edition. Even then they were granted a mere five pages, compared to sixty for public-school cricket. Essentially the cricket establishment, aided by propagandists in literature and the media, used the example of the leagues to reinforce the moral and technical paramountcy of amateur-led cricket over risk-avoiding professionals. The leagues were blamed simultaneously for producing batters who were dour accumulators or crude sloggers. A few observers challenged such stereotyping. The journalist Ivan Sharpe called league cricket 'the keenest cricket of all'. Fred Root, who experienced all forms of the game, rated league cricket far above county in terms of playing standards, competitiveness and administration.

The marginalisation of league cricket ensured that, for all its success in producing and training cricketers, it never played the same foundation role in English cricket as the grade system in Australia and New Zealand.[37,†] The MCC and the counties used league clubs as feeding stock without even giving them a consultative role in the administration of English cricket. Southern clubs and counties blocked competitive cricket throughout the south of England.

---

* Published in 1933 and much anthologised, although its depiction of the actual cricket is rotten.

† This was observed acutely by a future editor of *Wisden,* Norman Preston, in an analysis of the success of northern counties in the pre-war championship.

Chapter 18

THE FIRST WOMEN'S TEST MATCHES

The formation of the Women's Cricket Association in 1926 was a great moment. The WCA recruited players who wanted to develop the sport along formal lines rather than rely on random social encounters. It organised fixtures and coaching opportunities and recruited affiliates. It made a crucial early decision to adopt the MCC Laws of Cricket with only one modification – a 5-ounce ball instead of the standard 5½ ounces. In another pivotal decision it formed county associations. But the most important move of all was to found a journal, *Women's Cricket,* edited by Marjorie Pollard, the principal evangelist and strategist of English women's cricket for over two decades.

Pollard faced down personal unpopularity and constant criticism that she made women's cricket too elitist and middle-class. The WCA was drawn heavily from the middle classes and elite institutions in the south – but to a degree that was arguably inevitable at the time. English girls and women were unlikely to have played cricket at all unless they came from well-to-do families. Given the cost of equipment and travel – and the enduring expectations in the period that married women would give priority to husbands and families over their own pursuits – it was hard for English women to play organised, regular cricket without substantial means and supportive households. The WCA tried to reach out to women's workplace teams and others with working-class and lower-middle class teams, and give opportunities to their members, with some success.[1] But the biggest obstacle to

English women's cricket, then as later, was its absence from the great majority of state schools. Pollard was criticised for subservience to the privileged men controlling English men's cricket. She had little choice: it was the only way that women could get access to decent grounds, all controlled by men. She was criticised for insisting on conservative standards of dress and deportment for women cricketers. Here, too, Pollard felt she had no other option. Women's cricket had to combat constant hostility from men: she could not afford to make men feel threatened or undermined by women's cricket, or give the media excuses to print mocking stories of women playing cricket in bathing dresses.[2]

In this period and after, England's women cricketers showed little interest in feminist agendas, although the first international captain, Betty Archdale, was the daughter of a militant suffragette and had herself worked for the fiery feminist Labour MP Ellen Wilkinson, later famous as the organiser of the Jarrow march of the unemployed.[3] Their prime focus was to play cricket regularly on decent grounds. Pollard's approach was vindicated by the growth of the WCA, whose affiliations trebled from its foundation to the eve of the Second World War, to reach 105 clubs, eighteen colleges and eighty-five schools.[4] Women had played matches at major clubs and county grounds, spectatorship at important matches was high, media coverage more respectful and two English women – the all-rounder Myrtle Maclagan and the wicketkeeper-batter Betty Snowball – were presented as sporting celebrities.

The two announced themselves in the first women's Test series, England in Australia and New Zealand in 1934–35, and the Australian series in return in 1937. England won the first series 2–0 with one draw and overwhelmed New Zealand. The return series was shared 1–1 with one draw. Neither tour had any recognition from the MCC or its wholly owned subsidiary, the ICC: they arose by invitation and exchanges between women. Although far below those of men's Ashes Tests, the crowds in Brisbane, Melbourne and Sydney totalled over 30,000, far above expectations on both sides. The matches in

England also pulled in thousands of spectators, and extensive and serious reporting in newspapers. Most significantly, the BBC gave them radio coverage and Pollard became the world's first female radio commentator.[5]

England's women received no fee or even expenses for playing. Those on the first tour had to pay for their own clothing, equipment and travel. The WCA did not select them on merit but invited applications from women who could afford the tour and judged themselves 'of good club standard'. The England team for the home series was less socially exclusive, including two products of workplace teams, Muriel Lowe and Betty Belton. It also included the first married player, Joan Davis; and Eileen Whelan, who would continue her career after the war as Eileen Ash.[6]

Although the WCA dominated the organisation of English women's cricket, in terms of participation more than twice as many women who played cricket regularly before the war (estimated at about 10,000) did so in leagues under the auspices of the England Women's Cricket Federation. Membership largely comprised the workplace teams provided for women by employers – some enlightened, others with an eye to recruitment and retention, particularly when the labour market for women tightened with the approach of war again in the 1930s. EWCF members were far more inclusive in approach than the WCA, especially in terms of membership fees, dress and deportment. Against that, the federation was run by men, while the WCA early on had barred men from its administration. Despite occasional spats, the two organisations stayed on reasonable terms and the barriers between them were much weaker than those between the men's leagues and the counties and the MCC. At the end of the 1930s, the WCA admitted league clubs to its membership. This removed the need for the EWCF and its disappearance left women in sole charge of English women's cricket for the next sixty years.

In Australia, women's cricket flourished in the prosperous 1920s and associations were formed in each state except Tasmania. Progress was not checked by the Depression and 1931 saw the formation of a central Australian Women's Cricket Council. It was this body that issued the invitation for the WCA tour and organised an interstate competition to select the players to meet it. Relations were unruffled by Bodyline. The AWCC deferred to the English captain, Archdale, on playing times and use of the six-ball over instead of the Australian eight-ball.[7]

New Zealand women made slower progress, although the game was taken up by more and more secondary schools. There was enough demand for organised school fixtures to generate the Auckland Women's Cricket Association in 1928, and for similar efforts in Wellington, Otago and Canterbury in 1932. Two years later, the New Zealand Women's Cricket Council was formed and initiated a representative White Ferns women's team. Although thrashed by the visiting English in 1935, its performance won the respect of watchers and local media, and earned an invitation to visit New South Wales the following year.[8]

In the Netherlands during the 1930s, women playing hockey began to turn to cricket as a summer game. A few clubs formed the Nederlandse Dames Cricket Bond in 1934, which organised a league and opened contacts with England and Australia. Its biggest success was to secure a visit from the Australian women en route to England in 1937. The Dutch team (on its own matting wickets) was outplayed by the Australians in two matches, although they were left drawn. However, they had the satisfaction of playing international cricket for their country seventeen years ahead of Dutch men, and in two-innings matches, which Dutch men have yet to play against anyone anywhere.[9]

Chapter 19

BRADMAN, BODYLINE AND EMPIRE

The Bodyline crisis was historic in many ways. It marked a transition in cricket from a contest of individual skills and tactical choices in key moments to a strategic campaign for supremacy.

It was profoundly shaped by the media and by the state of communications technology, which both inflamed the public mood and prevented commentators and fans alike from understanding what was really happening. Above all, Bodyline played out against a background of deep economic and social crisis, with unprecedented political tensions between England and Australia. As a result cricket, promoted as a binding force for the British Empire, tore it apart.

The story begins with the arrival of Bodyline's intended victim. Don Bradman was a largely self-taught genius. The solitary game he invented for himself – endlessly hitting a golf ball against a water tank behind his family's modest up-country home – has long passed into legend. Like W. G. Grace, he owed much to his mother, Emily. Like Denis Compton, he excelled in other sports, and he gave up cricket for tennis for two years when he left school. These 'lost years' clearly had no impact on his development and he announced himself with a century at every level of Australian cricket. He was the youngest to score a Sheffield Shield century and, after a tough debut, the youngest to score a Test century.

Bradman emerged into a confident Australia enjoying a decade of prosperity, in which extensive public works and land grants to veterans had cut unemployment to 7 per cent.[1] The catchphrase of the time was 'everything goodo'. Unfortunately, much of this prosperity rested on loans from the City of London, whose demands for repayment would deepen the economic and political crisis caused by the Depression. But during the 1920s, most families had plenty of money to spend playing and following cricket. Attendances swelled, especially for the three Ashes tours by England but also for the revived Sheffield Shield first-class competition, to which Queensland was added in 1926–27. Newspaper coverage of cricket expanded in Australian cities, and in Melbourne and Sydney a new means of following the game arrived through radio, where listeners could hear not only expert summaries of important matches by the great veteran Monty Noble but also live ball-by-ball commentaries, in which Australia was far more advanced than England. Station 3AR was the first to broadcast live passages in a Test match, Australia's Ashes victory in Melbourne in 1924–25.[2]

It was certainly 'everything goodo' for Australian batters in the 1920s. Heavy scoring became commonplace on sedated pitches, on which cricket balls quickly lost any properties of bounce or swing. First-class cricket has only seen two first-class totals of more than 1,000. Both were scored by Australian teams in home matches in this period. In one of them, Australia's heaviest scorer, Bill Ponsford, passed 400, beating the record then held by the famous English amateur Archie MacLaren. Characteristically, the MCC asked the state of Victoria to withdraw first-class status from the fixture (against Tasmania) to hand back the record to MacLaren.[3,*] Victoria stood by their champion and his record.

On the Test scene, Australia began the 1920s with eight successive Test victories over England teams weakened by war, injury to Jack Hobbs and confused selectors. They also whitewashed South Africa. They were led by a gigantic personality in every sense, Warwick

---

*   Ponsford scored another 400 in this period and a 352 in the all-time first-class record score of 1,107 against New South Wales. He glimpsed at his score on the giant board and said, in all seriousness, '352. By cripes, I am unlucky.' Jack Pollard, *The Illustrated History of Australian Cricket.*

Armstrong (one of the six leading players to join the strike of 1912), who faced down hostile administrators at home even more fiercely than opponents on the field. His biggest asset was a pair of fast bowlers, Jack Gregory, from a celebrated Australian cricket dynasty, and Ted McDonald. They inspired the same reactions as Jeff Thomson and Dennis Lillee in the 1970s, and in much the same way: Gregory by extreme and unpredictable pace; McDonald not as fast but with exceptional control of movement through the air and off the pitch. Together they terrorised several English batters who had been decorated for bravery in the First World War. Armstrong's use of them would later be cited as a justification for England captain Douglas Jardine's Bodyline tactics. They initiated the general modern practice of opening the bowling attack with the two fastest bowlers in the team.

Meanwhile, England had found the best opening partnership in cricket history, Jack Hobbs and Herbert Sutcliffe; added Patsy Hendren to the middle order; and boasted a superlative wicket-taking workaholic swing bowler in Maurice Tate. For the home series in 1926 against Australia, they recruited a fast bowler with little county experience, so youthful-looking that King George V queried his age in surprise when the teams were presented to him.[4] More would be heard of Harold Larwood. But the prime contributors to England's lone Test victory, which regained the Ashes, were Hobbs and Sutcliffe and Wilfred Rhodes, recalled at forty-eight. He not only took six wickets but guided England's new amateur captain, Percy Chapman, just as he regularly took charge on the field at Yorkshire.

Chapman, a bibulous charismatic lightweight, took a strong team to Australia in 1928–29 to defend the Ashes. It included Larwood but Tate was still the spearhead. The batting was strengthened still further by the left-handed stalwart Maurice Leyland, and the imperious right-handed Walter Hammond, the world's best slip fieldsman and, when he chose, a hostile fast-medium seam bowler. It faced an ageing Australian side in transition, led by the veteran Jack Ryder.

Bradman forced his way into this side aged just twenty, after a few appearances in the Sheffield Shield for New South Wales, marked by heavy and fast scoring. During the season he would total 1,690 first-class runs, still a record.⁵ Rivalry between the two great players would dominate Anglo-Australian cricket until Hammond's sad, defeated retirement in 1946–47.

Bradman had an unhappy first Test, scoring just 19 in two innings, in a match lost by Australia by the record margin of 675 runs. He would never forget or forgive the decision by Chapman (supposedly a debonair amateur) to bat again and set Australia – with two men absent, injured and ill – a target of more than 700. Bradman was dropped for the only time in his Test career. He atoned on his return with a century and in the rest of the series added 449 runs in six innings.

Already a popular favourite and a magnet for spectators, Bradman's status in Australia was transformed by his tour of England in 1930. He scored a record aggregate of 974, including a record innings of 334. Bradman scored his runs quickly and generally with an aura of total impregnability. He drove Chapman out of the England captaincy.

Australian supporters could follow his triumphs by radio, for this was the first overseas series to reach them in this way, with an immediacy conveyed by the newly invented radio telephone. English commentaries were picked up on headphones and then relayed by Australians in their own words to some 350,000 valve sets. People invited their neighbours over to listen in the middle of the night. With an average of five listeners per receiver, it was estimated that one-third of Australia's population tuned into some part of the series.⁶

On his return to Australia, Bradman attained a status as a national figure transcending sport. He made a series of triumphal progresses by car, train and, alarmingly, by air. The adulation of the crowds put huge strain on a reclusive personality.⁷ By then the economic and social conditions of Australia had been transformed, and Bradman was called on to provide hope for an angry nation brought low, as most believed, by its English creditors.

The Depression that followed the crash of 1929 struck Australia hard. By the end of 1932, world trade had fallen by one-third in volume and one-half in value, and there was a general collapse in the value of Australia's exports of primary products – wool, wheat, butter and mutton. Unemployment climbed from 11 per cent at the end of 1929 to 29 per cent by the time Jardine's England team arrived in 1932.[8] The Australian census of 1933 reported that two-thirds of households were living on an income less than the basic wage. There was no unemployment relief other than niggardly ration orders known as 'sosso'.[9]

The impact of the Depression quickly spilled into Australian politics and relations with the UK. These were already inflamed by a dispute over the performance of Australian forces in the First World War and, in particular, British generalship at Gallipoli where 8,709 Australian soldiers had died.[10] They deteriorated still further when the James Scullin Labor government in Australia insisted on the appointment of an Australian governor-general instead of choosing from a list of candidates selected by King George V and the British government.[11]

The Depression dried up British loans to Australia and made the City of London press for repayment of those it had made in the expansionist 1920s. It preached retrenchment and deflation at Australian state and federal governments. In 1930, amid Bradman's run-making spree in England, the Bank of England's Sir Otto Niemeyer and Commonwealth Bank Board chairman Sir Robert Gibson delivered this message to all state prime ministers at a special meeting in Melbourne.[12] Scullin's federal government had already been rebuffed when it sought to defer interest payments on a massive British war loan. The UK trade commissioner in Australia urged the British government to seize the opportunity 'for bringing Australia back into the fold not only chastened but more appreciative of the value of the Imperial tie'. The *Observer* newspaper commented that British money markets were determined that 'Australia must be taught a lesson'.[13] Sending out an England cricket team packed with fast bowlers captained by Jardine, already notorious for his hatred of Australians in general, would be an important part of this lesson.

Significantly, the newspaper, the official and the bankers ignored the possibility that Ramsay MacDonald's Labour government might show some fraternal solidarity with its counterpart in Australia. Imperial relations, whichever elected governments were in power, were always managed by the same financial and administrative elite. In the event, both Labour governments fell within a few months of each other in 1931, under pressure to implement similar spending reductions, and were replaced by Conservative-dominated coalitions. MacDonald stayed on as prime minister in a coalition government courtesy of Stanley Baldwin, the Conservative leader, after the General Election of 1931. So too did his voluble Dominions secretary, Jimmy Thomas, who would play a key role in the Bodyline crisis.

Within Australia the Depression produced intense political and social conflict. Jack Lang, the populist Labor prime minister of New South Wales, defaulted on a British loan. The new Conservative federal government of Joseph Lyons bailed out the state but then collected the money from state banks over the head of Lang's administration. Lang was allowed to open the new Sydney Harbour Bridge, financed by British loans, and was then dismissed by the state governor-general in a move that foreshadowed the even more controversial dismissal in the 1970s of the Labor federal prime minister Gough Whitlam. In a febrile atmosphere, some Australians feared social breakdown. They included Bradman, who briefly drilled with a local private militia formed to preserve law and order.[14]

Before its fall, Scullin's Labor government had infuriated the British by imposing a general protectionist tariff on all imports and banning those deemed non-essential. The Australians did not exempt British goods or give them any preference. One incidental beneficiary was Australia's sporting goods industry, especially its cricket balls. Larwood later complained that they quickly lost their shine and swing, and gave them as a partial explanation for his adoption of Bodyline.[15]

Trading relations did not improve when Lyons replaced Scullin. He maintained his predecessor's policy. The most he conceded to the British at the Imperial Economic Conference in 1932 was to raise tariffs even higher on non-British imports.[16]

The planning of Bodyline

Everything about Bodyline was premeditated and rehearsed to a degree then unknown in cricket at any level. C. L. R. James wrote: 'Bodyline was not an accident [or] a temporary aberration. It was the violence and ferocity of our age expressing itself in cricket . . . The totalitarian dictatorships cultivated brutality of set purpose.'[17] The peak of the Bodyline crisis coincided with Hitler's ascent to government in Germany – and attracted more attention in most British media.

Plum Warner, in multiple and conflicting roles as administrator and journalist, tried to deny responsibility but was in the thick of it, as chief selector and manager of Jardine's tour. He also planted himself on the tour programme planning committee.[18] In 1930, he had himself written, 'England must evolve a new type of bowler and develop fresh ideas and strange tactics to curb [Bradman's] almost uncanny skill.'[19]

Bodyline describes a method of bowling that aimed the ball at the batter's body rather than the stumps. In a dramatic breach with the ethics of the game, it used physical intimidation as a tactic to secure a batter's dismissal. It had forerunners in both England and Australia. We have already cited the post-war assault by Gregory and McDonald. In England there were two notable exponents of what was called 'leg theory', below-express bowlers who bowled to a packed leg-side field to restrict scoring and induce catches from ill-chosen strokes by frustrated batters. One was Frank Foster, the amateur pre-war captain of Warwickshire. His left-arm, fast-medium leg theory helped his unfashionable county win the Championship in 1911 – and then subdue Australia in that winter's Ashes series as opening partner of the great Sydney Barnes. Foster, in a troubled retirement, explained his methods to Jardine and would publicly repent the use Jardine made of them. The other was Fred Root, who carried Worcestershire's attack in the 1920s and helped to wear down the Australians in the Ashes series of 1926. He played with Larwood in his debut Test, and mentored him. Later he would write that Larwood was no bully and hated hitting batters.[20]

There were two other important English progenitors of Bodyline. Percy Fender had experienced and never forgotten either Gregory and McDonald or the implacable captaincy of Armstrong. As Jardine's predecessor and mentor at Surrey, he instilled the same attention to forming a plan and sticking to it. Nottinghamshire captain Arthur Carr gave Jardine his chosen instruments – his county's opening pair of Larwood and Bill Voce. Although short and apparently frail in physique, Larwood's near-perfect action made him the fastest bowler in England at a young age. Voce was not quite so fast, but his left-arm deliveries had a knack of hitting batters in the ribs. Carr mentored and nursed them both, building up Larwood's strength and aggression by converting him to beer and gin. In county games, he exploited the fear they both induced in opponents.[21]

Jardine became England captain in 1931 almost by default, as the best available amateur. Both he and Larwood had toured Australia in Chapman's winning side of 1928–29, and knew that they had to find a way to restrict and dismiss Bradman. His Australian form since 1930 had been astounding, with two big centuries in the inaugural series against the West Indies and an average of more than 200 against South Africa, and he had scored heavily and rapidly in the Sheffield Shield.

At this point Jardine saw one of the most fateful newsreels in sports history. Newsreels were not a new medium, but they were hugely enhanced by sound and a wartime invention, the long-distance lens. Jardine watched a passage of Bradman against Larwood at the Oval in 1930 after rain had livened the pitch. It seemed to confirm the reports that he had retreated. Jardine exclaimed: 'I've got it. He's yellow.'[22]

Jardine meant that he considered Bradman a coward. The

England captain now had his strategy: pummel Bradman into submission or at least quiescence on his leg stump. He then did something unprecedented for that era of cricket: the amateur England captain invited professionals Larwood and Voce to dinner at the fashionable Piccadilly Hotel in London to discuss his strategy on equal terms. Their county captain, Carr, was also present. Rather than giving orders or allowing them to decide their methods for themselves, Jardine explained candidly the demands his strategy would make on them physically and mentally, and checked whether they were ready for them.[23]

England's final selection signalled their intentions for Australia. There were four outright fast bowlers. Besides Larwood, Voce and Bill Bowes, Warner had insisted on the amateur Gubby Allen, his Middlesex protégé. Hedley Verity, already established as a substantial left-arm spin bowler, was chosen for support and containment duties when the fast bowlers needed a rest. Tate, hitherto England's spearhead, was chosen late. Jardine did not like him and had no plans to use him in the Tests. On the long sea voyage to Australia (where the amateurs and professionals for the first time shared first-class passenger status) Jardine gave his team instructions to reinforce his strategy psychologically: no fraternisation with the opposition, general hatred of everything Australian, and no assistance to Australian – or for that matter, English – media.

The Bodyline series

England's early matches boded well for Jardine's strategy. Bradman was not on top form, managing only 103 scratchy runs in six innings and clearly discomfited by the short-pitched bowling even to orthodox fields. Bob Wyatt, the vice-captain, was the first to set the so-called Bodyline field, packed with leg-side catchers, rather than Jardine, who released himself to go fishing. Off the field, Bradman was coping with financial anxiety, a dispute with the Australian Broadcasting Corporation over his journalistic work, and health problems. He withdrew from the first Test at Sydney: Jardine claimed that the prospect of facing Larwood had given him a nervous breakdown.

The first outing for what became Bodyline was nearly its last. Stan McCabe played an innings of epic daring, repeatedly hooking short balls from the fast bowlers – including the first he received from Larwood – to the boundary and making Jardine flustered for the only time in the series. But he got no support from the other batters, who could not cope physically or in some cases mentally with the new attack. England piled up a big lead, bowled Australia out cheaply in the second innings and needed just one run for victory.

English and Australian media cast around for a name for the new form of attack. The English generally settled on 'fast leg theory'. The Australians evolved Bodyline from a description of bowling 'at or near the body line' through a series of punctuation changes. The last was by a sub-editor, Ray Robinson, who would become one of Australia's' greatest cricket writers.[24] The English refused to accept the term although it was far more descriptive and accurate than their own.

Bradman returned for the second Test at Melbourne, in place of his state captain Alan Kippax, a great stylist and popular favourite who admitted openly that Larwood was too fast for him. The wicket was much slower than Sydney, and Jardine made a serious error in dropping Verity for Bowes and an all-pace attack. At first the move seemed to pay off, when Bradman was out first ball to Bowes, playing a very poor delivery onto his stumps. It inspired Jardine to a rare display of emotion, an impromptu jig. But it was Bowes' only wicket in the series. Bradman redeemed himself with a not-out century in the second innings in a total of only 191. Australia's spinners, Bill O'Reilly and Bert Ironmonger (who was nearly fifty), dismissed England cheaply and the series was level.

Simmering Australian fury at Bodyline, and Jardine in particular, erupted at the third Test in Adelaide. *Wisden* would describe it as 'one of the most unpleasant in history', although it aimed this remark mainly at the Australian crowd. Larwood hit the Australian captain, Bill Woodfull, a terrific blow in the chest, from which he took several minutes to recover. Jardine promptly said, 'Well bowled, Harold,' and moved the fielders from orthodox positions to the leg-side cluster for Bodyline. All this was done to intimidate the non-striker – Bradman.

Worse still, the Australian wicketkeeper, Bert Oldfield, was almost killed trying to hook Larwood. The ball was simply too fast for him and he top-edged it into his skull. He murmured chivalrously, 'It's not your fault, Harold,' but the record crowd of more than 50,000 never heard it. Nor did radio listeners or newspaper reporters. All Australians knew was that their wicketkeeper had been struck down by Larwood. Woodfull (who had been dismissed, as had Bradman) rushed onto the field in a dark suit. Normally quiet and polite, he was shouting. Larwood was not alone in fearing a riot and a mob attack on England players. Only Jardine kept his calm – as he persisted with the Bodyline field.[25]

Aggravated by a media leak, Adelaide began a war of cables between the ABC and the MCC. The ABC fired off a provocative cable condemning Bodyline as 'unsportsmanlike'. They added: 'Unless stopped at once it is likely to upset the friendly relations existing between Australia and England.' Most of the ABC members who decided to send it, after a vote, had not seen the injuries to Woodfull and Oldfield. It was dispatched to appease the angry spectators and Australian media, to whom they released it. It reached English media before the MCC, because an Australian journalist sent it to Reuters in England by express cable while the ABC decided to save money by sending their text to the MCC at normal rates.[26]

The MCC were outraged at the challenge to the sportsmanship of their chosen captain, team and managers. They sent a cable back to say so and challenged the ABC to cancel the rest of the tour. This was well calculated to discomfit the ABC. Whatever Australians thought of the England team, they paid to watch it in record numbers. Australian cricket, stricken financially by the Depression, could not afford to lose the receipts of the last two Tests.

Then came a new flashpoint. A supposedly private exchange between Woodfull and Warner was leaked to the press. Warner tried to visit Woodfull on the treatment table after his injury with a message of consolation. Woodfull refused to see him, with an icy message: 'There are two teams out there. One is trying to play cricket and the other isn't.' Warner almost collapsed in shock. He then worsened the media furore by making a false statement that he and Woodfull had made peace and become the best of friends, which Woodfull publicly denied.

Warner by then had lost the confidence of the England party he was supposed to manage. Jardine called a team meeting to discuss his strategy and his own form as a captain. Warner tried to speak and was told by the forthright professional Tommy Mitchell, 'It's nowt to do with thee!' This was a historic moment: no professional had ever spoken thus to a gentleman administrator without penalty.*,27 During the tour Jardine enjoyed the loyalty of all his professionals, although they sometimes chafed at his stern discipline and evaded it. Any objections to Bodyline came from two amateurs, Iftikhar Ali Khan Pataudi (an Indian prince) and Gubby Allen (who had been born in Australia and spent much of the tour with relatives).28

The leak was generally blamed on Australia's opening bat, Jack Fingleton, who was a professional journalist. He denied it and blamed Bradman.29 Whoever was responsible, this was a departure: such exchanges were kept private. It would open an era when cricketers leaked routinely either for money or (as Fingleton claimed of Bradman) in pursuit of a cricketing objective, in this case the ending of Bodyline.

Further cable exchanges followed in the gap between Adelaide and the next Test at Brisbane. The ABC climbed down and met the MCC's main demand, to withdraw the charge of bad sportsmanship. It did set up a committee of inquiry into Bodyline, composed mainly

---

* Mitchell would later lose his Test career after a rude remark to his amateur captain, Bob Wyatt.

of veteran players. They devised a Law against bowling 'which *in the opinion of the umpire,* [our emphasis] is bowled at the batter with intent to intimidate or injure him'. The MCC refused to adopt it, partly from genuine doubt whether any umpire could discern intent and more importantly to preserve their monopoly of law-making in cricket. They eventually legislated against Bodyline tactics in 1935, outlawing the use of 'direct attack' on the batter.[30]

By then the tour had been saved. England took the Ashes by winning the Brisbane Test. Their hero was middle-order batter Eddie Paynter, who rose from a high fever in a hospital bed to play a vital innings of 86. England also won the last Test in Sydney. Jardine cruelly refused Larwood's request for a rest after the Ashes were won, although he was showing signs of severe stress injuries from bowling on hard surfaces in ill-fitting boots. He then ordered Larwood to bat as a nightwatchman.* The infuriated bowler whacked 98 the next day. Informed of his score by his partner, he mishit his next shot and was caught by Ironmonger, one of the worst fielders in international cricket history. Larwood's front foot was broken, but Jardine made him bowl on – to intimidate Bradman. He was allowed to limp off the field – as it turned out forever in Test cricket – only when Bradman was dismissed by Verity.[31]

England had won the series 4–1. Jardine's strategy had prevailed against Bradman and forced him to adopt desperate means of scoring in his four Test matches. It is a measure of Bradman's greatness that his final batting average of nearly 57 was regarded as failure.

The Australians at least got their money's worth, with 1.28 million spectators spending more than £100,000 in admissions alone.[32]

Jardine's strategy might have been less successful had not Australia refused to retaliate. Woodfull as captain set his face against it. His

---

* A nightwatchman is an inferior batter sent in just before close of a day's play to prevent the dismissal of a better one.

prime bowling resources were the leg-spinners Clarrie Grimmett and Bill O'Reilly, and the left-arm slows of Ironmonger. His fastest strike bowler was Tim Wall, well below Larwood's speed. Public pressure forced the selection of a supposedly more hostile bowler, 'Bull' Alexander. He proved innocuous.[33]

One Shield bowler had already discomfited Bradman even more than Larwood: Eddie Gilbert of Queensland. As an indigenous Australian, Gilbert could not travel to matches or anywhere else outside a reservation without a permit. Such controls, reminiscent of formal apartheid in South Africa, persisted in his state until the 1970s.[34] He had adapted boomerang throwing to generate terrific speed from arm and wrist action alone after very little run-up. In a state match, Gilbert delivered, in Bradman's own words, the fastest over he ever received.[35] Two deliveries dumped him on his back before he was clean bowled for a duck. Gilbert also enjoyed success with eleven wickets in two matches for Queensland against the visiting West Indians and South Africans.

But there was no question of picking him against the English. After the over against Bradman, he was persistently no-balled by state umpires, in spite of filmed evidence that his action was legal. There is no evidence that Bradman initiated this, but there was a clear commercial motive for state umpires to protect Australia's leading run-scorer and crowd-puller, just as there had been when Jack Marsh, an earlier indigenous fast bowler, had threatened to subdue Victor Trumper. By the time of the English tour, Gilbert had modified his action to appease the umpires, at the cost of pace and rhythm.

Throughout his brief Shield career, he encountered persistent racism, including from teammates. He lingered on for a few more years, and dismissed Bradman again in a Shield game in 1936, this time for 31, in a spell of five wickets. He was then discarded by the Queensland Cricket Association. They made him launder and return his white clothing before sending him back to the reservation. He died years later, poor and forgotten in a mental asylum.[36]

Media coverage

Hostility and misunderstanding were made worse by the media. While Australians could follow along with events as they happened thanks to ball-by-ball commentaries and newspaper accounts, English cricket lovers had to contend with news reports that were often delayed, and frequently censored or slanted. Newsreel film took at least three weeks to arrive, and usually had a gung-ho pro-English commentary. The footage of Oldfield's near-fatal injury was described as 'Oldfield is hit – and Larwood is the unlucky bowler.'[37] There were few English newspaper reporters in Australia and their copy was of necessity terse and cabled. A radio-telephone link had recently been established but it was expensive and unreliable. The key English newspaper was the London *Evening Standard*. Because of the time zone it would carry the first reports on each day's play. They could have sent a young E. W. Swanton, who understood cricket, but he had been too slow in getting to the only public telephone in the county ground in Leyton to be first with the news of the record partnership of 555 by the Yorkshire openers Herbert Sutcliffe and Percy Holmes. As punishment, the newspaper sent its tennis correspondent instead. Jardine broke his policy of not speaking to the press and carefully guided his reports home.[38]

English listeners in the night were able to hear a ball-by-ball commentary by Alan Fairfax, constructed from cables. Fairfax, an Australian Test player and tourist in 1930, left the Australian set-up to make a new career in England. Perhaps in pursuit of this, he often omitted to mention the injuries to his former teammates.[39]

Both sets of reporters or commentators naturally sought to please their own public. *The Times* minimised Oldfield's injury while highlighting the 'wild shouting' from Australian crowds (within a few years the paper would downplay Nazi atrocities in support of Neville Chamberlain's policy of appeasement). Its leader column pronounced it inconceivable that Jardine would adopt a form of attack 'that in the time-honoured phrase is "not cricket".' Even Neville Cardus praised

England and proposed a statue to Larwood. In fairness, Cardus was one of the first English journalists to condemn Bodyline later. Even the left-wing *Daily Herald* condemned the 'undignified snivelling' of the Australians, while the *Star* denounced the ABC's initial cable as 'the cheapest possible insult'.[40]

When the Bodyline series ended, attention focused on Australia's coming tour of England in 1934. There was a serious prospect that it might be cancelled, but politicians, business leaders and grandees saved it in the interests of trade and the British Empire. The full story remains opaque because three sets of key papers are missing or defective: records of Australian state associations, records of the British Dominions office and MCC records, which fell into the custodianship of Warner, an interested party, during the Second World War.[41]

In England, a key role was played by the glad-handing Dominions secretary, Jimmy Thomas. He was in office on sufferance of the huge Conservative majority after the 1931 election, and completely cut off from his base in the Labour party and the trade unions. His one reliable supporter was the king, whom he entertained with his jokes and stage working-class accent. One at least was genuinely funny. The king asked him if the financial crisis of 1931 was serious. Thomas replied quickly: 'Well, sir, if I were you, I would put the country into your wife's name.'[42]

Even with the king's support, Thomas could not afford to lose a Dominion on his watch and pressed actively for a settlement. He was well briefed by Sir Alexander Hore-Ruthven, the governor-general of South Australia. Unusually astute and sensitive to Australian attitudes, it was a disaster that he was absent in England during the Adelaide Test. On return to Australia, he relayed the damage to British commercial interests if ABC cancelled the 1934 tour. Australian resentment of Bodyline had progressed 'even to the extent of reluctance to buy English goods, which businessmen inform me is going on to a certain extent in [Adelaide] today'.

Thomas passed on these concerns to his Tory Cabinet colleague,

Secretary of State for War Lord Hailsham – who happened also to be the president of the MCC.[43,*]

On the Australian side, the federal government warned the ABC that a rupture would hit trade and drive down agricultural prices, already at record depths.[44]

After many more exchanges of cables, the MCC tacitly agreed that Bodyline would not be used against the Australians and that Jardine would not be England captain.

Even without Australian and political pressure, the MCC and English opinion generally moved against Bodyline after the Ashes series. One factor was the West Indies visit to England in 1933, when their two fastest bowlers, Learie Constantine and Manny Martindale, bounced English batters. They were not as hostile as Larwood or Voce, but when Wally Hammond had his chin cut by a bouncer, he declared that if this was Test cricket he was done with it. Jardine, still captain, characteristically faced down the West Indian attack and scored his only Test century. He then took a sub-strength England team, with only Verity from his Ashes party, on the inaugural tour of India, his birthplace. He had a mixed reception, pleasing Indians with some gracious speeches and, better still, a public row with the viceroy. On the other hand, he gave further exhibitions of Bodyline through his fastest bowler, Nobby Clark of Northamptonshire, in which one victim was the son of the Maharaja of Patiala, the leading princely patron of Indian cricket. Knowing that Warner and the MCC were moving against him, Jardine announced that he had 'neither the intention nor the desire' to play against Australia in 1934. In a final tilt at English media, he gave this scoop to an Indian journalist.[45]

Larwood had returned injured and alone from the Ashes tour when Jardine and his Ashes colleagues went on to New Zealand. On

---

* Hailsham was secretary of state for war, an apposite post at the height of the Bodyline rift with Australia. Hore-Ruthven would become the Earl of Gowrie and governor-general of all Australia.

ship, he met his county captain Arthur Carr. Instead of protecting Larwood from the media, Carr, himself a journalist, encouraged him to tell his story. This conversation resulted in a series of incendiary ghostwritten articles and a book. They accused Bradman of lacking courage, Woodfull of poor technique and Australian complainers generally of being 'effeminate', an especially pejorative term in the 1930s. The MCC then demanded Larwood apologise for his bowling in Australia using a poorly chosen emissary, Sir Julien Cahn, the wealthy flamboyant cricket patron whom the committee themselves despised. Larwood angrily refused, ruled himself out of the first Test in 1934 with a non-existent injury (he played for his county on the opening day) and then out of the second with a further outburst against 'squealing' Australians and 'politicians trying to hound me out of Test cricket . . . They feared I would burst the Empire.'[46]

Despite a return to peak bowling form for his county, Larwood never played for England again. He drifted out of cricket altogether and escaped a lacklustre existence running a rationed sweetshop in post-war Blackpool to a new life in Australia – with help from two players he had injured in the Bodyline series, Fingleton and Oldfield.[47]

With no Bodyline against them, the Australians won back the Ashes in the summer of 1934 under Woodfull. Bradman resumed his dominance, scoring a double and a triple century, and averaging 94.75. But the stress of Bodyline endured and he suffered from nervous exhaustion throughout the tour. He collapsed after the last Test with appendicitis and nearly died of the ensuing peritonitis, reviving only after a desperate visit from his wife Jessie.[48] He then missed a season of cricket, including Australia's tour of South Africa, which was led by popular veteran Vic Richardson.

On returning to cricket, Bradman was captain of his new state of South Australia and then of Australia, replacing Richardson in both cases. His captaincy of Australia began badly with two defeats against Gubby Allen's visitors and a semi-public row with the leading Catholic members of his team, O'Reilly and Fingleton. One of his most epic innings, in partnership with Fingleton, produced victory in the third Test and he won the series from 2–0 behind, still the only time this has happened.

Allen was popular (as most visiting English captains are when they lose): attendances and receipts broke records again. Bodyline was successfully buried, although its memory would revive any time one side had some dominant fast bowlers.

Chapter 20

THE EXPANSION OF TEST CRICKET

The last peacetime English summer without Test matches was 1927,* the consequence of three new countries acceding to membership at the Imperial Cricket Conference of 1926: West Indies, India and New Zealand. The ICC minutes record no explanation for this decision, nor indeed any discussion. To an extraordinary degree, it seems to have been the personal decision of Lord Harris, who had visited both India and the West Indies shortly before, and had been a major influence in forming their boards of control, both under British tutelage.[1]

There had been no great agitation for Test match status in the three new members. Of the ICC founder members who admitted them, only England had any intention of playing all three. South Africa, a white supremacist state long before formal apartheid, refused to play India or the West Indies while Australia continued to deny equality to New Zealand. The new countries themselves would not begin to play Tests against each other until after the war.

Their elevation consolidated cricket's status as an imperial game. The 1926 ICC meeting, at Harris's behest, adopted a new definition

---

* Pedants might object that 1970 was another, when England played five matches against the Rest of the World in substitution for the cancelled series with apartheid South Africa. These matches were promoted and sponsored and broadcast at the time as Test matches: the England players chosen were up against the greatest assembly of cricket talent in history. Their status was rescinded some years later. Alan Jones, the Glamorgan opener, made his only England appearance in one match. His Test cap was deservedly restored to him.

of Test cricket as 'between sides duly selected by recognised governing bodies of cricket representing Countries within the Empire'. As at its foundation, the ICC gave no consideration to the US claim to full international status and by 1926 it was already too late to arrest cricket's decline there, even in Philadelphia, its epicentre.

The new countries were allotted Test matches in the margins of the programme already established for the founder members. West Indies got three in England in 1928, New Zealand three in 1931 and India a single Test in 1932. These matches were of three days. This gave them a lower status than Ashes Tests, which were allotted five days or more, but also demonstrated the elasticity of Test match status. Second-string England teams played Test matches in the West Indies in 1929–30 and 1934–35, in New Zealand in 1929–30 (the only year in which two entirely separate teams have played Tests for England) and in India in 1933–34. New Zealand hosted an almost full-strength England side led by Douglas Jardine in the aftermath of Bodyline in 1932–33, which enabled Walter Hammond to break the Test scoring record with a triple century and to average more than 500.

Ashes Tests were still substantially more important in number, spectatorship and media following than any others. Seventy-five of the ninety-two Test matches played between 1928 to 1939 involved England, of which twenty-four were Ashes Tests.

Nonetheless, the expansion of Test match cricket marked a watershed. The first fifty years had been dominated to the exclusion of all else by the white Test-playing countries of England, Australia and South Africa. New life was being injected.

Cricket in India from 1914–45

Before the First World War, two types of cricket, based on divergent and contrasting principles, had emerged on the Indian subcontinent.

Left in office under the careful eye of a British resident but deprived of real power, Indian princes deployed their prodigious wealth to build teams and lure star players – rather as Gulf states such as Saudi Arabia and Qatar have done with football and other sports in the modern era.

Some princes, such as the appalling Maharajkumar of Vizianagram, used cricket as a means of ingratiating themselves with the British, who welcomed allies in the face of the growing power of the Congress independence movement. Vizianagram notoriously courted the viceroy, thus securing the captaincy for the 1936 Indian tour of England, a role to which he proved hopelessly unsuited.

The pioneer of princely cricket was Bhupinder Singh, Maharaja of Patiala. In 1911, he captained the first non-sectarian Indian team to tour England. It contained six Parsis, five Hindus, three Muslims and two Dalits (or 'untouchables', the lowest stratum in the Indian caste system). One of them, the left-arm spinner Palwankar Baloo, established himself among the greatest Indian players of all time.

Patiala's tour was a success, but it set a disastrous precedent. His rivals envied the political and social benefits (private audience with the king, polo matches, invitation to the Trooping of the Colour etc) that came Patiala's way. Thereafter, princely rivalry marred India's cricket, especially after India's admission to the ICC.

When the MCC invited India for its first tour of England as a Test-playing nation in 1932, Jardine (who had been born in Mumbai) was seriously put forward as captain of India.[2] After much squabbling, one of the most obscure maharajas, Porbandar, ruler of Kathiawar, was chosen for the job. Over his summer campaign, he notoriously scored fewer runs (two) than he owned Rolls-Royces.[*,3] A combination of royal and high-born incompetence, capricious selection policies and cultural deference from tour administrators held back India's international cricket for four decades. Only in 1971 would India win a Test match against England away. Meanwhile, the Bombay Quadrangular became a premier social and sporting

---

[*] Porbandar played three innings across four matches (high score 2; average 0.66) before wisely deciding to drop himself to allow the great C. K. Nayudu to lead India in their inaugural Test at Lord's.

tournament, attracting vast crowds, and much copied in other urban centres. Mahatma Gandhi's Congress Party believed that it played into the British policy of 'divide and rule', and tried to stop it.[4] Despite repeated and sometimes successful attempts to enforce a boycott, the competition (reclassified as the Pentangular in the final years of the Raj when a fifth team known as 'The Rest', including Buddhists, Jews and Sikhs was added) continued through much of the Second World War. The final of the 1944–45 renewal was watched by more than 200,000 spectators.[5] The Muslims secured a one-wicket victory in a famous match. Seventy years later, Shaharyar Khan, who attended the Pentangular as a young man and later became head of the Pakistan Foreign Service and in retirement chairman of the Pakistan Cricket Board, told us how much the Bombay Pentangular had meant. He explained that these matches 'especially between the Hindus and Muslims, had the intensity of an Ashes Test match. As in England and Australia, cricket had entered the domain of mass public appeal in India. From there it was only a short step to the India–Pakistan matches that followed shortly after independence.'[6]

Khan was correct about the drama of communal cricket. However, a new basis of competition evolved in India during the 1930s in the shape of the Ranji Trophy. Named after Ranjitsinhji, whose experience of cricket in India did not extend beyond the occasional social match, the teams were formed along regional rather than communal lines. The Northern India side, embracing many of the areas that were shortly to become Pakistan, contained Muslims and Hindus when it played its inaugural fixture in December 1934. This communal blindness made the Ranji Trophy a better fit with Gandhi's vision of a multicultural India than the Pentangular.

White South African cricket

South Africa took time to live up to its status as a member of the ICC. It flopped in the 1912 Triangular Tournament so assiduously pressed by Abe Bailey. The tournament itself flopped too: such a disaster that it has never been repeated.

In its early years the national team could pull off occasional eye-catching victories on matting wickets at home. Abroad they were often hopeless. The 1924 tour of England was a fiasco. Replying to England's 438 in the first Test, South Africa were bowled out for 30 (Arthur Gilligan 6/7). South Africa lost their first two matches by an innings and their third by nine wickets. Resources were so depleted that George Parker, who had never played a first-class match, was plucked out of the Bradford League. Aubrey Faulkner was recalled at the age of forty-two, but failed to make an impact.

From the early years, South Africa were held together by some splendid cricketers. Herbie Taylor was captain of the national team from late 1913 till the disastrous summer of 1924. Norwegian-born Buster Nupen, who lost an eye in a childhood accident, and was shot through both knees during the Rand rebellion, was described by a perhaps overgenerous Jack Hobbs as the 'most dangerous off-spin bowler the world has ever seen'.[7] Nupen did not get many chances to practise his art because South Africa paid a price for refusing to play emerging non-white nations. Significantly K. S. Duleepsinhji, Ranji's nephew, and at the time one of the finest players in the world, was not selected for the 1930–31 MCC tour of South Africa.

After a 5–0 thrashing in Australia in 1932 (only partly redeemed by a 2–0 victory over New Zealand immediately afterwards), South Africa endured a chasm of three years without a Test. The long-awaited return to Test cricket proved glorious: a 1–0 victory over England, Bruce Mitchell influential with 488 runs at 69.71. South Africa were then thrashed by Australia at home, followed by another long gap till the notable 1939 England tour, which ended with the famous 'timeless' Test. This 'Durban monstrosity', as it was christened by Neville Cardus, endured for ten days before ending in a draw when the England team needed to dash for the boat home.

Chapter 21

THE SECOND WORLD WAR AND ITS AFTERMATH

Test cricket stopped completely during the Second World War, while first-class domestic cricket continued only on the Indian subcontinent and briefly in Australia and New Zealand. However, for the game as a whole, it was a dynamic and inventive era – and one that remains wrongly neglected.

As in other aspects of life, cricket in England became more open, democratic and improvisational to meet the demands of survival and eventual victory in war. It was enriched by an influx of talent from service personnel and civilian workers from the Empire. Wartime cricket could be described as a simultaneous set of tours by all the other Test-playing countries except India, although the latter supplied 2.5 million servicemen to Dominion forces and uncounted numbers of labourers and merchant seamen.[1]

The war brought new opportunities for young players, including those from poor backgrounds, to play cricket – often for the first time. As in the First World War, participation in the services and wartime production provided new outlets for women's cricket, less dependent on the traditional controllers of the male game.

Internationally, English and Dominions cricketers took the game to every theatre of war in which they participated. To paraphrase Winston Churchill, they played cricket on the beaches, on the landing grounds, in the fields, in the streets and in the hills, in places which had never seen cricket before. They improvised cricket under bombardment and under terrible privation in prisoner-of-war camps.

The outbreak of war

The West Indies were touring in the summer of 1939, with an ageing but still dynamic Learie Constantine and the world-class George Headley, who scored a century in each innings of the Lord's Test. The tour was abandoned after the Oval Test as war clouds gathered and the West Indian players headed home to escape the prospect of U-boat attacks. They would not play another Test match till 1948.

The County Championship was at once cancelled following the declaration of war on 3 September, with Yorkshire declared champions. Poignantly, Hedley Verity ended their last match at Hove early, taking seven Sussex wickets for nine runs in six overs. The Yorkshire team headed back home by coach through blacked-out roads crammed with traffic fleeing an expected all-out German bombing attack.[2]

The Oval was converted into a prisoner-of-war camp. Lord's escaped this fate, although the Nursery ground was taken over for use by the RAF and Plum Warner returned as acting secretary to supervise the evacuation of the Long Room and its treasures. Warner maintained traditional fixtures including Oxford and Cambridge and visits to and by public schools. Far more important, as we shall see, Lord's also became a setting for morale-boosting ad hoc charity matches of teams featuring current and former stars.

Overseas, the West Indian Inter-Colonial Tournament was cancelled. It failed to return after the war, leaving the West Indies without a formal first-class competition until the Shell Shield launched in 1965–66. In South Africa, the Currie Cup was cancelled. Australia's Sheffield Shield continued to run in 1939–40, but not thereafter. Friendly interstate matches were played to raise funds, but these stopped in December 1941 as the war effort intensified.* New

---

* After the fall of Singapore and the Japanese conquest of the Dutch East Indies and New Guinea, Australia became a frontline state in danger of invasion. The Japanese bombed Darwin and their midget submarines sank shipping and raided Australia's long and virtually defenceless coastlines. Indian first-class cricket was

Zealand's Plunket Shield was also played in 1939–40, but then suspended. India was the exception. Both the Ranji Trophy and the Bombay Pentangular (apart from 1942–43) continued undisturbed. Denis Compton, Reg Simpson and Joe Hardstaff, stationed in India, turned out in the Pentangular: Compton also played three games for Holkar in the Ranji Trophy in 1945.*,3 Ceylon's visit to India in 1940–41, and India's return visit in March 1945 marked the only international contests played during the war.

Sir Home Gordon, the noted (and reactionary) cricket writer and statistician, famously described the outbreak of war as 'a grim Test match against Germany' in which 'the Ashes of civilisation were at stake'.[4] Now much mocked, this language was widely emulated. Warner remarked that 'if Goebbels had been able to broadcast that the war had stopped cricket at Lord's it would have been valuable propaganda for the Germans'.[5,†] The *Cricketer* noted: 'The most strenuous opposition to Nazi aggression has been provided and is still being provided by countries in which cricket is played.' (This was written before Hitler's invasion of the non-cricket-playing Soviet Union.) It added: 'The whole underlying spirit of the game is antagonistic to Teutonic regimentation.'[6]

---

disrupted by the Japanese bombing of Madras and invasion of Assam, and even more by the heavy-handed British response to Gandhi's Quit India call in 1942. A future Test nation, Ceylon, suffered two serious Japanese naval raids in 1942 and 1944. The West Indian islands had their defence virtually taken over by the Americans, even before their entry into the war, over fears of Nazi U-boats and subversion. There were high losses among West Indian merchant seamen: one was the father of Garry Sobers, then aged five. The weakness of British power in all these countries would have a lasting influence on cricket, which we have tried to trace elsewhere.

* Indian wartime cricket was dominated by the colossal scoring rivalry between the two stars, Vijay Merchant and Vijay Hazare. Compton's not-out double century for Holkar was not enough for them to chase a fourth-innings total of 867 in a completed match that yielded more than 2,000 runs and nearly 700 six-ball overs.

† Warner was right. The infamous Lord Haw-Haw, whose broadcasts were much followed in Britain, specialised in giving details of local English scenes.

Official Nazi briefing on cricket before the intended invasion of Britain in 1940 itself acknowledged that 'cricket best personifies the British Imperial system and the British sense of values', although it sneered that cricket inculcated 'the strength to suffer boredom' and that 'in cricket, English self-conceit, English pride and English vanity have been raised to a sort of divine service'.[7] Before the war, the Nazis – even Hitler personally – had shown a passing interest in cricket. His sports supremo, the upper-class Hans von Tschammer und Osten (who cultivated prominent British appeasers) urged English cricket clubs to tour Nazi Germany, an invitation taken up by an amateur team from Worcestershire who played a 'Test match' at the infamous Berlin Olympic stadium.

In 1942, after the fall of Singapore at the lowest point of the war, the austere production minister Stafford Cripps tried to clamp down on sport as a waste of resources. Warner rallied service chiefs in support of wartime cricket, citing its contribution to service charities and its 'definite use in a very pleasant atmosphere for sailors, soldiers and airmen and those engaged on war work'.[8] Cricket had many supporters and protectors among the Labour ministers in the wartime coalition, including the First Lord of the Admiralty, A. V. Alexander,[9] its cricket-loving leader Clem Attlee and, perhaps surprisingly, the working-class hero Ernest Bevin,* who became a personal friend of Constantine.[10] (By now in his forties, Constantine remained a major attraction, travelling extensively and playing fifty-four wartime matches for twenty sides, in between welfare duties for West Indians in the wartime workforce, coaching,† campaigning with his friend C. L. R. James for West Indian independence and

---

* As foreign secretary in the post-war Labour government, Bevin attempted to initiate a thaw by inviting the Soviet Marshal Voroshilov to the Test match against India at Lord's.

† His pupils included Margaret Brown, mother of one of the authors, who under his guidance opened the bowling for St Swithun's girls' school in Winchester.

winning a landmark court case when excluded on racial grounds from a London hotel.)[11,*]

Even more than the First, the Second World War provided new opportunities for women's cricket, above all through the conscription of 1.5 million women into the services and factory work, more than compensating for the takeover or dispersal of the girls' public schools, which had been the main nursery of the women's game. Both women and men benefited from the emphasis on sport as a means of raising morale, fitness and efficiency, and this was especially true of the half million in the auxiliary armed services. Some civil defence teams were mixed, to make up numbers. Two pre-war internationals, Betty Archdale and Myrtle Maclagan, were prominent in women's service cricket, which Archdale established in Singapore and Colombo when stationed there with the Wrens.[12]

The war also extended cricket's global footprint into any country visited by Dominion forces, including Iceland, Ethiopia, Iran and Iraq,[13] and more lastingly Papua New Guinea and the Gulf states.[14] Before evacuating Yugoslavia in the Nazi invasion of 1941, the British ambassador staged a patriotic cricket match in Belgrade.[15] In Arcadia, Florida, British forces were surprised to be beaten by a local team with a strong surviving cricket tradition.[16]

Egypt and Libya became major theatres of cricket for Dominion sides confronting Rommel. They played in conditions that ranged from the opulent Gezira Club and the even more luxurious Maadi Club, to the streets of Tobruk under bombardment.[17] The Egyptian clubs saw matches between many current and future Dominion Test stars, including England's Wally Hammond and Freddie Brown, Australia's Lindsay Hassett, New Zealand's Martin Donnelly, South Africa's Bruce Mitchell, Dudley Nourse and the dynamic much-decorated and multitalented bowler Bob Crisp.[18] For one future

---

* The exclusion was prompted by the fear of offending visiting American military guests. Franklin D. Roosevelt never had the political strength to desegregate the armed forces he sent to liberate countries from Nazi and Japanese racial tyranny. His successor, Truman, did this in a single day by executive order.

England cricketer, who had enlisted underage, the hard wickets of Egypt were a vital education: Jim Laker switched from being a run-of-the-mill fast bowler to off-spin.[19] Egyptians appear in accounts of these matches mainly as servants, not even as spectators, although important matches were broadcast on Egyptian state radio.[20] It is possible that these Dominion matches set back the cause of Egyptian cricket by identifying it as a sport for privileged Anglophile collaborators.*

Two ad hoc teams were especially important in bringing cricket to deprived wartime spectators. The British Empire Eleven was founded by a cricket-crazed teenager, Desmond Donnelly,† and raised more than £15,000 for wartime charities.[21] It was dominated by a talented West Indian, Bertie Clarke, who had played in the West Indian Test team of 1939 and stayed on in the UK to qualify as a doctor. Clarke would have a post-war county career with Northamptonshire and Essex, and play in countless club matches, with an interruption for a short prison sentence for performing abortions when they were still unlawful.

The London Counties Eleven, a more establishment body, played 180 wartime matches. The two teams met occasionally and were studded with famous names: one fixture brought Frank Woolley out of retirement against the rising star Compton. Harold Larwood and Bill Voce bowled together again for Nottinghamshire even though the county had treated both shabbily after Bodyline. Larwood was still so fast in retirement that he had to be taken off.[22] Herbert Sutcliffe rejoined the army but was invalided out with persistent sinus and shoulder trouble. He still played wartime charity matches, and scored his final century in aid of the Red Cross.[23]

---

* Dominion forces, especially Australians, were generally unpopular in both world wars among ordinary Egyptians. This can be seen in the Cairo Trilogy of the great novelist Naguib Mahfouz.

† Donnelly went on to a political career as a maverick MP in five different parties, a journalist and a failed businessman.

Despite difficult travel conditions these matches were immensely popular. They were aided by one wartime innovation – double summertime, intended to allow more war work to be completed in the evening shift before German bombers arrived. It allowed cricket to be played in good light until 8 p.m. In 1943, forty-seven wartime matches were watched by more than 200,000 spectators.[24]

The game endured to varying degrees under Nazi occupation. In the Netherlands cricket carried on largely without interference, and despite desperate privation in the winter of 1944. The bombing of Rotterdam in 1940 destroyed the Netherlands' only cricket emporium, but Dutch players eked out their equipment and renewed cricket balls with boot polish. Private motor transport was almost non-existent for the occupied population, but they travelled long distances by homemade tricycle to fulfil the annual programme of 300 fixtures arranged by their cricket association. Despite their own shortages, the celebrated De Flamingo club donated equipment and even a grass wicket to British prisoners of war in German hands.[25]

In Denmark cricket continued in highly restricted conditions and even joined the resistance, thanks to businessman Frederick Ferslev, who set up a cricket bat press under the nose of the Nazis in the basement of one of their own workshops.*

Cricket had flourished in the Channel Islands when they became fashionable resorts for English families in the Victorian age. But the sport virtually disappeared from the islands under Nazi occupation, which took over buildings and land, built colossal fortifications with slave labour and left the islanders very short of food. The game only survived throughout the war among the boys of Victoria College.†

---

* Tim Brooks has recently told his remarkable story in *The Batmaker of Copenhagen*.

† We are indebted for this information to an old Victorian, Mr James Wooldridge. We have no information about wartime cricket in Corfu, occupied successively by the Italians and the Germans.

Cricket disappeared in Japanese-occupied Malaya, Hong Kong and Shanghai. The Japanese seem to have made no use of it to recruit Indian prisoners of war into their 'Indian National Army' under Subhas Chandra Bose. For British and Dominion prisoners of war, even to talk about cricket – let alone play it – required prodigious physical and moral effort. Conditions were better in German and Italian camps, where the Red Cross sent occasional supplies of basic equipment. Special rules were devised to accommodate cricket in constricted conditions at Oflag IX-A/H camp. A sketch of cricket there by Terence Prittie, later a noted military historian, was smuggled out and published in the *Cricketer* in 1942. Improvised matches and tournaments involved more than three-quarters of the inmates.[26]

After the fall of Tobruk, Freddie Brown and Bill Bowes had a harder time at the Italian prisoner-of-war camp at Chieti, on the Adriatic. Mussolini's incompetent fascist regime left the guards almost as deprived as the inmates, from whom they stole anything of value, including donated equipment and tools. The prisoners became too weak to play any sort of cricket for more than a few hours at a time until conditions improved in the summer of 1943 and organised matches became possible. Brown kept up morale with talks on cricket and eventually captained one of the camp teams.[27]

Prisoners in Japanese camps endured horrifying deprivation and organised cruelty. But the cricketers among them still arranged matches even when they were barely strong enough to lift a bat. One inmate, Jim Swanton, gave a guarded account in the 1946 *Wisden* of how he was sent from Changi to work on the Burma railway, losing five stone in weight and contracting a form of polio. He was more forthcoming in his autobiography twenty-four years later, recalling: 'My 1939 *Wisden* was in such demand that it could be lent out only for periods of six hours.'[28] Swanton's copy may have been the most read volume of *Wisden* in history. Geoff Edrich was similarly reduced to six stone in weight and survived malaria by selling his wedding ring in exchange for quinine. He went on to play for Lancashire after the war, where he was admired for an impervious indifference to the fastest bowling.[29]

More than a hundred first-class cricketers were killed in action in the Second World War, about one-third of the toll in the First.[30] In both wars, the casualty figures for the Indian subcontinent are grossly under-recorded in Western sources.

Hedley Verity was the most high-profile wartime casualty. After joining up with the Green Howards, he was posted to India, Persia, Syria and Egypt. Leading an assault in Sicily in 1943, Verity was hit in the chest by shrapnel. Captured by the Italians, he died as a result of his injuries, characteristically thinking first and last of the men under his command.[31]

Many post-war talents announced themselves during the war. For England, Laker, Alec Bedser and Trevor Bailey were notable examples, and for the West Indies Clyde Walcott, Everton Weekes and Frank Worrell. Virtually all of the celebrated 'Invincibles' touring team, which Don Bradman took to England in 1948, had done war service. Two exceptions were Neil Harvey, still a teenager, and Bradman himself. He volunteered for the Air Force, but to the astonishment of the Australian public, the most gifted batter of all time was found to have defective eyesight. Transferred to physical training duties, he broke down with fibrositis. He therefore spent most of the war as a stockbroker and it was far from certain that he would return to cricket afterwards.[32]

By 1945, with the war against Japan still in progress, England celebrated victory over the Germans with a hastily arranged five-match series of Test match quality between an England team captained by Wally Hammond and an Australian Services Eleven side, captained by Lindsay Hassett and dominated by Keith Miller, a new and charismatic all-rounder from the Australian Air Force. It attracted crowds totalling more than 367,000, and produced much fine cricket as each side won two matches and drew the other.

A further representative match was held at Lord's against a Dominions Eleven. Since Hassett was unavailable to captain, the most senior alternative was Constantine. Warner, who was managing the team, characteristically prevaricated before eventually doing the right thing. He wrote later (with some delicacy):

> In this country certainly, on the cricket field colour does not excite the feeling and prejudice that exists in some parts of the Empire. It was however necessary to secure both the consent and the co-operation of the rest of the Dom side and I went into the dressing room . . . I think I sensed that for a moment there was a slight hesitation but after a very prominent member of the side had agreed that [Constantine] was the proper choice one and all fell into line.[33]

This was the first time that a team of white players of Test quality (including a South African, Desmond Fell) was captained by a black man in a first-class match. Constantine's team won, and he contributed a fast 40 and a brilliant run-out in his final first-class game.

Lessons not learned

Some observers, such as the future *Wisden* editor Norman Preston, noted the strengths of one-day cricket as played in the war and suggested that it might become a foundation of English cricket as grade cricket had served New Zealand and Australia.[34] But traditionalists, led inevitably by Warner, defended the paramountcy of three-day cricket. Warner commented that 'the one-day match would play havoc with our time-honoured weeks and festivals and raise many financial and staff problems'.

In 1942 the MCC and the first-class counties set up an advisory committee of grandees led by Sir Stanley Jackson. It deliberated for eighteen months and came up with a blueprint for post-war cricket, reflecting the wartime emphasis on planning that had produced the Beveridge Report, presaging the welfare state. It was no match for Beveridge's radicalism, rejecting proposals for a one-day cup, and for Sunday play in county and Test matches, even though Sunday cricket (with start times to allow for attendance at church or chapel) was another major wartime innovation.[35]

The advisory committee envisaged a return to the primacy of first-class county cricket led by amateurs. It ended the experiment in 1939 with eight-ball overs, to the general relief of bowlers. Two changes were misguided. They made a new ball available after 55 overs (instead of 200 runs) in the knowledge that new balls were actually very scarce (as were English fast bowlers post-war). Worse still, the committee decided that umpires had to offer batters the chance to appeal against bad light, something which would become a vehicle for lost play and gamesmanship (especially when exploited by Bailey).[36]

Chapter 22

AFTER THE WAR

Among the twelve teams that relaunched the County Championship in early May 1946,[1] twenty-three players were in their forties and only two were younger than twenty-five. The average age of the Glamorgan team was thirty-eight while the captain was forty-eight. The age factor limited the supply of fast bowlers. England's pace attack against the 1946 Indian tourists included three men in their late thirties: Bill Bowes, Bill Voce and Alf Gover. The find of that summer was twenty-seven-year-old Alec Bedser (who had fought alongside his twin brother Eric at Dunkirk).

Professional cricket's elderly feel during this post-war period reflected the lack of serious cricket over the past six years, with many young men away on national service. Britain, meanwhile, was charting a course towards becoming a more equal and democratic society. Clem Attlee's Labour government, elected in July 1945, nationalised much of British industry, consolidating the welfare state and creating a National Health Service; all financed by punitive taxation on the rich.

The MCC did not adapt. The distinction between amateur and professional was maintained. It was still deemed especially important for county teams to be led by an amateur captain. There is an enduring legend that Surrey appointed the wrong Major Bennett to lead them in 1946. His batting return was actually a little better than some other amateur captains but cricket correspondent E. M. Wellings reported that he was 'utterly lost as a county captain'.[2]

The best amateurs ran their teams in a professional spirit, with strict discipline and game plans that denied any advantage to opponents. With these methods, Wilf Wooller drove his unfashionable county, Glamorgan, to win the championship in 1948. His feud with another captain in the same mould, Freddie Brown of Northamptonshire, became famous. Stuart Surridge won five championships in a row at Surrey and passed these methods on to his successor, Peter May, to win another two. One captain during this period, Colin Ingleby-Mackenzie of Hampshire, was a throwback to the carefree gentleman amateurs of pre-war seasons. A flamboyant batter who loved parties and horse racing, he led his team to the championship in 1961, when it was said that his personal charm induced many generous declarations from opponents. His team relied strongly on its professional spine of Henry Horton, Roy Marshall and Jimmy Gray as batters and the hard-working, prodigiously accurate Derek Shackleton as a seam bowler.

There were just 1.8 million spectators in 1950, despite a visit from the scintillating West Indian team. In 1958 (a very wet summer with a weak New Zealand team as visitors) more than 700 days of first-class match play attracted fewer spectators than one football club, Arsenal, to its forty-two league matches.[3]

In 1953, to much ironic commentary, the counties managed to persuade the chancellor of the exchequer, Rab Butler, to let them off entertainments duty (a tax on admission fees for commercial amusements). By then, English cricket was yielding a meagre £36,000 to the exchequer, although this was still too great a burden for most of the counties.[4]

In 1929 there had been 205 so-called amateurs in first-class cricket. By 1959 this number had contracted to thirty-nine, with some paid 'assistant secretaries', the title allotted to Trevor Bailey at Essex. In 1952, England bowed to the inevitable, and appointed a professional captain. Len Hutton, unlike Wally Hammond in 1938, refused to turn amateur. Hutton constantly struggled against the fear that the MCC establishment viewed him as a stopgap, even after he had won two

Ashes series. Its preferred replacement was David Sheppard, amateur captain of Cambridge and Sussex and a fine batter, although well short of Hutton's class. Sheppard did step in for two matches at home against unfancied Pakistan when Hutton was sidelined by back pain and stress, and but for the demands of his religious vocation he might have got Hutton's job in Australia. The Gentlemen v Players annual fixture, dating back to 1806, was not abandoned till 1963. This opened the prime minister of the day, Sir Alec Douglas-Home, to ridicule. 'At the very time when even the MCC has abolished the distinction between amateur and professional,' mocked his Labour opponent, Harold Wilson, 'we are content to remain, in science and industry, a nation of gentlemen in a world of players.' Sir Alec, an all-rounder who played for Oxford University, Middlesex and the MCC, remains the only British prime minister to have played first-class cricket.*

Rowland Bowen wrote that the post-war years 'constituted a period of delusion', during which the game failed to come to terms with social change sweeping the country. In his history of English cricket, Derek Birley agrees: 'The old regime was back in force, reactionary as ever.'[5] From today's perspective in the third decade of the twenty-first century, these criticisms are arguably overstated. Cricketers, in common with the country as a whole, had been engaged in total war against Nazi barbarism for six years. It was understandable that they should favour continuity over change.

After all the mayhem, there was a comforting regularity about the structure of the post-war season, with the seventeen counties for the most part playing each other twice. Visiting teams were not parachuted in for the Tests, as happens today. They toured the country, starting with the traditional first match of the season against the Duke of Norfolk's Eleven at his country seat of Arundel in Sussex and ending at the Scarborough Festival, giving a structure to the season.

---

* Four of his first-class matches were in Argentina.

In those pre-climate change days, the County Championship started in early May rather than the start of April as it does today, coming to a close in early September. This meant that all-round sportsmen could enjoy parallel careers as winter footballer and summer cricketer. In 1950, Denis Compton, the most talented batter of the post-war decade, played for Arsenal in the FA Cup final alongside his brother Leslie. The following Saturday they turned out for Middlesex. Ken Taylor of Yorkshire, England and Huddersfield Town, found time to prepare for a third career as a student at the Slade School of Art. The last double cricket and football international (and a regular answer to quiz questions) was Arthur Milton of Arsenal and Gloucestershire. He had such modest earnings and savings from a long career that he became a postman on retirement, although he enjoyed the outdoor life so much that he kept his bicycle to deliver newspapers.[6] In 1964, Jim Standen won a European Cup Winners' Cup medal as West Ham goalkeeper, as well as bowling Worcestershire to its first victory in the County Championship. Cricket was the first love of Geoff Hurst, England's 1966 World Cup hat-trick hero. A wicketkeeper-batter, he played one first-class fixture for Essex. Had he been born thirty years earlier, Manchester United's Phil Neville, Lancashire's most promising cricketer for a generation when he turned out for the second eleven, might have followed a similar path.

This was the era of the schoolmaster cricketer, who would wait till the summer holidays before turning out for his county, as Micky Walford of Sherborne School and Jack Meyer of Millfield did for Somerset. Old professionals such as Jack Simmons of Lancashire carried on into their late forties, seemingly eternal, scoring runs, taking wickets and imparting wisdom.

The historian Stephen Chalke has resurrected this lost world in a series of works that exploit the techniques of oral history to show that cricket, as played in the post-war era, was in meaningful ways an accurate reflection of the social democratic egalitarianism of the period. The team rather than the individual came first, while money didn't count for much – largely because there wasn't any. The county cricket system was intrinsically linked to the communities it served, recruiting talent that would otherwise be lost. Chalke conveys the camaraderie that reconciled many players to an arduous season with long journeys, poor accommodation and minimal physical and mental support.[7]

Notwithstanding their disappearance from the county game, amateur influence remained strong in cricket's governance. In the early post-war period it was leavened by a new MCC president. Prince Philip, Duke of Edinburgh, Princess Elizabeth's husband, was a reformer, especially interested in outdoor recreation for disadvantaged young people. He was an active cricketer, whose career had begun on the park pitches used by his school at Gordonstoun. With help from Gubby Allen and the historian H. S. Altham, he promoted the Youth Cricket Association with the aim of bringing cricket to the 80 per cent of British schoolchildren who had no access to it in public schools or the leading grammar schools. It promoted group coaching in indoor settings and trained 15,000 coaches in two decades, based on *The MCC Cricket Coaching Book*. This concentrated strongly on orthodoxy batting: right-handed boys taught by it in the 1950s remember its injunction to keep the left elbow well up, even though they did not hold the bat, let alone hit the ball, with their elbows. In this way the coaching book played an unintended role in creating the defensive batting that raised such concern in the 1960s.

League cricket generally thrived post-war, although as before it did not attract English players who still had ambitions to represent their country. It gave tremendous opportunities for overseas players to earn good money and complete the residential qualifications (slightly relaxed from pre-war) for an English county. It drained a great deal of post-war Australian talent, including Bill Alley of Somerset, George Tribe of Northamptonshire and Bruce Dooland of Nottinghamshire (who taught Richie Benaud to bowl his wicket-taking 'flipper'). By contrast the leagues developed a great deal of talent for the West Indies and Pakistan, notably Garry Sobers, who developed at least three additional styles of bowling as a professional and tightened his batting technique enough to dominate in any conditions. The first year in which *Wisden* reported league cricket was 1959. Its spectators could watch the West Indians Sobers, Frank Worrell, Sonny Ramadhin, Conrad Hunte and Collie Smith, an all-round talent tragically killed that year in a car accident, with Sobers at the wheel. Pakistan supplied Fazal Mahmood, India Vinoo Mankad. Middleton's professional was the West Indian fast bowler Roy Gilchrist, who terrorised helmetless opponents with head-high 'beamers'. Two years later he would be replaced by a more important talent: Basil D'Oliveira.

Meanwhile, in the south, the Club Cricket Conference resisted any form of competition, preferring to keep places in club teams for incompetent wealthy enthusiasts.[8]

While domestic cricket stagnated, not only in England, international cricket experienced dynamic growth. From the (retrospective) beginning of Test cricket in 1876–77, 274 official Test matches were played up to the Second World War, of which nearly 90 per cent involved England. The same number were played in just thirteen years after the war, and more than 40 per cent did *not* involve England.[9] No longer an irregular addition to each country's first-class programme, Test series become the mainstay of their finances. The post-war England team was heavily reliant on players who had begun their Test careers before the war. The big discovery was Alec Bedser of Surrey, a superlative swing and seam bowler, often compared to Maurice Tate. His Test career would eventually end the same way: after carrying the England attack almost single-handed for years, he was discarded on an Ashes tour by a captain who believed in express pace.

The batting looked stronger: Hammond seemed as commanding as before the war, Compton as prolific and improvisational, Hutton as reliable, in spite of a wartime fracture that shortened his arm. England were induced to play a series in Australia prematurely, in 1946–47, largely to revive imperial links, which had been frayed by the fall of Malaya and Singapore and the East Indies, where British power failed to protect Australia from the threat of invasion.

An ageing team, starved at home under austerity and then feasting on the sea voyage, was simply outmatched by the Australians. They had a hostile opening attack, which was a counterpart to Jack Gregory and Ted McDonald after the First World War, in Keith Miller and Ray Lindwall, a bowler whose classical action was modelled on Harold Larwood's. Their back-up bowlers offered many seam and spin options, and could strangle batters on good wickets and dismiss them on bad ones.

The big issue was whether Bradman, dogged by health and financial worries, would return. Patriotic appeals and success in some non-competitive trial matches made up his mind. In the first Test, he had made an uncertain 28 runs and then survived what the English thought was an obvious slip catch. He stayed at the crease and the umpire accepted his contention that he had jammed the ball into the ground first.

This incident was intensely discussed and still is. It opened an era of focus on individual decisions by umpires. Hammond swore, Bradman ignored him and went on to score 187 and add a double century and three fifties in the rest of the series. Hammond had his own worries: the series was an exhausting failure for him as both batter and captain. He retired, disappearing to South Africa. An attempted return for his county, Gloucestershire, was an embarrassment.

England lost the series 3–0. They did even worse at home in 1948 under Hammond's successor, the amiable Yorkshire amateur Norman Yardley, when Bradman brought over a team known as the Invincibles. At Leeds they became the first Test team to chase down a total of more than 400 for victory.

In the final Test at the Oval, Bradman walked out for his last innings. He needed just four runs to make certain of a Test average of 100. He got a standing ovation from the crowd and the England players – and was then bowled second ball for a duck by the homespun Warwickshire leg-break bowler Eric Hollies. Described by the great commentator John Arlott over the radio, it became one of the most famous and replayed moments in cricket history. Bradman's

Test average of 99.94 is higher by nearly forty runs than that of any other great batsman with a major career.*

The pendulum then shifted dramatically, as England won three Ashes series in a row. In 1953, led by Hutton, they won the last Test after two others were improbably saved with contributions from Bailey as batter and bowler, which included deliberate time-wasting. Crucially, England had acquired a potent accomplice for Alec Bedser: Fred Trueman, the best English fast bowler since Larwood. The Surrey 'spin twins', Jim Laker and Tony Lock, were deadly on their own pitch: Laker a master of controlled off-spin, Lock an aggressive slow-left-armer, especially since he was rarely called for throwing his suspect quicker ball.

The Ashes win was gained in the Coronation year. Alongside the conquest of Everest and the Stanley Matthews FA Cup final, it fed into wider expectations of a new Elizabethan age of achievement, which added to establishment pressures on Hutton.[10,†]

England travelled to Australia in 1954 in the old-fashioned way: a six-week journey by ocean liner after the unhappy experiment the previous winter by air to the West Indies, stopping off en route to pay tribute to the grave of Hedley Verity in Italy.[11] Once there, England secured the 1954–55 Ashes after a massive loss in the first Test, for which Hutton was blamed for electing to field at a sweltering Brisbane. He then dropped England's stalwart, Bedser, but was too embarrassed to tell him personally and relied on all-out pace from two new stars. There was no Trueman, after his alleged misconduct in the troubled West Indies tour, but Brian Statham was his equal in pace – and remorselessly accurate. Frank Tyson was even faster, some believe the fastest bowler in English history. Several of his deliveries

---

* But it is exceeded by the unsung West Indian Andy Ganteaume, discarded for slow scoring in his only Test innings of 112. At the time of writing the Australian batter Kurtis Patterson boasted a Test match average of 144.

† A fine magazine, actually called *Young Elizabethan*, promoted this mood among schoolchildren as did the more popular *Eagle* comic.

in county cricket famously bounced over the batter and hit the sightscreen behind him. A well-read and thoughtful man, he expressed irritation on the field by quoting poetry.

In 1956, now captained by Peter May, England held the Ashes after one last great all-round performance by Miller gave Australia victory at Lord's. The selectors made some inspired recalls in batting – Compton, Sheppard and Cyril Washbrook – and Laker took 27 wickets *apart* from the 19 at Manchester.

Benaud turns the tables

The pendulum swung back after the imaginative appointment of Richie Benaud as Australian captain. Benaud had enjoyed a stop-start career as a leg-spinning all-rounder in the 1950s. He tightened his bowling and added to his repertoire with advice from legendary Bill O'Reilly as well as Bruce Dooland. Apart from superb close fielding, combative late-order batting and an attacking mindset on the field, Benaud, a working journalist, was a master of press and public relations off the field.

Benaud outgeneralled the introverted and defensive May. His team overpowered injury-hit England in 1958–59, winning four Tests to none. Australia's extra element was a set of bowlers suspected even in their own country of illegal methods. Ian Meckiff, a left-arm seamer, appeared to have a bent arm, which made his deliveries hard to detect; Gordon Rorke was a 'dragger', a fast bowler who used the back-foot no-ball rule to deliver the ball from a shorter distance than the Laws allowed. The English media complained, although neither captain May nor manager Freddie Brown did. The controversy generated a purge against bowlers with suspect actions in both countries. This was mainly the result of a private agreement between Bradman and Gubby Allen. One feature of this was that umpires would not no-ball suspect bowlers during matches but instead report them to the authorities (though this did not stop English umpires no-balling the South African Geoff Griffin out of Test cricket in 1960).

Test cricket relationships had become more important than the Laws of the game.[12]

There was also an agreed change to the Laws against dragging, so that the ball had to be delivered with some part of the front foot behind the bowling crease in front of the stumps. The change was cursed by Trueman and many pace-bowling successors since and blamed for many injuries, but it ended dragging and made it much easier for umpires – and later, cameras – to detect no-balls.

England and Australia agreed not to select suspect bowlers, and Meckiff was dropped for Australia's tour of England in 1961. To support the superlative left-arm opening bowler Alan Davidson, the selectors sent three seamers with impeccable actions: one, the teenaged Graham McKenzie, would have a long career.

The first Test was a high-scoring draw. The Australians, led by Harvey in place of the injured Benaud, dominated at Lord's despite a late collapse in pursuit of a small target. Trueman, at cut pace, wrecked Australia at Leeds to level the series. At Manchester, England twice seemed poised for victory. Australia had a small second-innings lead and one wicket to fall. Davidson was still in and launched a violent assault on Laker's off-spin successor, David Allen. But England still had a reachable target, which was even more reachable after a domineering 76 from Ted Dexter. Benaud in desperation switched himself to bowl round the wicket into footmarks left by the England pace bowlers. It would at least create unpredictable bounce. Almost immediately, Dexter was caught behind. Then Benaud bowled May, second ball, behind his legs, a basic error in technique by England's best batter. The patient opener Raman Subba Row and Brian Close quickly followed. Ken Barrington alone remained of the frontline batters. The target was still just over three an over, a trifle by modern standards, but when Barrington and the wicketkeeper John Murray left in rapid succession, England abandoned all thoughts of winning. Australia wrapped up victory with half-an-hour to spare: Benaud had six wickets without attempting much spin. The series loss and Australia's consequent retention of the Ashes were blamed on a defensive mindset that had left English batters incapable of controlled aggression. So much for brighter cricket by carefree amateurs. May left the scene at the early age of thirty-one.

Post-war cricket in New Zealand

New Zealand's Test programme expanded after the war but they generally remained international whipping boys. They produced three players of international class – batters Martin Donnelly and Bert Sutcliffe and the all-rounder John Reid – but these were not enough to carry a team of enthusiastic but less-talented colleagues. New Zealand were especially hampered by the lack of quality in the bowling and their cricket continued to be held back by climate, distance, Australian neglect* and the dominance of rugby union.

In 1949, expertly led by Walter Hadlee, founder of a magnificent cricket dynasty, New Zealand were good enough to draw all four Tests in England, and the series marked the end of three-day Test matches. They were popular tourists everywhere for their sporting behaviour and, in India and Pakistan, for their willingness to tour at all.

Quietly, the New Zealanders prepared for better times by making their domestic competition, the Plunket Shield, more competitive and strengthening the links between the centre and the provinces. In 1956, after twenty-five years of attempts, they won a Test match. It was at home and the last match of a dead rubber against a below-strength, experimental West Indies. In 1961–62, led by Reid, they won two Tests against South Africa and shared the rubber.

Playing South Africa in Johannesburg on Boxing Day 1953, their team received the news of the Tangiwai railway disaster, among the worst in history. The 151 victims included Nerissa Love, fiancée of the team's opening bowler, Bob Blair. The already shaken New Zealanders were then battered by the South African pace bowlers.

---

* Australia overpowered New Zealand in a one-off Test match in 1946 and did not play another until the 1970s.

Sutcliffe had to retire hurt but returned at 81 for 6, still bleeding into the bandages around his head. He carried the score to 154 when the ninth wicket fell. Everyone assumed the innings closed but Blair, although still distraught, stunned everyone at the ground by walking out to join him. Sutcliffe gave him a brief hug and the two then smashed 25 from an over by the miserly off-spinner Hugh Tayfield. This story has been made into a book, a play and a movie. Blair subsequently moved to England, and married thirty-three years after his loss.[13]

Women's cricket

Women's cricket after the war presented a similar pattern to men's. There was more international competition but domestically the game could not break free of the constraints imposed by economics – and men.

Nineteen Test matches were played by women between 1947 and 1961, compared to seven in the 1930s. In the same period, men played nearly 300. Nearly all women's Tests involved three countries: England, Australia and New Zealand. In 1960–61 England toured South Africa and played four Tests against a white-only team.

One Test match stands out in this period: Australia against England in Melbourne in February 1958. England's captain Mary Duggan took seven wickets for six runs as Australia were all out for 38. Australia still got a first-innings lead because Betty Wilson also took seven wickets to bowl out England for 35. Wilson then scored a century in the second innings. England clung on to a draw at 76 for 8: four more wickets to Wilson giving her 11 for 16 runs. She was the first cricketer to complete a Test match double of a century and 10 wickets, twenty-two years ahead of the first man, Ian Botham against India.

Another significant milestone was Faith Thomas's lone Test for Australia. She was the first indigenous person to play for her country. More indigenous women have represented Australia than indigenous men, despite the women's team playing far fewer matches.[14]

None of the women players was paid, and each had to cover their passage and expenses. Those selected for the England tour of Australia and New Zealand in 1948–49 had to find a sum equivalent to more than £8,000 in today's purchasing power.[15] Not surprisingly, women's cricket was largely restricted to well-to-do women with supportive families or employers. In England, the cost of clothing to meet the strict standards of deportment of Marjorie Pollard was another obstacle to lower-income women and girls. Pollard's policy of placating male administrators and combatting patronising or embarrassing media coverage remained a necessity after the war. This was especially true of access to decent grounds – all controlled by men.

The WCA was still heavily concentrated in English girls' public schools. Girls were not encouraged to play cricket in the state secondary schools created by the Butler Education Act of 1944 and few teachers could coach it. There was no improvement when comprehensive schools fused the division between grammar schools and secondary moderns. One of these, Holland Park, soon became a magnet for 'progressive' families in London. Its head teacher announced in 1960 that, 'Girls will not enjoy a game in which they have neither aptitude nor interest.'[16]

Part Four

THE EMPIRE STRIKES BACK

Steeped within the tradition of Constantine, Headley, and Worrell, came the artistic genius of Sobers and the ideological radicalism of Richards . . . It was politics, and ideological power struggle, and it was recognised by the world as such.

SIR HILARY BECKLES, 'The Radical Tradition in the Culture of West Indies Cricket', 1994

I can never forget Lucknow and the ground by the Goomti river.

A. H. KARDAR on Pakistan's first Test match victory over India, 1954

Cricket is a subtle game. In form and appearance it can be gentle, even idyllic, yet violence is always there.

MIHIR BOSE

Chapter 23

THE WEST INDIES EMERGE AS A MAJOR POWER

From its origins until the second half of the twentieth century, cricket was run by white men. The first half century of Test match cricket was built around the Ashes contest between England and Australia. When a tripartite system emerged, the third country was racist South Africa.

With the collapse of the Empire, newly liberated nations emerged as an independent force. In some, above all the West Indies and Pakistan, cricket became part of an independence movement. A small group of players came to symbolise the emergent anti-colonial consciousness. This was the global context as the West Indies emerged as a world-beater after a long struggle to break free of the legacy of racism and colonialism, culminating in the overdue appointment of a black captain, Frank Worrell.

Some of the imperial legacy remained, particularly the inter-island rivalries. But the intense stratification of West Indian cricket by race and class was dissipated, and Worrell could nurture and fuse multiple talents into a team that won Test matches and hearts alike.

The post-war story began when they overpowered a second-string and injury-hit England side led by the forty-five-year-old Gubby Allen in 1947–8. The series launched the three Ws: Clyde Walcott, Everton Weekes and Frank Worrell. Born within two miles of each other in Barbados, they were a remarkable concentration of batting talent from a small space: Walcott fearsome in power, Worrell supremely elegant, Weekes remorseless and dominant. Walcott and Worrell came from middle-class backgrounds; Weekes was poorer, and had to battle racism and snobbery.[1] Walcott could keep wicket while Worrell, a right-hand bat like the others, also bowled left-arm orthodox spin or seam.

George Headley returned and became the West Indies' first black captain, for just one home Test. But even if he had not been injured in the first Test, the selectors had agreed to replace him with the usual white man. The first was Gerry Gomez, who had played Tests before the war. The second was John Goddard, a less accomplished player than Gomez, let alone Headley. But he rose above them both in social class as a member of the Goddard's rum family. He remained captain on the West Indies' first tour of India even though Headley had recovered. The West Indies won a high-scoring series 1–0. Weekes had a record-breaking run of five consecutive centuries. Worrell was missing. In an early sign of his independent mind, he asked the West Indies Cricket Board for more money, marking himself down as a 'cricketing Bolshevik'. The board refused and Indians got their first sight of him with a Commonwealth team of English league professionals instead of the West Indies. Worrell's act of rebellion earned him hostility in his native Barbados and led him to relocate to Jamaica.

He returned for the West Indies tour of England in 1950, for which Goddard was reappointed captain. The West Indies looked strong in batting but looked very short of bowling, especially spin. The selectors took a chance on two virtual unknowns, Sonny Ramadhin of Trinidad and Alf Valentine of Jamaica.

Ramadhin was a genuine mystery right-arm spinner, who could turn the ball sharply either way with no obvious change of action. Like all bowlers of his type, he was accused by his victims of an illegal action, charges fed by his habit of bowling with his sleeves rolled down. Valentine was an orthodox slow-left armer with great powers of spin and a dangerous 'arm ball', which (unlike his English contemporary Tony Lock) had an entirely legal action. Ramadhin's selection was politically significant as the first 'East Indian' (denoting Asian family origins) to represent the West Indies.

The surprise selections proved devastating. England won the first Test, but then Ramadhin and Valentine bowled the West Indies to three overwhelming victories, their first on English soil. Both the victories and the impromptu calypso-singing celebrations by West Indian supporters, early members of what would become known as the Windrush generation, gave the English cricket establishment a serious shock. The celebrations were the first visible demonstration that Britain was becoming a multiracial society.

Valentine took 33 English wickets in four Tests in his first series, Ramadhin 26, while six other bowlers shared 18. One factor in their success was the speed at which they bowled their overs, which gave batters no time to rest. Obituaries of Valentine said that he could bowl a maiden over in ninety seconds. At Lord's, when the West Indies won by 326 runs, they bowled 231 overs mostly in tandem, of which 145 were maidens. Over rates were not recorded then but we have calculated that the West Indies bowled more than 25 overs an hour for much of their time in the field, far higher than today's required rate of 15.

The partnership of Ramadhin, the introverted East Indian, and Valentine,* the extroverted 'African', was a powerful symbol of Caribbean unity.

Goddard did not contribute too much to the results but he didn't have to, and his captaincy was generally admired. He was criticised for keeping his match-winners on for too long and having no idea how to support them in the field if they were put under pressure. This criticism was magnified when the West Indies lost 4–1 in Australia in a series billed as a world championship. Australia snatched one

---

* Valentine signed thousands of autographs on the tour and prepared dozens in advance to hand out from the team coach. He was delighted to receive his first pair of glasses in his life, through the new NHS, but they made no difference to his batting, which was among the worst in modern times. He took more first-class wickets in his career than he scored runs. A highly ethical man, Valentine had a noble post-playing life. Settling in Florida, he and his second wife fostered dozens of troubled children.

victory by 3 wickets and another by 1 wicket. In neither case was Goddard able to produce a plan B or rally his team. The fielding throughout the series was ragged and the batting repeatedly fallible against Australian pace, both signs of poor preparation. He gave way as captain to another white man, Jeff Stollmeyer, but would return.

The West Indies' next major series, at home to England in 1953–54, was one of the most turbulent in cricket history. All the fissures in West Indian cricket – between races, classes, and islands down to individual clubs and players – intersected with the separate political struggles in each island against colonialism. The English side brought conflicts of their own, in the shape of an establishment conspiracy against Len Hutton as a professional captain and poor relationships between individual players.

Hutton's uncompromising approach to winning and giving opponents no quarter was magnified by intense pressure from local white spectators to beat the 'restive natives' and maintain the prestige of the ruling class. Such was the anxiety about the political situation in the islands that ahead of the tour the players were given a briefing by a Cabinet minister, Minister of Labour Walter Monckton. This was unprecedented. So was the decision to fly the whole team to the West Indies instead of giving them a chance to bond on the usual sea voyage. As an omen of future troubles, the aircraft developed a technical fault and barely made it to the pre-jet era stopover in Gander, Newfoundland.[2]

The English team and accompanying media regularly aggravated tense on-field situations by displays of grievance and, sometimes, open racism. Umpires were intimidated by crowds and players. West Indians including Stollmeyer were abused by fans from other islands. Several English players received complaints about off-field behaviour, some justified but none resolved by what would now be judged a fair process.

All these issues would have been a major challenge for Hutton's introverted leadership. He was further handicapped by the strange decision to give him an amateur player-manager, the kindly schoolmaster Charles Palmer of Leicestershire, blurring lines of authority. *Wisden* 1955 called this an experiment that should never be repeated. It never has been.

This tangled skein has been brilliantly unravelled by the historian David Woodhouse in his book *Who Only Cricket Know*. This is especially true of his analysis of the multiple causes – rum, gambling, class-based and anti-colonial protests – of the bottle-throwing riot in the British Guiana Test, the first of its kind anywhere in Test cricket, which shocked players, administrators and media alike.[3] Woodhouse also does justice to the cricket, much of it scintillating. England levelled the series from 2–0 behind. They won the third, at Georgetown, after a superb spell of pace bowling from Brian Statham. The fourth was a high-scoring draw. England's second victory came in the last at Kingston. Trevor Bailey took seven wickets for thirty-four on a blameless pitch, and Hutton overcame his troubles in a magisterial double century.

One great West Indian vanished from the scene, George Headley. A well-subscribed public collection had paid for his recall from England, but he could no longer cope with the English pace attack. Another announced himself.

In the final Test of 1953–54 the selectors replaced Valentine with a teenage slow-left-arm bowler who had made just two first-class appearances for Barbados. Garry Sobers was just five years old when he lost his father, a merchant sailor sunk at sea during the war. His mother raised him and his brother in a single-room shack on a tiny income. In the stratified West Indian club structure, patrons propelled him into important teams. In the second, the police, he served as a bugler. Like Don Bradman, he was almost lost to another sport, in his case football as a goalkeeper.

Sobers made a stuttering start to Test cricket, although he worked his way up the batting order. In four series in three countries, his top score was 66 and he took just 14 wickets at a cost of over 40 apiece. The selectors kept faith with him on the evidence of class. He rewarded them at home by breaking Hutton's Test batting record. His undefeated 365 was scored against a Pakistan attack weakened by the loss of a key bowler, but still required intense discipline, signalled by its lack of a six, and was nearly four hours shorter than Hutton's innings.

Sobers would go on to become the most inspirational and versatile cricket player of all time, a left-handed batter able to score with power and grace on all sides of the wicket with the full swing of the bat, which has always delighted aficionados. To this he added the ability to bowl almost anything with his left hand, adding wrist spin, seam movement, swing and outright pace to his original orthodox spin. His fielding was superlative anywhere, especially at short leg where he stood closer to the batter than anyone before him.

There were clouds in his career, especially when he had to captain and mentor a weak Test team, and he showed naivety in a visit to white Rhodesia. But he never lost the love of fans. Sobers became a global cricketer, playing league and county cricket in England, state cricket in Australia and numerous exhibition matches for private teams in other countries, apart from his commitments to Barbados and West Indies. He needed the income, for his earnings were far below what such a great player would command later. In all cricket, he batted almost 900 times for nearly 40,000 runs and bowled more than 92,000 deliveries for close to 2,000 wickets.[4] By the end, his left shoulder and right knee had taken a terrible toll. His playing career finished in 1974 before one-day internationals took off. He played only one – and scored a duck.

The campaign for Worrell

Stollmeyer departed after two more Tests against the next visitors, Australia. Worrell, his vice-captain, was passed over as his successor for another white man, Denis Atkinson. He had no credentials to outrank Worrell, or indeed Weekes and Walcott. The West Indies lost the series 3–0. The Australians, captained by the affable Ian Johnson and carrying no colonial baggage, enjoyed a friendly, incident-free tour.

Goddard was mysteriously recalled to the captaincy. He took as tour manager a largely experimental team to New Zealand, performed capably with the bat and won the series comfortably. On the strength of this, he was given the captaincy of the party to England in 1957. It contained some fine young players: Sobers and Rohan Kanhai as batters, Wesley Hall as a pace bowler, Collie Smith as an all-rounder, besides the three Ws, and Ramadhin and Valentine. Valentine had the mysterious condition known as the yips, an inexplicable loss of rhythm that seems especially to afflict bowlers of his type. Against a powerfully rebuilt England team, the West Indies would depend heavily on Ramadhin.

He began well, taking seven cheap wickets in the first innings of the first Test. The West Indies built a big lead through Smith and Worrell, and then Ramadhin took two more cheap wickets. The match was then transformed by a partnership between Peter May and Colin Cowdrey of 411. Its heroics were marred by their pragmatic but ugly method of taking a long stride forward and intercepting Ramadhin's deliveries with their pads. He appealed for LBW several dozen times for deliveries that would almost certainly have hit the wicket. Under the Laws as they stood at the time, the umpires were obliged to refuse the appeals if the point of impact was outside the off stump. Batters could therefore get their pad outside the line and kick the ball away. Goddard had no answer to these tactics except to force Ramadhin to bowl 98 overs, an unwanted record that still stands. Ramadhin did not dismiss either batter and he was broken by the ordeal for the rest of the series. Though praised at the time, May's and Cowdrey's strategy was a triumph for negative and cynical cricket over one of the most magical spin bowlers in the history of the game. Even the English were embarrassed but it was not till 1972 that the Laws were finally changed to outlaw their pad-play.

The West Indies lost three of the four remaining Tests heavily. Goddard retired but still the selectors did not ask for Worrell. The new choice as captain was Gerry Alexander, who had played just three Tests. By strict West Indian caste standards he was not white but mixed race,[5] but he was a former captain of Cambridge University. Alexander was an ethical, conscientious and empathetic captain, under whom Sobers, Kanhai and Hall established themselves, as did a world-class spin bowler in Lance Gibbs and an excellent opening bat, Conrad Hunte. However, his appointment was an outrage to popular feeling. A press campaign for Worrell was already under way. It acquired new momentum with the return of C. L. R. James to write for the *Nation* in his native Trinidad. James's special contribution was to link the captaincy issue with the ongoing struggles against class and colonialism.[6]

Alexander's reign began with the home victory against Pakistan, followed by an overwhelming series win away in India. He drew heavy criticism from West Indies supporters for his decision to send home the hyper-aggressive fast bowler, Roy Gilchrist. There were solid reasons – Gilchrist was a troubled character who bowled potentially lethal beamers at opponents – but he was seen by many as a martyr, a poor black man victimised by a privileged white one. Comparisons were made with Worrell's sympathetic mentorship of him in the closing stages of the English tour of 1957.[7] Matters came to a head when Alexander painfully lost an attritional series at home to an England side captained by his friend Peter May. West Indies lost one Test heavily, after another bottle-throwing riot. All the others were drawn. Alexander was now beset by the pro-Worrell campaign, which James had turned against him personally. At the end of the series, he stepped down. The selectors finally accepted the inevitability of Worrell, who had been vice-captain during the England tour – and Alexander graciously agreed to swap places with him.

The struggle over the captaincy was fuelled by the persistent myth that only white men had the leadership qualities to create a united, disciplined West Indies. In the end, it established that only a black captain could achieve this.

The greatest series of all

Worrell's first assignment could not have been harder – away to Australia. His team was well-resourced if he could make its elements gel. Its main weaknesses were the lack of a reliable opening partner for Hunte and of an out-and-out pace partner for Hall (although Sobers had now added fast-medium to his repertoire). Ramadhin and especially Valentine had been revitalised, Gibbs was established and Sobers could also supply two types of left-arm spin. Worrell had established an excellent ongoing relationship with his Australian opposite, Richie Benaud, with a shared commitment to play positive cricket. Worrell further committed his team to accept umpires' decisions and to respect their opponents. He was a natural motivator and mentor but treated all his players as individuals and adults. On the field, he always gave the impression of a plan and encouraged this with long conversations with his bowlers. Between them, he and Benaud served up the most pulsating series of all time. It was watched by nearly a million people, almost equal to the previous Ashes series.[8] The opening day of the first Test at Brisbane set the tone for what followed. Three West Indian wickets fell cheaply but then Sobers scored one of his most electrifying Test centuries. He was supported by Worrell, Joe Solomon (of British Guiana, a reliable presence in the middle order), Alexander and a whirlwind 50 from Hall. The West Indies closed on 453 from 104 eight-ball overs, an unheard-of scoring rate. Worrell fretted that the West Indies had left Australia too much time to make a worthwhile reply and he was right, since they made over 500. The West Indies slumped in their second innings. Worrell and Solomon saved it from disaster but the Australian target of 233 was well within reach. Wes Hall then produced an inspired spell that reduced Australia to 92 for 6. Benaud and Alan Davidson, their two all-rounders, counter-attacked when Hall had to be rested. They reached 226, seven runs to win, when Davidson was run out attempting a sharp single by a direct hit from Joe Solomon, the West Indies' best outfielder, at midwicket.

Suddenly the game took a new course.

Worrell gave the ball to Hall for the last eight-ball over. He instructed Hall not to attempt a bouncer. Hall ignored the instruction. Benaud hooked, got a top edge and was caught behind by Alexander.

Two wickets to fall. The next pair, Ian Meckiff and Wally Grout, pinched a sharp single. Hall picked up the ball and made a wild attempt to throw down the stumps at his end. The ball could easily have gone for 4 winning overthrows. Instead, Valentine, an indifferent fielder, heroically backed up.

Grout spooned an easy catch to Kanhai at square leg. Hall rushed over to grab it himself and dropped it. One more run. Three to win off three balls.

Meckiff hit Hall towards the leg-side boundary. But the grass in that part of the ground was thick. Hunte cut the ball off as the batters ran two and turned for the third. Hunte delivered a perfect throw to Alexander, who ran out Grout.

The last man, Lindsay Kline, emerged to face the last two balls. He pushed one to cover and the two batters scampered for a winning single.

They may not have noticed that the fielder was Solomon. The photograph shows clearly that Solomon should have thrown to the bowler's end. Worrell was coolly poised over the stumps and would have run out Kline by a long way.

Instead Solomon aimed at the stumps at the batting end. Alexander, standing a long way back to Hall, had no chance to gather the throw. Solomon had only one stump to aim at. He hit it. Meckiff, the non-striker, was run out.

Nobody quite knew what had happened. Finally, both sides realised that they had just played the first tied Test match.* Benaud came

---

* There are detailed accounts of the last over in two fine biographies of the main protagonists, Hall and Solomon: *Answering the Call* by Paul Akeroyd and

onto the field to embrace Worrell. The two teams celebrated together long into the night. The Queensland administrators complained and later threw away the scorebook.[9]

The rest of the series was almost as good. A big win for Australia in the second Test, a big win for West Indies in the third, with another century by Sobers. Gibbs and Valentine (in his last great performance) span out Australia, and Sobers for the first time took up his ultra-short catching position on the leg side.

In the next match, Kanhai scored two centuries and Gibbs took a hat-trick. A West Indies victory seemed certain when the last Australian batter, Kline, joined Australia's adhesive middle-order batter, Ken Mackay.

Almost instantly, Sobers appealed for a short-leg catch against Kline. It was rejected. All the West Indians were certain it was a catch but followed Worrell's instructions not to show it. The last pair then survived ninety minutes to save the match.

Australia had the better of most of the final Test but were made to struggle hard for a victory target of 258. They lost 8 wickets and there was a contentious decision in their favour when it seemed that a batter had been clean bowled. The final winning run was a bye that just missed the stumps.

The West Indian batting had been either spectacular (Sobers and Kanhai) or solid and consistent (Hunte, Worrell and Solomon). Alexander was a revelation. Freed from his unwanted captaincy, he scored a fifty in every Test match and claimed twenty-three victims behind the stumps. Seymour Nurse was a new batting star. Hall reached greatness as a fast bowler, Gibbs as a spinner. Valentine, Worrell and, in several styles, Sobers were fine support. The fielding, previously a weak spot, was consistently good and had earned them the tied Test.

Joe Solomon and the Spirit of Port Mourant by Clem Seecharan and Ian McDonald. Solomon attributed his success to early practice in knocking down mangoes with stones. There has been just one tied Test since, between India and Australia in Madras in 1986.

They were given a ticker-tape parade on departing from Melbourne, attended by a crowd whose lowest estimate was a quarter of a million. No team has received a similar honour. The West Indies had saved Test match cricket from attritional extinction.

Three of the most popular West Indians were inducted into state teams: Hall in Queensland, Kanhai in Western Australia and Sobers in South Australia. All three made major contributions as players and generated a big uplift in spectators and receipts. To accommodate them the Australian board opened the Sheffield Shield to overseas imports, seven years ahead of a similar move in the English County Championship.[10]

Worrell had two more series as captain. At home, he led the West Indies to a 5–0 whitewash against India. A new young wicketkeeper, Deryck Murray, began a long residence and would become influential as a players' 'shop steward'. Hall acquired a fearsome opening partner, Charlie Griffith, widely suspected of throwing. The Indian captain, Nari Contractor, was nearly killed when he ducked into a Griffith bouncer: Worrell led the blood donors who saved his life, but Contractor never played cricket again and the young Nawab of Pataudi became captain in his place, overcoming the loss of an eye in a car accident while at Oxford.

Finally, Worrell led the West Indies to England where they repeated the 3–1 series victory of his first tour. Hunte, Kanhai, Sobers and a new talent, Basil Butcher of British Guiana, carried the batting; Griffith, Sobers, Gibbs and Hall took the wickets. Worrell's leadership and coolness at critical moments were vital. At one such moment, in the Lord's Test, when England had a chance of victory and were attempting a sharp single, Worrell fielded the ball and remembered that the England batter, Derek Shackleton, was the same age (thirty-eight) as himself.

Instead of shying the ball at the stumps, he calmly decided to outrun Shackleton and break them in person. Hall was then bowling, for the second time in three years, an over in which all the results were possible. The run-out set up the dramatic return of Colin Cowdrey, who had broken his arm. His heroics passed into legend, although he did not face a ball. His partner, David Allen, blocked out the remaining deliveries for a draw.

Worrell was knighted on retirement, the first overseas cricketer so honoured since Bradman. He managed the West Indian team against Australia in 1964–5, having secured the succession for his protégé Sobers over Hunte. Worrell was appointed warden of the University of the West Indies and a Jamaican senator. He seemed destined for a distinguished role in public life when in 1967 his life was cut tragically short by leukaemia.

Chapter 24

INDEPENDENCE AND SEPARATION

After Partition in 1947, India remained a member of the ICC, with headquarters operating out of Bombay (now Mumbai), leaving Pakistan without a central structure let alone Test status. Pakistan's infrastructure was wretched, with only two turf wickets, both in Lahore, and no Test grounds.

Anthony de Mello, president of the Board of Control for Cricket in India, blackmailed Pakistan. Either Pakistan could have first-class and Test cricket within the Indian structure, or remain outside and have neither. The ICC (and MCC) sent out signals it preferred India to remain, for cricketing purposes, a single country.[1] This vision held out the prospect of Pakistan as a minor cricketing nation, probably contributing the occasional player to the Indian team, as Ireland did for England after Partition in 1922.

Fazal Mahmood resolved the matter. The most talented member of Professor Aslam's brilliant Islamia College team, Mahmood had earned a golden reputation in the years running up to independence. In early 1947, he was picked for that winter's all-India tour of Australia. Mahmood could accept this offer as a Pakistani because at that point the Attlee government planned to quit India in June 1948, after the tour was over.

Then the British panicked and brought forward independence. By the time the All-Indian team assembled for pre-tour training in Poona (now Pune) in August 1947, Partition was under way and the Punjab in flames. The training camp was abandoned, and players ordered to return home to pack their bags and say goodbye to their families.

Mahmood faced the task of returning to what had suddenly become a foreign country in the headwinds of the greatest mass migration in history. A Hindu mob attacked him on the train journey from Poona to Bombay. He would have been lynched but for the intervention of his travelling companion, Indian cricket legend C. K. Nayudu, who defended Mahmood with a cricket bat. When he got back home to Lahore, Mahmood cabled Lala Amarnath, the Indian captain, explaining that he could not make the Australia tour.

Had Mahmood become an Indian cricketer, de Mello's plan to turn Pakistan into a tributary of India would almost certainly have worked. Instead, Mahmood shamed the ICC into giving his country Test match status when he bowled Pakistan to victory against a strong MCC side in Karachi. At this point India, to their credit, proposed their northern neighbour for ICC membership.

Once Pakistan got Test status, Mahmood bowled them to victory after victory, starting with the defeat of India in the ancient Islamic centre of Lucknow in 1952, moving on to a famous triumph at the Oval over England in 1954.

Subcontinental cricket after independence

India were not short of quality players, yet the brilliance did not lead to success for a team that retained an apologetic air of post-colonial deference. England pace bowler Fred Trueman, making his international debut in the Headingley Test in 1952, reduced India to 0 for 4, the worst ever start to an innings in Test cricket, with batters backing off to square leg.

The captain, Vijay Hazare, India's most experienced batter, dropped himself down the order in an attempt to avoid the onslaught. Historian Mihir Bose excuses Hazare on the slender grounds that he suffered a thigh strain, nevertheless adding that a 'whole generation of Indian batters were branded as cowards'.[2,*]

Administrators treated players with arbitrary contempt. The red carpet was rolled out for visiting teams, but India's own players had to make do with third-class rail travel and second-class hotels. When Amarnath complained, he was investigated for misconduct.[3,†] Through almost three decades of Test cricket, India failed to strike on a stable, settled captain. Four were tried in a five-match series against West Indies;[‡] five different ones appeared in consecutive Tests in 1959.[§] In the 1960s, India were not felt to merit a full five-Test home series in England.

Meanwhile, Pakistan could not sustain the early victories. The dictatorship of Ayub Khan, who dislodged Iskander Mirza – like many Pakistani leaders, an exceptional cricketer – in a military coup in 1958, imposed a conformity on Pakistan society that found its way into the cricket field. 'When war is not on,' observed the field marshal, 'the best place for the promotion of team spirit is the cricket field.'[4] It is not surprising that some of the best players – above all Khalid Ibadulla and Mushtaq Mohammad – disappeared into English county cricket.

Visiting teams stayed away. Australia only played two Tests against Pakistan in the 1960s. The West Indies did not play against Pakistan at all between March 1959 and February 1975. MCC relations with Pakistan were damaged by the calamitous 'A' tour in early 1956. A

---

[*] Trueman clearly scarred the Indian psyche. Polly Umrigar, who scored heavily in the tour games but found it hard to score in the Tests, particularly struggled. He was bowled three times backing away to Trueman during the series.

[†] When Amarnath asked de Mello for more money, the administrator responded by launching twenty-three allegations of misconduct against him. At a board meeting on 10 April 1949, Amarnath was suspended from both domestic and international cricket.

[‡] They were Polly Umrigar, Ghulam Ahmed, Vinoo Mankad and Hemu Adhikari.

[§] Ahmed, Mankad and Adhikari were followed by Datta Gaekwad and Pankaj Roy.

group of England players, led by captain Donald Carr, kidnapped the Pakistan umpire Idris Baig, forced him into the back of a rickshaw, took him to their hotel, and poured buckets of water over him. Brian Close, Ken Barrington and Jim Parks were involved in the 'prank'.

The episode prompted riots, forcing the closure of the British Embassy, while the England players were thereafter accompanied by guards. Pakistan would have sent the team home but for Field Marshal Lord Alexander of Tunis, that year's MCC president. He took control of the situation, got personally in touch with the president of Pakistan's cricket board, Iskander Mirza, apologised and offered to order Carr's team home.[5] The two men had served together on the North-West Frontier in the 1930s, and the situation was resolved. This episode put on display the racism, chauvinism and cultural arrogance of English teams visiting the subcontinent – repeated three decades later when England captain Mike Gatting insulted a different Pakistani umpire, Shakoor Rana.

It sometimes felt as if Pakistan were fighting a rearguard action against the world. For two decades, opening bat Hanif Mohammad embodied this spirit of heroic resistance. Just 5 foot 7 inches, Hanif again and again clung on amid the wreckage of the Pakistan batting order. In the first Test of the West Indies tour of 1958, he sculpted the greatest (and bravest) defensive innings in the history of the game.

When West Indies captain Gerry Alexander asked Pakistan to follow on 473 runs behind, more than three-and-a-half days remained. Hanif stayed at the crease for 999 minutes, facing a bowling attack that included Garry Sobers, Alf Valentine, Collie Smith and the lethal Roy Gilchrist. Batters did not use thigh pads in those days, so the fastest deliveries thudded constantly into Hanif's unprotected upper thigh, leaving a deep indent. His upper cheeks were black in the pre-suncream days as layers of skin had burned off. We visited Hanif not long before his death at his home in Karachi. His fingers were like the twigs of an old tree, twisted, bent and broken by twenty years of cricket. In his playing days, they did not use X-rays and the fingers were left to mend themselves.

India played three five-Test series against Pakistan between 1952 and 1960. There was no further engagement for eighteen years because of the 1965 and 1971 wars between the two countries. Cricket resumed in 1978, to be curtailed by a further lull for a decade after 1987. There have been no Test matches since 2007 and at the time of writing any resumption is a remote prospect.

On the playing field, cricket has been burdened with the density of history, meaning, current conflict and recent memory. In the early contests in particular, neither side was prepared to lose. In 1954, Vinoo Mankad took his team to Pakistan. At the end of a five-Test series the scoreline was 0–0, the first time this result had been recorded. The scoring rate rarely exceeded two runs an over, often much less. The two teams played out their second consecutive 0–0 series draw when Mahmood led Pakistan to India six years later. Remarkably every single one of the fifteen first-class matches on that tour ended in stalemate.

Despite the violent context of past and future wars, whenever the two teams have met, Indian and Pakistani spectators have often greeted each other warmly, in contrast to the hostility between national politicians, whose sabre-rattling has often provided a sombre background. While the players have been paralysed by this bloody history, the humanity of spectators has frequently demonstrated the belief that cricket can somehow find a way to reconciliation.

In recent times, alas, much has changed. As the respected historian of Indian cricket Prashant Kidambi has told us, this is 'no longer the case with the Indian cricket board and the fans themselves: a series of recent incidents (on and off the field) testify to how cricket has become a stage on which anti-Pakistan feelings are constantly projected.'

Chapter 25

THE BATTLE AGAINST APARTHEID

In 1948, D. F. Malan's National Party, which had sympathised with the Nazis during the Second World War, swept to power in South Africa, bringing with it a 'scientific' methodology that gave a spurious authority to an apartheid system based on racially structured segregation. England, Australia and New Zealand made no complaints. White Commonwealth teams loved their tours of South Africa, with visits to vineyards, game parks and parties. Players were instructed that 'colour, as a topic of conversation, was strictly out'.[1]

Few made a fuss. The cricket commentator John Arlott was appalled by what he saw during George Mann's 1948–49 tour of South Africa. Asked at immigration to state what race he belonged to, he replied 'human'.[2] He refused to join future tours. David Sheppard, the post-war batting prodigy who quit cricket to join the Church, boycotted South Africa for the same reason.[3]

During the twenty years after the war, England played fifty-five Tests against Australia and thirty-eight against South Africa. These ninety-three Tests were one more than those played against the other four Test countries combined. South Africa received three England visits, Pakistan just one, below full strength, as were the three to India.[4]

There was cricketing logic behind this concentration. South Africa were not an especially attractive team but they were competitive. Their batting was mainly defensive and attritional. In the 1950s they had two mean fast bowlers, Neil Adcock and Peter Heine, and a world-class off-spinner, Hugh Tayfield. Their fielding was always good and Colin Bland, on the 1965 tour, was the first player since the Australian Aboriginals in 1868 to attract crowds to displays of throwing skills.

English tours of South Africa were profitable, even though segregated crowds reduced their potential receipts and there was no television income because the white supremacist government was afraid of television's subversive potential.

South Africa's withdrawal from the Commonwealth in 1961, fuelled by international pressure against white minority rule, could and should have marked the turning point. Departure from the Commonwealth meant that South Africa automatically forfeited membership of the ICC. In principle this meant that South Africa had no right to play Test cricket.

In July that year, however, South Africa sought a change in the ICC constitution to retain full membership.[5] England, Australia (who both retained a double vote) and New Zealand supported South Africa. India, Pakistan and the West Indies opposed. The result was deadlock.

The ICC decreed that Test matches against South Africa had no standing. In theory South Africa was out of world cricket. The white cricket-playing countries simply ignored the ICC. When Australia challenged South Africa in 1963–64, it made it clear that the series was official. The MCC continued to award caps to players for South African matches. To this day these matches remain part of the official cricket record in defiance of the ICC ruling.

In the winter of 1966–67, South Africa claimed a first series victory over Australia. The brothers Graeme and Peter Pollock, all-rounders Mike Procter and Eddie Barlow, wicketkeeper-batter Denis Lindsay and others formed by far the best side South Africa had ever produced. In the winter of 1970–71, a brilliant white South African team demolished a visiting Australia team 4–0, the country's last official Test series for twenty-two years.

The D'Oliveira affair

We have already seen how a multiracial cricket culture had developed in South Africa by the 1880s. We have also charted the exclusion of people of colour from official cricket over the following decade. They were cut out of schools and had no access to pitches, unless as groundsmen or gardeners. Their exploits were never reported in the white press. Indeed, the racist ideology that dominated South Africa well before formal apartheid began in 1948 required the belief that black people were incapable of playing the game.

Africans could have turned to other sports. Yet they didn't. There is a poignant paradox here. Black South Africans subscribed to the doctrines about cricket propagated by the MCC. The records show they walked before being given out, treated their opponents with respect, and adhered to the spirit and the letter of the laws of the game. Their umpires were stern and impartial. The players linked cricket to Lord's, headquarters of the MCC, and believed that Lord's embodied the values they yearned for but did not possess. Yet the MCC was complicit in the barbarous system that blighted their lives.

The D'Oliveira cricketing dynasty is a fine illustration of these painful contradictions. Its patriarch Lewis D'Oliveira, a tailor, was born around the time of the Anglo-Boer War and was for many years captain of St Augustine, a Cape Town club founded by a British pastor at the end of the nineteenth century. Go into the club house today and you'll see a photograph of Lewis: tall with distinguished, finely chiselled features; a martinet who insisted on the highest standards. The ball, he instructed, must always be hit along the ground, as Don Bradman did, never up in their air. The games themselves were played in squalid conditions. There were no club houses or changing rooms. But standards had to be maintained. Players who turned up with soiled whites or dirty boots were sent home. At club functions, they were expected to wear blazers and ties.

Like Krom Hendricks, Lewis's son Basil was born in Bo-Kaap on the edge of Cape Town. He grew up when apartheid was at its most brutal and systematic. During the week he worked for a printing firm and at weekends played cricket. Sometimes these games would be broken up by police. To the day he died he carried the dent on his skull where he was struck by a police baton before being carted off to jail.

Basil D'Oliveira was his father's son. He didn't drink or smoke, and always walked when he was out (though he disobeyed his father's rule against hitting sixes). In 1956, aged twenty-five, he was appointed captain of the first South African team to be chosen on non-racial lines. This team, which entertained Kenya at home in Cape Town and then made a return tour to East Africa, included players from all the non-white racial unions – Malay, Indian, African and 'coloured'. D'Oliveira could reasonably have claimed he was the first ever captain of the national South African team.

At this point a glorious opportunity opened up. Frank Worrell's West Indies agreed to tour. The rules of apartheid would not allow the official South African team to play the West Indies, but did allow non-white teams from a foreign country to play non-white opposition within South Africa.

The West Indies agreed to tour for £5,000 plus expenses. The fee was meagre but everything we know about Worrell suggests that he took on the challenge in order to put black cricket on the map. It was called off with just weeks to go following protests from the emerging anti-apartheid movement. Organisers sent Worrell a letter saying the tour would be 'a conspiracy between colour bar sportsmen and the South African government to persuade – by fair means or foul – non-colour bar sportsmen to accept apartheid and an inferior status in the sporting world'.[6]

Whatever the rights or wrongs of this argument (and at the time anti-racist campaigners such as C. L. R. James argued in favour), cancellation was the cruellest possible blow to South Africa's non-white cricketers, whose chance to play against the best players in the world had been taken away not by the South African government but by their own people. D'Oliveira was crushed – but his shattering disappointment set him off on an alternative course of action that would help to force white South Africa out of international cricket for good.

In August 1959, D'Oliveira wrote a letter to John Arlott pleading for a job in English cricket. Late in life, we asked D'Oliveira why he chose Arlott. He replied that he had heard him talking cricket on BBC World Service radio 10,000 miles away, and 'I liked his voice'. This intuition about Arlott's wisdom and humanity was acute: he was one of the few members of the English cricket universe with the capacity to understand why the letter – scribbled by a barely literate D'Oliveira on green ink from his home in Bo-Kaap – mattered.

Arlott, a former policeman and failed Liberal party candidate, knew the political consequences that might follow if he found a position for the Cape Coloured* cricketer. With the help of John Kay, cricket correspondent for the *Manchester Evening News,* Arlott found D'Oliveira a post as a professional at the Lancashire League club Middleton. In late March 1960, a few days after sixty-nine anti-apartheid protestors were killed in the Sharpeville massacre, D'Oliveira was on a plane to London.

He struggled at first on Middleton's damp turf wickets, quite unlike what he was used to in Cape Town, but painstakingly ascended the ladder into first-class cricket. In early 1966, he was brought into the England Test team against the West Indies, then the best team in the world. From that moment on he was a dagger pointing at the heart of apartheid. The MCC was scheduled to tour South Africa over the winter of 1968–69. If D'Oliveira, the cricketing legend from

---

* This term is offensive today because it is a reminder of the insidious racial classifications of the apartheid era. D'Oliveira, who referred to himself as Cape Coloured, tackled this problem in his book, *The D'Oliveira Affair.* 'I am not certain of the sociology of our past and when I am asked "What is a Cape Coloured?" I can only repeat what we grew up to understand it to be. A Cape Coloured is somebody who is not Indian, not African, but a combination of either Indian and white or African and white. Out of this mixing a new race was born. In South Africa, if you are mixed you are coloured and that's the end of it.'

the Bo-Kaap, was selected, it would blow apart the doctrine of the white man's superiority.

John Vorster, a cynical but astute politician who became prime minister following the assassination of Hendrik Verwoerd in 1966, was wide awake to this problem. He tried to bribe D'Oliveira with the offer of a lucrative coaching contract, mediated via the South African tobacco giant Rembrandt, in return for making himself unavailable. After D'Oliveira refused, he turned his attention to the MCC: the more fruitful approach. As we have seen, the English cricket establishment had long been implicated in and a collaborator with South African racism.

Research from Professor Bruce Murray has established that Vorster personally masterminded the plot to ensure that D'Oliveira never made the plane to South Africa. Those drawn into Vorster's web included the former British prime minister Sir Alec Douglas-Home, MCC treasurer Gubby Allen, MCC secretary Billy Griffith and Sir John Nicholls, British ambassador to South Africa, whose diplomatic telegrams back to London unctuously preening himself on access to Vorster can be studied in the National Archive in Kew.

The evidence, hidden during the apartheid years, shows that the MCC allowed Vorster to be an invisible but decisive presence when the MCC selectors chose the touring party to South Africa. Arlott wrote in the *Guardian*: 'No one of open mind will believe that he was left out for valid cricket reasons.'[7] Uproar followed. Promising Middlesex player Mike Brearley sacrificially damaged his chances of playing for England by helping to lead the protest. The former England cricket captain David Sheppard interrupted his stellar career in the church to join him. The MCC panicked, then reversed its decision. Vorster cancelled the tour. Undeterred, the MCC invited South Africa to tour England in the summer of 1970, a plan abandoned following a campaign led by student activist (and future Labour Cabinet minister) Peter Hain. After that, apartheid South Africa was out of world cricket and, soon enough, world sport.

The careers of two magnificent sportsmen bookend the story of

South African racism. The non-selection of Hendricks in 1894 consolidated racial segregation, while D'Oliveira helped to set in motion the process that unravelled it.

The white bubble

For over seven decades apartheid cricket required an extraordinary degree of collusion from its domestic players, supporters, reporters and administrators. In effect, they had to live in a 'white bubble' in which they simply did not acknowledge the existence of cricketers of other races. White children might play cricket informally with those of other racial backgrounds – but never formally once they went away to school.[8] There were acts of individual support by adult whites to non-white cricketers, but no move to advance them into first-class domestic cricket, even those who might have strengthened the Test side during a long period of mediocrity. Long before formal apartheid, many potentially great South African players were victims of this system – none more so than Frank Roro, often compared to Bradman or George Headley, and the first South African to complete a hundred recorded centuries.[9]

This process of denial also required complicity from all of South Africa's white visitors, who were encouraged to see all local people of other races as servants in the lavish hospitality of white hosts or as local entertainment. For example, Percy Chapman's visitors in 1930–31 knew about Roro and some fine black contemporaries, but made no effort to seek them out. They concentrated on their social duties as guests.[10]

All through the 1950s, the English cricket establishment knew that South African cricket – and South African sport generally – was racially segregated. Long before D'Oliveira, Denis Foreman had been classified as Cape Coloured and migrated to England to pursue a footballing and cricketing career at Brighton & Hove Albion and Sussex.[11] In football, he was followed by Albert Johanneson, the first black footballer to play in an FA Cup final.[12] Athletics supplied the case of Precious McKenzie, who moved to England and then New Zealand to achieve recognition as an international lifter.[13]

The British Table Tennis Association had the honour of being the first British sport to boycott South Africa. In 1958 a group of prominent sportspeople signed a letter to *The Times* calling for South Africa's exclusion from the Commonwealth Games in Cardiff that year. They included four cricketers. Three were noted 'anti-establishment' figures – David Sheppard, Maurice Tremlett of Somerset and Alan Wharton of Lancashire[14],* – but the fourth was the unobtrusive M. J. K. Smith of Warwickshire. Ironically, he would captain the last MCC side to tour South Africa before the D'Oliveira affair and entertain the architect of apartheid, Hendrik Verwoerd, in the England dressing room.[15],†

Before the MCC team under Peter May left for South Africa, they received a briefing from the MCC president: on no account raise racial questions in front of their hosts. The president was Walter Monckton, who had briefed Len Hutton's team ahead of the troubled West Indies tour several years earlier. As chair of the Monckton Commission, he would later pave the way to independence for Zambia and Malawi. The MCC tour manager, Freddie Brown, collected copies of an unsolicited gift to the tour party – Trevor Huddleston's anti-apartheid book *Naught For Your Comfort* – and threw them into the Bay of Biscay.[16] Two players on that tour, Jim Laker and Alan Oakman, were involved in an incident when Oakman, driving a car with Laker as a passenger, seriously injured a black cyclist.

---

* Wharton is an interesting emblematic figure of English cricket in the 1950s. An all-rounder and one of the best outfielders in England, he was unlucky to receive only one Test match cap. He was also a teacher and a long-serving magistrate, and the informal 'shop steward' for the Lancashire players. He was not sufficiently deferential to the reactionary Lancashire committee of the time and they were glad to see him depart to Leicestershire with good playing seasons still in him.

† Another ironic signatory of the 1958 letter was the England football captain Johnny Haynes, who would play out his distinguished career with (white) Durban FC under apartheid.

The white policeman at the scene described the victim as a notorious, habitual drunk and delayed the England players only to allow onlookers to seek their autographs.[17]

In 1961 white supremacism found its ultimate expression when the South African wicketkeeper-batter John Waite published his autobiography. He wrote: 'One excellent reason we are not ready [for mixed-race sport] is that there are no African, Indian or Cape Coloured rugby footballers, cricketers or athletes whose ability or exploits would justify their selection ahead of White candidates for South Africa.'[18] Waite would have been aware not only of D'Oliveira, but also of the Abed brothers. Dik Abed would have a great Lancashire League career with Haslingden, and then play and coach in the Netherlands. His brother Lolo was a better wicketkeeper than Waite himself.[19] Other talents ignored by Waite were Cecil Abrahams[20] and Taliep Salie.[21]

Waite's book passed unchallenged by the English cricket establishment and its media. It was politely reviewed in *Wisden* 1962 by, of all people, John Arlott, who forced himself to say: 'It puts the South African view [meaning the official white South African view] with maximum force, dealing with the problem of "Why White Cricketers Do Not Play Non-White Cricketers In South Africa".'[22]

The MCC's treatment of D'Oliveira remains a scandal. But there is an even greater scandal: at no time during the long era of racial segregation in South African cricket did it take any interest in the fate of its excluded cricket population.

Part Five

THE SECOND GOLDEN AGE

Cricket was my first love. I would genuinely have swapped the dream of a winning goal at Wembley for a century against the Australians at Lord's.
BRIAN CLOUGH

Cricket is the easiest sport in the world to take over. Nobody bothered to pay the players what they were worth.
KERRY PACKER

When the Asian bid won, it was a defining moment for the balance of power of world cricket. It was clear that things would never be the same.
EHSAN MANI

Chapter 26

CRICKET REINVENTS ITSELF

From the 1960s, television became a constant thread in the fabric of cricket. It generated new shorter forms of the sport, domestically and internationally, which progressively challenged the primacy of the longer first-class game and the techniques associated with it. Television brought new income to cricket directly and from commercial sponsorship, especially a long relationship with the tobacco industry strong enough to defy public health policy for several decades. New styles of commentary and analysis, and dramatic technical innovations, made this form of spectatorship not only easier but often more satisfying than a journey to watch a match live in a faraway and often ill-maintained stadium. Television played a prodigious role not just in bringing cricket to hundreds of millions of people who had never seen it. It also weakened the links between cricket and locality, and the control by local people of the cricket on offer to them. Over time it turned cricket lovers into another niche set of consumers of cricket 'content'.

A technological transformation

Operating in increasingly competitive markets, both commercial and state broadcasters virtually demanded forms of cricket with fewer 'dot balls' (deliveries from which no runs were scored), greater ease of capturing highlights and drama, a guaranteed result, and less loss of play to weather. The big loser was first-class domestic cricket, although this still served as the gateway to international selection. But over time, international Tests and one-day matches also came under threat – because they were less attractive to broadcasters and sponsors unless they involved one or more of those who became known as the Big Three (India, England and Australia).

Television generated changes not only in cricket's format and playing conditions but also in playing techniques and on-field tactics, making the game quicker and more exciting. As broadcasters competed to show cricket, they had to manufacture drama from the coverage itself. This involved turning commentators and cricketers into personalities, while real or synthetic personality clashes had to be heightened. Radio, especially, had to turn the commentary box itself into a form of daytime soap opera.

Even before television, commercial interests had discovered the power of cricket and individual cricketers to promote their products and services. This brought unprecedented outside wealth into cricket but turned administrators into pitiful clients of broadcast organisations and their owners, advertisers and sponsors. The revenues occasionally drew administrators into abandoning other objectives, especially preserving the aesthetic and moral qualities of the game.

Although television initially opened cricket to larger audiences, administrators would then shut them out again by exclusive private deals with broadcasters, which ended cricket's presence on free-to-air television. They salved their consciences by congratulating themselves on the new investment this allowed them to make in the 'grass roots', even when most of the money from these deals was used to prop up existing structures, or, in some countries, as a new source of patronage.

Cricket had to compete for this new wealth against other sports with more global adherents and better professional administration, especially football: the already established gap between revenues and professional earnings in both sports widened to a chasm. Television and associated commercial revenues did 'trickle down' to professional cricketers, but the top stars and leading personalities collected far more than the workaday ones. Television did at last bring worthwhile earnings to female cricketers in the twenty-first century.

Television coverage encouraged the growth of illegal betting markets, especially on individual events within passages of play. Punters could watch them unfold in real time and the impulse to bet encouraged a volatile spread-betting market (see chapter 29), ripe for 'spot-fixing' and other forms of corruption.

The arrival of new communications technology intensified all the trends described above. Most recently the advent of social media has created new forms of participation in cricket and markets for it. Led by India, entrepreneurs devised entirely new forms of cricket and forms of ownership, which bypassed official structures. These turned more and more star players into itinerant mercenaries, although the Indian Premier League owners still encouraged local associations for commercial reasons: they wanted local live spectators to provide exciting cut-away shots for television. At the same time, these technologies have re-energised cricket's historic roots, offering local clubs and teams the opportunity to televise themselves.

Cricket gets faster and shorter

Put simply, cricket since the 1960s has become the victim of a continuous search for ways to speed up the game. After decades of resistance to short-form cricket, the English authorities[*] introduced three different competitive forms of it in rapid succession. All three were attractive to television and sponsors: one of them was designed to be played on Sunday afternoons, defying long resistance by sabbatarian lobbies.

In 1962 counties played a maximum of thirty-two championship matches. By 1969 the figure had shrunk to twenty-four.[1] By 2023 the

---

[*] As we shall see, the structure and names of English administrative bodies went through significant change in this period: at the beginning, this term covers the MCC and the Advisory Committee on County Cricket, and from the late 1960s the Test and County Cricket Board.

number had shrivelled to fourteen, mostly at the beginning and end of the season, when weather and pitches were least certain and spectatorship most reduced, none in the peak holiday month of August.

In England, the first new competition was the Gillette Cup, launched in 1963. Gillette picked up its sponsorship for a bargain £6,500: it was not even formally sponsorship but a guarantee for counties against loss if their one-day matches had to go into a second or even third day. Reflecting the fast over rates still expected at the time, the initial contest was for 65 overs an innings, a potential 130 overs in a single day (compared to the present 100). The first final was contested between Sussex and Worcestershire: Sussex gained their first major trophy, defending a total of 168 all out. The Sussex captain, Ted Dexter, was an exceptionally attractive batter who filled grounds. But as a captain he employed defensive run-strangling fields, to the disgust of his opponents who had maintained conventional ones.[2] The first year's scoring rates remained sedate by later standards: there were only two innings above 300 and only two others with a scoring rate above four an over. One-day fielding restrictions would not be introduced until the 1980s in Australia.

The next two one-day competitions deepened cricket's relationship with tobacco. The John Player League, which began in 1969, was a Sunday 40-overs-an-innings competition for counties. Despite six years' experience of the Gillette Cup, some players still found it difficult to adjust to the new short format. In one early John Player match, Somerset's accurate off-spinner Brian Langford established an unbeatable record by bowling eight consecutive scoreless overs at Essex batters indoctrinated by the first-class habit of 'seeing off' the most dangerous bowler.[3]

The third one-day entrant in 1972 was the Benson & Hedges competition. It began with regional leagues (to encourage local derbies) and concluded with a three-stage knockout. Opportunities were given to teams outside the County Championship. It never quite gained the following of the other two one-day competitions, but was nonetheless the longest-lasting sponsorship deal in English cricket history, expiring only after government legislation against tobacco advertising in 2002.

Cricket and tobacco[4]

From Victorian times onwards, competing tobacco firms made use of celebrity endorsements from cricketers and other sporting personalities. The 1880s saw a bizarre promotion: two matches of mixed representative teams from England and Australia playing as Smokers v Non-smokers. This was discontinued by the tobacco industry, possibly because the non-smokers won both matches by large margins.

From the 1920s to the 1950s many other famous cricketers followed W. G. Grace, whose image had inevitably been used to promote John Player's Navy Cut, in endorsing brands of cigarettes. Jack Hobbs extolled Sarony, claiming that there was 'nothing throaty' about it, and Army Club announced that it was the only choice of Australian cricketers: men whose 'prowess depends on eye, nerve and wind'. In the immediate post-war era, Denis Compton, Len Hutton and Godfrey Evans helped John Player to sell Medium Navy Cut cigarettes, although Hutton also endorsed a rival brand, Craven A.

As cricket attendances dropped dramatically in the 1950s, the tobacco industry stopped using the game and its players to sell its products. Public opinion was also turning against tobacco. The British Doctors Study, commonly known as the Doll Report after its principal author, Richard Doll, gave in 1954 the first authoritative evidence of the association of smoking and lung cancer, and two years later that of smoking and chronic obstructive pulmonary disease.[5] The tobacco industry resisted the study and continued to blame Britain's mephitic air quality.

Even more influential was the bestselling 1962 report by the Royal College of Physicians on 'Smoking and Health', which sparked a demand to end tobacco advertising on television. The industry tried to forestall this with a voluntary code removing any heroic or manly associations with cigarettes. One facet of this applied to cricketers: top stars could not be shown smoking but bucolic villagers were allowed.

Despite this effort, the Television Act 1964 gave the postmaster general the power to ban tobacco advertising. The tobacco industry went in search of alternative forms of promotion. First into the field were Rothmans, which sponsored the teams organised as the International Cavaliers by the veterans Compton and Evans. From 1965 to 1968, they played a series of non-competitive limited-over matches against English counties and other ad hoc celebrity elevens on Sundays, which were then still a rest day in Test and county cricket.[6]

The boredom of an English Sunday afternoon before the liberalisation of the 1980s is incomprehensible to modern generations. It was therefore no surprise the matches were instantly popular with live spectators and TV viewers. Although prohibited from advertising directly on either BBC network, Rothmans gained a great deal of exposure by simple association.

However, the company got no benefit from being a pioneer. The Test and County Cricket Board saw the success of its Sunday cricket competition and decided to copy it, pushing out Rothmans in favour of John Player. Like Gillette, it got a bargain. John Player between 1976 and 1978 gave the TCCB one-quarter of what it gave to Team Lotus for its sponsorship of Formula One racing cars and drew almost the same benefits from regular television coverage. The company used its corporate name in its sponsorship of cricket, not the name of any brand, which enabled it to circumvent the BBC ban on cigarette advertising on television. More importantly, it allowed the company to present itself as the saviour of English cricket, and suggest that similar national institutions would founder without its support.

The TCCB gave the company virtually complete freedom to exploit cricket. It even allowed it to offer samples to teenage spectators at grounds. It helped the tobacco industry generally to fight off government regulation. Donald Carr, TCCB secretary, cited its support for youth cricket. And when the TCCB decided to expand one-day cricket in England, it did not hesitate to enlist another tobacco sponsor – Benson & Hedges.

One tobacco promotion failed. The Lambert & Butler Cup in 1981 was a one-off oddity, sponsored by Imperial Tobacco as part of the relaunch of a once-popular brand. It staged 10-over contests between county sides of just seven players each at floodlit soccer pitches. Lancashire won the only final, at Chelsea's Stamford Bridge – but with only 2,564 spectators. The organisers and the TCCB had forgotten that soccer pitches are small and rectangular, and their grass is much thicker. Batters had almost no option but to hit sixes, and the crowd got bored with them and even more with the time taken to retrieve them. The Lambert & Butler Cup was a forgotten warning to the creators and promoters of the Hundred.[7]

In 1997, Tony Blair's Labour government came to power with a landslide majority – and a campaign promise to ban tobacco sponsorship of sport and live events. The Benson & Hedges Cup had its last year in 2002, which finally saw passage of the Tobacco Advertising and Promotion Act. This ended the marriage of nearly sixty years between English cricket and tobacco – in which the former had always been the submissive partner.

Tobacco promotion continued in India and Pakistan, where Imperial Tobacco – through its Wills brands – was a major contributor to cricket. In February 2001 when the Indian government threatened a ban, the BCCI protested and cited the essential financial support by Imperial for Indian cricket. The Pakistan Tobacco Company, another subsidiary of Imperial, began a long relationship with Pakistan cricket in 1978.* Through Wills, it financed an expansion of one-day cricket as well as first-class and age-group cricket, major improvements in grounds and facilities, and promoted links between Pakistan and

---

* Two vivid and opposing accounts of this relationship are given by Arif Abbasi in *Not a Gentleman's Game* and by Taher Memon and Salim Parvez in *Another Perspective*.

Indian cricket centres. India passed legislation against tobacco promotion through sport in 2003 but it was readily circumvented.

In 2023, former Indian Test opener Gautam Gambhir berated a group of famous ex-players including Sunil Gavaskar and Kapil Dev for promoting tobacco. This is a rare example of a cricketer campaigning against tobacco, although Gambhir's action appears to have been a response to an ongoing cricketing dispute rather than an act of principled hostility.[8] In the same year, the BCCI announced that tobacco would not be allowed to sponsor Indian cricket – a prohibition that would have been otiose if the law had been working properly. It was promptly relaxed for the 2023 World Cup.

In 2021, the International Cricket Council banned cricketers from advertising gambling on their shirts at ICC events, but there has never been any matching ban on tobacco. The ICC appears to have abandoned this responsibility to member countries.

International one-day cricket catches on

One-day internationals (ODIs) began accidentally when a one-day fixture was inserted into the Ashes series of 1970–71 in compensation for a washed-out Test match at Melbourne. It would be the first of many. Within less than thirty years, the total number of ODIs overtook the total number of Tests, which began in 1877.*

Short-form cricket allowed for the first men's global cricket contest, in the World Cup of 1975, involving eight countries and sponsored by the insurance company Prudential for a then staggering £100,000.

The prime aim of ODIs was to produce faster scoring, long thought essential to bring back spectators. It took a while but scoring rates would eventually rise in all forms of cricket. Previously unorthodox strokes (the sweep, the 'inside-out' forcing stroke) became canonical;

---

* From 1971 to October 2023, 1,846 Test matches were played. The same period saw nearly 5,000 one-day internationals. In 2005 the first T20 international was played – intended as a one-off. By October 2023 more than 2,000 T20s had been played.

new ones (the reverse sweep) were perfected. Short-form cricket led to a major improvement in outfielding and throwing, but gave fewer opportunities for close catchers and specialist wicketkeepers, replaced over time by less competent ones who could contribute with the bat. Short-form cricket would later create specialist careers for fast-scoring batters or containing bowlers, and so-called 'bits and pieces' players – capable, but not supreme in all aspects of the game. Above all, the tension of 'battling for the draw' by determined defensive batting against hostile bowlers and thickets of close fielders would disappear.

Several operational changes emerged in the following years. One stemmed from the 1987 World Cup, held in India and Pakistan, where fading light reduced playing hours for matches. Their length was therefore cut from 60 to 50 overs an innings. This became the standard length for all one-day internationals and the highest level of domestic one-day matches. Third-country international umpires were used in the potentially explosive Pakistan–India series of 1989. The 1992 World Cup in Australia staged night matches with white balls against black screens. It also entrenched the 'powerplay' (limits on boundary fielders in the first 15 overs of the game).

Overseas stars and English professionals

For the 1968 season England relaxed residential qualification rules to allow counties to sign an overseas star instantly and a second one after the first had completed three years' service. England was not the first to do so: Australia amended its Sheffield Shield rules to allow West Indians Garry Sobers, Rohan Kanhai and Wes Hall to play in the Sheffield Shield. But England was a bigger market than Australia and the impact of its relaxations was far greater. Indeed, it was one of the biggest factors in the creation of modern global cricket.

Overseas stars had already contributed substantially to English county cricket, especially the influx of post-war Australians such as George Tribe of Northamptonshire, and the voluble, rumbustious Bill Alley of Somerset, who had abandoned Test ambitions. The reform ensured that overseas stars could negotiate their own terms, not shackled by county wage structures, and make good money in a long English summer when most of them would not normally be engaged. After intense competition, Nottinghamshire secured Sobers for a reputed £5,000, about double the earnings of an English Test star. (In the same year the Manchester United star George Best signed a contract for £1,000 *a week.*)[9]

The overseas imports raised the playing standards of all the counties they signed for – and the tempo of cricket in all the formats they played in. They were especially important in attracting spectators to the new one-day competitions, in which Lancashire's two imports, West Indian batter Clive Lloyd and Farokh Engineer, India's ebullient wicketkeeper-batter, made a major contribution to their success.

For their part, the imports gained experience of varying English conditions that had been previously alien to them. Every competitor Test nation to England benefited, and England lost what had previously been a strong home advantage. From 1926 (the year of expansion of Test status) to 1970, England won 41 per cent of their home Test matches. From 1970 to 2000 their success rate was 26 per cent.[10] Every member of the West Indies side that won the first men's World Cup in 1975 had played county cricket. South Africa, before and after cricket exile, supplied Eddie Barlow, Barry Richards and Mike Procter. Contentiously, some South African players qualified for England instead during the country's exile, notably Robin Smith and Allan Lamb.

County cricket created a community of the world's best cricketers. They met regularly as teammates and opponents, instead of haphazardly in national or private tours. The best white South African exports could play cricket at a high level in a multiracial environment, and the experience turned most of them against apartheid. Many found that they were being underpaid at home. The biggest impact of this discovery came in Pakistan, where the players revolted against their administration in the 1970s, but it would also contribute to the success of Kerry Packer's recruitment and, later, to the rebel South African tours.

The overseas stars were generally popular with their counties but some critics fretted about their displacement of English players, especially younger ones still in development. Alec Bedser, the long-serving chairman of selectors, grumbled in 1980 that overseas players occupied half of the top places in both the batting and the bowling averages.[11]

Conditions, meanwhile, improved slowly for English professionals. Perhaps inspired by the terms given to overseas stars they began to assert themselves, although reluctantly, as John Arlott learned during his term as president of the fledgeling Professional Cricketers' Association. He later recorded: 'Cricketers were the only body of wage-earners with no freedom of choice of employment, no representation, no arbitration, no protection of independently framed conditions of employment. Most administrators believed that this state of affairs should continue, while many players were alarmed by the possible consequences of trying to redress it.'[12]

The association was founded by the Somerset and England fast bowler Fred Rumsey, an enterprising and undeferential character. Rumsey received essential support from Jack Bannister of Warwickshire, who served at different times as treasurer, chairman and secretary. By 1970 the PCA had secured virtually 100 per cent of potential members – but it still had to be funded by the TCCB, the employers' organisation. In the next decade it secured its members a group retirement scheme, a minimum wage and representation on the TCCB's registration and disciplinary committees.[13]

Some players stood up for themselves. Ray Illingworth sought a new contract at his county. When Yorkshire refused this, he decamped to Leicestershire, proved his worth as captain and revived his England career in that capacity.

In the late 1960s the best paid professionals at the most successful counties, Surrey and Yorkshire, might earn between £1,000 and £1,200, broadly in line with average male earnings. Test match fees were £100, a winter tour £1,000. Without international selection, professional cricketers were already lagging behind professional footballers, who had secured the end of their maximum wage in 1961. A journeyman player in the top division in this period enjoyed about double the basic earnings of a top county professional cricketer.[14]

In 1964, Harold Wilson's Labour government took office. His canny sports minister, Denis Howell, appointed an advisory Sports Council to promote wider engagement in all British sport and pledged government funding. The MCC realised there was no hope of funding for English cricket if it was run by a private members' club. It therefore established, in 1969, a new and supposedly accountable governance structure, the Cricket Council. The TCCB became responsible for the first-class game. The MCC remained custodian of Lord's and the game's lawmaker, the National Cricket Association, was to run everything else, especially youth cricket. By far the most influential of these was the TCCB, although crucially the MCC continued to administer all three. Notable exclusions from the new governing structure were the leagues and women's cricket.

In 1965 the ICC at last ditched its association with the British Empire and changed its name to the International Cricket Conference. Equally important, it admitted associate members, including Canada, Netherlands, Fiji and Ceylon. The USA was allowed in – six decades too late. The ICC, still an MCC side-hustle managed at Lord's, preserved the 'white veto' for England and Australia, and allowed South Africa to keep observer status.

At the very end of this period, English cricket finally aligned itself with the rest of the world in a vital area of match conditions. From 1979 all Test pitches were to be fully covered against rain on match days and two years later all first-class pitches. This ended a long period of confusion, shifting regulations and outright local defiance of authority.[15] For years counties had chafed against the loss of match play and revenues from rain. But the decisive factor was the power of television. Radio commentators could fill time and entertain listeners when rain stopped play; television could not cope with long hours of sodden empty pitches. 'Sticky wickets', drying unevenly after rain, disappeared and became an increasingly baffling metaphor. The shift favoured batters, especially overseas ones, against bowlers: both groups asked for this to be assessed when examining historic averages. Traditionalists complained that the shift reduced the skill sets of both groups, and pointed to the greater incidence of draws and contrived finishes in county cricket afterwards.

The power of the establishment was not extinct, as shown by choice of England captains: Dexter, Colin Cowdrey, M. J. K. Smith, Tony Lewis and Mike Denness (professional, but a safe establishment man and a protégé of Cowdrey). Captains who had risen up the ranks such as Illingworth and Close found themselves under constant pressure from administrators, and were sacked at the earliest opportunity. The final hoorah of the amateur dream came with the recall of (ex-amateur) Mike Brearley to lead England in the 1981 Ashes series. The decision was vindicated by Brearley's empathetic man-management and tactical sense. His performance as a player was less compelling.

The Kerry Packer revolution

The most powerful factor in creating the conditions for this new Golden Age was the most controversial. In the late 1970s a parochial dispute over broadcasting rights erupted into a global cricket conflict that pitted players and administrators against each other. It turned the communications mogul Kerry Packer into an ogre to some and a saviour to others. Packer's revolution, however, had straightforward economic origins. The world's best cricketers were underpaid and their televised cricket was underpriced.

Channel 9 in the early 1970s was one of the weaker links in the communications empire that Packer inherited from his domineering father, Sir Frank. Television growth in Australia was stagnant. Sporting coverage, always valuable in winning and binding an audience, became still more valuable after two developments. One was the introduction of colour TV in 1974, in time for the coverage of the first men's cricket World Cup in 1975. Australia's narrow defeat by the West Indies in the exciting final drew hundreds of thousands of all-night viewers. The second was a requirement by Gough Whitlam's Labor government that half of all daytime transmissions had to be local in content.

Packer's initial move into sport was his first love, golf. But cricket offered much more. Played in a confined space where the action was easier to track, it required fewer cameras and offered far more individual duels and dramas. Above all, a five-day Test match meant at least 350 advertising slots within thirty hours of local content.[16]

For months the Australian Cricket Board refused to meet him to discuss his generous bid for three years of exclusive coverage of major Australian cricket matches. England's TCCB blocked him. So he was immediately interested when approached by two well-connected men. John Cornell was the partner and business manager of the comic actor Paul Hogan, later to become famous as Crocodile Dundee. Austin Robertson was a former Australian Rules football star with superb cricket contacts. When Cornell and Robertson pitched Packer their enhanced scheme of private exhibition fixtures, he gave the go-ahead for an ambitious campaign of covert recruitment.

Packer offered a minimum of A$20,000 (then worth about £13,000)* for twelve weeks' work each year for three years, far in excess of what a star could earn in any Test-playing country at a time when none had any guarantee of total earnings in a single year. Only the English had any professional structure. Australians were still, essentially, amateurs dependent on benign employers for time off to play first-class and Test matches, as were the West Indians and Pakistanis. Packer's offer was a once-in-a-lifetime opportunity, especially since it promised to leave county contracts intact. An important sweetener was travel and accommodation for wives and families – a major grievance for English, Australian and West Indian players.

---

* In 1977 the Australian dollar was close to parity with the US dollar.

Packer had no difficulty finding recruits – and recruiters. Ian Chappell, his first pick, had pressed for an A$30,000 index-linked salary for Test players (Australia like England was undergoing high inflation). In his final full year of Test cricket before retirement he had earned A$5,000. Dennis Lillee calculated that after taxation and expenses his Test match appearances were worth just A$30 a day. Rodney Marsh had a ready comparator: in his last full Test year (with a benign employer), he managed A$12,000 from all sources; his brother Graham, then the golfer ranked sixteenth in the world, earned US$120,000.[17]

This explains why Packer found little difficulty in hiring recruits, though there were notable absentees. Geoffrey Boycott turned down Packer, partly on principle and partly for fear of damage to his benefit. Graeme Pollock was a victim of the West Indian Board's policy that none of its players should play with South Africans unless they were already playing together in English county cricket. A plea for an exception to this policy for Pollock, on the basis of his publicly expressed opposition to apartheid, was reluctantly refused.[18] Jeff Thomson was lost to Packer because of his habit of signing contracts he had not read: Packer's rival, David Lord, held Thomson to the one he had already signed.

Packer's shrewdest signing was off the field. Richie Benaud gave his enterprise huge legitimacy, not only as a public face, but as expert adviser on media and public relations and handling the ACB. Benaud picked out its three most influential figures: Bob Parish the chairman, the treasurer Ray Steele and Sir Donald Bradman.[19] The recently retired Garry Sobers gave Packer even more legitimacy when he became one of his ambassadors, picking up more money for ceremonial duties than in many years of playing at the highest level.[20] Fred Trueman signed up, but Jim Laker declined. BBC TV's Irving Rosenwater became Packer's scorer. The greatest problem was in recruiting leading umpires, after Dickie Bird refused.[21]

The TCCB, with the backing of the ICC, announced a prospective ban from Test cricket from October 1977 for any player who 'has played or has made himself available to play in a match previously disapproved by the [International Cricket] Conference'.[22] Packer fired back at the TCCB and the ICC in the English courts, seeking an injunction against them for restraint of trade. Despite a bravura performance by Boycott as a witness for the TCCB, the result was complete victory for Packer. In non-legal language, Doug Insole summed up the result as 'a good stuffing'.[23] The case cost the TCCB and the ICC between them £250,000 and Mr Justice Slade's findings were so emphatic as to rule out any prospect of a successful appeal, even if they could afford it.[24]

The judgment struck down over a hundred years of the establishment governance of cricket and the ideology it imposed on the game. Such a ban, the judge said, would 'substantially restrict the area in which it will be open to professional cricketers to earn their livings. It is common ground that the rules of an association which seek substantially to restrict the area in which a person may earn his living in the capacity in which he is qualified to do so are in restraint of trade.' He rejected moral charges against the Packer players:

> A professional cricketer needs to make his living as much as any other professional man. It is straining the concept of loyalty too far for authorities . . . to expect him to enter into a self-denying ordinance not to play cricket for a private promoter during the winter months, merely because the matches promoted could detract from the future profits made by those authorities, who are not themselves willing or in position to offer him employment over the winter or to guarantee him employment for the future.

It took two years for a settlement to be reached: all-but complete surrender to Packer. His Channel 9 would get exclusive rights to cricket in Australia for ten years. Packer's subsidiary, PBL, was to have exclusive marketing rights over Australian cricket – and cricketers. Effectively, PBL acquired control over every representative

Australian cricketer and leased him back to the ACB. When he had gained everything he wanted, Packer withdrew from the field and left the administration of cricket in the hands of his former enemies in the establishment. But their absolute power over players in each country had been struck down forever.

The income of international players leapt as a response to Packer's competition for their services. In England, the Test match fee quintupled from £210 to £1,000 and overseas tour fees grew from £3,000 to £5,000. The PCA gained permanent recognition, and with its new authority it secured its members a minimum seasonal wage of £4,500, the right to winter pay, and a guaranteed retirement fund. The association also secured an easing of the registration rules to allow players more freedom to change county. Taken together, all the changes induced a rise in the counties' wage bill from £700,000 in 1978 to more than £2 million in 1988.[25]

Packer accelerated the shift from long-form to short-form cricket. To inject more run-scoring into the latter, he introduced the novel concept of inner circles, separating the infield from the outfield, in order to prevent defensive field settings. Packer's branding and coloured clothing would be preserved in all televised cricket. Because his matches unleashed a succession of ultra-fast bowlers on unreliable pitches, they also led to the general use of batting helmets.

The experience of playing well-rewarded, fiercely contested matches with the best players in world cricket contributed much to the development of great players, including Imran Khan, Michael Holding and Joel Garner. Packer's enticement of established Test stars gave opportunities for new players to experience Test cricket, most notably England's David Gower and Australia's Allan Border. One popular beneficiary was England's specialist wicketkeeper Bob Taylor, who had a long international career he might otherwise have been denied.

Packer's innovative televising of cricket made the game more exciting to viewers, but also more intimate, offering them close-ups of players and pitch-side interviews, and letting them eavesdrop on their on-field remarks. It gave new value to players with dramatic personalities and manufactured them for hitherto anonymous ones. Action replays and analysis gave viewers more claim to expertise, and generated more off-field discussion and controversy. Packer's marketing of the game presented cricket as another competitive form of mass entertainment rather than an elevated art appreciated only by an initiated elite. All these trends have become permanent.

Chapter 27

TEST CRICKET WIDENS AND DEEPENS

Kerry Packer smashed the paternalist structures that had shaped cricket since the eighteenth century. For a little while longer global cricket remained under the control of the white countries that still governed the game. But not for long.

Independently of Packer, the 1980s and 1990s saw a decisive shift in influence over world cricket away from England and Australia in favour of the Indian subcontinent, itself dominated by the power of an Indian economy opened to market forces after years of state socialism.

This shift was signalled by an Indo-Pakistani coup that snatched the right to host the 1987 World Cup, to the fury of the English establishment. The English monopoly of cricket's greatest international tournament was broken. The event went to Australia and New Zealand jointly in 1992, then to three Asian countries, India, Pakistan and Sri Lanka, in 1996.

The long-delayed arrival of Sri Lanka as a full member in 1981 (having discarded its colonial name of Ceylon in 1972) brought another Asian vote to the ICC. All the Asian cricket powers formed the Asian Cricket Conference, which organised tournaments independently of the ICC.

In the 1990s the ICC finally broke clear of formal English control, electing its first non-English chairman in the great West Indian Clyde Walcott, although initially retaining its headquarters and small administrative staff at Lord's. This development would alter the game beyond recognition. The ICC shifted from Lord's to new headquarters, first in Monaco then lastingly to Dubai, in a move that was very much more than merely symbolic.

Sri Lanka arrives at the top table

Sri Lanka's belated arrival as a Test team in 1982 meant that four major world religions – Christianity, Hinduism, Islam and Buddhism – were represented on the Test stage. It was reasonable to ask whether any nation had to wait so long – or been so ready – when they joined the club.

The nationalist movement in Ceylon achieved independence in early 1948, a few months after India. At this point Ceylon and Pakistan had been the two most likely candidates for promotion to Test states. Ceylon's tour of Pakistan over the winter of 1949–50 had the air of a run-off. Ceylon lost both unofficial Tests, and any immediate prospect of Test status, by massive margins.

In subsequent decades Ceylonese cricket was dogged by poor infrastructure and dreadful governance. Some of the best players (such as Clive Inman) went abroad. There were moments of glory, followed by years of mediocrity. In the mid 1960s, Ceylon suddenly beat a strong Pakistan A-side and then India in short order. This led to an invitation to tour England, an audition for Test status, but political infighting in Colombo meant the tour was cancelled.

In 1983, Garry Sobers became national coach. He clashed with the management and soon quit, but not before insisting on the selection of one raw teenager.[1] Arjuna Ranatunga would in due course come to embody an emerging national consciousness. Sobers himself had done the same, following in the footsteps of his mentor, Frank Worrell. W. G. Grace, Don Bradman and Abdul Kardar fall into the same category.

Arjuna joined a troubled team at a difficult time. Five of its senior members, led by the captain Bandula Warnapura, received twenty-five-year bans for joining the 1982 rebel tour of South Africa. Civil war deterred Test sides from visiting,[2] which helps explain a lamentable show in the 1987 World Cup.

Arjuna came from a tough school. When he was thirteen his father was stabbed by political opponents and the family house burned to the ground. A Buddhist, he was dismissed as a 'sarong Johnnie' at the start of his cricket career.[3] He challenged the 'Brown Sahib'* mentality that dominated Sri Lankan cricket until his arrival. This brought him into conflict with the authorities, who sacked him several times.[4]

They always brought him back. He was the only player with the authority, wisdom and pugnacious management skills to mould the Sri Lankan side, which came together under his command in the mid 1990s. This team, like Sobers' West Indies of the 1960s, reinvented world cricket, with a self-confidence that until then had been outside the scope of post-colonial Sri Lanka.

In 1992, Arjuna chose Muttiah Muralitharan, a twenty-year-old Tamil off-spinner who would become one of the greatest and most significant bowlers of all time. At the Boxing Day Test against Australia in 1995, local umpire Darrell Hair no-balled Muralitharan repeatedly for throwing.[5] Some captains of Sri Lanka might deferentially have given into calls to send him home. Arjuna refused, rallying his players behind Muralitharan, who was from that point a popular hero. It was a moment of national definition: Sri Lanka had come of age.

The following year Sri Lanka, 66 to 1 outsiders, won the World Cup.[6] Arjuna's team played their own way. Muralitharan led an irregular army of spinners (only two seamers) who strangled opposition batters while Sri Lanka's fearless pinch-hitting opener Sanath Jayasuriya ran riot against world-class bowling attacks. In the final, Aravinda de Silva tamed Shane Warne with a match-winning century. The previous year he had charmed Kent supporters as the first Sri Lankan overseas county star, establishing a lasting image of

---

* A term used, mostly derogatively, to describe South Asians who imitated a Western lifestyle.

elegance and technique, maintained by the next generation's stars, Mahela Jayawardene and Kumar Sangakkara.

Few sporting triumphs can have meant so much to a nation. Tensions had been brewing ever since the Sinhala Only Act of 1956 had made Sinhalese the only official language. From then on Tamils were increasingly excluded from mainstream society.[7] By the time of the World Cup victory, civil war had been raging for thirteen years. Muralitharan played almost his entire career against the shadow of war, which ended amid terrible bloodshed in 2009. A highly principled man, he made deep personal efforts to unify his nation and raise relief funds for victims of the civil war, and the tsunami that devastated the island in 2004.

Cricket was extinguished in the war-torn Tamil areas during this period, though it continued in Colombo. The Tamils nevertheless respected cricket. When the touring New Zealanders planned to abandon their 1992 tour following a bomb blast, they were contacted by a Tamil Tiger. He said the team 'are very safe. We are all cricket people . . . We don't attack visitors.' New Zealand stayed.[8]

Muralitharan made a relatively modest contribution to Sri Lanka's greatest result, victory in the World Cup final. He took just one Australian wicket (his rival, Warne) although he was the most economical bowler. But in 1998 he took 16 wickets in a one-off Test victory against England at the Oval – after England were sent into bat and scored 445. Sri Lanka's coach Roy Dias explained the unconventional decision to make England bat first in simple terms. He wanted to give Murali the best chance of bowling England out twice.

Bangladesh

In 1947, East Pakistan – the future Bangladesh – was isolated, poverty-stricken and deprived of resources, despite the fact that it contributed a major part of Pakistan's foreign income through exports of jute and tea. Its language, Bangla, was not recognised. Central government enforced Urdu, spoken by a tiny elite. Many Bengalis felt that they had swapped the British Empire for another one that was even more remote and overbearing.

This situation was reflected in cricket. East Pakistan had an in-and-out presence in the first-class Quaid-e-Azam Trophy, named after Jinnah and an imitation of the English County Championship. It had no representative on the Board of Control for Cricket in Pakistan, a keenly felt insult. Only one player with any form of East Pakistan credentials ever represented the country. His name was Niaz Ahmed, and he was not a Bengali but a migrant from India.

By the late 1960s parts of East Pakistan were falling outside central government control and Sheikh Mujib's Awami League was demanding almost total economic, fiscal, legislative and military separation. In the west, Zulfikar Ali Bhutto's Pakistan People's Party led a democratic movement against the Ayub Khan dictatorship. Ayub was floundering when a lifebelt was thrown to him. The cancellation of the winter tour of South Africa because of the Basil D'Oliveira affair left the MCC with the problem of how to provide employment for contracted players over the winter of 1968–69. For Ayub Khan's government, an MCC tour offered a measure of legitimacy for his politically bankrupt regime.

Ayub Khan at first promised that the MCC would not play in Dacca (now Dhaka), capital of East Pakistan, but he went back on his word when Dacca's exclusion from the tour schedule gave rise to Bengali fury. The senior England players were summoned to the presidential HQ in Rawalpindi. 'We had the meeting,' recalled Tom Graveney 'and when it was over we had got Dacca, the place everybody had assured us we would not have to visit, back on our programme.'[9]

The England team were first dispatched on a hastily arranged tour of Ayub Khan's regional strongholds in the Punjab. At Bahawalpur, where a rowdy and impatient crowd awaited, the players arrived ninety minutes late. Panicking officials ordered the England team straight out to play. Cowdrey stood his ground. 'No Englishman,' the captain imperturbably declared, 'ever started a game of cricket without first having a cup of tea.'[10]

When the MCC party reached Dacca, the city was in the hands

of rebels. According to the opening bowler, John Snow, the touring party asked to leave, only to be told 'in no uncertain terms that our coach would not reach the airport'. Snow said the week that followed was 'probably the most nerve-wracking in my life. Day and night we could hear gunfire – some of it only yards from our hotel as the students patrolled the streets armed with rifles, seeking out people they believed to be corrupt.'[11] The Test match went ahead, with Niaz Ahmed on board. He bowled 12 overs in a drawn game and never played for Pakistan again.

The MCC got out of Dacca intact and made it to Karachi in time for the third test. Rioting – prompted not by politics but by fury that local hero Hanif Mohammad had been removed from the captaincy – caused the game to be abandoned on the third day, and the England team fled to the airport with Alan Knott stranded on 96 not out. Three weeks later, in worsening health and shaken by a failed assassination attempt, Ayub Khan resigned. Two years later East Pakistan collapsed into civil war. India gave first covert then open support to the Bengalis, marching its army into East Pakistan, where the exhausted Pakistani army surrendered.

Mystery surrounds this tour. Why did the MCC, supported by the Foreign Office, send its cricketers into a war zone? In the national archive at Kew, the very substantial diplomatic traffic around the tour is not available, suggesting that – like so many post-colonial records – it was either destroyed or withheld. It may be relevant to note that the Foreign Office was at the time eager to lend as much support to Ayub Khan, a British ally at the height of the Cold War, as it could.

Cricket-wise, the new state of Bangladesh emerged in rotten shape. Pakistan's first tour in 1980, nine years after the independence war, was abandoned after fans rioted when the team moved up country to Chittagong. According to reports, rioters stormed the Pakistan dressing room and attacked the players.[12] One of those players, the future Pakistan cricket captain and later prime minister Imran Khan, would face worse treatment when after his cricket career he entered politics.

Bangladesh took a major leap forward after the appointment of Gordon Greenidge, former West Indian opening bat, as coach in 1996. Victory over Kenya in 1997 brought ICC status;[13,*] two years later, the fledgling nation announced itself to the world by defeating Scotland and then Pakistan (a result viewed by some as suspicious)[14,†] at the World Cup. But Greenidge was sacked midway through the tournament after suggesting the board's bid for full ICC status, and Test match status, was premature.[15]

Bangladesh's promotion to the top table in 2000, engineered with India's support, was contentious. In cricketing terms, Kenya had the stronger claim, having achieved more during the 1990s.[‡] Greenidge may have felt vindicated, following from afar as Bangladesh lost twenty-six of its first twenty-seven Tests. Fourteen of these were innings defeats. The sole draw, at home to Zimbabwe, would almost certainly have been another loss were it not for two days of straight rain.[§]

After a miserable World Cup campaign in 2003, Australian Dav Whatmore – who'd already done much to professionalise the Sri Lankan scene – took charge as coach. A first legitimate Test draw and a maiden win came in quick succession, and the 2007 World Cup proved a coming-out party for Bangladesh. India were dispatched during the group stage; world-number-one South Africa were seen off in

---

* Bangladesh advanced to ICC membership in two stages. In 1997 it was allowed ODI matches and in 2000 it was granted full Test match status.

† The outspoken but not always reliable former Pakistan opening bowler Sarfraz Nawaz recently claimed in conversation with BOL News, an Urdu news channel, that there was spot-fixing during the match. Pakistan, eventual finalists, were already guaranteed to top the group having won their first four games. The Qayyum report, published the following May, exposed widespread corruption in Pakistan cricket.

‡ At the 1996 World Cup, Kenya dramatically defeated the West Indies, skittling the former champions for 93. In 1998, they beat India in an ODI game. Though Kenya continued their charge in the early 2000s – beating Sri Lanka at the 2003 World Cup en route to the semi-finals – sadly their cricket has since fallen away.

§ Skittled for 107 on the opening day, Bangladesh were 125 for 3 – and still 199 behind – at the close of day three. The weather meant no play was possible on days four and five.

the Super Eights. With youngsters Tamim Iqbal, Shakib Al Hasan and Mushfiqur Rahim ensconced in the side, it got better: a World Cup quarter-final berth in 2015; Shakib's ascent to number-one-ranked all-rounder status; and maiden Test triumphs over England, Sri Lanka and Australia.*

Bangladesh have failed to build on that momentum. Structural problems remain unresolved. The board has grown rich, yet little has been done to improve the domestic scene: there have been regular complaints about the standard of umpires and pitches. Despite a population of 170 million, and the presence of the Bangladesh Premier League since 2012, the country has failed to produce a steady stream of talent. Two decades after being awarded Test status, questions have lingered about Bangladesh's ability to compete. Yet cricket has provided a welcome balm for a country where large swathes of the population are trapped in poverty. For Bangladeshis, the game is a unique form of entertainment and a source of national pride. In September 2024, their team completed a 2–0 Test series victory in Pakistan. Several stars dedicated their performances to the protestors who had just overthrown the long-serving dynastic prime minister Sheikh Hasina.

South Africa returns

The return of Test cricket to South Africa in 1992 ended a wretched twenty-five years that brought little credit to the white cricket establishment. Despite being a founder member of the ICC and historically a major tour venue for the white countries, South Africa as a nation was not missed in the first three World Cups or any part of the new international cricket scene in which power and patronage was flowing rapidly to Asian countries. The best white South African players could not achieve the highest playing standards except in county cricket in

---

* England were seen off in October 2016, Sri Lanka beaten in Colombo in March 2017, before Bangladesh claimed victory over Australia in August 2017.

England, and they could not achieve international recognition except by changing nationality.

South Africa's domestic cricket opened in small, incremental steps for non-white players. But a significant majority rejected these limited advances because apartheid and repression continued, and even intensified, off the field. Despite some factional disputes, a common front held around the slogan 'no normal sport in an abnormal society'. Following the fall of apartheid, in a textbook example of political survival, former South African captain Ali Bacher (who had played a central role in the rebel tours, of which more later) entered into alliance with the African National Congress and negotiated the return to Test cricket. The team that returned relied heavily on white players (Graeme Smith, Shaun Pollock, Jacques Kallis, Allan Donald, Gary Kirsten, Jonty Rhodes): it was too late for excluded great players to resume their Test careers or for the brilliant all-rounder Clive Rice to enjoy one at all.*

New Zealand emerges

The arrival of one-day cricket gave New Zealand more international opportunities in a format well-suited to them. They were innovators, the first team to exploit fielding restrictions when they batted and the first to see the run-choking possibilities of spin and slow-medium pace. Above all, New Zealand cricket found a champion: Richard Hadlee. New Zealand cricketers have always been a tight, intimate group in which family ties were important: two Howarths and two Crowes, Cairns father and son, and the three Hadlee brothers performed for them internationally.

---

* Zimbabwe's national team meanwhile emerged out of civil war and nation building. It too was heavily dependent on top white players, especially the Flower brothers, Andy and Grant, in batting and Heath Streak in bowling. An early victory over Pakistan was marred by corruption allegations against the Pakistan captain Saleem Malik, and the suspicion that he and teammates threw the result.

As part of a talented Nottinghamshire side led by Rice, Hadlee converted himself deliberately from an out-and-out paceman to one of the greatest of all fast-medium swing bowlers and a genuine all-rounder. He lifted New Zealand close to parity with their neighbours Australia after a century of condescension. In the Brisbane Test of 1985–86 (which they won) he took the nine Australian wickets in an innings, and unselfishly caught the tenth off another bowler.

Fittingly, Hadlee played his last Test for New Zealand in 1990 as a knight, by which time he had taken over a third of New Zealand's wickets during his career. Only Sydney Barnes for England and Muralitharan for Sri Lanka have made a bigger contribution to their country's attack. Chris Cairns, son of Lance, succeeded Hadlee as strike bowler and late-order batter; Danny Morrison was a fine bowling partner; Nathan Astle and Craig McMillan were run-scoring batters; and Stephen Fleming was even better and an authoritative captain. New Zealand were prepared to take risks on youth. A schoolboy left-arm spinner, Daniel Vettori, made his debut in the late 1990s and would complete a career more than fifteen years later as one of the best all-rounders in the world.

India breaks out of deference and defeat

Indian cricket had a strong domestic following in the 1960s and many talented players. But they were poorly rewarded and even worse administered, with recurring crises over captaincy and team selection. Placid pitches inhibited the development of Indian pace bowlers and the ability of Indian batters to face them overseas. It took over thirty years of Test cricket for India to win anywhere overseas (against a still weak New Zealand side). They did not beat many teams at home except sub-strength ones on favourable surfaces.

Their administrators and managers overseas were dominated by princes and deferential Anglophiles. Keki Tarapore, the manager of the India team that lost all three Tests in England in 1967, infuriated his players by telling his hosts that India 'had come to learn' from English cricket.[16] The result was a defensive mindset focused on avoiding defeat, especially when it came to their neighbour, Pakistan, against whom India achieved twelve successive slow draws, home and away.

However, it is pleasant to note, especially in the light of recent developments, that India fielded Test sides with representatives of five major faiths: Hinduism, Islam, Christianity, Sikhism and Zoroastrianism.[17,*]

Indian cricket saw a big upturn in the early 1970s, based on a disciplined, middle-class Indian captain, Ajit Wadekar, in place of the English-educated prince, the Nawab of Pataudi, and backed by a resolute, non-deferential, 'tracksuit' manager, Hemu Adhikari. Wadekar had a quartet of spin bowlers who could win matches anywhere: Bishan Bedi, tantalising slow left-arm; Erapalli Prasanna[†] and Srinivasaraghavan Venkataraghavan, contrasting off-spinners; and Bhagwat Chandrasekhar, who purveyed mystery wrist-spin at almost medium pace. They were backed by two superb close catchers, Eknath Solkar and Abid Ali, who were also fill-in seam bowlers and could bat anywhere in the order. After first punishing him for leaving Indian domestic cricket to join Lancashire, the Indian cricket board gave India back its ebullient wicketkeeper-batter Farokh Engineer, the most recent representative of a distinguished line of Parsis to play Test match cricket.

Sunil Gavaskar was a world-class opening bat combining courage, technique and stamina, later joined by his stylish brother-in-law, Gundappa Viswanath. This combination won away series in the West Indies and, in front of delighted supporters (and an elephant) at the Oval, secured victory in England for the first time. They then beat a sub-strength England 2–1 at home and briefly were rated, informally,

---

* Farokh Engineer was the last Parsi Test cricketer for India in 1974–75, a sad commentary on the first of India's religious communities to adopt cricket.

† It was characteristic of Indian cricket at the time that Prasanna was regularly unavailable because he could not abandon his professional career as an engineer.

world champions.* Engineer, Bedi and Venkataraghavan had careers and incomes from English county cricket, but their colleagues made little from playing in or even for India. Gavaskar was a sign of the future: an astute businessman who knew how to market himself.

In the late 1970s, as their great quartet of spinners was ageing, Indian cricket acquired a new bowling hero, their first serious pace bowler since Amar Singh and Mohammad Nissar in the 1930s. Kapil Dev came from the unfashionable (and distinctly un-Indian[†]) northern city of Chandigarh. This signalled a wider spread of Indian cricket talent. As a promising teenager he worked intensely under a great coach, Desh Prem Azad. Late swing and immense stamina were his greatest assets, to which he added explosive middle-order batting and superb outfielding.

Dev had an uneasy relationship with his formidable contemporary Gavaskar, with whom he regularly alternated the captaincy depending on which group of selectors was in power. His big century (in partnership with tailenders) in the 1983 World Cup saved India from ruin against Zimbabwe in the preliminary rounds. In the final, his athletic catch to dismiss Viv Richards helped his team defend a small total and achieve an upset victory against the West Indies. Followed intensely on radio and (often publicly) on television, Kapil Dev inspired a new generation of Indian cricketers, including Rahul Dravid, Sourav Ganguly, V. V. S. Laxman and Sachin Tendulkar.

In Tests, Dev's captaincy was admired for its boldness compared to the defensive, calculating Gavaskar. It produced only four victories out of thirty-four, but he contributed a decisive century to the second tied Test match, against Australia in Madras in 1986–87. Dev had the talent and application to remain an essential part of his team's batting and bowling for the last eight years of his career: despite a serious knee injury, he did not miss a single Test or one-day international.

---

* Arunabha Sengupta's *Elephant in the Stadium* is an acute and entertaining account of India's winning series and its domestic impact.

† It was designed in alien functional geometric grids by Le Corbusier.

He nudged just ahead, by three wickets, of Hadlee's then record total of 431 victims and had also scored more than 5,000 Test runs, an all-round performance still unequalled.[18]

The end of the state television monopoly in 1994 was a major milestone for Indian cricket, part of an economic shift from state control to a more dynamic (if less equal) free-market model. Satellite broadcasters produced exciting coverage and injected huge new revenues into the game, boosting players' incomes and followers. Sachin Tendulkar was an especial beneficiary: his early experience playing at Shivaji Park in Mumbai encouraged millions of aspirant imitators.

Pakistan: socialism, success and scandal

The 1960s saw a major expansion of domestic first-class cricket in Pakistan, partly to spread support for Ayub Khan's military regime to outlying areas. Many mismatches resulted, including the victory by the widest margin in cricket history when the mighty Railways team downed some eager youngsters from Dera Ismail Khan by an innings and 851 runs.[19] But the general pattern was bland pitches producing elongated draws, with colossal spells by defensive spin bowlers. Partly due to foreign exchange problems, Pakistan played few Test matches and did not win many of those they did.[20]

Once Ayub Khan was gone, Pakistan adopted a 'state socialist' model of cricket led by Abdul Hafeez Kardar, who as captain had played a leading role in establishing Pakistan as a force in the 1950s. Kardar encouraged state organisations, especially banks, to recruit players for their own first-class teams, in a major expansion of domestic cricket. Employers' teams have had a varied but enduring presence ever since. They brought security to Pakistan's cricketers but players were still ill-paid for their talents, as they discovered from first-class county cricket in England and international tours. This led to a players' revolt in the late 1970s, which ended Kardar's long dominance over Pakistan cricket. The revolt was led by Asif Iqbal, a brilliant talent for Pakistan and Kent, and an equally talented shop steward.

Another rebel, Mushtaq Mohammad, fourth of the great family of five cricketing brothers, and with the longest experience of county cricket at Northamptonshire, replaced the always diplomatic Intikhab Alam as captain. Mushtaq was an assertive captain who refused to defer to administrators.[21] With this new approach, Pakistan became a team that did justice to its formidable talents, including Asif Iqbal, Majid Khan, Zaheer Abbas, Javed Miandad, the mercurial but inventive opening bowler Sarfraz Nawaz, and Imran Khan, transformed from a raw teenager into a world-class all-rounder.

Mushtaq bequeathed this fine team to a young successor. Miandad was a superb batter, especially in difficult situations, and had an acute cricket brain, but at this early stage of his career was a poor man-manager and provoked another players' revolt. This propelled Imran to the captaincy, although injuries and boredom with series against lesser sides led him regularly to withdraw in favour of Miandad. The two formed a memorable partnership, based on deep mutual tolerance and understanding, in a successful era of international cricket for Pakistan.

One of Imran's great contributions was his support (and theatrical coaching) for Abdul Qadir, a magical leg-spin bowler. He revived this almost forgotten art, proved its value in one-day cricket, and would be a precursor and inspiration for Warne in the 1990s.

Meanwhile Imran mentored Pakistan's greatest pair of pace bowlers, the left-arm Wasim Akram and the right-arm Waqar Younis, and transmitted the secrets of a great Pakistani invention – reverse swing (a phenomenon in which an old ball deviates unexpectedly at pace). Now commonplace, the innovation (developed by Sarfraz Nawaz, who passed it on to Imran) inspired accusations of illegal tampering with the ball. There were other controversies over the quality of Pakistan's umpiring, with accusations taking off when Pakistan started to win matches regularly.[22]

The 1980s saw another expansion of Pakistan cricket, especially to outlying areas. This could be attributed to the allied factors of colour television (which rewarded viewers on its first day with the sight of

Imran's cousin Majid Khan scoring a Test century before lunch)[23] and a new surge of corporate sponsorship under the commercially acute leadership of a war hero, Air Marshal Nur Khan and his lieutenant Arif Abbasi.

By this point, Pakistan was again under military rule, this time by General Zia ul-Haq, who had overthrown and executed Prime Minister Bhutto. Zia aligned himself with conservative clerical forces but was politically astute enough to resist a clerical demand for a ban on televised cricket.[24]

The decade saw more frequent bilateral contests than any other between Pakistan and India, including some at one-day level in the new commercially driven cricket centres of the United Arab Emirates. One such contest produced the most-watched shot in cricket history – Miandad's six to beat India off the last ball.[25] Despite some crowd incidents and riots, these matches were generally benign and used by each side's supporters to signal their hopes for peace and family reunions. They inspired 'cricket diplomacy' by Zia – a serious attempt to settle the Kashmir issue at a Test match.[26]

Returning to Pakistan cricket after serious injury at Zia's behest, Imran inspired Pakistan's greatest moment – the 'cornered tigers' victory that had seemed impossible in the World Cup of 1992. He was helped in the final by his old comrade-in-arms Javed Miandad after the semi-final had been won by a new batting star, Inzamam-ul-Haq. It was the perfect end to a mighty career.

Chapter 28

FEATURES OF THE SECOND GOLDEN AGE

The West Indies remained the best team in the world. Viv Richards replaced Clive Lloyd as captain in 1985, maintaining the Lloyd formula of dominant batting, especially through his own aura at the crease, and relays of fast bowlers at sluggish over rates offering few opportunities to score when they were not taking wickets.

The production line of scarcely playable fast bowlers was maintained when Malcolm Marshall and Michael Holding were succeeded by Curtly Ambrose and Courtney Walsh. Two new fast bowlers, Patrick Patterson and Ian Bishop, inspired real fear in their opponents. Continued international success masked long-term weaknesses in West Indian cricket, however, including the familiar inter-island rivalries, a weak first-class structure, limited television coverage and commercial sponsorship, and better opportunities in American sports for young West Indian athletes – especially through scholarships at colleges. Most important, the top West Indian cricketers could not make a decent living without committing themselves to an exhausting year-round schedule of playing overseas.

An astute administrator, the former opening bat Allan Rae, recognised these weaknesses and produced a plan for all West Indian governments to contribute to a common fund to keep the best players on an annual retainer. It was rejected, another victim of the islands' determination to keep control of their own players.

This period saw the advance of players from smaller West Indian islands as well as the four traditional centres of Barbados, Trinidad,

Jamaica and Guyana. Richards himself was Antiguan and identified with African-Caribbean nationalism and culture. He sported a wristband in Rastafarian colours, encouraged descriptions of West Indian cricket in terms of reggae rather than calypso, and publicly praised his 'African team'.

In the 1990s the left-handed Brian Lara replaced Richards, reminding onlookers of Garry Sobers with his high backlift and striking power. In the great man's presence he broke Sobers' long-standing Test record with an unbeaten 375 against England in Antigua in 1994.

He broke it again ten years later, in the same place against the same opponents, with the only quadruple century in Test cricket. He also scored the only first-class 500, in a drawn match for his English county, Warwickshire. (Warwickshire's coach Bob Woolmer watched both Lara's 501 not out *and* the innings it surpassed, Hanif Mohammad's 499 in Karachi in 1959.)

Shivnarine Chanderpaul, who accumulated unspectacular runs in long innings, broke into the West Indian team in the 1990s. An unorthodox two-eyed stance led him to be undervalued in a twenty-year career as the anchor of an increasingly weak batting side. Neither he nor Lara (a temperamental and isolated captain) nor the long-serving Ambrose and Walsh, could overcome the team's limitations. The West Indies were dethroned by Australia in the 1994–95 series, and have not won a Test series against them since.

England subsides

The less said about England the better. The 1980s had begun on a memorable note with the Ashes victory in 1981, overseen by Mike Brearley and seized for them by Ian Botham and Bob Willis. The rebel South Africa tour of 1982 ended the careers of Alan Knott and Geoffrey Boycott, and deprived England for three years of Graham Gooch, overcoming early setbacks to emerge as a dedicated and consistent opening bat.

Willis, who was captain when England lost in Australia in 1982–83, was succeeded by David Gower, England's most graceful batter, but without the tactical acumen or motivational powers to get the most from a transitional team. His highest achievement was to regain the Ashes at home in 1985 from a similarly transitional Australia, after winning an away series against India. His five Test victories were all gained in these two series: England could not beat anyone else, home or away, in five others, which included two consecutive annihilations by the West Indies. Gower was replaced by Mike Gatting, a brave, earthy professional of a different mould, who retained the Ashes unexpectedly in Australia in 1986–87. From this point, results went into a prolonged downturn.

By the end of the 1990s, according to *Wisden* unofficial rankings, England were the lowest-ranked Test-playing country, lower even than newcomer Zimbabwe. This period was full of one-cap wonders. In the lost Ashes series of 1989, England called on twenty-nine players. The year before, the selectors went through four captains (and twenty-three players) as the team was thrashed by the West Indies. In a last flicker of choosing 'the right sort of chap' as captain, the selectors turned to Colin Cowdrey's son, Chris, who had not played Test cricket for three years. He scored five, took no wickets and his team went down to another heavy defeat.

A new body, the England and Wales Cricket Board or ECB, took responsibility for reversing the decline. It was formed as a limited company in succession to the TCCB, and also incorporated the Cricket Council, which had dealt with the non-first-class game. The first chair of the new body was Lord MacLaurin, who as CEO of Tesco had modernised and transformed a sleepy retail giant. He was expected to have the same effect on English cricket and persuaded the counties to accept a two-division Championship with promotion and relegation.

In two respects, the changeover to the ECB was disastrous. One impact was accidental: the ECB lost sight of an ambitious programme, Clean Bowl Racism, inherited from the TCCB. Its unfulfilled recommendations would resurface twenty years later, in the intense debate over racism in English cricket.

Almost as momentous was MacLaurin's fatal recommendation for English cricket to be removed from the so-called 'protected list' of sports events that had to be shown free-to-air. Instead, he proposed to rely on a gentlemen's agreement to achieve this result. The gentlemen's agreement was finally broken in 2006 – after cricket achieved its greatest viewing figures in the 2005 Ashes series. Sky Television paid a huge sum to acquire it and the television audience shrivelled permanently, especially among lower-income families.

Women's cricket yields its autonomy

In the 1980s and 1990s female cricketers came under increasing pressure to cede control of their affairs to national men's cricket associations. It was the only way in which the women's game could attract the investment and commercial income to allow it to break out of its status as a strictly amateur, leisure pursuit. New Zealand women were the first to merge in 1992.

English women's cricket came under particular pressure to take this course. The WCA could not finance England's women cricketers, especially on tour, where they had to pay their own travel costs and take unpaid leave from work. Three selections could not afford to tour India in 1978 and dropped out of England's World Cup squad. The WCA could not host any international tourists between 1979 and 1984. England did host a women's World Cup in 1993, in which their team gained a surprise victory in front of 2.5 million BBC viewers. But the tournament was a shoestring operation, bailed out by a late charitable donation, and in the England–Holland match the players had to roll the pitch themselves.

In 1998 women were finally admitted to membership of the MCC. It required three separate votes and attracted some ridiculous and offensive resistance from opponents. But it was achieved and there was great symbolism in the fall of the MCC as a male bastion. In the same year, without much resistance, the WCA gave up over seventy years guidance of women's cricket in England to become part of the new ECB. It would take another sixteen years for England's women to be paid to represent their country, but the modern era of English women's cricket had begun.

The first Golden Age had been defined by the genius of a handful of cricketers from England, Australia and South Africa. The second Golden Age was created by the genius of numerous countries: Australia, post-apartheid South Africa, the West Indies, India, Pakistan, Sri Lanka, New Zealand and even, on occasions, England. Bangladesh and Zimbabwe had their moments too. This profusion of talent was exhilarating and unprecedented. The one-day game, and the new freedoms as well as disciplines it imposed, brought a dazzling and unpredictable pace to Test cricket. This was an era in which the short and longer forms of the games co-existed and cross-fertilised, to inspiring and innovative effect.

The 1990s saw a glorious restoration of spin, led by Shane Warne of Australia and Muttiah Muralitharan of Sri Lanka. Not far behind them were India's Anil Kumble and Pakistan's Saqlain Mushtaq and Mushtaq Ahmed, Abdul Qadir's successor.

Warne has some claim to being the best bowler of all time, not just for the number of international wickets he took (1,001, one every fifty-one balls) but the number of top-quality batters whom he baffled – none more so than Gatting, victim of his very first delivery in an Ashes Test, pitching outside his legs and hitting off-stump, the so-called Ball of the Century, which would have made him a legend if he had achieved nothing else.

Warne, a shrewd amateur psychologist, occasionally claimed to have invented a new mystery ball, which he termed the zooter. In fact, he was an orthodox leg-spinner, and he did not have much of a googly. He had phenomenal accuracy and control, and could drop his leg-break anywhere at will with varying degrees of spin, mixing them up with the occasional 'slider', a straight unspun delivery that hardly bounced. Immense stamina gave him a long career, while his self-belief sustained him through a serious shoulder injury, suspension after taking an illicit weight-reducing drug, and other off-field scandals.

Muralitharan took more international Test and ODI wickets for Sri Lanka than Warne for Australia – 1,334, one every forty-seven balls. He had to as he was usually the sole attacking threat, whereas Warne was supported by seamers as good as Glenn McGrath (remorselessly accurate), Brett Lee (express pace) and the late swing of Jason Gillespie. In Warne's early days he often bowled in tandem with a thoughtful off-spinner, Tim May, and sometimes a leg-spinner, Stuart MacGill, who would have had a longer and much more significant career but for the misfortune of being at his peak during the era of Warne.

Muralitharan was a unique bowler. A combination of an exceptionally supple wrist and strong shoulder and a deformed elbow gave him an extraordinary action, which produced far more spin than a conventional off-spinner. He was able to add a genuine mystery ball, the *doosra* (Urdu for 'the other one'), which span from leg with no obvious change of action. The doosra was invented by Saqlain Mushtaq, who, unlike his imitators, was judged to have a 'clean' legal bowling action. All the others were regularly accused of throwing the doosra, that is, illegally unbending the elbow in the delivery. The accusations nearly ended Muralitharan's career, but science eventually came to his aid. Biomechanical and video analysis showed that many other bowlers of different types unbent their arm to the same degree, including McGrath, generally thought to have a model action. The ICC then relaxed the limit against unbending the elbow from five degrees to fifteen, which was also identified as the smallest angle that could be detected and called a no-ball by an on-field umpire with the naked eye. This compromise did not satisfy many purists and it was not enough to reprieve several previously potent international bowlers. Whatever its motives, the ICC's decision kept alive a major innovation. Spinners generally got more opportunities, spectators saw more variety and faster over rates, and the tyranny of fast short-pitched deliveries in the 1980s was broken.

Part Six

CRICKET'S UNDERSIDE

The London gamesters intend to go to law for the money, there being upward of £100 depending upon the game. This is the thirteenth match the London gamesters have played this year and not lost one match.
Appleton's Original Weekly Journal, 1732

I never cheated. I never appealed for a decision unless I thought the batsman was out, I never argued with the umpire, I never jeered at a defeated opponent.
C. L. R. JAMES, *Beyond a Boundary*, 1963

From early on there was a lot of 'You lot sit over there near the toilets', the word 'P***' was used constantly, no one ever stamped it out.
AZEEM RAFIQ, on the racist culture in English county cricket, 2021

Chapter 29

CORRUPTION AND SCANDAL STAIN CRICKET

By the end of the twentieth century, corruption in cricket was as rife as it had been in the eighteenth century, with its effects hugely magnified by modern technology.

Scandals struck every major cricket nation and many minor ones. They were generally described as match-fixing, but the bigger problem was the property of cricket that makes it so compulsive for statisticians – the number of measurable events and individual contests within a match or a phase of play.

To arrange an entire result required the deliberate underperformance of at least the majority of a team of eleven – and even then could be frustrated by brilliant performances by the non-compliant minority or even an outstanding player. To arrange a single unexpected event or outcome of a phase of play required only one player or, at most, a few. Known as spot-fixing, it gave those who knew about the arrangement an opportunity to bet on a certainty at long odds.

The opportunities and rewards of spot-fixing grew explosively because new technology facilitated the growth of a huge new unlicensed betting market, primarily in the Indian subcontinent and the Middle East, which was quickly taken over by organised crime. As early as 2000, the *Times of India* estimated the total value of betting on Indian cricket matches at between $6 billion and $9 billion.[1]

One specific event was a trigger: India's unexpected World Cup win in 1983 dramatically increased the following and earning power of its stars, and introduced them to new social milieus in which dark and criminal money was regarded as legitimate.

Bookmakers became more and more brazen in their approaches to players, sometimes under pretence of offering commercial or acting opportunities in the burgeoning Bollywood industry where many of them laundered money. The ready access of bookmakers* made it easy to accuse players of corruption but also harder to prove. It poisoned relationships within teams, dividing those who took bribes from those who refused and reviving ancient grudges. It blighted the reputation of great players and teams. For years fans, media and administrators alike had accepted that players sometimes made poor decisions or had spells of bad form. After the corruption scandals, all such episodes became tainted with suspicion.

Spot-fixing became especially lucrative because of the new medium of spread betting. Instead of betting on the result at a bookmaker's set odds, punters were offered a 'spread' of outcomes, as it might be forty to fifty runs in a phase of play, and invited to stake on a 'down' bet for each run short of the lower end or an 'up' bet for each run in excess of the upper range. Mobile telephones and the internet made it possible to grow this new betting market on a continental or even global scale, although its last link depended on the ancient and barely traceable 'hawala' system, where instructions given in one country were fulfilled by a trusted intermediary in another.

Spot-fixing was also facilitated by the proliferation of inconsequential cricket matches, such as one-day contests in non-traditional cricket centres. Weak or avaricious members of cricket teams could persuade themselves that they were doing no harm by a single act with no obvious impact on the result of a 'meaningless' match. Poorly paid players and those whose families were vulnerable to organised crime were especially prey to the temptations of spot-fixing.

---

* The notorious underworld leader Dawood Ibrahim achieved a family connection with Pakistan's great batter Javed Miandad when their children married each other.

Finally, the scandals were aggravated by an inconsistent response from national cricket authorities. They showed themselves too ready to ignore or conceal evidence of wrongdoing and to protect the clean image of their nation's cricket. National authorities were often unwilling to cooperate on bilateral scandals – notably Australia and Pakistan during the 1990s – and the ICC was slow to act.

The first public anxiety about corruption hastened the end of the career of the magnificent Pakistani all-rounder Asif Iqbal. Captaining an unsuccessful Pakistan tour of India in 1979–80, he was accused of allowing a bookmaker access to the team. Asif denied this (and plausibly so) and was forced to do so again nearly twenty years later. He retired, exhausted and embittered after the series.

In 1992, Sri Lanka became the first team to be accused of throwing a Test match. They had outplayed Australia for four days and were poised for a historic victory before a sudden collapse in pursuit of a modest target allowed Australia to win by 16 runs. Their captain Allan Border called it 'the greatest heist in cricket history'. An official inquiry produced no hard evidence but noted the presence of a bookmaker among the Sri Lankan players. It damaged the local reputation of two of the team's greatest players, Arjuna Ranatunga and Aravinda de Silva, but otherwise achieved no significant result. This inquiry was suppressed and would only re-emerge years later in the wake of greater scandals in India, Pakistan and South Africa.[2]

The tainted years

Saleem Malik was a brilliant batter but a bad character, not only personally corrupt but an instigator of a culture of corruption within the team. He was openly accused of this by three of his own players: Rashid Latif, Basit Ali and Aamir Sohail. The first two retired (in their twenties) in disgust in the midst of a southern African tour.[*] Several

---

[*] Latif faced personal threats for his stance and on his return to Pakistan needed the protection of armed security from the MQM-P, the political party that controlled Karachi (personal testimony to the authors).

matches conducted by Malik as captain came under special suspicion, especially Pakistan's crushing defeat by newcomers Zimbabwe, who had never won a Test before.[3]

Malik shifted the focus to Australia when an Australian newspaper accused him of attempting to bribe two spin bowlers, Shane Warne and Tim May, to bowl badly in the vital first Test of their tour of Pakistan in Karachi in 1994. Warne and May refused, and Warne took eight wickets in a (genuine) thrilling last-wicket victory by Pakistan.[4]

Independently of Malik, Warne and Mark Waugh (twin brother of the future captain, Steve) were forced to admit that they had indeed given information to a bookmaker they knew only as 'John'. He would later be identified as M. K. Gupta, a self-proclaimed leader of the new industry of match- or spot-fixing and a protagonist in a series of other major scandals. They claimed that the information was innocuous but they were both fined by the Australian Cricket Board. The board kept this quiet but the affair was revealed by journalists three years later. Inevitably, the cover-up led to speculation that worse offences were being concealed and other players protected.[5]

This was not the last of Gupta. Hansie Cronje was the second captain of post-apartheid South Africa. His austere, aloof and overtly religious personality concealed a deep appetite for money and luxury goods.[6] Mohammad Azharuddin, one of the most elegant batters in Indian history, was a Muslim from a modest middle-class background in Hyderabad. Promoted to the Indian captaincy in 1990, his unassuming lifestyle changed when he moved to Mumbai, formed connections with Bollywood and criminal racketeers, divorced his wife and married a minor Bollywood actress, Sangeeta Bijlani.[7]

In 1995, both Cronje and Azharuddin began taking money from Gupta, although they denied that they had carried out Gupta's instruction to influence cricket matches, and both would break with him and find other paymasters.[8] Test matches and one-day internationals under each captain came under increasing suspicion in the

1990s. Cronje was open about the offers he received, and shared them with selected teammates and sometimes his entire team. When rebuffed by its stronger members, he would pass them off as one of his heavy-handed jokes.

Two well-informed pieces of investigatory journalism into match-fixing were dismissed by the Indian authorities, but sensationally reinforced courtesy of an incendiary article by the former Test all-rounder Manoj Prabhakar. Initially a fixer and a bookie's runner and recruiter, he turned whistleblower after being discarded at the end of the 1996 World Cup. Prabhakar alleged that the entire Indian team was being run by match-fixers and that a senior unnamed player had offered him a vast sum to sabotage a one-day match in Sri Lanka. His claims led to two inquiries in which he declined to name names, and which generated no action from the authorities except a deduction from his benevolent fund.[9]

In Pakistan, meanwhile, a series of inquiries into fixing and corruption took place, heavily influenced by changes in cricket administration and government. The first (under the cricket administration of Arif Abbasi and the government of Benazir Bhutto) resulted in Saleem Malik's restoration – and a sharp rift with Australia.

In 1997 the rival government of Nawaz Sharif took over and appointed a cricket administration led by the former Test star Majid Khan. Majid initiated an administrative inquiry into all the known allegations of fixing and corruption. Its preliminary findings condemned both Malik and Wasim Akram, as well as a third player, Ijaz Ahmed, and led Majid to procure a full judicial inquiry under the senior judge Malik Mohammad Qayyum.

Qayyum's report was delayed by the 1999 World Cup (which produced fresh allegations not only against Pakistan but other countries). More importantly, a new military government under General Pervez Musharraf overthrew Sharif. It set up yet another inquiry under another judge into the 1999 allegations and sat on Qayyum's completed report for many months.

There were credible rumours, which General Musharraf did not discourage when we interviewed him in retirement, that his government encouraged Qayyum to soften his conclusions on senior players. In the event, his report banned only two – an over-the-hill Malik for life, and a confused young fringe member of the team, Ata-ur-Rehman (his lifetime ban was lifted in 2007). Qayyum condemned and fined star players including the batters Inzamam-ul-Haq and Saeed Anwar, and the spin bowler Mushtaq Ahmed, while Wasim Akram was banned from captaincy but not as a player.

Akram came under suspicion again in 1999 for his much-contested decision to bat first in the World Cup final at Lord's, and he and the whole team for their loss en route to unfancied Bangladesh, though no conclusions were reached.

The cricket careers of Cronje and Azharuddin both ended in 2000 when an incriminating recording of a conversation between Cronje and a criminal bookmaker called Sanjeev Chawla came to light.[10] Cronje was instantly dismissed as a captain and player, and an official public inquiry was set up under Judge King. In it, Cronje named Azharuddin as the man who had introduced him to Gupta, through whom he had become enmeshed in match-fixing and crime. This revelation triggered a thorough inquiry by India's Criminal Bureau of Investigation (CBI).[11]

Cronje emerged from the King inquiry a ruined man, banned for life from cricket. He had been forced to admit taking payments he knew to be intended for match-fixing and attempting to suborn teammates into assisting him.[12] Nonetheless, he received widespread support from fans, administrators and teammates.[13] Many saw him as a martyr to devious Indians. He was beginning to restore his life and reputation when he was killed in an air crash in 2002, an event that predictably spawned many theories that he was murdered to prevent further damaging revelations.[14]

The CBI inquiry into Azharuddin failed to sustain criminal charges against him but found him guilty of misconduct, aggravated by his role as captain. This led to a lifetime ban. Azharuddin also had wide support in most echelons of Indian cricket and in the media. After a decade of campaigning, he won an acquittal in court from match-fixing. He also secured election as an MP on the Congress ticket.[15]

One by-product of the Azharuddin inquiry was that Prabhakar was finally compelled to name the player he alleged to have tried to bribe him to underperform. It was none other than Kapil Dev, India's finest all-rounder and a national hero. Kapil was eventually cleared, but lost his job as India's national coach.[16] Even the most respected cricketers could not escape accusations of corruption. A decade later, three Sri Lankan greats provided another illustration when Mahela Jayawardene, Aravinda de Silva and Kumar Sangakkara were falsely accused by a local politician of throwing the 2011 World Cup final.[17]

England was not immune from controversy. Chris Lewis was an England all-rounder of African-Caribbean origin, talented but with a reputation for volatility. Discarded from the England side in 1998, he had not endeared himself to the authorities when he called the selectors 'full of shit'. Nonetheless, he did his duty to them in reporting an amazing offer to him of £300,000 to bribe three current England players to underperform in the forthcoming Test match against New Zealand at Old Trafford. He named the attempted bribers but not the three players concerned.

According to Lewis, the ECB did not ask for the names; according to the ECB, he refused to give them. The match went ahead with just four members of the ECB aware that it might be the subject of a conspiracy. They themselves did not report the matter to the police until weeks later, with Lewis accompanying them. He named the three England players concerned but understandably asked not to be identified. The story (without any names) then appeared in the *News of the World* and the ECB aggravated its fractured relationship with Lewis by presuming that he had leaked it, although almost certainly it came from a police source. The ECB then issued a statement saying that there were no grounds for complaint against any English player.

Lewis felt betrayed for doing the right thing and was convinced that the ECB would have done nothing about it but for the furore surrounding the Cronje story, which had just broken.[18]

The Cronje affair, and the cascade of rumour and scandal it set off inspired the ICC's intervention against fixing and corruption. Paul Condon was appointed head of a new ICC Anti-Corruption Unit. At fifty-three, he had been the youngest ever commissioner of London's Metropolitan Police, with a reputation as an astute political operator and a diligent investigator. He would need both qualities in his task, given the determination of ICC full members to keep control of their own separate inquiries, and the welter of conflicting evidence from unreliable sources, accused players, criminal bookmakers and go-betweens. Condon and his unit were to report to a new Code of Conduct Commission, under the British peer, Hugh Griffiths.[19]

In quick time, Condon produced a report in June 2001 that acutely analysed the sources and forms of corruption in cricket, besides passing or confirming judgment on individual players.

He found that 'corrupt practices and deliberate underperformance have permeated all aspects of the game'. He described unregulated betting, the root of corruption, as 'fragmented and secretive . . . where long-term record-keeping is anathema'. He made a staggering estimate of its annual volume: $500 million on matches between India and Pakistan alone, with a further $200 million on other India matches.[20]

Condon suggested that corruption might have begun in English county cricket in the 1970s, citing unsubstantiated rumours about collusive results between Surrey and Lancashire in different competitions. He pointed to players' vulnerabilities to threats of violence, and the relatively poor pay and short careers of international cricketers as elements that encouraged corruption, but judged the main factors to be greed and opportunity. He had harsh words for the ICC (his paymasters): its governance was inadequate, and its staff too limited and naïve to have met the challenge of corruption, while national boards had been too lenient to their best players.[21]

Recognising the impossibility of controlling illegal betting, Condon called for a comprehensive training and awareness programme for all international players, match officials and administrators. At his prompting, the ICC appointed regional security managers, with a police or military background, to control access to players at their teams' hotels. Most contentiously of all, the new Code of Conduct Committee banned mobile phones in team dressing rooms, except one for emergency use by the team manager.[22]

These measures did not eliminate corruption in cricket, particularly after the proliferation of largely unregulated leagues of T20 and even shorter forms of cricket in the 2010s. But they represented a permanent shift of power from national boards to the ICC.

The most notable scalp of the ICC's new security regime was the mercurial West Indian all-rounder Marlon Samuels, banned for two years in 2008 for taking money for giving team information to two prominent bookmakers. In 2023, he received the dismal distinction of a second ban, this time for six years, following a corruption offence in a T10 contest in Abu Dhabi. It was a vivid illustration of the added peril of new competitions in places of weak cricket governance, with players who were effectively itinerant mercenaries.[23]

Another notable case was the conviction of a young Essex bowler, Mervyn Westfield, for deliberate underperformance in a 40-over game, after being introduced to a bookie by his senior county colleague Danish Kaneria, the Pakistani leg-spinner who remains the country's highest Test wicket-taker as a slow bowler. Kaneria did not face criminal charges but was given a lifetime ban by the ECB after disciplinary proceedings. When we interviewed him after a cricket match in Karachi in 2015, he protested innocence, but finally admitted his guilt in 2018.[24,*]

However, the standout case was the three no-balls bowled by two Pakistan fast bowlers, Mohammad Amir and Mohammad Asif, in the

---

* Kaneria was the second Hindu and the sixth non-Muslim to play Test cricket for Pakistan. In exile from any organised cricket in Pakistan, he was still a brilliant bowler, as we discovered when playing alongside him at a private club.

Lord's Test in England in 2010, at the behest of their captain, Salman Butt. All three thought that they had been bribed by a match-fixer. In fact, they were victims of a smartly executed sting operation by the English Sunday tabloid newspaper the *News of the World*.

There was no actual betting market for no-balls to corrupt: the fake fixer paid the bribes as a test to establish whether the players and agent could be trusted. When the players and the agent were eventually tried in an English criminal court, it was hard to identify the offence of which they might be accused. In the event, this relied on their acceptance of a bribe knowing that it was intended to corrupt them.[25]

The *News of the World* sting was predicated on an exceptionally accurate scenario of how cricket matches and passages of play were corrupted, and of relationships in Pakistan cricket between fixers, agents, captains and players. Addressing the jury at the outset of their trial, counsel for the Crown, a cricket-loving Sri Lankan Aftab Jafferjee, told them about the underworld beneath all international cricket of 'influential but shadowy figures' in Dubai, Mumbai, Karachi and London, and a black market where 'simply breathtaking' sums of money were gambled. He warned them that they would find it 'near impossible . . . to watch future games of cricket without a sense of disquiet'.[26]

The corruption of cricket especially relied on the strong hierarchy within teams and tour parties, with younger players expected to serve and obey their seniors. This well described the most powerless of those accused – the teenage prodigy Amir, from a poor village near Rawalpindi. As instructed, when he was approached by a real bookmaker he reported the incident to his captain. Instead of protecting him, Butt delivered him to the power of their tyrannical, corrupt agent.[27]

Amir rightly attracted some sympathy, including from his English opponents, and especially from two commentators, Michael Holding and Mike Atherton. Butt's arrogance and dishonesty won him none. The third player, Asif, was a highly talented bowler in the veteran stage, with a history of drug offences. Significantly, he delivered his required no-ball far more discreetly than Amir's, a massive overstep that drew gasps from commentators and within the Lord's crowd.

From the newspaper's point of view, the success of the sting was magnified by the response of the Pakistan Cricket Board chairman Ijaz Butt, who accused England of corruption in the one-day series accompanying the Tests. The intervention brought the two sides very close to blows. Predictably, the whole affair led to a flurry of accusations against other players (one other tourist, Umar Akmal, was subsequently punished for a different corruption offence)[28] and generally confirmed the impression of the underworld of cricket set out by Jafferjee.

All four men served terms of imprisonment. Amir was released first. He was young enough, at twenty-four, to enjoy a second international career under a very different captain, the high-principled and supportive Misbah-ul-Haq, and play an important role in Pakistan's 2–2 shared Test series in England in 2016. His greatest performance on return came the following year: 3 wickets for 16 to wreck a powerful Indian batting line-up and win Pakistan the ICC Champions Trophy.

In September 2024, the ICC anti-corruption chief, Alex Marshall, retired after a seven-year tenure. He congratulated the ICC and its compliant members on their efforts to clean up the game and encourage whistleblowers, singling out Sri Lanka. But he warned of the ongoing risk from burgeoning T20 and T10 competitions not regulated by the ICC. 'I am confident that the cricket you watch is safe and clean,' Marshall concluded. 'But I am also absolutely sure that corruptors are constantly looking for a route into the game, particularly in badly run lower-level franchise leagues.'[29]

The threat of match-fixing has meanwhile begun to appear in women's cricket – an oblique tribute to its recent global success. Betfair reported that from 2015 to 2018 its betting turnover on women's cricket rose from £15 million to £685 million.[30]

Chapter 30

THE RETURN OF RACISM

In this chapter, we return to the depressing theme of white dominance of the upper stratum of world cricket. We observed its origins in the imperial game before the First World War. We saw it continue tacitly in England, more evidently in 'white Australia' after the Second World War, and brutally codified and enforced in South Africa. Changes in the composition of English and Australian society, and independence and majority rule for South Africa, led many to believe that racism had been driven out of cricket in these nations.

However, racism had been embedded in cricket ever since the global expansion of the game in the Victorian epoch. Discrimination was built into the constitution of the ICC. It is therefore not surprising that prejudice and racism have remained stubbornly present at all levels of the sport.

The 1960s saw a revolution in British social attitudes, epitomised by the culture war around immigration and race that convulsed the Conservative Party. The main protagonists were party leader Edward Heath and Enoch Powell, his defence spokesman. In April 1968, Powell told an audience in Birmingham: 'As I look ahead, I am filled with foreboding. Like the Roman, I seem to see the River Tiber foaming with much blood.' The allusion to the Roman poet Virgil was a dramatic warning against what he saw as the consequences of immigration. It came just as pressure was building to block Basil D'Oliveira's selection for the winter tour of South Africa.

Heath responded decisively. His decision to sack Powell, more courageous in retrospect than it seemed at the time, was a pivotal moment in British public life, opening the way for a seemingly more tolerant, multicultural society in the coming decades. This was reflected in cricket. In the final two decades of the twentieth century, Roland Butcher, Gladstone Small, Devon Malcolm, Chris Lewis and many other English cricketers came from a West Indian heritage. Nasser Hussain became England's first cricket captain of Asian origin.

The cancellation of the 1968 tour of South Africa was a tactical climbdown forced on the cricket establishment by public outcry. Within two years it was business as usual. South Africa were invited to tour England. The plan was abandoned after Peter Hain, student activist and future Labour Cabinet minister, led a campaign of disruption.

South Africa's last hope of white-only Test cricket – a tour of Australia in 1971–72 – was extinguished by Sir Don Bradman. He was converted by a conversation with the cricket-loving trade union leader and future premier, Bob Hawke, and then himself confronted John Vorster over apartheid. It was a service to cricket that equalled his astonishing playing career.[1,*]

The establishment would not give up, however, and the early 1970s saw attempts to restore cricketing links. These were only abandoned after the 1977 Gleneagles agreement, when Commonwealth countries combined to block any sporting connection with apartheid. At this point, the 'rebel tours', a series of lavishly funded attempts to overturn South Africa's sporting isolation, began.

In all there were seven tours, two of which involved English teams. The first was led by the future England captain Graham Gooch. He defended himself on the grounds that 'we had taken up the right of an Englishman to earn a living where and in whatever legal way he chooses, which is normally one very good reason for being English'.[2]

---

[*] As in England in 1970, the South Africans were replaced by a multinational team, including the Pollock brothers, led by Garry Sobers. Sobers rewarded Bradman with 254 in the third unofficial Test, rated by him the greatest innings he had ever seen, in the *Sydney Morning Herald*, 6 January 1972.

Mike Procter captained a strong South African team. There was a second English rebel tour in the winter of 1989–90.

The TCCB had no choice but to ban the players. The alternative would have been a formal split between white and non-white cricket. Yet official sympathy for the rebels was widespread. Having served his ban, Gooch was quickly forgiven, restored to the national team and later appointed captain. The off-spinner John Emburey went on both tours, and was restored to favour *twice*. Much-loved voices, such as *The Times* columnist John Woodcock and *Test Match Special* commentators Brian Johnston and Christopher Martin-Jenkins, supported South Africa's readmission to world cricket. Martin-Jenkins even acted as master of ceremonies at a South African Cricket Union banquet. This deep understanding between the English cricket establishment and South Africa lasted up to the collapse of apartheid.[3]

By contrast the West Indies team that toured South Africa in 1982–83 and returned the following year were banned for life[4] and some were ostracised.* The Sri Lankan rebel team that toured South Africa in 1982–83 were handed twenty-five-year bans.[5] Australian rebels Terry Alderman, Trevor Hohns and Carl Rackemann, like their English counterparts, returned to represent Australia after taking part in rebel tours of the mid 1980s.[6]

Prejudice and the 'Tebbit test'

In England, sympathy towards apartheid South Africa was accompanied by a certain contempt towards non-white cricketing nations. Pakistan's rise as a cricketing power in the 1980s was met with hostility, petulance and allegations of cheating. Mike Gatting was an unfortunate choice to lead England on the 1987–88 tour of Pakistan. His notorious on-field row with Shakoor Rana, a Pakistan umpire, disgraced English cricket, as did opening bat Chris Broad's refusal to walk when given out caught behind. Worst of all, the TCCB awarded

---

* The ban was lifted in 1989, too late for most players to resume their careers.

Gatting's squad a £1,000 'hardship bonus' in an apparent endorsement of the conduct of the England team.[7] Two years later six members of the party that toured Pakistan (Bill Athey, Chris Broad, John Emburey, Bruce French, Neil Foster and Tim Robinson) would join Gatting when he led the final rebel tour to South Africa.[8]

This bigotry was echoed in the British press. Pakistani cricket supporters were 'excitable',[9] its umpires were cheats and the great batter Javed Miandad was 'cricket's Colonel Gaddafi'.[10] An article in *Wisden Cricket Monthly* headlined 'Is it in the Blood?'[11] suggested that foreign-born, and especially black, players were incapable of giving 100 per cent for England. This language was encouraged by politicians. Referring to Britons of Pakistani or Indian origin at international matches in 1990, the Conservative politician Norman Tebbit wondered: 'Which side do they cheer for?'[12] There were no similar comments about Britons with New Zealand roots who supported the All-Blacks.

For a time, black cricket had flourished in Britain. As the historian Michael Collins has written: 'By the mid 1970s and up to the mid 1990s, England's black settlers and their children had built up an immensely rich ecosystem of cricket: community clubs, workplace teams, leagues and cup competitions.'[13] Selectors tapped into this extraordinary talent pool. From 1980 to 1997 fourteen black men (though no women) played for English national teams, taking part in 251 Test matches. But in the twenty-eight years following 1997, only six male players (and two women) have done so.[14]

Class plays a role in this calamitous decline: children at private and public schools are more likely to have access to much better facilities. Hence the importance of organisations such as the Haringey Cricket College, set up in the aftermath of the 1981 Brixton riots to give places to local, often unemployed young men and women.[15]

By the mid 1990s, says Collins, 'there were thirty-three active professional cricketers who had either come to England from the Caribbean as children, or who had been born in England to parents of Caribbean origin'. Fifteen trained at Haringey. The Sports

Council called it the 'most successful sports academy in the world'. It was closed when the money ran out in the late 1990s, with the English Cricket Board deaf to desperate appeals for funds. The last English-born black cricketer to have played Test cricket for England was Michael Carberry. After batting with great courage in difficult circumstances on the troubled 2013–14 Ashes tour of Australia, Carberry was dropped. In an interview six years later, he spoke of how 'the people running the game don't care about black people', adding that 'racism is rife in the game'.[16]

The ECB estimated in 2018 that an astonishing 30 per cent of all recreational cricket players are of South Asian origin – but these represent only 5.8 per cent of male professional first-class cricketers.[17] A recent report claimed that privately educated white cricketers were thirty-four times more likely to play professional cricket than state-schooled British South Asians.[18]

The alienation goes back a long way. Reflecting on his experience of playing in the Bradford League in the 1970s, Lord Patel describes 'a feeling of not belonging'.[19] Rather than battling against prejudice, many South Asians chose to break away from traditional English cricket. In Yorkshire, Asian cricketers formed the Quaid e Azam league in 1980;[20] likewise, the Gujarati Metropolitan Cricket League (GMCL) launched in London in 1993.[21] Both still exist; the National Cricket League, a spin-off of the GMCL, is another bastion of South Asian cricket – with over 90 teams from across London and Essex as of 2025.[22]

In the 1980s, a player from the famed Indian Gymkhana Club turned up for Essex trials, only to be asked 'Was the Air India flight late?' He rejected the club's offer, and now works as a taxi driver.[23] Counties have also been slow to hire Asian coaches, even though they could encourage, develop and recruit a much wider talent pool into their squads.[24]

This is the ugly background to the allegations made by the Yorkshire player Azeem Rafiq, in September 2020, that he was on the receiving end of racism, harassment and bullying. Yorkshire launched an independent investigation into his claims, and other players came forward to support Rafiq. A year later, the club acknowledged that he was the 'victim of racial harassment and bullying', but Yorkshire still faced criticism for 'downplaying racism' and its hosting of international matches at Headingley would later be suspended by the ECB.[25]

In 2021, against a backdrop of the global Black Lives Matter and Me Too movements, and allegations of racism in cricket, the ECB appointed an Independent Commission for Equity in Cricket. Independently of its deliberations, the board implemented an anti-discrimination code of conduct across all levels of the game.[26]

In June 2023, the commission delivered a scathing report with forty-four recommendations, led by a demand for an 'unqualified public apology' from the ECB for the ongoing existence of racism, sexism, elitism and class bias in English cricket, its impact on victims and the historic failure to address it. The board gave that apology immediately and promised action within three months.[27]

The report presented overwhelming evidence of the under-representation of people of African-Caribbean and Asian origin at all levels of English cricket, of elitism and class-based discrimination, and the subordinate treatment of women. One eye-catching recommendation was the target of equal pay for all professional female cricketers by 2030. It also set the objective of equal representation for women throughout the administration of the game.

As to class, the report took special aim at the 'talent pathways' for boys into the county professional game and the bias they created for boys at independent schools who benefited from time, facilities and specialist coaching. It called for a State Schools Action Plan from the ECB, but again offered little guidance on its contents.

It is hard to argue against any of the report's recommendations – yet it also missed opportunities to recommend others, failed to address deeper problems in access to English cricket, and lost the chance to generate a reforming consensus in English cricket. It cited well-known central initiatives such as the MCC Foundation, ACE and Chance to Shine but not thousands of unheralded initiatives by local clubs. Anyone who plays recreational or club cricket in England and Wales for any length of time will have noticed clubs that have flourished by embracing diversity in contrast to those that are moribund as a result of reserving themselves for a privileged few. Another unheralded success story in English cricket is the participation of older people (although the commission noted the persistence of ageism without further analysis). Speaking personally, we have often played socially against teams that include three generations of the same family.

It noted prejudice against LGBTQ+ people and disabled people in English cricket, but decided not to research this. This was a regrettable omission: both groups have specific issues with stereotyping and under-provision, as we were told in our conversation with the Graces Cricket Club[28] and in private conversations with disabled cricketers.*

Above all, the commission did not look deeply enough into the basic issue of unequal access to cricket. While calling for a state schools plan for cricket, it did not look at the reasons why cricket has disappeared from them, including the pressures on school budgets and a lack of suitable playing surfaces, especially in inner cities. It did not look at the shrinking provision for cricket by local authorities, the number that have outsourced their leisure provision to companies that know nothing about cricket, nor the fact that pitches and practice facilities are becoming progressively worse and frequently dangerous.

In April 2024 the then prime minister Rishi Sunak announced a £35 million government investment in grass-roots cricket, including greater provision in state schools.[29] Keir Starmer has shown no interest in cricket nor has his sports minister, Stephanie Peacock. In August 2025, Labour's Culture Minister Lisa Nandy described the Sunak scheme as a 'fantasy', telling the BBC that 'There was not a single penny of funding actually attached to it.'[30]

---

* We regret our own inability to tell the full story of disabled cricket here.

The commission recorded one statistic that deserved much more attention than it received. It compared the participation rates in cricket in independent schools against others. Predictably the independents came out much better: the survey revealed that while '*16.8 per cent of children at private schools were playing cricket once a week during school hours,* [our emphasis] only 7.2 per cent of children at maintained state schools and 6.2 per cent at academies were doing so (during the academic year 2021–2022).'[31]

That italicised figure indicates that six out of seven children at English private schools were *not* playing cricket weekly. If English cricket is in retreat even as part of an expensive private education, it may be in worse shape than anyone imagines.

Racism has also infected every level of Australian cricket. We have already explored historic discrimination against Aboriginal cricketers, but more recently, John McGuire – an indigenous batter who remains the only man to have scored more than 7,000 runs in Perth club cricket without making the state side – claimed he was racially abused in every single game that he played.[32]

The cricket writer and broadcaster Jarrod Kimber recalls an incident at his childhood club, where players put up a sign at the bar stating 'No black blokes allowed'. When one of the few non-white players complained, he was told to calm down and accept the 'joke'.[33] After Sri Lankan cricketer Roshan Mahanama claimed that Glenn McGrath had called Sanath Jayasuriya a 'black monkey' during a one-day international in 1996, Australian cricket authorities dismissed the allegation as a publicity stunt.[34] In 2006, Dean Jones, wrongly believing that he was off air, referred to the South African batting star Hashim Amla as a 'terrorist'.[35] Usman Khawaja, an Australian Test batter of Pakistani heritage, records he was racially abused by players and parents in junior cricket.[36] Still today, he is regularly stopped and questioned outside team hotels while wearing Australia kit.[37]

In South Africa, meanwhile, the collapse of apartheid in the early 1990s had seemed to offer a new beginning and a team that reflected Nelson Mandela's rainbow vision.

The reality was very different. Makhaya Ntini, who became South Africa's first black cricketer in January 1998, has described feeling 'forever lonely'. He claims teammates wouldn't sit with him at meals and that the situation was so uncomfortable that he preferred to run to grounds rather than catch the team bus.[38] Ashwell Prince describes similar experiences and has also claimed that when black players were racially abused in Australia in 2005, the leadership group urged them to keep playing regardless.[39] Paul Adams feels that racial stereotyping underpinned the description of his bowling action as 'stealing hubcaps off moving cars'; his teammates used to revel in singing a song where he was labelled as 'brown shit'.[40]

When Adams made these allegations in July 2021, his former captain Graeme Smith and former teammate Mark Boucher held arguably the two most important roles within Cricket South Africa.[41] Boucher's apology to Adams seemed a tacit admission of guilt – but the charges brought against him were dropped when Adams decided not to testify. Boucher subsequently claimed the charges were 'unjustified' and caused 'considerable hurt and anguish'. Neither he nor Smith faced disciplinary action.[42]

At least Ntini, Prince and Adams were able to progress to the national side. By contrast, the wicketkeeper Thami Tsolekile was groomed as Boucher's successor only to be cast aside after three Tests.[43] Likewise, Khaya Zondo was pencilled in to play a one-day international in Mumbai in 2015, then deselected at the last hour when Dean Elgar was parachuted into the squad. A report found that Zondo 'was a victim of the exclusionary culture which persists within the cricket ecosystem'.[44]

Racism exists well beyond the national set-up. Playing domestic under-19 cricket, Aaron Phangiso realised he was being paid a fraction compared to his white counterparts.[45] Journalist Niren Tolsi has written that black bowlers would often be picked at junior level, but not given the opportunity to bowl. Meanwhile, racially motivated sledging has been prevalent at all levels of the game.[46] White players and administrators have too often preferred to ignore the racism and bigotry present within a system Prince describes as 'broken'.[47] Without a genuine desire for change, it is hard to see how it can be fixed.

There has nevertheless been much to celebrate in the thirty-two years since South Africa returned to international cricket, not least the country's victory in the 2025 World Test Championship final. This triumph was achieved under the leadership of Temba Bavuma, the first black African cricketer to make a Test century for South Africa and the first to captain the team.

Part Seven

WAITING FOR THE BARBARIANS

The Englishness is in the lie, in the cult of the honest yeoman, and the village green, in the denial of cricket's origins in commerce, politics, patronage and an urban society.
MIKE MARQUSEE, *Anyone But England*, 1994

I see the IPL becoming bigger than the NFL, NBA and the Premier League.
LALIT MODI, *The Times*, 2010

The ICC reacts as though it is primarily a members club: its interest in enhancing global development of the game is secondary.
LORD WOOLF, 2012

Chapter 31

PERMANENT REVOLUTION

England's County Championship lingered into the new century like an embarrassing elderly relative at a family reunion. The new ECB tinkered constantly and with little success. It gave priority to forms of cricket that were easier to sell to television and commercial sponsors. The first-class counties now numbered eighteen following Durham's admission in 1992, but there was a growing gulf in playing standards and match receipts between the strongest and the weakest.[1] The counties were compensated by the ECB for the loss of players on central contracts, introduced after long resistance from counties in 2001. But there was no way to measure the intangible losses from reduced spectator loyalties to counties missing their stars. These were not mitigated by relaxed registration regimes and changes in employment regulations that allowed short-term signings of overseas players. In 2012, the Australian Marcus North set a record by playing for six different counties in nine seasons.[2,*]

The ECB sought intermittently to 'rationalise' the number of counties (i.e. eliminate the weakest), with powerful support from England's coach Duncan Fletcher. The counties were ill-placed to resist, being, financially, clients of the body of which they were nominally in control. In 2008 (two years into the Sky television deal) they received a combined £30 million a year from the ECB, far more than their own resources from match and membership income and local sponsorship.[3] The ECB's power was supplemented when three

---

* North was equalled a few seasons later by Yasir Arafat of Pakistan.

counties – Durham (as a condition of first-class status), Glamorgan and Hampshire – invested heavily in new stadiums. The ECB's allocation of international fixtures became a major influence on the finances of half the counties in the championship.[4]

Eventually they bypassed the counties altogether: the introduction of the city-based league the Hundred in 2021 shunted the surviving reduced County Championship to the worst ends of the season, starting outlandishly early at the beginning of April, reserving the prime viewing time of August for the new competition.

Australian success

Australia have been the dominant men's cricket team of the twenty-first century, winning 167 Test matches against all-comers, losing sixty-six and drawing forty-three up to the end of November 2025.[5]

Two major developments in Australian cricket during this period powered their success. One was the arrival of a T20 league, the Big Bash, in 2005–06. Originally based on the six states in the Sheffield Shield, it was converted in imitation of the IPL into a city-based franchise league in 2011–12. By 2016–17 it had joined the IPL as one of the only two cricketing entries in the list of most attended sports leagues worldwide.[6] The Women's Big Bash, based on the same cities, was established in 2015. Both have made a major contribution to the earnings of leading Australian players, and given younger players an opportunity to learn from domestic and imported stars.

The other event was tragic: the death of a popular player, Phil Hughes, in 2014 after a blow to the upper part of his neck. His death led to the design of a new and better helmet, as well as new research into the under-recorded incidence of concussion in cricket. Players were no longer encouraged or even allowed to continue to play on recovery from concussion and 'like for like' substitutes had to replace them.[7]

In 2021–22, Scott Boland, a seam bowler rather in the style of Glenn McGrath, made a sensational entry into the Australian Test team at the relatively advanced age of thirty-two after a delayed apprenticeship for his state of Victoria and intermittent one-day international selections. He took 6 wickets for just 7 runs as England collapsed to 68 all out in the third Ashes Test at the MCG. He was only the second male First Nations player, after Jason Gillespie, to represent Australia in a Test match, and inspired new efforts by Cricket Australia to reach out to indigenous communities.[8] When Brendan Doggett was picked for the first Test of the 2025–26 Ashes series in Perth, he and Boland became the first pair of First Nations Australians to be included in the same national side.

Names such as Kasprowicz, Hilfenhaus and Starc (of Slovenian origin) in this period suggest that Australian cricket had finally managed to attract recruits from the waves of post-war non-British migration from Europe. But Australian cricketers of South Asian origin (about 4 per cent of the Australian population) remained rare,[9] and those of Southeast Asian origin even rarer. In the 1990s, Richard Chee Quee (with a very mixed ethnic heritage) became a cult hero as the second Australian of Chinese origin to play in the Sheffield Shield, but he was pigeonholed as an entertainer rather than a serious cricketer. No South Asian Australian since has played at a top level in either men's or women's cricket in Australia.[10]

Although Australian cricket has always prided itself on being more democratic and socially diverse, recent analysis revealed that its post-war Ashes teams were just as likely to be privately educated as England's. The proportion of privately educated players has been just under a third for both countries, and has risen at almost the same rate in the past decade. A major difference is that private education favours batters disproportionately in England whereas in Australia, for reasons yet to be identified, it is an advantage to all types of player.[11]

The West Indies – an ongoing eclipse

West Indies' performances deepened the desertion rates of players and fans alike, threatening to create a vicious spiral of decline. Only in the new form of T20 did the team assert itself, with victories in two Twenty20 World Cup finals. The second in 2016 was won with four consecutive sixes by Carlos Brathwaite in the final over bowled by Ben Stokes. The West Indian commentator, Ian Bishop, could only scream: 'Carlos Brathwaite – remember the name!'[12] Brathwaite's career neatly summarises the problems the West Indies have faced in retaining their best international players. As of November 2025, aged thirty-seven, he had made a total of 88 appearances for them: three Tests, forty-four one-day internationals, forty-one international T20s. He is unlikely to make any more. This contrasts with numerous appearances in the franchise leagues of India, Australia, Pakistan, Sri Lanka and Bangladesh, and a handful in the even shorter format of the English Hundred.[13]

With a small and fragmented television audience, and consequent lack of opportunity for sponsorship, there was not enough money to give a good living to professional players in domestic cricket. The West Indies' problems were made worse by a lack of leadership at every level, and a faction-ridden administration at war within itself and with the players. Unlike New Zealand the West Indies Cricket Board resisted reform and unification, and preserved the power of each island association.[14] It went through nine captains in two decades after Brian Lara departed for the easier life of a celebrity cricketer, with bitter words towards his administrators for converting talent into mediocrity.[15] Since Lara's departure, no West Indian batter except the obdurate Shivnarine Chanderpaul has averaged 45 in Test cricket, and since Courtney Walsh retired, no West Indian bowler except Kemar Roach has taken 200 Test wickets. It was no surprise that the West Indies Cricket Board submitted to the embrace of American-Antiguan financier Allen Stanford: it was spared financial ruin by his timely exposure as a fraud.[16]

A transformed New Zealand[17]

In June 2021, New Zealand, a country with a population of 5 million and a cricket administration with annual revenue of £28 million, won the inaugural World Test Championship against India, population 1.4 billion, cricket board annual revenue £380 million. New Zealand cricket had finally managed to shake off its lingering inferiority complex towards its superlative rugby union team.

These successes were a rare triumph for far-sighted cricket administrators, who made the most of the country's limited but unique resources. They had reacted sharply to scandal in 1995 when three leading players – two of them future captains, Dion Nash and Stephen Fleming – admitted to smoking dope on their tour of South Africa. It was surprising that they could afford it. Even with international fees, New Zealand cricketers complained that they could not earn enough to support their families.

The administrators set up a fundamental review under John Hood, a future vice-chancellor of Oxford University. He recommended a reconstruction of the board, replacing the amateur administrators appointed by the provinces with a centralised team of professionals. Unselfishly, the provincial appointees accepted their extinction and appointed an unusual CEO, Chris Doig, a cricket lover better known as a leading operatic tenor. Doig tripled cricket's revenues in the five years to 2000, boosting attendances and making the game more attractive to television and sponsors. The top New Zealand players secured the first full-time contracts in 2001, and the Players Association then negotiated better terms for all first-class cricketers and for full-time coaches. Doig established an academy and a high-performance centre. He streamlined the match structure and made the critical decision that the same six provincial associations should play each other in all formats, including T20 when it arrived. This kept players together as a unit through the season. New Zealand's best cricketers were accommodated rather than resisted when they sought to join the IPL. He improved New Zealand's low-scoring seaming pitches – but also promoted superior drop-in pitches (one of Packer's lasting innovations) to create attractive new cricket centres. Better pitches and better coaching together ensured a rise in the batting average for all first-class cricket in New Zealand from 28 in 1999 to 32 in 2021, the highest of all Test-playing countries.

Doig and his successors were determined to prioritise the national team. The provincial associations fell in line and even consented to give players the role in provincial matches that they fulfilled in the national team. The country's performances vindicated this policy and it developed more world-class players than at any period in its history: Stephen Fleming as batter and exceptional captain; Daniel Vettori, left-arm all-rounder; Trent Boult and Tim Southee as an opening attack; Ross Taylor and Kane Williamson as batters. More of their players were now in demand overseas, in English and Australian first-class cricket or in T20 franchises, which further developed their talent and experience.

New Zealand's administrative reforms were widely admired: Ireland sought to replicate them on its journey to full member status. However, they owed much to New Zealand's special environment: a prosperous country with a strong social and political consensus, a tradition of self-reliance, and a general appetite for sport and outdoor life. It received an external boost from the arrival of white South African cricketers who gave up on their chance of selection in their native land, as well as cricketers with roots in the Indian subcontinent. However, these new sources of talent may have helped to continue the under-representation of Māoris and Pacific Islanders, despite the evangelism of Ross Taylor, himself of Pacific descent.

Women's cricket in the twenty-first century

The absorption of women's cricket by the ICC in 2005 brought two major financial benefits. Women's cricket became part of the ICC's development programme for all countries and women's participation a metric for funding. Secondly, the ICC added Women's World Cups into its bundle of events for the sale of media rights: this generated huge increases in media funding and sponsorship. From 2006 to 2010 the ICC cited an increase from forty-five to ninety-six in the number of member countries where women played organised cricket.[18] Several new members, notably Brazil and Thailand, actually prioritised women's cricket because it offered more opportunity for international advance than men's. The Thai women vindicated this strategy by progressing rapidly into the finals of the T20 World Cup in 2020, thirteen years after their international debut in which they were bowled out for 40 by Nepal.[19] Infuriatingly, their passage into the 2023 Women's World Cup was blocked thanks to a contentious ruling by the ICC in favour of the full member countries whom they would have displaced.[20]

In 2009, Claire Taylor of England became the first woman to be chosen as one of *Wisden*'s Five Cricketers of the Year, a tribute to her role in winning the Women's Ashes for England. In 2008, England's women cricketers were paid for the first time, as coaches for its Cricket Foundation. In 2011, they were given touring and match fees. In 2014, eighteen of them secured central contracts,[21] and there were also payments for partners and children to join them on tours. At grass-roots level, there was an increase of more than 500 per cent in the number of clubs offering girls' or women's cricket (despite the merger of many famous women's clubs into men's) and a similar increase in the number of girls playing cricket at school.

However, the administration of English cricket remained male-dominated. Men outnumbered women by two to one on the ECB Board.[22] At international level, the ICC Women's Committee could do no more than put up proposals to the male-dominated Development Committee. It took more than a decade for it to appoint the first woman to its main board in 2018, Indra Nooyi. England's Clare Connor joined her shortly afterwards.[23]

Umpiring, coaching and scoring at all levels of English cricket were still dominated by men, and there were regular complaints about the disempowerment of women in club and county administrations. The Womens Cricket Southern League and several other prominent leagues stayed independent of the ECB, keeping their autonomy and their own sources of finance.[24]

As in the men's game, there were powerful barriers against working-class and ethnic-minority female cricketers. Mahika Gaur, Isa Guha, Issy Wong and Sonia Odedra were the only international players of Asian origin, Sophia Dunkley and Ebony Rainford-Brent the only black Britons.[25] England women cricketers continued to complain about pressures to dress and behave in a conventional feminine style,[26] although globally, female players were far more open than men about same-sex relationships.[27]

The ECB gave women's cricket a boost in 2021 through the introduction of the Hundred competition, which invented eight new teams with men's and women's squads to replace the existing counties. Pandemic restrictions forced the new competition to show both women's and men's matches on the same day. This brought totally new live and televised audiences for women's cricket.[28]

In April 2021 the Australian women's team recorded their twenty-second consecutive one-day international victory, overtaking the record set by the men under Ricky Ponting in 2003. They added two more to a sequence in which they scored their runs 50 per cent faster than their opponents and averaged two-and-a-half times more in each partnership. They were the world's best-supported female cricketers. The women's Big Bash created eight semi-professional teams in 2015, followed in 2017 by the grant of semi-professional status for the best domestic players. With a BBL contract on top, they could achieve a minimum retainer of A$36,000 (£20,000), while a full international player could expect earnings five times greater. Superstars such as Meg Lanning, Alyssa Healy and Ellyse Perry earned even more and gained greater recognition, Healy not in the least overshadowed by an illustrious uncle (the record-breaking Test wicketkeeper Ian) or a famous husband, express opening bowler Mitchell Starc.*

---

* Healy and Starc were the third husband and wife to play international cricket after Roger and Ruth Prideaux for England in the 1950s and 1960s and Guy and

Australia's dominance was broken in 2017 by England and India. They contested a thrilling 50-over World Cup final at Lord's, snatched by England in front of 30,000 spectators when the seam bowler Anya Shrubsole took six wickets.[29] The domestic television audience of 1.1 million was higher than for many live Premier League football matches: India's presence drove the overseas viewership to an estimated 180 million.[30] Australia were back in the final five years later, thrashing England by 71 runs in a high-scoring final in Christchurch thanks to 170 from Healy. However, they lost their crown in 2025, defeated in a thrilling semi-final by eventual champions India at Navi Mumbai.

Rasanjali de Alwis for Sri Lanka in the 1980s and 1990s. They were followed by three married women couples: Katherine and Natalie Sciver-Brunt of England, Marizanne Kapp and Dane van Niekerk of South Africa, and Lea Tahuhu and Amy Satterwaite of New Zealand.

Chapter 32

THE ICC EXPANDS CRICKET GLOBALLY

In 1993 the ICC took its first formal steps away from English tutelage. It renamed itself the International Cricket Council, abolished England and Australia's veto powers, and appointed its first non-English chairman, Sir Clyde Walcott. However, it remained primarily a talking shop and forum for lobbying over tournament hosting rather than the governing body of a global sport. Each member had almost total responsibility for the administration of cricket in its territory and bilateral relationships with other full members. The organisation remained in a few spare rooms at Lord's, with a secretariat from the MCC.

In 1997 it turned into an incorporated body, with a president instead of a chairman and an executive board. This was a statement of intent.[1] But when one Australian, Malcolm Speed, succeeded another, Dave Richards, in 2001, he found a body that was 'poorly regarded, under-resourced, politically and culturally unstable and ... everybody's punching bag when it came to cricket's problems'. He was shocked to discover that it was functioning with a part-time media manager during the international media fall-out from the corruption scandals.[2] But Speed was wrong to call it under-resourced.

Ehsan Mani was chair of the ICC Finance and Marketing Committee from 1996 till 2002. During this period the Pakistani chartered accountant effected a financial revolution in world cricket.

Mani grasped that, while a resounding success, the 1996 World Cup had demonstrated the limitations of the existing system of cricket rights. The same applied to the 1999 tournament in England. In both cases the rights were sold as 'one-off' events by the hosts, who kept the lion's share of the income. Mani's solution would transform the finances of global cricket.

Overcoming fierce resistance from members, Mani arranged for the ICC to auction rights in a 'bundle'. In 2000 the ICC offered TV and sponsorship rights to all its forthcoming international tournaments by competitive tender, including the World Cups of 2003 and 2007.

After fierce competition the bundled rights were sold for $550 million, an unimaginable sum of money for the time, and monumental in comparison to the ICC's *total budget* in 1993 of just £100,000.[3] When a similar exercise was carried out for 2007–15 the process raised $1.5 billion. Cricket, run for so many years on a shoestring, suddenly had access to wealth beyond its wildest dreams.

The question was whether the ICC would use this wealth wisely. At first it did, devoting massive resources from its swollen revenues to growing the game. In 2001 it expanded its executive team and created a new post of head of development, the New Zealander Andrew Eade.

This was a symbolic moment. The ICC was seizing control for growing the game from national boards, which had proved haphazard and at times self-interested. Eade gave new energy to the five development offices already set up in the 1990s, charging them with organising regional tournaments, as well as strengthening governance and playing standards in associate countries.

The ICC also established a high-performance programme for the leading associate members (Kenya, Canada, the Netherlands and Namibia), headed by the former England Test batter Bob Woolmer. He urged more competitive qualifying tournaments for the World Cup in 2003 and for a clear development pathway for associates.[4]

Mani (who became ICC president in 2003) and Malcolm Speed commissioned a wide-ranging review of the structure of world cricket, examining the volume of cricket being played, the economics of the game, and the preferences for formats of players and administrators.[5]

International cricket took off. At the start of 2001 the ICC had fifty-three members: ten full, with Test status, thirty associates with an established structure of organised cricket and a further thirteen affiliates, countries or territories where cricket had become a recognised competitive sport. Over the decade this number all but doubled, as the ICC admitted fifty-one new countries at the lowest, affiliate level.[6]

The most important immediate step was the expansion from twelve to sixteen teams for the 2007 World Cup, hosted by the West Indies. At this tournament Ireland announced its transformation from romantic backwater to independent cricket power.

Irish cricket arrives on the global stage

Irish cricket made an international breakthrough in the twenty-first century, from a combination of factors. Ed Joyce led several talented Irish players in taking the risk of seeking a professional career in England, including Eoin Morgan, Boyd Rankin, Tim Murtagh, William Porterfield, Paul Stirling and the brothers Kevin and Niall O'Brien. Their success and experience would eventually return to Ireland as players or coaches. Ireland's cricket administration became much tauter and directed under an experienced CEO, Warren Deutrom.[7] The ICC handed greater revenues to associates, which coincided with a long boom in the Irish economy. Irish cricket became significantly richer, and clubs could afford to offer professional contracts to experienced players and coaches. The ICC created a new competition – the Intercontinental Cup – to drive up first-class playing standards in the more advanced associate members (including Ireland and Scotland): its advocate, Bob Woolmer, was convinced that it would also drive up their one-day standards.[8] They expanded the entrants to the 2007 World Cup in the West Indies and gave Ireland a pathway to qualification for the first time.

Ireland qualified for the Super Eights round of the 2007 World Cup after a thrilling tie with one full member, Zimbabwe, and victories over two others, Bangladesh and, most sensationally, Pakistan. The result was overshadowed by the death of Bob Woolmer (by that point, Pakistan's national coach) on the same day. In the next 50-over World Cup, in 2011, Ireland overcame England for the first time with a century off 50 balls by Kevin O'Brien. For financial reasons alone, Deutrom was anxious to push Ireland further, into full member (or Test match) status. It would mean not only a bigger share-out of ICC revenues but a far greater number of bilateral one-day contests against other full members. He gained his objective in 2018, when Ireland secured their first Test match – at home in Malahide – against Pakistan. Ed Joyce was allowed to return to the fold for Ireland ahead of time after his one-day career with England. Again, O'Brien came to the fore, with a fifty and a century, which saved Ireland from a likely innings defeat. In their first Test match against England at Lord's, Ireland led England on first innings, thanks to Tim Murtagh, who had learned his trade there leading the Middlesex attack.

As of June 2025, Ireland had played ten Test matches and won three of them – a decent record compared to the opening ten Test matches of most other cricket nations. But none counted for the World Test Championship and most were one-off matches rather than series, and against lesser cricket powers. With long gaps between them in an irregular programme, many of Ireland's best players have understandably given priority to franchise competitions. Ireland's first-class structure (created as a condition of Test match status) has disappeared. No domestic first-class matches were played in 2023 and just four in 2024, only one of these between domestic Irish teams. Ireland's example is likely to convince future nations that Test status is not worth the bother and expense, when T20 offers an easier pathway into international competition.

Since 2000, in addition to those ten Test matches, the Irish men's team have played 241 one-day internationals and 203 T20 internationals. In the same period Ireland's women have played a solitary Test match, 149 one-day internationals and 148 T20s.⁹ In spite of their recent successes, Ireland's men have yet to match Ireland women's appearance in five World Cups. With even less official support than Ireland's male cricketers for most of their history, Ireland's women's cricket depended on individual efforts by players and administrators. In 2001, after twenty years of independent life, the Irish Women's Cricket Union followed England's women in merging with their country's men's administration, on promise of more resources and attention.[10]

New cricket powers

Besides the Intercontinental Cup and the expanded World Cup of 2007, the ICC promoted new age-group and youth international competitions. The ICC hoped to create a recognised development pathway through continuous tours, although (as we shall see) one unintended and in many ways baleful consequence was to draw the best talent of associate countries to the notice of full members.

Formerly left to their own domestic devices, the forty or so associates were each given their own development officer, who promoted five-year plans to integrate their schools and club cricket, and create a clear development progression for all its domestic players. The Intercontinental Cup was created with four-day first-class matches for the leading associates, three each representing Africa, Asia, the Americas and Europe. This gave their players first-class averages and aspirations, but sadly had little commercial appeal to local media and sponsors without the potential for promotion to full member status in Test matches and one-day internationals.[11]

The inaugural competition took nine months to complete, with the semi-finals and final in the new made-for-television stadiums in the UAE. Scotland had an easy victory over Canada in the final: two countries with a long cricketing history and a nucleus of experienced players. Kenya departed in the semi-final, its team weakened by a players' strike. Bermuda maintained its status as a cricket nation outside the West Indies and its rotund spin bowler Dwayne Leverock began a journey to cult status.[12]

Two relative newcomers announced themselves. Malaysia had inherited at independence a strong infrastructure of clubs, grounds and administrators. It benefited from its location to host regional Asian tournaments. Nepal had none of these advantages and indeed struggled to find enough flat land for pitches. The game had been introduced as a private amusement for the elite by the ruling Rana dynasty. Indian traders introduced cricket to a wider population, especially after the overthrow of the autocratic Ranas in 1951. ICC membership in 1988 rewarded progress in schools and clubs, while promotion to associate status in 1996 generated new funding. The former Sri Lankan batter Roy Dias drove up technical standards, discipline and fitness among its international players of all ages. However, both Malaysia and Nepal were beaten in the Asian section by the UAE, a side made up entirely of expatriates from the Indian subcontinent.

The competition was designed to advance the leading associates as cricket powers. If anything, it set limits on their ambitions. Scotland's best player, Gavin Hamilton, was lost to English county cricket and one (runless and wicketless) Test for England. Malaysia's biggest talent, Arul Suppiah, never played for the country at all: instead his English public-school education at Millfield, a forcing house for cricket, took him to Somerset.[13] In recent years the same system has begun to siphon off young talent from the West Indies, thus accelerating the national team's decline. Barbados-born Jacob Bethell won player of the tournament in the West Indies Under-15 competition in 2017 before he was whisked away to Rugby School, and thence to Warwickshire and the English national team.

For all the ICC's earnest efforts, the biggest factor in the expansion of cricket may have been the global job market of the long boom years of the early 2000s, which exported millions of players and supporters, especially from the Indian subcontinent, to places where the game had never been played. New cable and satellite networks carried cricket programming to service them, and in a few countries, particularly Norway and Germany, governments promoted cricket clubs as a force for social integration.

Almost unknown before 2000, Norwegian cricket became so prosperous and well-organised that it was able to offer well-remunerated coaching holidays to leading Pakistani players, including the future captain Misbah-ul-Haq, and their families.[14] Some traditional cricket-playing small nations, notably Gibraltar and Greece, sputtered at the admission of so many new countries with no native players. The most successful new Middle Eastern cricket nation, Oman, took early steps to reserve team places for locally born players.

Bhutan's Buddhist monarchy concluded that cricket could contribute to the national objective of maximising gross national happiness after the remote and largely self-isolating Himalayan nation was won over to cricket by the advent of television in 1999. Bhutan was almost without expatriates to draw on, but several members of the ruling Wangchuck dynasty have played cricket for them. Bhutan has never progressed far in international competitions but enjoys significant home advantage: its leading cricket stadium at Thimphu is more than 7,500 feet above sea level. In 2022 the Yellow Dragons had the satisfaction of overwhelming their mighty neighbours from mainland China.[15]

Moroccan cricket was an unlikely beneficiary of the match-fixing scandals that tarnished cricket matches in Sharjah, and led their promoter, Sheikh Bukhatir, to search for a new setting. Bukhatir invested in a fine stadium in Tangier, hitherto renowned mainly as a haven for louche writers, artists and remittance men sent away by their families. Cricket took off rapidly in Moroccan cities in the early 2000s. There was a thriving competitive league and Bukhatir engaged two former Test all-rounders, Mohinder Amarnath of India and Gary Cosier of Australia, to coach a youthful and energetic national team. Pakistan played some televised one-day international matches in the fine stadium but the Moroccans found it difficult to entice international visitors of standing, and in 2004 they had to make do with a motley side representing the British Parliament, organised by Richard Heller, who became the only visiting captain to lose a series in Morocco.*

The ICC's expansionist efforts reached their apogee in its centenary year 2009 with the admission of the hundredth member, Chile. At that point it began to reduce its own support for cricket in new countries and expected them to generate more resources themselves. Countries were admitted on their own application, sometimes with limited evidence of cricket. Once in as an affiliate member, a country remained in, short of egregious maladministration. In this way the ICC acquired a somewhat random collection of members in varying stages of cricket development. It never devised a prospective membership category that might have enabled it to nurture cricket from its beginnings in each country.[16] The most romantic and inspirational of all these new members was Afghanistan.

Afghanistan gains Test match status

Until Afghanistan was admitted as a full member of the ICC in 2017, every Test-playing country had been at some point part of the British Empire. Afghanistan escaped that fate only by fierce resistance in its inhospitable terrain. The British had attempted to introduce the Afghans to cricket on the ill-fated excursion to Kabul during the first Afghan War between 1839 and 1842. They refused to follow the example of their southern neighbours in India. Instead they drove the British out of the country.

The Soviet invasion in 1979 sowed the seeds of Afghan cricket. Millions of Afghans fled as refugees to northern Pakistan, where they

---

* Bukhatir abandoned the venture, the stadium and pitch decayed, a new Moroccan cricket administration took over, and when Heller tried to organise a follow-up tour in 2008 he was informed that Moroccan cricket had virtually disappeared (and with it all its liquid and mobile assets).

learned to love the game. When the war ended, they took cricket back home with them. The Taliban's seizure of control in 1996 was a setback. The reactionary clerical and tribal regime at first banned all sports, regarding cricket as especially frivolous and foreign. Over time this bleak ideological hostility to cricket weakened and the beginnings of a national team emerged.

The ICC granted affiliate membership in June 2001.[17] The timing was crucial: three months before 9/11. The country's cricket could have fallen by the wayside; instead, Afghan cricket went from strength to strength. Advancing through the ICC's lower leagues, Afghanistan narrowly missed out on qualifying for the 2011 World Cup.[18]

Meanwhile, in a village in Nangarhar, 25 miles from the Pakistan border, a boy called Rashid Khan passed the days hunting with his slingshot.[19] Rashid's youth was itinerant: the Khans moved from Nangarhar to Peshawar, Jalalabad to Kabul – yet wherever they went, there was cricket. All his brothers bowled leg spin; as sixth in line, Rashid had to wait his turn to bat. He sent down twenty-five overs a day, forsaking loopy flight for quick, fizzing spinners.[20] He learned to turn the ball with his fingers as well as his wrist, to bowl a googly that came out as fast as his leg-break.

In October 2015, seventeen-year-old Rashid was picked for the first time – helping Afghanistan overturn a 2–1 deficit in a one-day international (ODI) series in Zimbabwe.[21] Two years later Afghanistan was awarded Test status. Rashid's rise felt emblematic: like Afghanistan's cricket, he'd appeared out of nowhere. By 2018, he was a global star: the fastest bowler to 100 ODI wickets,[22] the youngest to top the ODI rankings,[23] the poster boy for the newest Test nation.

In Germany Angela Merkel's 2015 refugee policy catalysed the rise of cricket. Once the sport was hardly played; by 2020 there were 300 German teams.[24] The national side – with its strong Afghan influence – has shot up the ICC rankings. Afghan exiles are making their presence felt in Belgium and Austria too, and at school and club level in Britain. An Afghan teenage refugee, Adnan Miakhel, became a television star in Freddie Flintoff's compelling series *Field of Dreams*, about his personal attempt to restore cricket to apathetic teenagers in his hometown of Preston.*,25

The progress of Afghan's male cricketers was not matched by their women. Both the Afghan Cricket Board and the ICC were so anxious to embed cricket in the country, under conditions of great economic, social and political uncertainty, that neither was willing to challenge traditional rural values and interest groups for the benefit of women's cricket. However, under gentle pressure from the ICC, the post-Taliban, Western-supported government cautiously encouraged women's participation and the ACB awarded central contracts to a number of women designated as its future representative team. This progress was undone when President Donald Trump reached a private deal with the Taliban to reduce American support for Afghanistan. The resistance of the Afghan army crumbled and the rout was completed when Trump's successor, Joe Biden, withdrew the remaining American forces.

Some Afghan female cricketers found exile in Australia and Canada. The restored regime appointed a new all-male Afghan Cricket Board at gunpoint and stopped women's cricket in its tracks. Women and girls in Afghanistan were subject to ever more vicious repressive decrees, excluded from jobs, education and public spaces.

The ICC's response was to appoint an all-male working party in Afghanistan. It has published no report of its work, and we have seen no evidence that it has ever spoken to any Afghan women at home or in exile. The ICC rejected a proposal to withhold some of the country's share of cricket's international revenues to support its exiled women cricketers. Afghanistan has retained its full member status and its men have continued to play international cricket (with intermittent success): it has been argued that banning them would extinguish Afghan cricket and the window it offers to the outside world. However, the fate of Afghan female cricketers suggests

---

* As of October 2024, Adnan had won a scholarship to a leading cricket school, Rossall, and represented Lancashire under-18s.

that the ICC has as little will as FIFA or the International Olympic Committee to protect the basic rights of the most vulnerable participants in its sport.²⁶

Two big prizes missed: China and the USA

From 2001 onwards, the ICC strove especially hard to capture the two biggest untapped cricket markets in the world: mainland China and the USA.

Cricket had a strong expatriate presence in China before the communist takeover, and survived in Shanghai until the Cultural Revolution. It was then displaced by decree for two generations by table tennis and basketball before a 1990s revival, with the help of celebrity-studded matches from the Hong Kong Sixes, including Ian Botham and Viv Richards.

From the beginning the ICC recognised that cricket in mainland China would require the government's active support and it cultivated relationships with Communist Party officials. A deliberate disregard of politics was apparent: ICC papers show no sign of debate over mainland China's human rights record or state control over recreational activities.*

The country was admitted to membership in 2001, followed quickly by a visit from Malcolm Speed with an ICC delegation. In the Chinese system, where children were assigned to different sports at the age of seven, the best natural athletes were directed into table tennis, gymnastics and athletics: cricket was a minority sport for duffers. This was a mirror image of the traditional sporting summer priorities at English public schools.

The Asian Cricket Council set up a committee to evaluate cricket in China. In May 2006 it urged the ICC to consider China as a 'special case' on economic grounds more than sporting ones. It estimated that 'the commercial values of cricket would increase by up to 40 per

---

* However, the ICC admitted Taiwan as an affiliated member in 2004.

cent once China has emerged as an international force'. It noted a recent estimate of the value of China's internal advertising market, 75 per cent derived from television, at $32.7 billion – compared to $2.8 billion for India.[27]

In subsequent years both the ICC and the Asian Cricket Council invested more money in China, especially to facilitate cricket's inclusion in the Asian Games of 2010, to be hosted in Guangzhou. Cricket made inroads at Chinese universities.[28] Unfortunately China did not show to advantage in the Guangzhou tournament, contested in the Twenty20 format by both men and women. The men lost both their matches, to Malaysia and a very under-strength Pakistan by 128 runs (a huge margin in 20 overs). The women did better, beating Malaysia and Thailand (by 1 run), but losing to Bangladesh, Pakistan and Japan, who thereby edged them out of a bronze medal.[29,*]

The ICC was fatally slow to see the benefits of including cricket in the Olympic Games, not only for the direct television revenues and the exposure, but also as a means of securing funding for cricket from national sports administrators. Within mainland China, rugby sevens (the faster, shorter form of rugby union) gained a huge advantage when it became an Olympic sport at Rio de Janeiro in 2016. It quickly displaced cricket as a university sport.[30]

The USA was an even bigger prize. In 2001 the ICC estimated that its sports and leisure market, 'the largest and most sophisticated in the world, had revenues of $15 billion'. It had more than 8,000 senior cricketers, more than any other associate member. However, the ICC also recorded that 'cricket remains a fringe activity, played almost exclusively by expatriate players from cricket-playing countries. It has yet to be marketed successfully into mainstream American society.'[31]

In 2000, efforts were made to develop an international standard ground for one-day matches at Walt Disney World in Florida.

---

* Against Japan the Chinese opening bowler Mei Chun Hua took 1 wicket for 3 in her four overs as Japan laboured to chase a winning target of 67 in the last of their 20 overs. China had scored their 66 but lost only six wickets, suggesting early tactical naivety by both teams in 20-over cricket.

These generated a sharp clash with the faction-ridden USA Cricket Association or USACA, led by the voluble and litigious Gladstone Dainty, which the ICC had tried to sideline. The clash signalled a basic battle for control of American cricket between its traditional base of Caribbean origin, and a wave of new and generally more affluent immigrants from the Indian subcontinent.

The two sides resumed talks in 2003, and 'Project USA' offered one-day international matches against full members in the United States (all profits to American cricket) and part-hosting (with a guaranteed place for the USA team) of the 2007 World Cup awarded to the West Indies. After further arguments nothing happened, and the ICC recorded caustically: 'We have never seen a sporting organization that combines such great potential and such poor administration as the USACA.'[32] Further USACA marketing initiatives followed: 'Project 15' was intended to help the USA play in the 2015 World Cup, while 'Destination USA' encouraged touring teams to play on neutral soil in the USA. New Zealand and Sri Lanka were induced to play each other in Florida, but the matches had poor attendances and television coverage, and made a financial loss.[33]

In recent years, the ICC's hopes of American entry into the global market for cricket continued to be frustrated. Local leadership remained divided, and the game remained identified with expatriates (mostly of Asian rather than Caribbean origin), disconnected from schools and colleges, and offering no academic and career pathways to compare with competing sports. American cricket has failed to replicate soccer's rapid advance and, crucially, there are no 'cricket moms' to rival the vital voter demographic that is the soccer mom.[34]

Kenya: a lost opportunity

The prime candidate for promotion to full member Test status at the turn of the twenty-first century was Kenya, where a thriving cricket scene drew on players of both African and Asian communities. On performances in associate cricket, they looked to have a stronger claim than the latest full members, Zimbabwe and Bangladesh, and their promotion would create a new focus for cricket in Africa. This may explain why the ICC allocated Kenya two home games in the 2003 men's 50-over World Cup.

Kenya derived an unexpected advantage when New Zealand refused to play there, citing security concerns, and gave them a walkover. They outperformed expectations in the tournament by qualifying for the semi-final, with outstanding performances from Kennedy Otieno, Thomas Odoyo, Maurice Odumbe and Collins Obuya.

But promotion never arrived. The weaker full members, Zimbabwe and Bangladesh, successfully resisted a proposal to limit them to international matches at home, Bangladesh benefiting from India's patronage.[35] The other full members had no financial motive to admit Kenya to a share of the massive new revenues in international cricket and to play unprofitable bilateral series. There were genuine concerns about the infrastructure of Kenyan cricket and its ability to produce successors to the World Cup stars.[36]

After their disappointment, Kenyan cricket went sharply into reverse, on and off the field. They had few opportunities and even fewer successes in one-day internationals despite their success in the World Cup. There was a players' strike; Odumbe was banned for match-fixing;[37] Obuya went to play for Warwickshire in the English County Championship. A weakened team lost to Scotland in the first Intercontinental Cup for associates. By 2005, just two years after their World Cup performance, Kenya cricket had no sponsors and was playing almost no international matches.[38]

Zimbabwe – and a retreat from politics

The collapse of cricket administration in Zimbabwe under Robert Mugabe provoked a major crisis. To say the least, it was unfortunate that Zimbabwe had been awarded hosting status in the 2003 World Cup, primarily staged in South Africa. When England refused to play their fixture there, for a mixture of ethical and security reasons, this threatened the ICC with a truncated World Cup and a resulting lawsuit for restitution of substantial sponsorship income. Its showpiece competition was further disrupted when New Zealand declined to play their match in Kenya.

The ICC gave walkovers to Zimbabwe and Kenya, and instituted a specific doctrine of avoidance of political or ethical issues. It would respect any ban on cricket contact imposed by a country's government against another country – but otherwise fine or sanction cricket administrations that made such decisions unilaterally. The ICC hoped that Tony Blair's government might resolve its dilemma by banning contact with Zimbabwe, but was disappointed when Blair contented himself with a 'personal opinion' rather than an outright ban.

Malcolm Speed produced a rationale for the ICC's policy at its annual meeting in 2004. His draft statement said: 'The ICC's role is to administer and promote the game of cricket. We do not judge the political regimes, policies, actions and ideologies of the governments of our members and in fact, we are not qualified to do so.' The ICC confirmed this policy in 2007 (again in relation to Zimbabwe, where not only cricket but every aspect of economic, social and civic life had collapsed further under Mugabe). Speed asked the ICC board to consider whether moral, as opposed to political, considerations should be taken into account: 'Is there a point at which external factors make normal sporting relations unsustainable?' The board discussed human rights abuses in mainland China (then being actively courted as a new cricketing power) and the boycott of South Africa in the apartheid era, before agreeing with Speed that 'sport should not be required to make these decisions'.[39]

The immediate result of this policy was that England played another one-day series in Zimbabwe in 2007–08, in which they crushed the unhappy, divided representatives of a disintegrating cricket nation. The no-politics, no-ethics policy has been applied by the ICC ever since, even on matters with a clear cricket dimension.

A Big Three cartel

In 2006, the long-serving Jagmohan Dalmiya lost his influence in the BCCI to I. S. Bindra, whose powerbase was the northern industrial city of Mohali. Bindra proposed that since India provided 80 per cent of the revenues of the ICC, it should enjoy 80 per cent of its voting power. India would set its own programme of future bilateral tours, independent of the ICC's and excluding some full members at will (though not at that time Pakistan, whose bilateral meetings were understandably popular and profitable). The ICC's international events would be limited to the World Cup, and more multinational events would be organised by the Asian Cricket Council and staged by its members.

The ICC warned that the Indian proposals would amount to 'India controlling world cricket', that they would cause a 'severe financial impact' to other full members apart from England, Australia and Pakistan, and starve the resources of the ICC development programme for the associates.[40] Constitutional obstacles frustrated the Indian agenda but it would return in the next decade, with a vengeance.

In 2011 the ICC produced a strategic plan, promising more global growth and inclusion of more cricket communities. But these pieties ran up against the self-interest of the full members. A frustrated Haroon Lorgat, the South African who succeeded Speed as CEO in 2011, pushed through an independent review of the ICC's governance by Lord Woolf, former Lord Chief Justice of England.

Famous for his incisive language, Woolf was shocked into even greater bluntness by the state of international cricket. He wrote: 'The ICC reacts as though it is primarily a members' club: its interest in enhancing global development of the game is secondary.' He condemned its 'self-interested or parochial decision-making' and called for independent ICC directors and a new funding model, based on the actual needs of *all* members. Taking direct aim at Indian power within the ICC, he pressed for a code of ethics to eliminate undue influence by one member over another, especially by the award or refusal of bilateral series. He proposed the uncoupling of Test and full member status, the end of full member control over the ICC's development programme, and in general, accountability of full members to the global cricket community.[41]

Associate members, most independent cricket media, and global cricket lovers in general pressed for implementation of his reforms but the full member representatives rejected it, led by the Indian representative, N. Srinivasan. He had moved up the hierarchy of the BCCI over five years as secretary and president, and in 2014 he became chairman of the ICC without reducing his commitment to India and Tamil Nadu. Srinivasan instantly threatened Indian withdrawal from the ICC's Future Tours Programme, which would spell ruin for most of the other full members. Srinivasan linked up with the English and Australian ICC representatives, Giles Clarke and Wally Edwards, to create a cartel within the cartel of full members.

The so-called Big Three met Woolf's recommendation to end the 1993 equal share-out of ICC revenues from its international events between full members – but not as Woolf intended. On the argument that they generated most of those media revenues, they demanded a bigger share for themselves, with a third going to India.[42]

The Big Three argued that the international revenues would be massively increased through the sale of the eight-year bundle of events for 2015–23, which had raised a mighty $1.5 billion. Every full member would be substantially better off even with a reduced share. Critics still protested against the Big Three's power- and revenue-grabbing, and pointed to the shrinkage of the ICC development programme, the abandonment of the proposed World Test Championship and the reduction of participants in the 2015 World Cup. Clarke argued vigorously in response that the elevation of the Big Three was the only way that India's raw commercial power could be contained and put to the service of world cricket. When Srinivasan was ousted from the ICC in 2015 in the light of a match-fixing scandal involving his son-in-law and his franchise team in the Indian Premier

League, Chennai Super Kings, his critics were delighted. The aftermath was a brief period of reform in Indian cricket administration imposed by the Indian Supreme Court.[43,*]

For the ICC, this episode allowed space for limited reform with partial implementation of the Woolf proposals. All affiliate members were automatically uplifted to associates and all 20-over matches between them became full internationals. The development programme was partially restored and a new share-out of revenues made some recognition of the needs of full members, now including Ireland and Afghanistan. The World Test Championship was restored, but excluded the weakest countries and imposed no obligation on each remaining country to play each other, enabling India to refuse to meet Pakistan in bilateral series. All these reforms preserved the cartel of full members and offered no pathway into first-class and Test cricket for associates.[44]

The ICC's sudden riches financed one great decade of cricketing evangelism, which doubled its member countries. But it has proved ill-equipped since then to grow international cricket, as we explain in the next chapter.

---

[*] Srinivasan retained his local cricket power base in Tamil Nadu.

Chapter 33

CRICKET COMES FULL CIRCLE

As the twenty-first century dawned, both long-form and 50-over cricket were in crisis. Apart from the World Cups (at irregular intervals and with constantly shifting formats and numbers of participants) both domestic and international cricket had static or declining appeal to live spectators and broadcast audiences alike. The response of the authorities, especially in England, was to shorten the game still further, and create a format of 20-over games in place of the previous lower limit of 40 or 50.

England pioneered a 20-over cricket competition, launched in midsummer 2003, to enable counties without lights to take advantage of the summer evenings. The first 20-over match, between Hampshire and Sussex, was presented with the eager boast: 'welcome to a revolution in cricket'. The early matches attracted five times the live audience of the previous year's longer-form Benson & Hedges matches, 30 per cent of it women.

Despite its success in England, the new format made little initial headway in international competition. There were just sixteen bilateral international matches in the four years between England's introduction and the first T20 World Cup in 2007. Ironically, India was the least enthusiastic country.

When the ICC proposed an international 20-over tournament in 2006, BCCI secretary Niranjan Shah mocked the idea ('Why not ten-ten, or five-five or one-one?') and complained that India would be at a disadvantage given their lack of experience.[1] The BCCI withheld its biggest stars – Sachin Tendulkar, Rahul Dravid and Sourav Ganguly – from the first World Cup to rest them for a more important home series against Australia. Auspiciously, M. S. Dhoni replaced Ganguly as captain.

Mr Shah had made a mistake. The first T20 men's World Cup was an exuberant product of cricket's dynamic economic and political landscape. The ICC's 50-over competitions were becoming jaded. The flagship 2007 World Cup in the West Indies had been overlong and chaotic, with a final (won by Australia over Sri Lanka) absurdly compelled to finish in darkness. Cricket needed a new competition to appeal to television companies, choosing to stage the first 20-over contest in South Africa, which had already introduced the format with success. India was persuaded to send a team (minus the three top stars) in exchange for being chosen as hosts of the World Cup in 2011.[2]

India's supposedly second-string team at once converted their home supporters to the new format through dazzling televised performances. Early on, Yuvraj Singh hit Stuart Broad, one of England's finest post-war bowlers, for six sixes in an over, matching the first-class feats of Garry Sobers and India's Ravi Shastri.

Like Malcolm Nash, Sobers' victim, Broad made the mistake of bowling conventionally good deliveries.[3,*] Singh and Dhoni, a positive and dynamic leader throughout the tournament, established a new image for Indian cricketers as 'streetfighters' from underprivileged backgrounds. Best of all from an Indian point of view, India won two tight matches against Pakistan, one in the preliminary rounds – a tie followed by a bowl-out – and then the final in the last over when defeat seemed certain. In both cases victory resulted from a rare error by Pakistan's Misbah-ul-Haq. He would become renowned for his calm captaincy and run-scoring under pressure – but these lapses of judgement haunted him for his whole career.[4]

---

[*] We do not know what kind of bowling Tilak Raj served to Shastri in his innings in the Ranji Trophy in 1984.

The global television audience for the final was 400 million, the majority in India, and Dhoni's team were given a massive and lengthy victory parade on returning home.[5] The victory checked a drift away from cricket viewing in India, and reinforced local efforts to overturn its existing structure and format.

Flamboyant Lalit Modi, an entrepreneur from a wealthy family, has taken most of the credit for the formation of the Indian Premier League – although he was exiled from it, and indeed India itself, in 2013. In fact, he was not alone in conceiving the idea of a city-based league of privately owned franchise teams in big cities to replace the long-established state associations.

The economic climate was right. Neo-liberal economic policies had replaced the state socialism of the ousted Congress governments. The economy responded with 9 per cent GDP annual growth and a massive transfer of population from the countryside to the cities.[6] Above all, television hugely increased its penetration of the Indian population. When India achieved World Cup victory in 1983, only a small percentage of households were able to watch it on television, but by 2000 the national Doordarshan network was available to 70 per cent of the population all over India, including rural areas. Before 1993, the BCCI had actually *paid* Doordarshan to broadcast cricket matches but this was overturned after a Supreme Court decision in 1995.

Modi understood that some of the world's most financially successful professional team sports – American football, baseball and basketball – did not need international competition, which had become the lifeblood of cricket worldwide. Both live and television audiences could be drawn to teams if they had a local identity, a collection of star players, and could provide entertainment and a sense of occasion during prime time on television week after week. He also recognised that women controlled television viewing in the great majority of Indian households. He believed that they could be won to cricket by associating it with Bollywood.[7]

Modi joined forces with a competitor, Madhavrao Scindia, from the princely house of Gwalior and president of the state cricket association of Madhya Pradesh. Their city-based league was rebuffed by the then all-powerful BCCI chairman, Jagmohan Dalmiya, who objected to the presence of overseas stars. This doomed the proposed league's commercial prospects.[8]

Modi returned to the fray with a powerful new ally, the politician Sharad Pawar, who had ousted Dalmiya in a bitter coup from the BCCI (although such was the confused governance of cricket that Dalmiya lingered for several years at the ICC). Pawar made Modi a vice-president in charge of marketing at the BCCI. Modi called in Andrew Wildblood of sports agency the International Marketing Group, who worked up a revised two-page proposal for a city-based franchise cricket league. They were both determined that the games would be screened live in the evenings on prime-time television – which dictated a shift to the new 20-over format. They pitched it to the BCCI and it was accepted.[9]

Modi staged a dramatic televised announcement of the IPL, attended by the same superstars withheld from India's team for the Twenty20 World Cup. He promised a six-week tournament in April 2008 with prize money of $3 million – before he had even sold the television rights.

Influenced as always by American sport, Modi turned the franchise bids and the subsequent player auctions into dramatic television. He managed to get a Bollywood presence into each bid, with the sole exception of low-key Rajasthan Royals, whose ownership was led by a shrewd expatriate, Manoj Badale. The BCCI made deals with seventy-seven major Indian and overseas cricketers to play for the franchise that bid for them successfully. The Rajasthan Royals had studied *Moneyball*, Michael Lewis's bestselling study of the financial and playing success of the unfashionable Oakland Athletics in major League baseball. At auction, Badale went for value-for-money players. Even at his reserve price of $450,000, Shane Warne was in that category, as player and captain. The top price was paid for India's winning Twenty20 World Cup captain, M. S. Dhoni, at $1.5 million by Chennai Super Kings. Again on the American model, a draft sold off the best uncapped under-19 Indian players for $50,000 each. This launched the career of one Virat Kohli.[10]

The new competition was an almost instant success. Expecting a loss of $4 million in its first year, IPL broadcaster Sony made a profit of $75 million and agreed to raise their payment to BCCI by a further $1.6 billion for the remaining nine years. Pawar, who was now combining (against ICC rules) the roles of BCCI president and food and agriculture minister, hailed the success of the IPL as an advertisement for modern India (under his government, of course.)[11] The defining innings of the first season was 158 off just 73 balls, with 10 fours and 13 sixes, by Brendon McCullum of New Zealand, for Kolkata. But the first winners were the underrated Rajasthan Royals. Badale hailed his captain, Warne: 'His cricketing acumen was extraordinary. His captaincy was a combination of meticulous planning and gut instinct.'[12]

Instantly the IPL affected virtually every other Test-playing country. Imitators appeared quickly – the Big Bash League in Australia, the Caribbean Super League and the Bangladesh Premier League. The Pakistan Super League thrived in the UAE, where, like the national side, it had been exiled after the terrorist attack on the Sri Lankan team in Lahore in 2009.

T20 facilitated a huge expansion of cricket to new countries and new populations, especially women.* It made all forms of cricket, including long-form versions, more exciting as players transferred to them the T20 skills they had made part of their routine. Critics accused T20 of lowering standards of play. It actually drove them

---

* The boundaries were shortened for the women's form, to facilitate the fast scoring and six hits, which were the prime viewer attractions for T20 – and the main determinant of winning. The same was done for the Hundred, England's answer to India's success with the IPL T20 franchise.

upwards, through the concentration and intensity of the new format, and the need for batters, bowlers and fielders to maximise the reward from every delivery.

England's immediate problems with the IPL centred on their two troubled stars, Kevin Pietersen and Andrew 'Freddie' Flintoff. Already semi-detached from the rest of their team through their celebrity status, they attracted strong bids. Distraction from the auction was blamed for their performance as part of an England side who were bowled out for 51 in the first Test of the 2008–09 series against West Indies. As if they had learned nothing from the Packer reverse in the High Court, the ECB tried to ban centrally contracted players from joining the IPL, and then demanded that they return from it by the end of April (then still the start of the English season), although the IPL still had weeks to run in May.[13] England then made a disastrous attempt to create a competing lucrative motive for their players to stay at home. This involved accepting a huge offer from Allen Stanford to stage a one-off match between England and his largely West Indian Superstars team. Stanford proved himself in succession a vulgarian, a sexist and a fraud.[14]

In 2021, the ECB took a second stab at creating a money-making domestic alternative to the IPL and its successor leagues, in the form of the Hundred, a format of 100-ball innings, delivered by bowlers five balls at a time or in ten-ball 'stints'. The disappearance of the 'over' was part of an avalanche of marketing babble, which infuriated traditionalists. We discuss the impact of the Hundred in the course of the next two chapters, as dispassionately as we feel able.[15]

A T20 playing revolution

Long-form cricket had traditionally encouraged batters who could score runs in a long innings without undue risk. The transformation to cricket of 40 or 50 overs an innings rewarded batters who could take as many singles and twos as possible. A run a ball (six an over), plus any wides or no-balls, nearly always generated a winning score. A run a ball – 120 (with the odd extra from a wide or no-ball) – soon proved a very poor score in T20.

The side that generated the most sixes and fours from their 120 balls were nearly always the winners. Much value was placed in T20 cricket on '360-degree' batters, who could score boundaries in any part of the field, although the first to claim the title, Tillakaratne Dilshan of Sri Lanka – inventor of the deliberate scoop over the wicket-keeper – predated the format in the 1990s and 2000s. Exponents of the reverse sweep were favoured by T20, but this shot was older still, counter-intuitively credited to Pakistan's ultra-defensive Hanif Mohammad as far back as the 1960s.

In fielding, T20 shifted emphasis from catching – and close catchers virtually disappeared – and rewarded ground fielding. With fine margins of victory and defeat in 20-over matches, saving runs off every ball delivered became imperative.

For bowlers, T20 restored some reward for taking wickets compared to 40- or 50-over cricket. Bowling sides were even less likely to dismiss all their opponents. But a bowler's wicket automatically denied opponents any runs from the delivery that captured it, and brought in a new batter who would be less likely to score boundaries off the next deliveries he or she faced. The most unexpected winners from T20 were wrist-spinners. By tradition, they had been shunned in limited-over cricket as too expensive (for all the evidence to the contrary of Pakistan's Abdul Qadir and his disciple Mushtaq Ahmed). In T20 cricket, leg-spinners became the most sought-after bowlers. Except in the closing overs when batters took on the risk of trying to club sixes, they were the hardest bowlers to 'line up' for boundaries and those most likely to reduce the rate of scoring by taking a wicket.[16]

T20 also generated a demand for data that spread out into other formats as well as club, college and school cricket. The sport has been profoundly influenced by the application of expertise and technology, much of it from disciplines far removed from cricket.* Systems designed to track the paths of missiles and ordnance were used to capture those of cricket balls, enabling the reviewing of on-field decisions.

The IPL transformed the economics of world cricket and the balance of power within it. Before its arrival, domestic first-class cricket was kept afloat by its cross-subsidy from international cricket. To make a worthwhile living from the game, players everywhere had to be selected for international cricket and keep on terms with the domestic clubs that alone made them eligible for selection. After the IPL and its imitators, domestic clubs remained in crisis – but they lost their economic hold on their best players, because they no longer needed representative international cricket.

In 2016, the Federation of International Cricketers' Associations (FICA) found that outside the Big Three of England, Australia and India, players were better off with contracts in the IPL and either the Big Bash or the Caribbean Premier League than they would be for playing a full schedule of international matches for their countries. In 2018–19, FICA identified 541 players with short-format contracts overseas with no need for earnings from international cricket. The ICC had already yielded to the top players at the end of 2017, when they left a gap of two months in the forthcoming Future Tours Programme to accommodate the IPL. Henceforward, international cricket, previously played continuously, was reduced to ten months a year. Apart from the World Cup in June 2019 there was no month between November 2018 and March 2020 without a short-format franchise league in progress.[17]

---

* In 1997, statistical expertise finally produced a solution – the Duckworth-Lewis-Stern method, named for its creators and its later custodian, Steven Stern – to a problem that had vexed one-day cricket since its inception: how to create a fair result when play was curtailed.

When the pandemic struck in early 2020 it brought Tests and one-day internationals to a halt, although England later hosted Tests against Pakistan and the West Indies under quarantine conditions. T20 leagues continued in six countries, including India, Australia and England.

Repeatedly, the best international stars abandoned bilateral series by their countries, especially the poorly remunerated West Indians. South Africa were also badly hit: they lost their first-choice pace attack for their bilateral ODI series against Pakistan in April 2021. Recently, they sent what was described as a third eleven to a series in New Zealand: their captain had never played a Test match. To South Africa's immense credit, they did not lose sight of the importance of Test cricket, becoming world Test champions in 2025. The IPL and its imitators also created a new market for the coach. Mahela Jayawardene and Stephen Fleming, former captains of their countries, have made their coaching careers in the IPL rather than in international and first-class cricket.[18]

Below-strength teams for bilateral series outside the Big Three obviously reduced their appeal for live spectators and, even more importantly, for television. Test series had already seen a general reduction from five to three matches: more and more were reduced to two, even those that determined points in the World Test Championship, because television companies would not bid enough for them.

In the early stages of the IPL, Test and ODI performances were the main identifier of the 'marquee players' who attracted the highest bids. But in less than ten years, franchise clubs were offering new pathways to talented players outside international cricket and the domestic clubs that fed it.

By ending Indian cricket's dependence on international revenues, the IPL consolidated India's dominance over the ICC as paymaster rather than a profit-sharing partner. Before the IPL the BCCI had derived only 2 per cent of its broadcast revenues from domestic sources. After ten years, the IPL was earning the BCCI well over two-thirds of those revenues. Income from ICC events was puny in comparison.[19]

In many ways the financial success of Indian cricket was welcome. Sadly, however, India has used its economic dominance to flex political muscle, opening itself up to criticisms that it has exploited its influence with the ICC to make arbitrary changes to tournament rules at the expense of other countries.

Chapter 34

CRICKET REBORN

In this penultimate chapter, we look at the forces that have led cricket to make a full circle and those that may bring it to a full stop.

Commercial profit-making cricket, driven by media revenues, will dominate the game for a long time. We are not as gloomy as some commentators about the consequences. But major costs and risks to cricket lie ahead at this point of the circle.

The biggest of these arise from extreme weather events and environmental degradation, which could render cricket literally unplayable by many of its devotees. Other risks are more insidious. Cricket's success in generating television and media makes it a competitor to every other form of entertainment. This has generated an increasingly desperate search for novelty by which to keep viewers engaged, with distinctive identifying features being wiped out.

We began with the earliest recorded matches in Georgian England between teams of itinerant players with rich owners or commercial sponsors. They attracted people into organised spaces to watch entertainment, to sell goods (principally food and drink) and services (mainly betting), and they had a symbiotic relationship with the media (then in the form of local newspapers).

This model persisted for about a century and a half. Then in the early Victorian age, we saw cricket acquire a different purpose and structure. This began in English public schools, founded or refounded to educate the sons of families with new wealth from industry and commerce (and offering them, thanks to trains, a safe way to send them away from home for months at a time). The heads of these families wanted their sons to keep their wealth intact, and not to lose it in the aristocratic manner from drinking, gambling and whoring. Cricket kept boys on school property, away from these three sources of temptation.

From there it was a short step to character-building. The game became a training ground for manly chaps to take up responsible positions in English social life and overseas, and to inspire respect and obedience in the lower orders. At their best, the ethics of nineteenth-century cricket embraced unselfishness, personal honesty, fairness, respect for opponents, and the prevalence of law over power and status. At their worst, they became overlain with snobbery, patriarchy, imperialism and racism.

In this era, cricket's governors beat back a series of upstart commercial entrepreneurs through the recruitment of W. G. Grace, the first international sporting icon. From their chosen instrument, a private members' club, they exported long-form versions of cricket to Britain's Empire. These versions happened to be well-suited to their long leisure hours, but they also provided a rationale for the cult of amateurism. The governors were astute enough to control the definition of 'first-class' cricket, to reserve it for their own chosen formats and to ensure that these were the ones most covered by the press. First-class cricket's diversity of skills, entertainment, drama and aesthetics, supported by brilliant writers, commentators and analysts, helped to prolong its life long after it became commercially unviable. It remained at the apex of cricket in every major cricket-playing nation even after breaking free of English tutelage.

But this structure of cricket is today clinging on to life and almost all forms of it are dependent on the bounty of commercial cricket.

The IPL and its imitation leagues have completed a return to the way organised cricket began – as a commercial entertainment built on hired performers with an ancillary function of selling goods and services and in a symbiotic relationship with the media. The scale of their activities is vastly greater than their distant predecessors and their centre of gravity has shifted to India from England. The re-commercialisation of cricket has turned it into a global sport, which its traditional administrators hardly attempted. It generates by far the greatest share of the sport's value, far ahead of live spectatorship, club membership, and playing or teaching the game.

In 2025, the data-gatherer Statista projected the total revenues from global sport at $118 billion. Exactly half would be derived from association football. American football would generate $29 billion, baseball $14 billion, basketball $12 billion.[*,1]

The same source projected the global revenues of cricket for 2025 at $3.8 billion, of which nearly two-thirds was derived from India alone.[2] As many as 90 per cent of all global cricket fans were Indian and that takes no account of expatriate Indians following the game.[3]

Cricket is, however, second only to association football in its numbers of global followers.[4] Organised cricket is now played in well over a hundred countries, and in significant numbers by women as well as men. It has many domestic and international contests but generates about one-eighth of the revenues of American football, a sport almost confined to one country and reliant on one major league.

Counter-intuitively, American sports may benefit from their international isolation and the strong loyalties they build up from repeated contests between the major domestic teams.[5] That feeds their power to generate media income and sponsorship. That is where value lies in all major sports. For all that live spectatorship still generates significant revenue for major events and their organisers, its main function is to provide a backdrop for the media audience of sport.

---

[*] All estimates of the global value of sports are contestable: in our selections we have done our best to compare like-with-like and assess cricket's order of magnitude as a global sport.

The dominance of India

India's cricket administration is the richest in the world by a distance. In its latest published year of account, 2022–23, its income was $781 million, swollen by a leap in revenues from the IPL.[6]

The ECB reported total revenues equivalent to just over $500 million in 2024. Three-quarters of this was derived from its sale of television rights, principally in the controversial agreement with Sky, which lasts until 2028.[7]

In 2023 Cricket Australia's total revenue was equivalent to US$213 million.[8] Then came Cricket South Africa, which had total revenue of $100 million in the year ended June 2024, boosted by three lucrative series against India.[9] The West Indies, New Zealand and Sri Lankan cricket administrations each reported revenues of about $60 million in their latest years of account.[10]

The Pakistan Cricket Board reported a big uplift in revenue for 2023, primarily due to being able to host international matches again after a long interval in exile. But total income was still only about $20 million.[11] In their latest annual reports the Irish and Afghan cricket boards showed total income of about $19 million and $10 million respectively,[12] and understandably were dependent on their share of the ICC's international revenues. We could find no reliable up-to-date revenues for the troubled Zimbabwe cricket administration.

These figures demonstrate a financial hierarchy in international cricket. India is at the apex, trailed by England and Australia. South Africa is a distant fourth. Sri Lanka, New Zealand and once-mighty West Indies are well down the field, but significantly better off than Pakistan and Bangladesh, which shows that a massive domestic following is no guarantee of major revenue. The newcomers to full member status, Ireland and Afghanistan, are financially dependent on the ICC.

Suppose, as many commentators believe, that T20 franchise leagues rather than national cricket administrations are the key to the future of cricket. In that case, India's dominance is even heavier.

A recent list put the total value of the IPL at just short of $11 *billion*. Its nearest follower was a virtual subsidiary of the IPL, the ILT20 established under the Emirates Cricket Board in 2023, valued at $15 *million*. That puts it ahead of the SA20, the Australian Big Bash League and the ECB's Hundred. The American entrant Major League Cricket – also with heavy Indian financial influence – was worth more than the established Pakistan Super League and Bangladesh Premier League.[13]

We have recorded past battles over the share-out of the revenues derived by the ICC from its 'bundles' of organised international cricket contests. The latest settlement, covering 2024 to 2027, produced a share of nearly 40 per cent, worth about $230 million, to India – the cricket administration with the least need of it. No other full member got 10 per cent or more. The England and Wales, Australian and Pakistan cricket administrations each got the next biggest shares, and there was a small uplift for South Africa, Sri Lanka, Bangladesh, New Zealand and West Indies. The associate members, now ninety-six in number – including the USA and China, the biggest targets for growing the game globally – shared less than $68 million, 11 per cent of the total.[14]

These figures show that India is the global cricket hegemon. The forms of cricket most likely to thrive in the future are those that adapt to the nexus of interests that shape Indian politics and society. Other forms of cricket will survive either by attracting a cross-subsidy from the profitable, Indian-dominated forms, or by developing niche markets that generate enough income to sustain them independently. Cricket lovers worldwide will have almost no influence over the game except as consumers of 'cricket products', especially those offered by franchises, which national administrations are forced to accommodate and strive to imitate.

Enter private equity

The IPL brought private equity into cricket many years after it had penetrated other sports. It has never looked back. Private equity concerns make money by the acquisition of assets that generate profits. Sporting assets are part of a revenue-generating portfolio in which their returns are assessed constantly against those of other possible acquisitions. If cricket yields less revenue than crematoriums, private equity will choose crematoriums and their owners will promote a different form of ashes.

As we have seen, the ECB looked enviously at the new stream of cricket investment generated by the IPL. It had failed to exploit the English introduction of T20 and allowed the benefits to pass into the hands of the counties. The board's solution was to create a new and unnecessary format – the Hundred* – with new teams separated from the counties, although using their grounds and the best of the talent they had developed. The ECB gave the Hundred a privileged place in the English cricket calendar, which marginalised first-class county and even Test match cricket, and downgraded the counties' hitherto successful T20 competition, the Blast.

The purpose of the Hundred was transparent – to create a cricket franchise product that could be sold to private investors.[15] This goal was delayed by various factors, including Covid, market uncertainties, a change of administration at the ECB and late resistance from the counties, who belatedly understood that the Hundred was a blueprint for reducing their number and eventually extinguishing the Championship. But in the 2025 season it finally succeeded in selling off a 49 per cent stake in the new teams it had created to private equity partners, with 51 per cent remaining with the team hosts.[16]

The sale generated a windfall of about £500 million for English and Welsh cricket, confounding pessimists who thought that the Hundred had been overvalued. The ECB announced a clever formula for sharing this out, calculated to disarm lingering opposition. A top slice worth £50 million would go to grass-roots cricket. Up to

---

* The Hundred format has not been followed in any other country, and we have found no evidence that it is played at recreational level or that it has inspired any playing innovations such as those produced by T20.

£225 million would be shared between all eighteen first-class counties and the MCC (as the host of the London Spirit squad at Lord's). Up to £150 million would go to the eleven counties that did not host a Hundred team. Any further proceeds would be shared by the eighteen counties and the MCC. The hosts were free to sell any of their 51 per cent stake in the Hundred team, but the formula again gave a preferential share of proceeds to recreational cricket and non-host counties.[17,*] All counties had to prioritise payment of debt (which had collectively reached about £200 million) or investment on infrastructure. They could not fritter their windfall away on players' or coaches' wages.[18]

In 2012, at the third attempt, the MCC had acquired for itself an impressive Royal Charter as a custodian of cricket's enduring values, roughly the same moment the club was throwing them overboard for good. Perhaps tactfully the Royal Charter was not mentioned as MCC members accepted the club link to the London Spirit franchise by a large majority.[19]

Some disappointed suitors for Hundred franchise teams expressed interest in acquiring established first-class counties. Hampshire and Northamptonshire were already privately owned, as was 90 per cent of Durham.[20] But it is fair to suggest that these suitors were not much interested in the counties' earnings from the first-class County Championship. They were looking at their share of revenue streams from other forms of cricket and the potential of their grounds as real estate.

There was applause for the financial gains to county cricket and the consequent relief to urgent debt problems. But these gains do nothing to secure a sustainable future for the county game.[21] Private equity and franchise cricket are here to stay. Sceptics point to the globalisation of franchise cricket, and the owners who have a stake in multiple teams in different locations. In particular, the Reliance

---

* The share-out excluded the national (formerly minor) counties and universities and colleges – and offered no specific benefits for women's cricket.

Group in India (run by the Ambani family) own the Mumbai Indians in the IPL as well as franchise teams in Cape Town, Abu Dhabi, New York and now the Oval. The biggest and costliest asset to owners of multiple teams is their players. They will want to use them throughout the year in all their franchises – and may consequently deny their services to their 'home' teams. This feeds into more general fears that franchise cricket is destroying the local roots and intimacy of cricket, and the ability of its devotees to control its future.

The brutal rejoinder to such criticisms is that if cricket fans are not willing to pay for the longer forms of the game, nor the organisations that sustain them and the incomes of their players, they should not be compelled to cross-subsidise them.

In some ways, cricket may be in better hands with commercial entrepreneurs than with its traditional administrators. They have an overwhelming imperative to achieve success on the field and off it. They cannot afford to let prejudice get in the way of playing talent – or spectatorship. They have a reputational incentive to stamp out any overt displays of discrimination or other antisocial behaviours in the teams that they own. If Yorkshire CCC had been commercially owned, it might have seen much earlier the senselessness as well as the repugnance of insulting and excluding the county's Asian-origin population.* Local roots are assets to any commercial sports team and reward private owners who nourish them. It is striking that none of the current Hundred franchise teams offers any form of membership or participation for supporters, especially children and young people. That may change when they acquire private investors, especially from the IPL. For example, no Hundred team has an academy or trials, but several IPL teams already offer academies in Britain.

---

* Yorkshire CCC in fact planned to go private in 2024 but this was abandoned under pressure from supporters.

T20 and passage into the international game

Twenty-over cricket has now established itself as the pathway for new nations to play international cricket, in preference to Test matches or 50-over one-day internationals. Indeed, it is unlikely that any new countries after Afghanistan and Ireland will invest in the domestic infrastructure required for Test match status even for the portion of the ICC's international competition receipts allocated to them by India.

By the end of 2023, 103 countries had played at least one men's T20 international match. Of these, seventy-seven had never played a longer-format international match. In women's cricket, the comparable figures are eighty-four countries that have played a T20 international and sixty-six that have never played anything longer.[22] Women's Test matches, never frequent, have virtually disappeared: just three were played in the whole of the calendar year 2024, compared to 171 women's one-day international matches and 176 women's T20 internationals in bilateral series alone.[23,*] At the beginning of 2025, England toured Australia in the Women's Ashes, playing one Test match (the first day-night Test at the MCG), three one-day internationals and three T20s. They lost every one, highlighting the biggest problem in international women's cricket: no one is a match for the Australians. It was therefore very welcome when they were knocked out of the 2025 Women's World Cup at the semi-final stage by eventual winners India.

Longer-format men's international cricket looked a little stronger in 2024. There were fifty-four Test matches played during the calendar year, of which forty-four counted for the World Test Championship. But sixteen of these matches were played in two-match series, giving

---

* Although no information is provided on the number of women's T20 matches played in multilateral tournaments and in preparation for the women's T20 World Cup that year.

players little chance to establish themselves and spectators no chance to appreciate the traditional ebb and flow of a Test series.[24,*]

The World Test Championship, launched in 2019 after long deliberations by the ICC to give purpose to the random bilateral encounters now customary between Test-playing countries, has suffered from a long timetable, lack of drama until its closing stages, a confusing points system, an unequal number of matches for contenders – and India's refusal to play Pakistan in the preliminary stages.

T20 cricket's advantage as an entry point for international cricket will be heightened by cricket's belated entry into the Olympic Games in 2028, a long-held ICC objective. T20 is the longest format for an international cricket competition that can be accommodated in the span of the Olympic Games. There is conflicting evidence about whether Olympic exposure makes an enduring difference to participation and spectatorship in countries where a sport is not already popular.[†] What is certain is that in dozens of countries cricket will benefit from Olympic-related government support and funding, especially in the school system. Now all that support will flow into 20-over cricket.

'Planet Stopped Play'

Of all major sports, cricket is one of the most vulnerable to climate change – particularly extreme weather events and environmental degradation. This is especially true on the Indian subcontinent – the epicentre of cricket's following.

High-level cricket requires a large well-prepared grass surface. As these become more challenging to provide, we may see a reversion

---

[*] Although the number of men's international T20 matches is only an estimate.

[†] Contrast the optimism of the ICC in https://www.espncricinfo.com/story/cricket-at-la28-cricket-confirmed-as-one-of-five-new-sports-at-la28-1403570 with the pragmatic analysis of the 2024 Olympics by America's National Sporting Goods Association, which has good commercial reasons for estimating any Olympic effect on sales https://nsga.org/news/is-olympic-participation-bump-a-myth.

to matting wickets (which disappeared from first-class cricket in the 1960s) and artificial surfaces.

Cricket cannot be played anywhere when it is too wet. Rain cancellations not only wreck the joy of players and spectators (although many famous players have been glad to play cards in the pavilion),* but also affect television coverage and the resulting sponsorship, and with them the income on which cricket has become financially dependent.

The hours of play required for major matches heighten the environmental risks. Strenuous physical exertion and continuous concentration is harder in extreme heat. It affects everyone on the field, including the umpire, but is a special hazard to batters and wicketkeepers who must wear heavy protective gear.

Major cricket grounds are increasingly exposed to extreme weather events: Galle in Sri Lanka was the worst casualty, destroyed by the tsunami in 2004 and since rebuilt – on the same site. The historic Bourda cricket ground in Georgetown, Guyana is below sea level, and most of the grounds in Bangladesh – a country frequently affected by flooding – are less than 40 feet above it. Virtually every ground in the West Indies, especially on the smaller islands, is at risk from hurricanes, which have become more prevalent and violent.[25] In temperate England, Worcestershire are considering moving from their historic ground in New Road because of how frequently it floods.

Poor air quality is affecting more cricket matches, especially in India. During the 2020–21 England cricket tour of India, both sides were compelled to play a Test match for six hours a day in the Narendra Modi Stadium in Ahmedabad when the city's population was officially advised to stay indoors.

Adverse weather and environmental degradation hit poor cricket fans harder than rich ones, and the oldest and the youngest most of all. Since 2019, *Wisden* has carried an annual review of cricket and the environment, written by Tanya Aldred, co-founder of the Next

---

* Ray Illingworth and Brian Close of England, Everton Weekes of West Indies and Saleem Altaf of Pakistan were noted bridge players.

Test, a not-for-profit group who work to raise issues of climate change and cricket. In 2020 it recorded the impact on Australian cricket of 'the terrible trifecta of heatwaves, drought and bushfires', while a breakout section reported a T20 international in a smog-infested Delhi in which players vomited openly on the pitch.[26] However, no demonstration was more vivid than Glenn Maxwell's double century, which won Australia's World Cup match in 2023 against Afghanistan. He made the second half after collapsing in spasms in heat of 34°C and humidity of 84 per cent.

In England in 2023, Just Stop Oil disrupted the Lord's Ashes Test match. England's wicketkeeper-batter Jonny Bairstow tackled a protestor, prompting comments that it was the best catch he had made in the series.* Extinction Rebellion, environmental activists with their own cricket team, staged a week of peaceful protest. The guest at the *Wisden* dinner that year was the global historian Peter Frankopan. He gave a 'post-apocalyptic' warning of the existential threat to cricket from extreme weather events and atmospheric pollution, particularly in the West Indies, India, Pakistan and Bangladesh.[27]

A few national boards responded to the crisis,[28] as did some individual cricketers, the most prominent being the Australian captain, Pat Cummins. Cricket Australia took the lead in issuing guidelines and protocols for players in extreme playing conditions.[29] But the board had provoked Cummins' first display of activism, protesting against its long-time sponsor Alinta Energy, a company heavily based on coal and gas. It earned him sharp personal criticism for his own carbon-heavy life as an international cricketer.[30] Cummins rode out the attacks and now leads Cricket for Climate, mobilising prominent cricketers and promoting the installation of solar panels in clubs.[31]

No famous cricketer has yet followed his example in the Indian subcontinent, where cricket lovers are potentially a colossal and

---

* Just Stop Oil protestors were outdone as disruptors by the MCC members in the Long Room, who abused the Australians after the controversial run-out of none other than Bairstow.

transformative voting bloc. While in power in Pakistan, Imran Khan made much of his project to plant 10 billion trees,[32] but he is now imprisoned. In India, the Green party is politically insignificant, and there have been no attempts to mobilise cricket against the established political and industrial nexus that is making India (and its cricket) hotter and more polluted.

The ICC accepted as a prime sponsor the oil giant Aramco, one of the world's greatest single sources of carbon emissions and owned by the oppressive Saudi state.[33] Critics were not appeased by Aramco's provision of recycling machines at tournament grounds. They suggested that cricket had followed football, Formula 1 and golf into the giant Saudi sportswashing business.

Profit over principle

As we have seen, the ICC's overriding principle in the 2000s was to expand global cricket and its revenues regardless of politics. Climate change is far from the only issue where that policy has come under increasing criticism.

The ICC attracted protest when it relocated its global headquarters to Dubai in 2004, for financial reasons, and perhaps also for its fine hotels and retail outlets. It did not discuss Dubai's total absence of cricket heritage or real concerns over human rights violations including its laws criminalising same-sex relationships.[34] Any LGBTQ+ employees or visitors are advised not to make public their sexual orientation.[35]

The ICC's Anti-Discrimination Code resulted in a penalty for the West Indian fast bowler Shannon Gabriel for a homophobic remark to Joe Root.[36] But the ICC has taken no steps against the member nations that discriminate against LGBTQ+ people, such as Afghanistan, Bangladesh, Pakistan, Guyana, Barbados and several other island nations in the West Indies. Nor has the ICC responded to the pressures on Muslim cricketers and fans in India, especially Indian-held Kashmir, including persecution for supporting Pakistan.[37]

In Ukraine, where cricket had begun to thrive in part thanks to the pioneering efforts of a dedicated South African teacher and coach, Kobus Olivier, the ICC failed to cover itself in glory. In early 2022, Ukraine's cricket association was given real hope to believe that its bid for associate member status would succeed and bring ICC funding with it. However, the application was rejected outright after the second Russian invasion on the basis that cricket had become impossible in Ukraine (even though it was still being played in the unoccupied parts that Western leaders were visiting regularly). The ICC declined a proposal to give Ukraine a suspensory associate status, or to support cricket efforts by Olivier for displaced Ukrainian families in Croatia.

The ICC had already suspended Russia for administrative irregularities unconnected with the invasion. The perceived effect was to apply no penalty to cricket in the invader state but only in the invaded one – anticipating by some years the policy of the Trump administration.[38]

Saddest of all is the ICC's response to the extinction of women's cricket and the general oppression of women in Afghanistan under the Taliban. Admittedly the ICC faces a genuine dilemma with Afghan cricket.[39] It may well consider that any gesture on behalf of women's cricket will have no effect except to threaten the future of Afghan men's cricket. Yet such dilemmas confront all proponents of 'constructive engagement' with repressive or totalitarian regimes. It is fair to say that the ICC has so far shown neither achievement nor transparency in its dealings with Afghanistan.

In December 2024, the ICC unanimously elected thirty-six-year-old Jay Shah as its chairman. Shah is the son of India's home affairs minister, Amit Shah, the second-most powerful member of the ruling Bharatiya Janata Party. In *Wisden* 2025, Lawrence Booth wrote in his Editor's Notes that the appointment ratified India's total monopoly control over world cricket and that '2024 was the year cricket gave up any claim to being properly administered, with checks, balances, and governance for the many, not the few.'[40]

Chapter 35

DOES CRICKET MAKE MONEY TO EXIST OR EXIST TO MAKE MONEY?

This book appears on the centenary of the first edition of H. S. Altham's* *A History of Cricket*, the first general history of the game from its distant beginnings. It originated in a series of articles by Altham for *The Cricketer* magazine, founded and edited by Plum Warner, and bore a preface by Lord Harris.

The endorsement of Warner and Harris gave Altham's work the blessing of England's cricket establishment and made it the authorised version of cricket history. Harris's preface (after a tribute to himself) celebrated its moral influence on any young cricketer. 'If he will but absorb a hundredth part of the cricket lore that has been assembled in this work, then he has laid up for life a store of value to which he can revert in his dullest moments and find food for much interesting contemplation.'[1]

Neville Cardus praised the book with characteristic eloquence in the *Observer*, ending: 'The book is monumental – Mr Altham has done the game a valuable service. Here is the history of cricket we have been waiting for these many years – a thoughtful book and a charming.'[2]

---

* H. S. Altham 1888–1965 was a first-class cricketer, much decorated soldier, historian, housemaster and cricket coach at Winchester College, administrator, treasurer and president of MCC, Test selector, and held many other cricketing roles especially in youth cricket.

Altham, who had a distinguished First World War where he was awarded a DSO and a Military Cross, was anything but a conventional establishment figure. He was renowned for his integrity, empathy and breadth of intellectual interests. He was no advocate of hierarchy: after the Second World War, with the support of the Duke of Edinburgh, he worked prodigiously to bring cricket to less privileged schoolchildren. The book fully deserved its final tribute from Cardus: it combined scholarship with passion.

But it is instructive that such a well-rounded figure as Altham could produce to great acclaim a history of cricket that mentions only one woman, the mother of W. G. Grace, and only three individual cricketers who were not white: Ranjitsinhji (admitted to English cricket as an amateur and a dubious prince), and, glancingly, Learie Constantine and C. B. Llewellyn. It is a heavily Anglocentric history, with some justification on the international scene. When published, England had taken part in 143 of the 157 official Test matches then played, while the other fourteen were contested between the other two Test nations, Australia and South Africa. Three new Test countries were admitted in rapid succession after publication: the West Indies, New Zealand and India. Altham recorded the first English overseas cricket tour, to the USA and Canada in 1859, but neither country appeared in his index and there is no account of what happened to cricket there after the visitors went home.

To a contemporary reader, Altham's history of cricket in general is overweighted with the deeds of English amateurs, especially public schoolboys, Oxford and Cambridge Universities, and even social clubs. That remains so in the versions revised and expanded with the help of E. W. Swanton in 1938, 1948 and 1962.

That is no criticism of Altham. It is a mark of how much cricket has changed in the hundred years since his first edition and how it can no longer be understood in his terms.

Altham's book also has an optimism that now reads as out of place. It carries a sense of inevitable progress to better forms of cricket, as Whig historians such as G. M. Trevelyan traced Britain's progress from autocracy and conflict to constitution, consensus and order. Although it conveys some of the economic context, especially in the difference between north and south, it is above all a romantic history of a sport shaped by the individual deeds of great performers assisted by wise, disinterested administrators.

A glancing quotation about the visiting South Africans in 1912 celebrated the treatment of cricket 'as a game not as a business'.[3] Altham's conclusion was uplifting: 'Despite all the uncertainties and the discouragements which the war has brought us in its train, cricket has never meant more to Englishmen than it means today.' He then cited a long passage from the Scottish author Andrew Lang:

> It is simply the most catholic and diffused, the most innocent, kindly and manly of popular pleasures. It is a liberal education in itself and demands temper and justice and perseverance. There is more teaching in the playground than the schoolrooms, and a lesson better worth learning very often. For there can be no good or enjoyable cricket without enthusiasm – without sentiment, one may almost say: a quality that enriches life and refines it, gives it what life more and more is apt to lose, zest.[4]

A century on, any history of cricket has to record over one hundred territories contesting some form of international cricket rather than three. Just twelve of these are playing the first-class and Test matches that Altham put at the summit of the game. It must look at why cricket thrives in some while others turn into cricketing failed states. It has many more great players and deeds to record but must also confront deeper issues of class, race, gender and power politics, which Altham in his time could pass over. In 1926 Altham could not have foreseen the transformation of spectatorship of cricket by radio broadcasting, let alone cricket's dependency on media-generated revenues.

Of course he could not anticipate, even in his final edition, the shift in the balance of power in cricket governance to India.

After the Second World War, Altham became acutely aware that the model of English cricket that he celebrated in his original volume was under threat. He chaired one of the many committees of inquiry set up to arrest this. He would have known how much it was struggling in a new landscape of sport and recreation. But he could never have contemplated the present scale of the threat to first-class cricket worldwide, and its compulsion to accommodate forms of cricket that have reverted to commercial entertainment without the aesthetic and moral qualities he believed made cricket a force for higher civilisation.

Almost nobody wants to revert to the cricket culture that Altham celebrated in 1926, which was based in part on imperialism and patriarchy. Still fewer would lament the extraordinary achievements of the last century: above all the rise of new cricketing nations; the enfranchisement of the women's game; the collapse of South African apartheid; the emergence of a brilliant new form of the game in the shape of one-day cricket.

But there was wisdom in Altham. He loved and respected cricket. He saw it as an end in itself, with its own values and institutions, independent of not just the state but also the market. This approach marks him out from the latest generation of cricket administrators. To explain the importance of this change, let's compare two Ashes series a century apart.

The attack on Test cricket

In 1926, the year Altham's history was published, Australia toured England. It was in some ways a disappointing series. The early Tests, then fought over an inadequate three days, were ruined by rain. In consequence the Ashes were still at stake when the teams met for the fifth and final match at the Oval in mid August. It was declared a timeless Test, meaning that it would be played to a finish in order to secure a result.

With England behind the game, Jack Hobbs and Herbert Sutcliffe came together on a sticky wicket (i.e. drying after heavy rain) at the start of the second innings. Showing skill, restraint and above all extraordinary discipline, the pair put on 172 before Hobbs was dismissed for exactly 100. The left-arm spinner Wilfred Rhodes, then forty-eight years old, ran through the Australian batting in the second innings, taking four wickets at little cost.

Herbert Strudwick was England's wicketkeeper, chosen above other candidates who were better batters. One hundred years later, England disastrously plumped for Jamie Smith, selected in preference to a superior wicketkeeper in the shape of Ben Foakes, on the grounds that he was a better batter. Smith, either the second or third best keeper in his county team according to opinion, dropped a crucial catch that may have affected the result of the second Test and therefore the series.

The decision by England selectors to choose Will Jacks, a part-time bowler who could also bat, as principal spinner sprang from a similar faulty logic. England selectors were resorting to bits-and-pieces players, who can be highly effective in one-day matches but proved hopelessly adrift in Test matches, the highest and most exacting level.

Harry Brook may potentially be as gifted a batter as Hobbs. During England's Ashes tour he lacked the application, mental discipline, patience and technical ability to cope against world-class bowlers on difficult pitches in Test match conditions. Brook has excelled on easy surfaces against second-rate opposition generally with little at stake, as he finally demonstrated when he came good at Sydney in the final Test once the rubber was already decided.

England took a one-day side to Australia. This helps to explain why one of the most talented teams to travel down under in recent decades lost the Ashes in the space of eleven days' play against a weakened Australian squad. But it is necessary to look deeper to identify the underlying causes of the debacle. We focus here on English cricket, but our conclusions apply to the game across the world.

Structural reasons for the Ashes fiasco

The Hundred was never primarily a cricketing project. From its inception, it functioned as a mechanism for the ECB to create ring-fenced assets that could be sold to external – largely overseas – investors. Former English cricket captain and *The Times* correspondent Michael Atherton was almost alone, early and consistently, in identifying this reality in Sky Sports commentary and his newspaper columns.

While much of the cricket media accepted the ECB's stated aims such as 'new audiences', 'simplification' and 'family appeal', Atherton repeatedly pointed out that the Hundred franchises were designed to be clean, tradable entities: centrally owned, brand-led and detached from English cricket's traditional ecosystem.

Events since have borne this out in the shape of sustained private equity interest, and the ECB's explicit prioritisation of investor confidence over domestic balance. The cost of this financialisation has been the ruination of the English summer. To make space for the Hundred (August exclusivity clauses were written into the calendar), the County Championship was pushed to the margins of the season – April, early May and September – when pitches are green, crowds are sparse, and conditions distort both performance and development.

The Championship was reduced to a background activity. Narratives were fragmented, achievements devalued and performances that once shaped Test selection became statistical noise. That displacement broke the pathway from county cricket to the England Test team. Selectors were left with a domestic structure that no longer reliably produced or revealed Test-ready players.

Into this vacuum stepped Rob Key (appointed managing director of England men's cricket in 2022) and coach Brendon McCullum. They attempted to make a virtue of necessity. With the traditional pipeline weakened, selection increasingly leaned on data analysis and player attributes in terms of technique and physical stature. (The early and persistent selections of Zak Crawley and Shoaib Bashir being examples of this approach.)

With first-class cricket no longer providing a robust proving ground, selectors were forced to infer readiness to play at the highest level. Advocates of 'Bazball' (England men's playing style under Brendon 'Baz' McCullum) presented this method as a conceptual revolution. In reality it reflected evidential poverty, with the results on display in the poor technique and lack of strategic intelligence displayed by England players in the 2025 Ashes fiasco.

This is not the first time that money has corrupted cricket. In the Georgian era, aristocrats opened the way to match-fixing by gambling huge sums. Before the First World War, as we have seen, plutocrats employed their vast wealth to ensure racist South Africa foundation status at the heart of the ICC. Today private equity moguls threaten the future of Test matches and the first-class game by promoting homogenous, globalised franchise cricket.

The refusal to confront reality

Sir Andrew Strauss, one of only three England captain to secure Ashes victories both at home and away, is the nearest contemporary equivalent to past grand viziers of cricket such as Lord Harris or Gubby Allen. His High-Performance Review was presented in 2022 as a serious examination of the future of first-class cricket and England's Test performance. It followed the now-familiar pattern: managerial language, structural tinkering and an avoidance of the fundamental issue that county cricket has been subordinated to franchised formats.

Sir Andrew has been involved in providing consultancy advice to potential investors in the Hundred. It is perhaps little surprise that the Strauss review did not recommend restoring Championship primacy or reclaiming the English summer for first-class cricket. Strauss's address to the MCC in 2023 on the 'Spirit of Cricket' became an opportunity for him to promote franchise virtues of flexibility, innovation and commercial alignment rather than to defend the domestic foundations of the game, or indeed anything resembling what Altham would have understood as the spirit of cricket.

The MCC's role is telling. For over 200 years, it served as the guardian of the Laws and the moral authority of the game. That authority rested on independence and a sense of history. Today, Lord's is treated primarily as a commercial asset – a venue competing in the same marketplace as Edgbaston, Old Trafford and Trent Bridge. The MCC – now a club where the wealthy are encouraged to jump the membership queue – no longer guards the guardians. The last institutional brake on the commercialisation of the game has gone.

The future of the county game

With Test grounds emerging as standalone commercial entities, counties have become tenants of diminishing importance. The trajectory is already visible: county cricket pushed to outgrounds and secondary venues; major stadiums reserved for Tests and franchise tournaments.

An example of this cultural and institutional hollowing-out is Warwickshire County Cricket Club. For much of its history, Edgbaston was the home of Warwickshire cricket, held in trust for the county and its people. The ground itself was gifted by the Calthorpe Estate explicitly for the benefit of Warwickshire, a civic and sporting inheritance rooted in place, identity and continuity. The ground existed to serve the county club, not the other way around. That relationship has now been inverted.

In recent years, Warwickshire has progressively diminished its own identity in favour of venue-led and franchise branding. The club rebranded Edgbaston as a standalone 'stadium', marketing it as an events and entertainment asset rather than a county cricket ground. Warwickshire cricket became secondary – sometimes barely visible – within its own home.

What was once a county club with a ground has become a ground with a county cricket club attached. Warwickshire is not an anomaly but a warning. It shows how easily historic identity can be sacrificed when administrators cease to understand their duty as custodians.

The ground gifted for the people of Warwickshire is now leveraged for franchises and corporate objectives, while the county itself is quietly diminished. In this sense, Edgbaston is a monument to English cricket's loss of memory. In chapter 4 we explained how in the early Victorian era cricket became part of what the political philosopher David Marquand has called the public domain (see p. 30). Today what was once common property is being handed over to private equity. This is not a problem uniquely faced by English cricket. There are now moves to sell the Australian 'Big Bash' to private equity. Earl Eddings, former chairman, has warned such a step would kill off Test cricket. The Australian cricket writer Gideon Haigh famously asked: 'Does cricket make money in order to exist, or does it exist in order to make money?'[5] Again, this is not a problem faced by cricket alone. Water privatisation has led to collapse of standards and degradation of infrastructure amid a drive for private profit at the expense of the public interest.

First-class cricket (deliberately slighted as 'red ball' by those who want to destroy it) may well survive, but stripped of prestige, audience and consequence. We are not merely losing structure but also meaning. The continuity between history, place and aspiration has been broken. Cricket is increasingly managed as content rather than culture. The silence surrounding this decline is structural. Much of the cricket media is financially or professionally entangled with the Hundred: through rights, consultancy, coaching roles and access.

In his masterpiece *Beyond a Boundary*, C. L. R. James argued that cricket is 'so organised that at all times it is compelled to reproduce the central action which characterises all good drama from the days of the Greeks to our own: two individuals are pitted against each other in a conflict that is strictly personal but no less strictly representative of a social group'.[6]

Cricket, wrote James, 'is structurally perfect. The total spectacle consists and must consist of a series of individual, isolated episodes, each in itself completely self-contained ... Within the fluctuating interest of the rise or fall of the game as a whole, there is this unending series of events, each single one fraught with immense possibilities of expectation and realisation.'

At the heart of this dramatic contest, he said, is 'the measured ritualism and the varied and intensive physical activity which take place within it'. For James (as surely for Altham), cricket was an art form. Today's cricket administrators, dazzled by financial deals, are reducing the game to a series of packaged and forgettable short-form encounters.

Re-embracing complexity?

We have followed two cycles in the history of cricket. It began as a short simple game and was slowly transformed into a long intricate one. Then under market pressures it has reinvented itself as a short and simple one again. Today we have a market full of identical 20-over contests with the same recurring casts of travelling stars. We are not convinced however that simplicity is a virtue in modern sport.

To a non-initiate, American football is a highly complex, mysterious and frankly dull game, with short bursts of play and long stoppages. But that is part of its appeal. It thrives on amateur analysis, punditry and argument.

Long-form cricket did not lose its following because it was too complex. With some help from the media, it engaged populations that were far less educated than today's. Illiterate followers could appreciate the contests, decisions and dramas taking place during a match – and create and influence them as players. The same was true of children. Without necessarily understanding all the Laws and tactics, they knew enough to follow the fortunes of individual players and teams, and to understand the subtleties of what their heroes were trying to achieve during the ebb and flow of a match. The complexity of long-form cricket generated amateur expertise and punditry, and built engagement. The marketers of the Hundred made a fundamental error in assuming that a crudely simple version of cricket was appealing and necessary for children.[7]

Nominally a team game, cricket is actually a sequence of solo actions: bowler bowls, batter receives, fielder reacts. Different skills and plans are required throughout, and fresh phases of play influence objectives and methods. All these properties are present in more variety in first-class, long-form cricket than in shorter forms. In particular, the first-class game allows for the possibility of a draw, which widens the range of skills and counterskills that players must deploy. In this way, first-class cricket creates the possibility of heroic roles for different types of cricketers. Old photographs of first-class cricket teams show a far wider range of physical ability than today. Such diversity lasted until at least the 1960s, when all players were expected to move athletically in the field.

Cricket's very sophistication and strangeness seem to render it well-equipped to help disadvantaged children. Apart from Freddie Flintoff's *Field of Dreams*, we have heard testaments to cricket from Syrian refugee children in the inspiring Alsama Project in Lebanon[8] and exiled children in Croatia from war-damaged Ukraine.[9] Earlier in our careers, we played against the Compton Homies, a team formed from disaffected youngsters in a lawless district of Los Angeles.[10] More recently we have played tapeball cricket on hillsides in the Hindu Kush and on the banks of the Indus River. In their entertaining odyssey through Latin America, Timothy Abraham and James Coyne discovered the special role of cricket in the rehabilitation work of the Refugio project.[11] Cricket could well circle back to its 'character-building' role once again.

We still obstinately hope that the authorities everywhere will promote the richness of first-class domestic cricket. Indian novelist Timeri Murari gave the world one of the finest expressions of that richness in his 2012 novel *The Taliban Cricket Club*:

> Why is the Taliban promoting cricket? You can't play cricket without understanding the essence of the game. Do the Talib know that they're encouraging the kinds of behaviour they

have been trying to suppress all these years? Because they are presenting us with the freedom to express who we are, to discover ourselves, to express our defiance on a playing field.[12,*]

---

[*] Timeri's novel starkly conveys the oppression of women in the first period of Taliban rule. This is even worse under the current one. The novel should be compulsory reading for the ICC.

ACKNOWLEDGEMENTS

Special thanks are due to our Editor Olivia Bays at Elliott & Thompson for making this book into a manageable length without losing any important or especially cherished content. And also to Tanya Aldred, Rob Smyth, Pippa Crane, Andrew Brassleay, Peter Moorby and Cathy Heath for essential fact-checking, editorial services, and meeting the demands of the index. At the MCC, Curator Neil Robinson and Librarian Alan Rees were as helpful as always and as resourceful in tracking exotic requests. So were all the staff at the London Library, whose unique subject catalogue places Cricket next to Cremation and therefore houses much Ashes literature. Ehsan Mani, former Chairman, gave us a generous look at his private collection of ICC papers, especially generous since we have not always been kind to the ICC.

We are conscious that we have been living through a golden age of cricket writing. The history of the game is being rewritten by a generation of brilliant and dedicated writers, examining the sport through the lens of race, class and imperialism, and climate. We have plundered much of their work. Some of these writers have been especially kind with their comments. We thank in particular André Odendaal, Richard Parry, Raf Nicholson, David Woodhouse, Roger Packham, John Goulstone, Mihir Bose, Robert Wainwright, Nicholas Brookes, Peter Della Penna, James Coyne, Charles Lysaght, Tim Kavanagh, Stephen Chalke, and Afzal Ahmed of Karachi, rightly nicknamed 'the Walter Cronkite of Pakistan cricket'. We alone remain responsible for errors of judgment and fact.

Acknowledgements

In this book we took inspiration and at times sourced material from the guests in podcast *Oborne and Heller on Cricket*, hosted by the Chiswick Calendar through which all the episodes can be heard (https://chiswickcalendar.co.uk/category/news-and-features/guest-blog/blogs-podcasts/oborne-heller-on-cricket/).We therefore thank our producers, Bridget Osborne and James Willcocks, especially for their interventions against obscure cricketing details. We also thank Roger Alton, sports columnist of *The Spectator*, for his appearances as a substitute host, especially for his insights into America's heritage of sporting literature and culture.

We thank our guests, some of whom had a second or even third innings. In order of first appearance: Nathan Leamon, former England data analyst and novelist; Peter Gibbs, first-class cricketer for Oxford University and Derbyshire, later novelist and screenwriter; Mickey Arthur, commentator and cricket coach; Stephen Chalke, historian of English county cricket and founder of Fairfield Books; ICC umpire Simon Taufel; Ehsan Mani, former chairman of ICC and Pakistan Cricket Board; cricket lover and Somerset supporter Lord (Jeffrey) Archer of Weston-super-Mare; comedian John Cleese, another Somerset supporter; former cricket captain and prime minister of Pakistan, Imran Khan; journalist, author and broadcaster Pat Murphy; journalist and sports historian Mihir Bose; Neil Robinson, curator MCC collections and heritage; Clare Connor, former England women captain and later senior administrator at ECB and ICC and first female president of MCC; Simon Hughes and Huw Turbervill of *The Cricketer*; Qamar Ahmed, doyen of Pakistan cricket writers; Indian cricket historian Prashant Kidambi; cricketer and human rights lawyer, Clive Stafford Smith; Timothy Abraham and James Coyne, recorders of cricket in Latin America and other distant (from England) locations and participants; Sana Mir, former captain of Pakistan women; Jill Rutter, public servant and cricket lover; Mo Allie, South African cricket writer; historian Arunabha Sengupta; Ted Dexter of Sussex and England (his last interview); David Leggat, New Zealand sportswriter (later tragically drowned);

Henry Blofeld; Fraser Simm, historian of Scots cricket; Lord (Peter) Hain, anti-apartheid protestor, later cabinet minister; Peter Della Penna, reporter and analyst of American cricket; Nicholas Brookes, historian of Sri Lankan cricket; Richard Verity, director of cricket at the Alsama Project in Lebanon; three young Alsama cricketers, Louay, Maram and Amani; Mahela Jayawardene, Sri Lankan master batsman and later captain; Ramachandra Guha, cricket historian; Andrew Hignell, recorder and historian of cricket in Glamorgan and Wales; Gowhar Geelani, cricket journalist and author in Kashmir; Andy Flower, Zimbabwe cricketer, protestor against the Mugabe régime, England cricket coach; Najum Latif, Pakistan cricket historian and personal friend of many great Pakistani players; Charles Lysaght, recorder of great or unusual moments in Irish cricket history; Athar Ali Khan, former international player for Bangladesh; Billy Cooper, professional trumpeter recruited by the Barmy Army; Ben Jones, collaborator with Nathan Leamon in showing influence of data on modern cricket; André Odendaal, former first-class cricketer and historian, restorer of records of cricketers who were victims of racism by the white masters of South African cricket; Rafaelle Nicholson, restorer of the 'lost' history of English women's cricket; Dame Angela Eagle MP and cricketer, victim in early life of sexism in cricket; Lonsdale Skinner, Surrey wicketkeeper whose career was blighted by racist episodes; Rob Eastaway, founder of the Googly community cricket initiative; Annie Chave, founder and editor of *County Cricket Matters*; Aslam Khota of South Africa, authority on the enduring legacy of racism in South African cricket; George Dobell, cricket journalist, anti-racism campaigner, co-founder Cricket Supporters Association; John Holder, Test match umpire; Lingard Goulding, Irish cricketer and educator; David Woodhouse, historian of West Indian cricket; Scyld Berry, author and journalist; Stuart Anthony and Chris Sherwood of the LGBTQ+ inclusive Graces Cricket Club; Micky Stewart, Surrey and England and later England cricket manager; Kobus Olivier, cricket coach in Ukraine, besieged in his home in Kyiv with his four dogs after the second Russian invasion; Matt

Thacker, managing editor of *The Nightwatchman* magazine; Ian Smith, dramatist, observer of influence of cricket on fellow dramatist Harold Pinter; Siddhartha Vaidyanathan, re-publisher of American Marxist Mike Marqusee's classic work, *War Minus The Shooting*; Jon Collett, advisor to the Pakistan Test team, now campaigning to save first-class cricket; Andy Nash, former board member of the ECB, now resisting its plans for the future of first-class cricket; Steven van Hoogstraten, former chairman of the Royal Dutch Cricket Association; Simon Heffer, author and historian, fighter against 'cricket pornography'; Alan Higham, cricket supporter and campaigner against the downgrading of first-class cricket; John McKenzie, dealer in cricket books and memorabilia; Mike Coward, Australian cricket historian and broadcaster; Sir Geoffrey Boycott, with cricket author Jon Hotten, his batting partner in the preparation of his memoir *Being Geoffrey Boycott*; SirWesley Hall, legendary West Indian fast bowler, who delivered the two most exciting overs in Test match history; Wendy Wimbush, former BBC scorer; Fernando Sugath and Will Dobson, who played cricket in a car park in Lebanon and other unlikely places, and their spectator, Tom Fletcher, former UK ambassador to Lebanon, and United Nations under-secretary-general for humanitarian affairs and emergency relief coordinator since 2024; Tom Greaves and Callum Widdows, captains of two thriving local community clubs and observers of the impact of cricket on wayward teenagers; Ed Smith, former England Test cricketer, later chief selector and now MCC president; Richard Parry, cricket historian helping to restore the narratives of the players excluded by racism; Aayush Puthran, cricket reporter and analyst and historian of Pakistan women's cricket; John Broom, author of studies of cricket in both world wars; Richard Sanders, historian of English football and how its organization and promotion made it a successful competitor to cricket; Tanya Aldred, journalist and co-founder of The Next Test; Russell Jackson, Australian journalist and recorder of the eccentric life of radical, groundbreaking cricket historian Major Rowland Bowen; James Harris, Glamorgan cricketer and chairman of the Professional Cricketers' Association. And (several repeat innings) Steven Lynch, obituarist of *Wisden Cricketers' Almanack*, and its editor, Lawrence Booth, who has turned the *Almanack*, of necessity, into a major work of social, economic and political history as well as cricket.

In other contexts, we benefited from extended contacts with Pakistani cricketers Misbah-ul-Haq, Younis Khan and Abdul Qadir, and Indian all-rounder Abid Ali. We thank them and all those above for their time and insights.

At the closing stages of the book Richard was laid up by a combination of arthritis, winter flu and a stroke. It was not much of a stroke, more a push to midwicket than a full-blooded straight drive, but it was a stroke for all that and a heavier burden than usual fell on Peter and Olivia to see the book through the last overs before close of play. The stroke teams at King's College and St Thomas' hospitals London enabled Richard to achieve any final work on it at all.

ENDNOTES

Introduction

1. Keith A. P. Sandiford, 'English Cricket Crowds During the Victorian Age', *Journal of Sport History*, vol. 9, no. 3 (1982), p. 8; https://www.jstor.org/stable/43609258
2. https://sideoncricket.blogspot.com/2019/11/county-championship-salary-cap.html#:
3. https://www.glassdoor.co.uk/Salary/Glamorgan-County-Cricket-Club-Salaries-E1819275
4. https://glamorgancricket.com/news/mipost-expand-partnership-with-glamorgan-to-become-a-principal-partner-of-the-club
5. https://en.wikipedia.org/wiki/2024_Rajasthan_Royals_season
6. https://www.espncricinfo.com/series/indian-premier-league-2024-1410320/rajasthan-royals-squad-1413568/series-squads
7. https://www.espncricinfo.com/cricketers/kunal-singh-rathore-1339031
8. https://www.bbc.co.uk/news/world-asia-india-61793888
9. https://www.business-standard.com/cricket/ipl/ipl-2024-auction-rajasthan-royals-entire-squad-and-playerssalary-123121801274_1.html
10. https://www.thetimes.com/sport/cricket/article/ipl-auction-mitchell-starc-lands-record-235m-contract-9vwz8xd6p

Chapter 1: Born in Obscurity

1. H. S. Altham, *A History of Cricket: Volume 1* (Allen and Unwin, 1926), p. 18
2. Rowland Bowen, *Cricket: A History of Its Growth and Development Throughout the World* (Eyre and Spottiswode, 1970), p. 29; Derek Birley, *A Social History of English Cricket* (Aurum, 1999) pp. 3–4
3. https://www.nationalarchives.gov.uk/currency-converter/. Unless otherwise stated, all future conversions into modern purchasing power derive from the same source.
4. Bodleian Library MS. Bodl. 264, pt. I, fol.022r, Bodleian Libraries, University of Oxford; https://digital.bodleian.ox.ac.uk/objects/8d17bc13-14b6-4a56-b3b5-d2e1a935c60d/surfaces/13215f56-47c3-48ec-8b70-d734e6975457/
5. Rafaelle Nicholson, *Ladies and Lords: A History of Women's Cricket in Britain* (Peter Lang, 2019), p. 25

6   Birley, *Social History of English Cricket*, p. 3
7   Bowen, *Cricket*, p. 30
8   https://www.independent.co.uk/sport/cricket/french-hamlet-claims-to-be-site-of-the-first-recorded-cricket-match-10478261.html
9   Bowen, *Cricket*, pp. 29–36
10 https://exploremyindia.in/amp/cricket-history/
11 Bowen, *Cricket*, pp. 36 and 261; Birley, *Social History of English Cricket*, p. 5
12 Altham, *History of Cricket*, p. 22; https://www.thecollector.com/history-of-cricket-worlds-second-most-popular-sport/
13 Birley, *Social History of English Cricket*, p. 10
14 Bowen, *Cricket*, pp. 41–2
15 Birley, *Social History of English Cricket*, pp. 4–5; Bowen, *Cricket*, p. 36
16 Brendan Cooper, *Echoing Greens: How Cricket Shaped the English Imagination* (Constable, 2024), pp. 43–8
17 David Underdown, *Start of Play: Cricket and Culture in Eighteenth-Century England* (Allen Lane, 2000), p. 4
18 https://www.cricketcountry.com/articles/death-of-jasper-vinall-earliest-known-instance-of-cricket-claiming-a-life-486328
19 Timothy J. McCann, *Sussex Cricket in the Eighteenth Century*, (Sussex Record Society, 2004) p. xxxix
20 Birley, *Social History of English Cricket*, p. 7
21 Bowen, *Cricket*, pp. 45 and 262
22 Birley, *Social History of English Cricket*, p. 8; Bowen, *Cricket*, p. 262
23 https://www.historic-uk.com/CultureUK/The-Stagecoach/
24 Bowen, *Cricket*, p. 42
25 Bowen, *Cricket*, pp. 42–3
26 Birley, *Social History of English Cricket*, pp. 8–10; Bowen, *Cricket*, p. 38
27 Dennis Brailsford, *British Sport: A Social History* (Lutterworth Press, 1997), p. 35
28 John Major, *More Than a Game: The Story of Cricket's Early Years* (Harper Perennial, 2007) p. 36
29 Ibid; Bowen, *Cricket*, pp. 47, 50, 72 and 262–3
30 Bowen, *Cricket*, p. 47
31 Birley, *Social History of English Cricket*, p. 12

Chapter 2: The Rise of the Leisure Class

1   Roger Munting, *An Economic and Social History of Gambling in Britain and the USA* (Manchester University Press, 1996), pp. 10–15
2   T. H. White, *The Age of Scandal: An Excursion Through a Minor Period* (Faber, 2010), p. 89
3   Michael Atherton, *Gambling: A Story of Triumph and Disaster* (Hodder & Stoughton, 2006), p. 178
4   Roy Porter, *English Society in the Eighteenth Century* (Penguin Allen Lane, 1982) p. 254
5   For an illuminating historical survey of match-fixing in all sports since ancient times, see Mike Huggins, 'Match-fixing: A Historical Perspective', *International*

Journal of the History of Sport, vol. 35, nos 2–3 (2018); https://insight.cumbria.ac.uk/id/eprint/4162/1/Huggins_MatchFixing.pdf

6 Duncan Stone, *Different Class: The Untold Story of English Cricket* (Repeater Books, 2022), p. 42
7 Birley, *Social History of English Cricket*, pp. 17–18
8 Birley, *Social History of English Cricket*, pp. 18–19; Bowen, *Cricket*, p. 513
9 Birley, *Social History of English Cricket*, p. 22
10 Ibid., p. 26–7 and 30–1; see also Gavin Mortimer, *A History of Cricket in 100 Objects* (Serpent's Tail, 2013) pp. 6–8
11 Birley, *Social History of English Cricket*, p. 27; Bowen, *Cricket*, p. 54
12 Bowen, *Cricket*, p. 55
13 Simon Hughes, *And God Created Cricket* (Black Swan, 2009), p. 42
14 Bowen, *Cricket*, p. 67
15 Birley, *Social History of English Cricket*, p. 31; Brailsford, *British Sport*, p. 55; Stone, *Different Class*, pp. 41–2
16 Bowen, *Cricket*, pp. 55–7
17 Stone, *Different Class*, p. 40
18 Ashley Mote, *The Glory Days of Cricket: The Extraordinary Story of Broadhalfpenny Down* (Robson, 1997), p. 125
19 Bowen, *Cricket*, pp. 45–6; Mortimer, *History of Cricket*, pp. 22–4. For a detailed history of the early cricket ball, see G. D. Martineau, *Bat, Ball, Wicket and All* (Sporting Handbooks, 1950) pp. 43–61
20 Birley, *Social History of English Cricket*, pp. 39; Bowen, *Cricket*, pp. 62–3 and 69; Hughes, *And God Created Cricket*, pp. 21–4
21 Bowen, ibid.; Hughes, ibid.
22 Birley, *Social History of English Cricket*, p. 21; Brooks, *Corner of Every Foreign Field*, p. 21. For a general aristocratic retreat into private recreation, Brailsford, *British Sport*, pp. 62–4
23 Bowen, *Cricket*, pp. 63–4; Stone, *Different Class*, p. 44
24 Peter Oborne and Richard Heller, '"Absent, Caught Fire" and other great moments from Scotland's cricket heritage', *Oborne & Heller on Cricket* [podcast], season 1, episode 35 (28 December 2020)
25 Ibid., 'Maurice Turnbull – and other heroes of cricket in Wales', episode 42 (15 February 2021)
26 Gerard Siggins, *Green Days: Cricket in Ireland 1792–2005* (The History Press, 2005), p. 10
27 Bowen, *Cricket*, pp. 70–3
28 Brooks, *Corner of Every Foreign Field*, pp. 58–9, 65, 69–70; Bowen, *Cricket*, pp. 267–8
29 Ibid.; Bowen, *Cricket*, p. 264
30 The evolution of early cricket reporting emerges in H. T. Waghorn's compilation *Cricket, Scores, Notes &c from 1730–1773* (William Blackwood and Sons, 1899)
31 Martineau, *Bat, Ball, Wicket and All*, pp. 81–7; Bowen, *Cricket*, p. 57
32 Bowen, *Cricket*, p. 267
33 Ibid., p. 268
34 Mortimer, *History of Cricket*, pp. 35–7
35 Birley, *Social History of English Cricket*, p. 33

36 Mortimer, *History of Cricket*, pp. 35–7
37 Porter, *English Society*, p. 366

Chapter 3: Technical Change

1 Birley, *Social History of English Cricket*, pp. 68–9; Bowen, *Cricket*, pp. 81–2; Mike Huggins, *The Victorians and Sport* (Hambledon & London, 2004), p. 31
2 For the round-arm controversy and its outcome, see Birley, *Social History of English Cricket*, pp. 64–6; Bowen, *Cricket*, p. 81; Hughes, *And God Created Cricket*, p. 48–9. Hughes, a professional bowler, casts the controversy as another attempt by privileged batters to suppress toiling bowlers.
3 Birley, *Social History of English Cricket*, pp. 73–4
4 Martineau, *Bat, Ball, Wicket and All*, pp. 75–80
5 Ibid., pp. 18–28
6 Chris Biddle, *The Budding Legacy: Celebrations of a British 'Grass Roots' Invention* (Chris Biddle Media, 2015), *passim*
7 https://www.espn.co.uk/cricket/story/_/id/22951876/a-collector-dream-continues
8 R. D. C. Evans, *Cricket Grounds* (Sports Turf Research Institute, 1991), pp. 10–14
9 Birley, *Social History of English Cricket*, p. 87
10 Biddle, *Budding Legacy*, *passim*
11 Robert Winder, *The Little Wonder: The Remarkable History of Wisden* (Wisden, 2013), p. 5

Chapter 4: A Struggle for Power

1 Birley, *Social History of English Cricket*, pp. 83–90; Huggins, *Victorians and Sport*, p. 56; Hughes, *And God Created Cricket*, pp. 67–72; and especially, John Major, *More Than a Game: The Story of Cricket's Early Years* (HarperCollins, 2007), pp. 178–90
2 Hughes, *And God Created Cricket*, p. 69
3 G. Derek West, *The Elevens of England* (Dart Publishers, 1985), pp. 1, 6 and 16
4 Peter Wynne-Thomas, *William Clarke: The Old General* (ACS Publications, 2014), pp. 6 and 67. This cites Richard Daft, *Kings of Cricket* (Tillotson & Sons, 1893); footnote: Birley, *Social History of English Cricket*, pp. 84–86; Stone, *Different Class*, p. 59
5 Winder, *The Little Wonder*, p. 5
6 Bowen, *Cricket*, pp. 87–8
7 Huggins, *Victorians and Sport*, pp. 170–1; Major, *More Than a Game*, p. 189
8 Major, ibid.
9 David Marquand, *Decline of the Public* (Polity Press, 2004) p. 32
10 Tony Money, *Manly and Muscular Diversions* (Duckworth, 1997) p. 64
11 Ibid; John Chandos, *Boys Together: English Public Schools 1800–1864* (Hutchinson 1984), p. 191
12 Richard Heller, 'Cricket Imagined . . . Ripping Yarns but Few Great Novels', *The Journal of the Cricket Society* (Spring, 2024); Eric Midwinter, *His Captain's Hand on his Shoulder Smote* (ACS Publications, 2019)

13 Keith Sandiford, *Cricket and the Victorians* (Routledge, 1994), p. 35 and *passim*
14 Chandos, *Boys Together*, p. 289
15 Sandiford, *Cricket and the Victorians*, p. 36
16 Ibid., p. 39
17 Ibid., p. 38

Chapter 5: The Impact of Grace

1 Hughes, *And God Created Cricket*, pp. 80–1
2 Simon Rae, *W. G. Grace: A Life* (Faber, 1998), p. 197
3 Hughes, *And God Created Cricket*, p. 81; footnote: Rae, *W. G. Grace*, p. 472.
4 Birley, *Social History of English Cricket*, p. 109
5 https://cricketarchive.com/Archive/Players/0/43/First-Class_Matches.html
6 Birley, *Social History of English Cricket*, p. 108
7 Birley, *Social History of English Cricket*, pp. 108–9; Bowen, *Cricket*, pp. 110–11
8 https://cricketarchive.com/Archive/Scorecards/194/194980.html; https://cricketarchive.com/Archive/Scorecards/194/194981.html
9 Huggins, *Victorians and Sport*, pp. 182–3; https://www.bioc.cam.ac.uk/about-us/history/the-colman-library/sir-jeremiah-colman
10 https://www.gettyimages.co.uk/detail/news-photo/sport-cricket-advertising-card-pic-circa-1920-dr-wg-grace-news-photo/79659442
11 Rae, *W. G. Grace*, pp. 144 and 341
12 Ibid., p. 343
13 Ibid., p. 2 and p. 79
14 Birley, *Social History of English Cricket*, pp. 105–6
15 Rae, *W. G. Grace*, p. 213; Hughes, *And God Created Cricket*, p. 88
16 Rae, *W. G. Grace*, p. 55
17 Hughes, *And God Created Cricket*, p. 86; footnote: Birley, *Social History of English Cricket*, p. 123
18 Rae, *W. G. Grace*, p. 475
19 Ric Sissons, *The Players: A Social History of the Professional Cricketer* (Kingswood, 1988), p. 254
20 Huggins, *Victorians and Sport*, p. 129
21 https://www.officialdata.org/uk/inflation/1908?amount=120000
22 Ibid.
23 Huggins, *Victorians and Sport*, pp. 182–3
24 Sissons, *The Players*, pp. 129–43, especially the table on p. 136
25 Rae, *W. G. Grace*, p. 327
26 Birley, *Social History of English Cricket*, pp. 111–12

Chapter 6: Women (Re-)Enter the Narrative

1 Nancy Joy, *Maiden Over: A Short History of Women's Cricket and a Report of the Australian Tour 1948–49* (Sporting Handbooks, 1950), pp. 14–15; Nicholson, *Ladies and Lords*, p. 36

2 https://www.andoveradvertiser.co.uk/news/25163408.back-pages-women-played-cricket-beer/
3 Nicholson, *Ladies and Lords*, p. 33
4 Rachael Heyhoe Flint and Netta Rheinberg (Angus & Robertson Publishers, 1976), *Fair Play*, pp. 18–19
5 Joy, *Maiden Over*, p. 22
6 Nicholson, *Ladies and Lords*, p. 43
7 Ibid., p. 29
8 Joy, *Maiden Over*, p. 29.
9 Isabelle Duncan, *Skirting the Boundary: A History of Women's Cricket* (Robson Press, 2013), p. 24; Joy, *Maiden Over*, pp. 32–3
10 Duncan, *Skirting the Boundary*, p. 15
11 Nicholson, *Ladies and Lords*, p. 50
12 Ibid., pp. 51–2
13 Ibid., p. 47
14 Ibid., p. 49
15 Ibid., p. 48
16 Ibid., p. 47; Duncan, *Skirting the Boundary*, pp. 32–3

Chapter 7: The Challenge of Association Football

1 Richard Sanders, *Beastly Fury* (Bantam, 2010), p. 68
2 Sanders, *Beastly Fury*, chapter 4
3 Ibid.
4 Keith Booth, *The Father of Modern Sport* (Parrs Wood Press, 2002), pp. 143–5
5 Stephen Chalke, *Summer's Crown: The Story of Cricket's County Championship* (Fairfield Books, 2015), pp. 60–1
6 Chalke *Summer's Crown*, p. 54
7 E. W. Swanton (ed.), *Barclays World of Cricket: The Game from A to Z* (Guild, 1986), p. 419; Altham, *History of Cricket*, p. 83
8 Sissons, *The Players*, pp. 86–8
9 Sissons, *The Players*, p. 81
10 Birley, *Social History of English Cricket*, p. 115
11 Ibid.; Sissons, *The Players*, pp. 74–5
12 Bowen, *Cricket*, p. 83; Altham, *History of Cricket*, pp. 89–90
13 Sissons, *The Players*, p. 74
14 Chalke, *Summer's Crown*, p. 63
15 'ICC appoints working group to review status of Afghanistan cricket: Women's first-class, List A classification to align with men's game', *Women's CricZone*, 17 November 2021
16 https://crickethistory.website/national/england/Minor_Counties_Championship.html
17 Sanders, *Beastly Fury*, pp. 139–40; Stone, *Different Class*, p. 71
18 Stone, *Different Class*, p. 72
19 Ibid., p. 74
20 Ibid., p. 75

21 https://oldebor.wordpress.com/2019/02/18/the-contrasting-path-of-amateur-and-professional-cricketers/
22 David Woodhouse, *Who Only Cricket Know: Hutton's Men in the West Indies 1953/54* (Fairfield Books, 2021), p. 92
23 Sissons, *The Players*, pp. 93–125 contains an exquisitely detailed analysis of players' earnings
24 Sissons, *The Players*, pp. 140–1
25 Ibid., pp. 174–80.
26 Huggins, *Victorians and Sport*, p. 155
27 Stone, *Different Class*, p. 89
28 Peter Gibbs, 'A chill wind beyond the boundary', in Lawrence Booth (ed.), *Wisden Cricketers' Almanack 2012* (Wisden, 2012), pp. 120–6

Chapter 8: The First Golden Age

1 Andy Bull, 'A history of left-handed batting', in Lawrence Booth (ed.), *Wisden Cricketers' Almanack 2020* (Wisden, 2020), pp. 85–91
2 Bowen, *Cricket*, pp. 167, 319
3 Chalke, *Summer's Crown*, pp. 92–93
4 https://oldebor.wordpress.com/2019/02/27/the-question-is-a-very-delicate-one-colonial-cricketers-in-english-cricket-before-1914/
5 Neville Cardus, *Cricket* (Longmans, Green and Co, 1949), p. 70
6 George Plumptre, *The Golden Age of Cricket* (Queen Anne, 1990), p. 7
7 J. B. Priestley, introduction to David Frith, *The Golden Age of Cricket, 1890–1914* (Lutterworth Press, 1978), p. 10
8 https://backwatersman.wordpress.com/2012/12/25/a-merry-christmas-with-arthur-ticker-mitchell-crickets-hardest-man/
9 Bowen, *Cricket*, pp. 141–2
10 Sissons, *The Players*, pp. 155–71
11 Keith Sandiford, 'England', in Brian Stoddart and Keith Sandiford (eds), *The Imperial Game: Cricket, Culture and Society* (Manchester University Press, 1998), pp. 26–7
12 Mihir Bose, *A History of Indian Cricket* (Andre Deutsch, 1990), p. 40

Chapter 9: Australia: Birth of a Cricket Superpower

1 https://www.sbs.com.au/news/article/a-brief-history-of-immigration-to-australia/cs4rmu3sr
2 Mariam Dixson, *The Imaginary Australian: Anglo-Celts and Identity, 1788 to the Present* (UNSW Press, 1999), p. 10
3 https://www.creativespirits.info/aboriginalculture/people/aboriginal-population-in-australia
4 https://www.statista.com/statistics/1066666/population-australia-since-1800/
5 Chris Harte, *A History of Australian Cricket* (Andre Deutsch, 1993), p. 192
6 Jim Kilburn and Mike Coward, 'Overseas cricket: Australia' in E. W. Swanton (ed.), *Barclays World of Cricket*, pp. 61–2; Harte, *History of Australian Cricket*, pp. 2–3

7   Kilburn and Coward, 'Overseas cricket: Australia' in Swanton (ed.), *Barclays World of Cricket*, p. 69; Harte, *History of Australian Cricket*, pp. 2–3
8   Richard Cashman, 'Australia', in Stoddart and Sandiford (eds), *The Imperial Game*, pp. 34–7
9   Kilburn and Coward, 'Overseas cricket: Australia' in Swanton (ed.), *Barclays World of Cricket*, pp. 72–3; and Harte, *History of Australian Cricket*, pp. 18, 32–3
10 Brooks, *Corner of Every Foreign Field*, pp. 59–61; Kilburn and Coward, 'Overseas cricket: Australia' in Swanton (ed.), *Barclays World of Cricket*, p. 73; Harte, *History of Australian Cricket*, pp. 9 and 12
11 Harte, *History of Australian Cricket*, pp. 25–27, 29–31; Kilburn and Coward, 'Overseas cricket: Australia' in Swanton (ed.), *Barclays World of Cricket*, pp. 70, 74
12 Harte, *History of Australian Cricket*, pp. 58–9
13 Ibid., p. 61 *et seq*
14 Ibid., p. 67; Bowen, *Cricket*, p. 99, 278; *Cricket Quarterly* (Spring 1966 and Winter 1966–67) cited in Keith Booth, *The Father of Modern Sport* (Parrs Wood Press, 2002), p. 163, note 318
15 Harte, *History of Australian Cricket*, pp. 72–76; Bowen, *Cricket*, p. 127; Brooks, *Corner of Every Foreign Field*, p. 63
16 https://www.onlymelbourne.com.au/thomas-wentworth-wills
17 Greg de Moore, *Tom Wills: First Wild Man of Australian Sport* (Allen & Unwin, 2008)
18 https://www.abc.net.au/news/2021-09-19/experts-add-weight-to-discovery-tom-wills-indigenous-massacre/100469428
19 https://adb.anu.edu.au/biography/wills-thomas-wentworth-4863
20 T. S. Wills Cooke, *The Currency Lad* (Digbys, 2013)
21 John Mulvaney and Rex Harcourt, *Cricket Walkabout, The Australian Aborigines in England* (Macmillan Australia, 1988), plate section caption
22 Harte, *History of Australian Cricket*, pp. 77–9
23 Ibid.; https://www.nma.gov.au/defining-moments/resources/aboriginal-cricket-team; https://www.espncricinfo.com/cricketers/johnny-mullagh-6846
24 Scyld Berry, *Beyond the Boundaries: Travels on England Cricket Tours* (Fairfield Books, 2021), p. 22
25 https://ia.anu.edu.au/biography/marsh-jack-13080
26 https://www.espncricinfo.com/cricketers/eddie-gilbert-5387; see also Mike Colman and Ken Edwards, *Eddie Gilbert* (ABC Books Sydney, 2002)
27 Jack Pollard, *The Formative Years of Australian Cricket 1803–93* (Angus & Robertson, 1987), pp. 181–82
28 Harte, *History of Australian Cricket*, pp. 101–4
29 https://www.theguardian.com/sport/2023/jul/26/why-ashes-the-burning-issue-of-obituary-behind-great-cricket-rivalry
30 https://www.theguardian.com/sport/blog/2009/jun/11/ashes-origins-england-australia
31 Harte, *History of Australian Cricket*, p. 131
32 Steven Lynch (ed.), *Wisden on the Ashes: The Authoritative Story of Cricket's Greatest Rivalry* (Bloomsbury, 2002), pp. 5–26, 18–19
33 Cashman, 'Australia', in Stoddart and Sandiford (eds), *The Imperial Game*, p. 45
34 Harte, *History of Australian Cricket*, p. 200

35 Ibid., p. 151
36 Sissons, *The Players*, p. 179
37 Harte, *History of Australian Cricket*, pp. 179–81
38 https://www.cricket.com.au/governing-the-game/ca-history
39 Harte, *History of Australian Cricket*, p. 169
40 https://www.australian-trains.com/blog/the-history-of-australian-rail.html
41 Louis Duffus and Michael Owen-Smith in Swanton (ed.), *Barclays World of Cricket*, pp. 253–4
42 Harte, *History of Australian Cricket*, p. 185
43 Lawrence Booth (ed.), *Wisden Cricketers' Almanack 2023* (Wisden, 2023)
44 https://www.espncricinfo.com/story/you-ve-been-asking-for-a-punch-all-night-143363
45 Lynch (ed.), *Wisden on the Ashes*, p. 140–5; Harte, *History of Australian Cricket*, p. 251

Chapter 10: New Zealand: Cricket's Farthest Realm

1 D. O. & P. W. Neely, *The Summer Game* (Russell & Dunworth, 1994), p. 11
2 https://teara.govt.nz/en/transport-overview
3 Greg Ryan, 'New Zealand', in Stoddart and Sandiford (eds), *The Imperial Game*, pp. 97–98
4 Ryan, 'New Zealand', in Stoddart and Sandiford (eds), *The Imperial Game*, pp. 102–3
5 Narelle McGluskey, 'The Willow and the Palm: An Exploration of the Role of Cricket in Fiji' (James Cook University, thesis submitted October 2005), pp. 81–2, https://researchonline.jcu.edu.au/1247/2/02whole.pdf
6 See Philip Snow's entry for Tonga in Swanton (ed.), *Barclays World of Cricket*, p. 127
7 Brian Stoddart, 'Other cultures', in Stoddart and Sandiford (eds), *The Imperial Game*, p. 140
8 Ibid., pp. 140–6

Chapter 11: South Africa: Cricket's Original Sin

1 H. G. Nahuys van Burgst, *Adventures at the Cape of Good Hope in 1806*, translated and edited by M. A. Bax-Botha (Friends of South Africa Library, 1993), p. 78
2 André Odendaal, Krish Reddy, Christopher Merrett and Jonty Winch, *Cricket and Conquest: The History of South African Cricket Retold, 1795–1914* (HSRC Press, 2016), p. 18
3 Bowen, *Cricket*, p. 85. Bowen places the first match at Green Point in 1808, but subsequent research has superseded him.
4 Ibid., p. 34
5 Ibid., p. 33
6 Basil D'Oliveira, *The D'Oliveira Affair* (Collins, 1969), p. 18
7 Ibid., p. 4

8 Richard Parry and Jonty Winch, *Too Black to Wear Whites: Krom Hendricks, the Remarkable Story of a Cricket Hero Rejected by the Empire* (Pitch Publishing, 2021), pp. xiii, 235
9 Bernard M. Magubane, *The Making of a Racist State: British Imperialism and the Union of South Africa, 1875–1910* (Africa World Press, 1996), p. 108
10 P. F. Warner, *Lords 1787–1945* (Sportsman's Book Club, London 1951) p. 60.
11 Odendaal et al., *Cricket and Conquest*, p. 256
12 Parry and Winch, *Too Black to Wear Whites*, p. xi
13 André Odendaal, *The Story of an African Game* (David Philip Publishers, 2003), pp. 82–3
14 Richard Parry and André Odendaal, *Swallows and Hawke: English Cricket Tours, the MCC and the Making of South Africa 1888–1968* (Pitch Publishing, 2022), p. 37
15 Denis Judd, *Empire: The British Imperial Experience from 1765 to the Present* (HarperCollins, 1996), p. 301
16 Odendaal et al., *Cricket and Conquest*, p. 227
17 https://www.cricketcountry.com/articles/monty-bowden-englands-youngest-test-captain-337536
18 John S. Galbraith, *Crown and Charter: The Early Years of the British South Africa Company* (University of California Press, 1974), pp. 143–53
19 Peter Bridger (ed.), *Encyclopaedia Rhodesia* (College Press, 1973)
20 'Lobengula, king of Ndebele', *Britannica*, https://www.britannica.com/biography/Lobengula
21 A. A. Thomson, *Odd Men In* (Pavilion, 1985), pp. v–vi. Introduction by Leo Cooper.
22 Peter Hain and André Odendaal, *Pitch Battles: Sport, Racism and Resistance* (Rowman & Littlefield, 2021), p. 85
23 http://cricmash.com/cricket-cards/reggie-schwarz-the-torch-bearer-of-the-googly
24 *South Africa News*, 10 January 1906, cited in Parry and Odendaal, *Swallows and Hawke*, p. 158
25 https://www.lords.org/lords/our-history/father-time-wall/1909-the-imperial-cricket-conference,-now-known-as#:~:text=It%20was%20at%20the%20end,those%20two%20countries%20and%20Australia

Chapter 12: Cricket Reaches the Indian Subcontinent

1 Ramachandra Guha, *A Corner of a Foreign Field: The Indian History of a British Sport* (Penguin India, 2002), p. 1
2 Bowen, *Cricket*, pp. 263–4
3 Prashant Kidambi, *Cricket Country: An Indian Odyssey in the Age of Empire* (Oxford University Press, 2019), p. 5
4 Guha, *Corner of a Foreign Field*, p. 8
5 Peter Oborne, *Wounded Tiger: A History of Cricket in Pakistan* (Simon & Schuster, 2014), p. 53
6 https://www.lords.org/lords/our-history/father-time-wall/1936-a-ball-strikes-a-sparrow-which-is-later-stuff
7 https://www.espncricinfo.com/story/ramachandra-guha-why-gandhi-would-have-been-appalled-by-the-gandhi-mandela-trophy-935051

8 *Bombay Times and Journal of Commerce*, 23 August 1843
9 Nira Wickramasinghe, *Sri Lanka in the Modern Age: A History* (Oxford University Press, 2015), p. 22
10 S. S. Perera, *The Janashakthi Book of Sri Lankan Cricket, 1832–1996* (Janashakthi Insurance, 1999), p. 29
11 Carl Muller, *Yakada Yaka: The Continuing Saga of Sonnaboy Von Bloss and the Burgher Railwaymen* (Penguin India, 1994), p. 11
12 Nicholas Brookes, *An Island's Eleven: The Story of Sri Lankan Cricket* (The History Press, 2022), p. 25
13 Perera, *Sri Lankan Cricket*, p. 30
14 S. P. Foenander, *Sixty Years of Ceylon Cricket* (Ceylon Advertising & General Publicity, 1924), p. 60
15 http://cricmash.com/cricket-during-wars/the-first-south-african-side-to-play-in-the-sub-continent-boer-prisoners-of-war-in-1901
16 *Times of Ceylon*, 28 February–1 March 1907
17 Brookes, *An Island's Eleven*, p. 16
18 https://glamorgancricketarchives.com/2021/01/16/alfred-holsinger-the-first-sri-lankan-professional-in-wales/
19 https://www.dailynews.lk/2019/05/25/sports/186471/dr-ch-gunasekara-appreciation

Chapter 13: West Indies: Destined for Glory

1 Bowen, *Cricket*, pp. 72–3; Tim Wigmore, *Test Cricket: A History* (Quercus, 2025), p. 67
2 Michael Manley, *A History of West Indies Cricket* (Pan Books, 1990), pp. 19–20
3 See for example, A. Derickson, 'A Widespread Superstition: The Purported Invulnerability of Workers of Color to Occupational Heat Stress', *Am J Public Health* vol. 109, no. 10 (October 2019), pp. 1329–35; doi: 10.2105/AJPH.2019.305246
4 Manley, *A History of West Indies Cricket*, p. 24
5 G. J. Heuman, '*The Killing Time*': *The Morant Bay Rebellion in Jamaica* (University of Tennessee Press, 1994), especially pp. 158–9
6 C. L. R. James, *Beyond a Boundary* (Hutchinson, 1963), chapter 4
7 See Everton Weekes' obituary in *Wisden* 2021
8 https://www.cricketcountry.com/articles/12-little-known-facts-about-garry-sobers-163571.
9 Woodhouse, *Who Only Cricket Know*, pp. 48–9.
10 https://www.espncricinfo.com/story/the-jewel-of-the-caribbean-240899
11 Manley, *A History of West Indies Cricket*, p. 21
12 Hughes, *And God Created Cricket*, pp. 123–4
13 C. L. R. James and P. Short, 'West Indies' in Swanton (ed.), *Barclays World of Cricket*, pp. 130–1
14 Brooks, *Corner of Every Foreign Field*, p. 74
15 Manley, *A History of West Indies Cricket*, p. 22
16 Brooks, *Corner of Every Foreign Field*, p. 75

Chapter 14: North America: Cricket's Failed State

1 P. David Sentance, *Cricket in America, 1710–2000* (McFarland, 2006), pp. 5, 7. See also Swanton (ed.), *Barclays World of Cricket*, p. 127
2 Sentance, *Cricket in America*, p. 8
3 Ibid.
4 Ibid., p. 7
5 Ibid., p. 10
6 Bowen, *Cricket*, p. 85
7 https://cricketarchive.com/cgi-bin/scorecard_oracle_reveals_results.cgi
8 George B. Kirsch, *Baseball and Cricket: The Creation of American Team Sports* (University of Illinois Press, 2007), pp. 50–1
9 https://www.dreamcricket.com/articles/history-of-american-cricket/150th-anniversary-of-the-first-english-cricket-tour-of-north-america/
10 John Marder and Vic Lewis, 'The United States of America' in Swanton (ed.), *Barclays World of Cricket*, pp. 127–30
11 Ibid; Bowen, *Cricket*, p. 121
12 https://www.dreamcricket.com/articles/history-of-american-cricket/history-of-american-cricket-part-vi–1880s/
13 Bowen, *Cricket*, pp. 120–1
14 Marder and Lewis in Swanton (ed.), *Barclays World of Cricket*, pp. 127–8; Bowen, *Cricket*, pp. 120–22, 158–60
15 Sentance, *Cricket in America*, p. 12
16 Tom Melville, *The Tented Field: A History of Cricket in America* (Bowling Green Press, 1998), p. 116
17 Ibid.
18 Timothy Abraham and James Coyne, *Evita Burned Down Our Pavilion: A Cricket Odyssey through Latin America* (Constable, 2021) p. 100
19 Melville, *The Tented Field*, pp. 115–18; Sentance, *Cricket in America*, p. 70
20 https://valeriesims.com/st-thomas-cricket-team-wins-match-1895
21 https://www.forces.net/news/north-bowl-navy-submariners-play-arctic-game-cricket; https://www.stuff.co.nz/sport/cricket/300132371/new-zealand-cricketing-icon-john-r-reid-dies-in-auckland
22 https://www.cbc.ca/news/canada/newfoundland-labrador/newfoundland-cricket-sports-history-1.5077024

Chapter 15: South American Odyssey

1 Abraham and Coyne, *Evita Burned Down Our Pavilion*, p. 9
2 Ibid. and p. 347
3 Ibid., p. 181
4 Ibid., p. 48
5 Ibid., p. 406
6 Ibid., pp. 169–70
7 Ibid., pp. 213–15; Kenneth E. Bridger in Swanton (ed.), *Barclays World of Cricket*, p. 80. See also https://www.pressandjournal.co.uk/fp/past-times/4044500/robert-clark-shackleton-endurance/

8 Abraham and Coyne, *Evita Burned Down Our Pavilion*, pp. 366–7
9 Bowen, *Cricket*, pp. 123–4

Chapter 16: The Uniqueness of Irish Cricket

1 Unless otherwise attributed, all references in this section are drawn from unpublished passages shared with us by the eminent Irish cricket historian and man of letters Charles Lysaght and our podcast conversations with him and Lingard Goulding, a towering figure in Irish sporting and educational history – Oborne and Heller, *Oborne & Heller on Cricket* [podcast], season 1: 'The glorious social and cultural heritage of Irish cricket with Charles Lysaght', episode 27 (2 November 2020); 'The man who discovered Eoin Morgan and other stories', episode 48 (29 March 2021); 'Behind the stumps but never the times in eight decades: The multiple lives of Lingard Goulding', episode 59 (6 July 2021)
2 Bowen, *Cricket*, pp. 37–8
3 Siggins, *Green Days*, p. 10.
4 Ibid., pp. 10–12; Swanton (ed.), *Barclays World of Cricket*, pp. 554–56
5 Ibid., pp. 14, 17; Wigmore, *Test Cricket*, pp. 523–4
6 Siggins, *Green Days*, p. 18
7 https://www.ighm.org/learn.html
8 Alan Bairner, 'Wearing the Baggie Green: The Irish and Australian Cricket', *Sport in Society*, vol. 10, no. 3 (2017), pp. 457–75; https://doi.org/10.1080/17430430701333851
9 https://history.howstuffworks.com/historical-events/when-irish-immigrants-werent-considered-white
10 Bowen, *Cricket*, p. 93; https://www.dib.ie/biography/lawrence-john-fortune-a9810
11 Siggins, *Green Days*, pp. 20–4
12 https://www.waterfordtreasures.com/charles-stewart-parnell-irish-nationalist-lost-english-cricketer/ (including a political cartoon of him being clean bowled)
13 https://www.espn.com/cricket/story/_/id/21858030/england-arrive-ireland-unloved-neighbours
14 Wigmore, *Test Cricket*, pp. 512–13
15 https://cricketarchive.com/Archive/Players/2/2287/2287.html
16 https://www.dib.ie/biography/boucher-james-chrysostom-jimmy-a0793
17 For a meticulously documented account of Bowlby's erratic career, see Charles Lysaght's article in the *Irish Times*, 7 February 2009
18 Siggins, *Green Days*, pp. 99, 101
19 https://www.nytimes.com/2015/03/05/sports/cricket/after-years-in-shadows-cricket-emerges-in-ireland.html
20 Wigmore, *Test Cricket*, pp. 510–14
21 https://stats.espncricinfo.com/ci/engine/stats/index.html?class=2;team=29;template=results;type=team
22 https://stats.espncricinfo.com/ci/engine/team/2234.html?class=10;spanmin1=01+Jan+2000;spanval1=span;template=results;type=team
23 Siggins, *Green Days*, p. 115

Chapter 17: The First World War and Its Aftermath

1 Chalke, *Summer's Crown*, pp. 112–13; an alternative version of the story can be found in John Broom, *Cricket in the First World War* (Pen & Sword History, 2022), p. 2
2 Broom, *Cricket in the First World War*, p. 8
3 Chalke, *Summer's Crown*, pp. 112–13
4 Broom, *Cricket in the First World War*, p. x
5 Oborne and Heller, 'Two testaments of cricket and war', *Oborne & Heller on Cricket* [podcast], season 1, episode 114 (13 March 2023) with John Broom; see also Broom, *Cricket in the First World War*, p. 205
6 Broom, *Cricket in the First World War*, p. 205
7 Stone, *Different Class*, p. 107
8 Jeremy Lonsdale, *A Game Divided* (ACS Publications, 2020) p. 15; Broom, *Cricket in the First World War*, pp. 119–20
9 https://polsci.institute/international-relations-world-history/india-contribution-british-war-efforts-wwi/
10 https://www.espncricinfo.com/cricketers/don-denton-12145
11 Broom, *Cricket in the First World War*, p. 128
12 Ibid., p. 130
13 Ibid., pp. 206–7
14 Birley, *Social History of English Cricket*, p. 213
15 Ibid.; see also Bull, 'A history of left-handed batting', in Booth (ed.), *Wisden Cricketers' Almanack 2020*
16 Birley, *Social History of English Cricket*, p. 212; Chalke, *Summer's Crown*, p. 115
17 Chalke, *Summer's Crown*, p. 115
18 Peter Wynne-Thomas, *The History of Cricket: From the Weald to the World* (HMSO, 1997), pp. 151–2; Chalke, *Summer's Crown*, pp. 16, 38
19 Chalke, *Summer's Crown*, pp. 116–19, 136–8
20 Dennis Brailsford, *British Sport: A Social History* (Lutterworth, 1992), pp. 116–17; C. L. Mowat, *Britain Between the Wars* (Methuen, 1954), p. 500
21 For changes to British leisure habits in the interwar period, including the impact of the new sports, see Juliet Gardiner, *The Thirties* (Harper, 2011), pp. 510–13, 624–6 (radio and dance music), chapter 20 (motoring, excursions, holidays), chapter 22 (cinema) and chapter 23 (for sports, significantly titled 'Not Cricket').
22 Birley, *Social History of English Cricket*, p. 253; Chalke, *Summer's Crown*, p. 135
23 Miranda Rijks, *The Eccentric Entrepreneur* (The History Press, 2009); https://www.espncricinfo.com/story/the-inflatable-philanthropist-391555
24 Chalke, *Summer's Crown*, p. 117
25 https://www.cricketmuseum.wales/sydney-barnes-a-great-welsh-bowler/
26 Harry Pearson, *Connie: The Marvellous Life of Learie Constantine* (Little, Brown, 2017), especially pp. 141, 160 for his relationships with teammates and the local community
27 Stone, *Different Class*, pp. 111, 116; Jack Williams, *Cricket and England* (Frank Cass, 1999) pp. 28–9, 64
28 Pearson, *Connie*, p. 128

29 Pearson, *Connie*, pp. 130–1
30 Peter Wynne-Thomas, *Arthur Carr* (Chequered Flag Publishing, 2017), p. 117
31 Williams, *Cricket and England*, p. 22
32 Lonsdale, *A Game Divided*, pp. 67–8
33 Ibid., p. 139
34 Sissons, *The Players*, p. 210
35 https://www.espncricinfo.com/story/indebted-to-james-seymour-233821
36 Neville Cardus, *Days in the Sun* (Hart Davis edition, 1948), p. 101
37 John Broom, *Cricket in the Second World War* (Pen & Sword, 2021), p. 138

Chapter 18: The First Women's Test Matches

1 Nicholson, *Ladies and Lords*, pp. 63–5
2 Ibid., pp. 82–3
3 Ibid., p. 90
4 Ibid., pp. 56–7
5 Ibid., pp. 62–5
6 Ibid., pp. 63–6
7 Duncan, *Skirting the Boundary*, pp. 62–3; Nicholson, *Ladies and Lords*, p. 77
8 Duncan, *Skirting the Boundary*, p. 63
9 Ibid., p. 59

Chapter 19: Bradman, Bodyline and Empire

1 Harte, *History of Australian Cricket*, p. 289
2 Ibid., p. 288
3 Ibid., p. 283.
4 Duncan Hamilton, *Harold Larwood* (Quercus, 2009), p. 72
5 Bowen, *Cricket*, p. 336
6 Charles Williams, *Bradman* (Little Brown, 1996), p. 55; David Frith, *Bodyline Autopsy* (Aurum, 2002), pp. 110–11
7 Williams, *Bradman*, chapter 4
8 Harte, *History of Australian Cricket*, pp. 318, 340
9 Williams, *Bradman*, p. 65
10 Frith, *Bodyline Autopsy*, p. 252
11 Harte, *History of Australian Cricket*, p. 341
12 Frith, *Bodyline Autopsy*, pp. 74–5
13 Harte, *History of Australian Cricket*, p. 340
14 Williams, *Bradman*, p. 83; Frith, *Bodyline Autopsy*, pp. 74–5; Harte, *History of Australian Cricket*, pp. 341–2
15 Hamilton, *Harold Larwood*, p. 186
16 Harte, *History of Australian Cricket*, p. 342
17 C. L. R. James, *Beyond A Boundary* (Serpent's Tail, 1994), p. 188
18 Harte, *History of Australian Cricket*, p. 339
19 Frith, *Bodyline Autopsy*, p. 41

20 Ibid., p. 23
21 Hamilton, *Harold Larwood*, chapters 2 and 4; Wynne-Thomas, *Arthur Carr*, especially chapters 8 and 9
22 Hamilton, *Harold Larwood*, pp. 128–9
23 Ibid., p. 130
24 https://www.cricketcountry.com/articles/bodyline-how-the-most-infamous-word-in-cricket-was-coined-20449
25 Hamilton, *Harold Larwood*, p. 144
26 https://www.espncricinfo.com/story/rewind-to-1933-a-near-riot-at-adelaide-oval-697733
27 https://oldebor.wordpress.com/2020/12/02/you-couldnt-captain-a-team-of-bloody-lead-soldiers-the-fall-of-bob-wyatt/
28 Hamilton, *Harold Larwood*, p. 170
29 Jack Fingleton, *Cricket Crisis* (Cassell Melbourne, 1947), p. 108; Frith, *Bodyline Autopsy*, pp. 187–90
30 Frith, *Bodyline Autopsy*, pp. 218–22, 408
31 Hamilton, *Harold Larwood*, pp. 170–7
32 Harte, *History of Australian Cricket*, p. 349
33 Wynne-Thomas, *The History of Cricket*, p. 160
34 Berry, *Beyond the Boundaries*, p. 22
35 https://www.cricket.com.au/news/3240234
36 https://ia.anu.edu.au/biography/gilbert-edward-eddie-6379; https://www.dailymail.co.uk/news/article-6591805/How-Aboriginal-bowler-Eddie-Gilbert-got-Don-Bradman-duck-died-tragic-drunk.html
37 https://www.espncricinfo.com/story/harold-larwood-154190
38 E. W. Swanton, *Sort of a Cricket Person* (Collins, 1972), pp. 13–15
39 Frith, *Bodyline Autopsy*, p. 112
40 Birley, *Social History of English Cricket*, p. 237; Hughes, *And God Created Cricket*, p. 182
41 Harte, *History of Australian Cricket*, pp. 342, 345; Hamilton, *Harold Larwood*, pp. 200–1
42 Narrated to Richard Heller by Lord Francis-Williams, former editor of the *Daily Herald* and press secretary to Clement Attlee as prime minister
43 Frith, *Bodyline Autopsy*, pp. 248–51
44 Ibid., p. 238
45 Hamilton, *Harold Larwood*, p. 210; Wynne-Thomas, *The History of Cricket*, p. 162
46 Hamilton, *Harold Larwood*, chapter 8 and pp. 214–16
47 Ibid., chapter 11
48 Williams, *Bradman*, pp. 1324–38

Chapter 20: The Expansion of Test Cricket

1 Wynne-Thomas, *History of Cricket*, pp. 171–6
2 Mihir Bose, *The Nine Waves* (Aleph Books, 2019), p. 64
3 Ibid., p. 30
4 Guha, *Corner of a Foreign Field*, pp. 33–6

5   Guha *Corner of a Foreign Field*, p. 20
6   Shaharyar Khan and Ali Khan, *Cricket Cauldron: The Turbulent Politics of Cricket in Pakistan* (IB Tauris, 2013), p. 7
7   https://www.theguardian.com/sport/2020/nov/17/buster-nupen-cricket-great-survivor-who-bewitched-hobbs-and-hammond

Chapter 21: The Second World War and Its Aftermath

1   https://www.history.org.uk/publications/resource/4825/india-and-the-british-war-effort-1939-1945?srsltid=AfmBOooo_vSzzpneYOqoIPY7d8fTMbSBt-JgkAd77rb50VrniZVSy0CE
2   Chalke, *Summer's Crown*, p. 153
3   Bose, *Nine Waves*, pp. 47–51
4   https://www.military-history.org/feature/war-culture-cricket-in-wwii.htm
5   Birley, *Social History of English Cricket*, p. 266
6   Broom, *Cricket in the Second World War*, p. 69
7   Ibid., pp. 18–19
8   Ibid., pp. 98–9
9   Ibid., p. 74
10 Ibid., pp. 99, 192
11 Ibid., p. 192
12 Nicholson, *Ladies and Lords*, pp. 96–101
13 Broom, *Cricket in the Second World War*, pp. 156, 158, 193–4
14 Hughes, *And God Created Cricket*, pp. 196–9
15 Broom, *Cricket in the Second World War*, p. 78
16 Ibid., p. 68
17 Ibid., pp. 78, 164
18 https://www.espncricinfo.com/cricketers/bob-crisp-44481
19 Broom, *Cricket in the Second World War*, p. 93
20 Ibid., pp. 90–1
21 Ibid., p. 221
22 Ibid., p. 81
23 Alan Hill, *Hedley Verity: Portrait of a Cricketer* (Mainstream Publishing, 2000), p. 181
24 Birley, *Social History of English Cricket*, p. 266
25 Broom, *Cricket in the Second World War*, p. 103
26 Ibid., pp. 103–4
27 Ibid., p. 105
28 E. W. Swanton, *Sort of a Cricket Person* (Fontana, 1974), pp. 121–30
29 Broom, *Cricket in the Second World War*, p. 101; see also John Woodcock (ed.), *Wisden Cricketers' Almanack 1983* (Queen Anne Press, 1983); and Matthew Engel (ed.), *Wisden Cricketers' Almanack 2005* (Wisden, 2005), pp. 1637–8
30 Chalke, *Summer's Crown*, p. 156
31 Broom, *Cricket in the Second World War*, pp. 131–2
32 Williams, *Bradman*, pp. 190–4
33 Pearson, *Connie*, p. 292

34 Broom, *Cricket in the Second World War*, p. 138
35 Ibid., p. 61
36 Hughes, *And God Created Cricket*, pp. 201–2

Chapter 22: After the War

1 https://i.imgci.com/db/ARCHIVE/1940S/1946/ENG_LOCAL/CC/
2 E. M. Wellings, 'Unthanked captains', *Wisden Cricket Monthly* (1986)
3 Wynne-Thomas, *History of Cricket*, p. 208
4 Sissons, *The Players*, p. 267
5 Birley, *Social History of English Cricket*
6 Mike Vockins, *Arthur Milton* (Sports Books, 2011), pp. 318–19
7 Stephen Chalke, *Runs in the Memory* (Fairfield Books, 1997); Stephen Chalke, *Caught in the Memory* (Fairfield Books, 1999)
8 Stone, *Different Class*, pp. 136–68
9 Wilde, *England: The Biography*, p. 23
10 Woodhouse, *Who Only Cricket Know*, pp. 95–7
11 Hill, *Hedley Verity*, p. 153
12 R. Benaud, *My Spin on Cricket* (Hodder & Stoughton, 2005), pp. 70–1
13 https://www.stuff.co.nz/sport/cricket/8788942/Almost-60-years-but-Bob-Blair-never-forgets; https://oztypewriter.blogspot.com/2014/12/bert-bob-and-boxing-day-bravado.html
14 https://www.espncricinfo.com/story/faith-thomas-the-first-indigenous-woman-to-play-cricket-for-australia-dies-aged-90-1369437; the match scorecard also contains a dismissal with resonance in Northern Ireland: caught Paisley bowled Christ.
15 Nicholson, *Ladies and Lords*, p. 111
16 Ibid., p. 138

Chapter 23: The West Indies Emerge as a Major Power

1 Lawrence Booth (ed.), *Wisden Cricketers' Almanack 2021* (Wisden, 2021), p. 123–6
2 Woodhouse, *Who Only Cricket Know*, p. 128
3 Ibid., pp. 244–51
4 https://www.espncricinfo.com/story/gideon-haigh-on-garry-sobers-legends-of-cricket-404515
5 Woodhouse, *Who Only Cricket Know*, p. 358
6 Ibid., p. 359
7 Ibid., p. 357
8 Harte, *History of Australian Cricket*, p. 476; Benaud, *My Spin on Cricket*, p. 8
9 Harte, *History of Australian Cricket*, pp. 473–4, 480
10 Ibid., pp. 480–1

Chapter 24: Independence and Separation

1 See the account from S. M. Hussain, quoted in the Pakistan v Australia Official Souvenir Brochure, Karachi 1959

2   Bose, *Nine Waves*, pp. 181–2
3   Ibid., pp. 169–87
4   Oborne, *Wounded Tiger*, p. 156
5   Oborne, *Wounded Tiger*, pp. 124–5

Chapter 25: The Battle Against Apartheid

1   Jim Laker, *Over to Me* (Muller, 1960), pp. 90–1
2   https://www.theguardian.com/books/2014/feb/28/my-hero-john-arlott-david-rayvern-allen. See also John Arlott, *Basingstoke Boy* (HarperCollins, 1990), esp. pp. 175–87
3   David Sheppard, *Parson's Pitch* (Hodder & Stoughton, 1964), p. 163
4   Wilde, *England: The Biography*, p. 245
5   https://knowledge.lancashire.ac.uk/id/eprint/9659/1/Iyer%20Usha%20Final%20e-Thesis%20(Master%20Copy).pdf, pp. 108–12
6   Peter Oborne, *Basil D'Oliveira: Cricket and Conspiracy* (Sphere, 2009), p. 58
7   *Guardian*, 22 October 1968
8   Hain and Odendaal, *Pitch Battles*
9   https://iol.co.za/sport/cricket/2021-12-05-remembering-frank-roro-south-africas-don-bradman/
10 Parry and Odendaal, *Swallows and Hawke*, pp. 257–9
11 Chalke, *Summer's Crown*, p. 193
12 https://thesefootballtimes.co/2017/11/30/the-tragedy-of-albert-johanneson-the-pioneer-who-paved-the-way-for-black-footballers-at-the-top/
13 https://www.insidethegames.biz/articles/1126429/commonweath-legend-precious-mckenzie
14 Hain and Odendaal, *Pitch Battles*, pp. 159–63
15 Parry and Odendaal, *Swallows and Hawke*, pp. 393–4
16 Wigmore, *Test Cricket*, pp. 152–3
17 Ibid; see also Parry and Odendaal, *Swallows and Hawke*, pp. 324–5
18 Hain and Odendaal, *Pitch Battles*, p. 67; Wigmore, *Test Cricket*, p. 155
19 https://iol.co.za/sport/cricket/2018-01-22-dik-abed-was-one-of-our-best-all-rounders/
20 https://iol.co.za/capeargus/sport/2007-08-17-sa-mourns-death-of-cricketer-cecil-abrahams/
21 Wigmore, *Test Cricket*, p. 165
22 Norman Preston (ed.), *Wisden Cricketers' Almanack 1962* (Sporting Handbooks, 1962), p. 1043

Chapter 26: Cricket Reinvents Itself

1   Chalke, *Summer's Crown*, p. 195
2   Chalke, *Caught in the Memory*, p. 75
3   Ibid., p. 200; Hughes, *And God Created Cricket*, p. 242
4   Unless otherwise stated, references in this section are taken from Daniel O'Neill and Anna Greenwood, '"Bringing You The Best": John Player & Sons,

Cricket and the Politics of Tobacco Sports Sponsorship in Britain, 1969–1986', *Eur J Hist Med Health*, vol. 80, no. 1 (11 August 2022), pp. 152–184; doi: 10.1163/26667711-bja10022
5 https://www.ctsu.ox.ac.uk/research/british-doctors-study
6 Hughes, *And God Created Cricket*, pp. 241–2; Guy Fraser-Sampson, *Cricket at the Crossroads* (Elliott & Thompson, 2011), pp. 23–4
7 https://cricketstuff.blog/2018/08/15/remembering-the-lambert-butler-floodlit-cup/
8 https://www.hindustantimes.com/cricket/disgusting-is-money-so-important-gautam-gambhir-blasts-virender-sehwag-sunil-gavaskar-endorsing-pan-masala-sachin-remark-101686660167569.html
9 Birley, *Social History of English Cricket*, p. 301; https://www.sportingintelligence.com/2011/01/20/from-20-to-33868-per-week-a-quick-history-of-english-footballs-top-flight-wages-200101/
10 https://stats.espncricinfo.com/ci/engine/team/1.html?class=1;spanmax1=31+Dec+1999;spanmin1=01+Jan+1970;spanval1=span;template=results;type=team
11 Wilde, *England: The Biography*, pp. 358–9
12 Sissons, *The Players*, p. 285; for Arlott's contribution to the association, see David Rayvern Allen, *Arlott: The Authorised Biography* (Aurum 2004), pp. 274–6
13 Sissons, *The Players*, pp. 285–7
14 Ibid., p. 312; https://www.salaryleaks.com/blogs/average-salary-premier-league-history
15 https://oldebor.wordpress.com/2022/05/17/the-extinction-of-the-sticky-wicket-the-confusing-history-of-pitch-covering/
16 Gideon Haigh, *The Cricket War* (John Wisden & Co, 2017), pp. 19–20
17 Ibid., p. 5
18 Manley, *History of West Indies Cricket*, p. 267
19 Haigh, *Cricket War*, p. 90
20 Ibid., p. 82
21 Ibid., p. 96
22 Wynne-Thomas, *History of Cricket*, pp. 228–9
23 Wilde, *England: The Biography*, pp. 384–5; Geoffrey Boycott and Jon Hotten, *Being Geoffrey Boycott* (Fairfield Books, 2022) p. 183
24 Wynne-Thomas, *History of Cricket*, p. 229
25 Sissons, *The Players*, pp. 296–8

Chapter 27: Test Cricket Widens and Deepens

1 Garry Sobers, *My Autobiography* (Headline, 2003), p. 171
2 Brookes, *An Island's Eleven*, p. 205
3 Kumar Sangakkara, MCC Spirit of Cricket Lecture, 2011. https://www.espncricinfo.com/story/kumar-sangakkara-s-mcc-spirit-of-cricket-lecture-522183
4 Brookes, *An Island's Eleven*, pp. 219–40
5 Michael Roberts, *Incursions & Excursions in and Around Sri Lankan Cricket* (Vijitha Yapa, 2011), pp. 112–13
6 https://www.thecricketmonthly.com/story/834255/the-lion-s-fairy-tale

7   Brookes, *An Island's Eleven*, p. 105
8   https://www.rnz.co.nz/national/programmes/eyewitness/audio/201857365/should-i-stay-or-should-i-go
9   Oborne, *Wounded Tiger*, p. 197
10 John Snow, *Cricket Rebel* (Hamlyn, 1976), p. 69. See also Oborne, *Wounded Tiger*, p. 198
11 John Snow, *Cricket Rebel* (Hamlyn, 1976), p. 69
12 https://dailyasianage.com/news/68013/imran-khans-antagonistic-approach-to-bangladesh
13 https://www.espncricinfo.com/story/when-bangladesh-strode-onto-the-test-stage-1086520
14 https://www.bolnews.com/sports/2020/05/sarfaraz-nawaz-reveals-pak-vs-ban-match-of-1999-world-cup-was-fixed/
15 https://www.cricbuzz.com/cricket-news/102119/19-years-on-gordon-greenidge-holds-no-grudge-over-sacking-bangladesh-cricket-cricbuzzcom
16 Personal testimony to the authors from Abid Ali, India's all-rounder of the 1960s and 1970s
17 https://www.cricketcountry.com/articles/11-religion-based-trivia-in-indian-test-cricket-173964
18 https://www.espncricinfo.com/records/most-wickets-in-career-93276. For Kapil and his influence, see Bose, *Nine Waves*, chapter 20
19 Richard Heller and Peter Oborne, *White on Green* (Simon & Schuster, 2016), chapter 14
20 Oborne, *Wounded Tiger*, chapter 10
21 Mushtaq Mohammed, *Inside Out* (published in Pakistan, 2006), chapter 11
22 Oborne, *Wounded Tiger*, chapter 19
23 Heller and Oborne, *White on Green*, chapter 19
24 Ibid.
25 Ibid., chapter 23
26 Oborne, *Wounded Tiger*, p. 315

Chapter 29: Corruption and Scandal Stain Cricket

1   Oborne, *Wounded Tiger*, p. 379
2   Simon Wilde, *Caught: The Full Story of Corruption in International Cricket* (Aurum 2001), pp. 44–5
3   Oborne, *Wounded Tiger*, p. 379
4   Ibid., p. 381
5   Wilde, *Caught*, chapter 5
6   Ibid., chapter 2
7   Bose, *Nine Waves*, p. 178; Wilde, *Caught*, pp. 94–5
8   Wilde, *Caught*, pp. 98–9
9   Ibid., pp. 62–4
10 Bose, *Nine Waves*, p. 277–9
11 Ibid., pp. 283–4
12 Ibid., p. 280; see also Wilde, *Caught*, pp. 187–9

13 Wilde, *Caught*, pp. 190–1
14 https://www.theguardian.com/sport/2003/aug/03/cricket.features
15 Bose, *Nine Waves*, p. 286
16 Ibid., p. 280
17 https://www.espncricinfo.com/story/sangakkara-jayawardene-called-up-in-investigation-into-2011-world-cup-final-1226004
18 Wilde, *Caught*, pp. 120–30
19 Malcolm Speed, *Sticky Wicket* (HarperCollins Australia, 2011), pp. 118–19
20 Ibid., p. 123
21 https://www.espncricinfo.com/story/condon-reveals-extent-of-corruption-in-cricket-106490
22 Speed, *Sticky Wicket*, pp. 121–3
23 https://www.espncricinfo.com/cricketers/marlon-samuels-52983
24 https://www.espncricinfo.com/cricketers/danish-kaneria-40043
25 Nick Greenslade, *The Thin White Line: The Inside Story of Cricket's Greatest Fixing Scandal* (Pitch Publishing, 2020) pp. 171–2
26 Ibid., p. 174
27 Oborne, *Wounded Tiger*, pp. 376–7
28 Ibid., p. 251
29 https://www.espncricinfo.com/story/retiring-icc-acu-head-alex-marshall-warns-of-corruption-threat-from-badly-run-t20-leagues-1450987
30 https://www.thesun.co.uk/sport/9455246/womens-cricketers-report-match-fixing-approaches-with-huge-surge-in-betting-on-sport/; and https://www.news24.com/citypress/sport/womens-t20-world-cup-rocked-by-match-fixing-claim-20230216

Chapter 30: The Return of Racism

1 Wigmore, *Test Cricket*, pp. 163–4
2 Mike Marqusee, *Anyone But England* (Verso, 1994), p. 197
3 Ibid., p. 203
4 https://www.espncricinfo.com/story/the-unforgiven-286356
5 https://counterpoint.lk/sri-lankas-rebel-tour-to-south-africa-in-1982/
6 https://www.theage.com.au/sport/cricket/rebels-the-85-south-africa-tour-20051210-ge1ekr.html
7 https://www.theguardian.com/sport/2008/nov/23/mike-gatting-shakoor-rana
8 https://www.theguardian.com/sport/2010/jan/11/rebel-tour-1990-england-players-south-africa and https://www.espncricinfo.com/series/england-tour-of-pakistan-1987-88-61761/pakistan-vs-england-2nd-test-63471/full-scorecard
9 https://www.theguardian.com/sport/2005/nov/20/cricket.englandinpakistan2005062
10 https://www.independent.co.uk/sport/cricket-javed-savours-the-fruit-of-his-labours-pakistan-typified-by-their-captain-have-excelled-at-almost-every-aspect-of-cricket-in-this-summer-s-series-writes-scyld-berry-1540559.html
11 https://i.imgci.com/link_to_database/ARCHIVE/CRICKET_NEWS/1996/JAN/422818_WISDEN_01JAN1996.html

12 https://www.theguardian.com/sport/1999/may/10/cricket
13 Michael Collins, 'Black Cricket, the College at Haringey and the England and Wales Cricket Board', *The Political Quarterly*, vol. 94, no. 1 (January/March 2023), p. 71; doi.org/10.1111/1467-923X.13228
14 Ibid., p. 72
15 Ibid., p. 73
16 Ibid., p. 78
17 https://www.telegraph.co.uk/cricket/2021/07/19/hundred-can-new-format-help-ecb-engage-british-asian-population/
18 Sasha Mistlin, 'White British cricketers from private schools 34 times more likely than young Asians to reach elite level', *Guardian*, 20 November 2021
19 https://www.wisden.com/cricket-features/bradford-and-the-question-of-british-asian-integration
20 Martin Charter and Tom Clark, 'Final Report. Sustainability, Cricket Gear, Clothing and Apparel: Report on Cricket Gear', University for the Creative Arts, 1 October, 2023 p. 65; https://cfsd.org.uk/wp-content/uploads/2023/06/Sustainability_Cricket-Gear-Final-July-2022-Updated-June-2023.pdf
21 https://www.wisden.com/cricket-features/british-asian-cricket-passion-glory
22 https://nationalcl.play-cricket.com/home
23 https://www.dailymail.co.uk/sport/cricket/article-10453739/SPECIAL-REPORT-lack-diversity-Middlesex-Sportsmail-visits-besieged-county.html
24 https://www.theguardian.com/sport/2020/dec/24/english-cricket-has-a-diversity-problem-among-its-coaches
25 https://www.bbc.co.uk/sport/cricket/59166142
26 Lawrence Booth (ed.), *Wisden Cricketers' Almanack 2022* (Wisden, 2022), p. 1470
27 Lawrence Booth (ed.), *Wisden Cricketers' Almanack 2024* (Wisden, 2024), pp. 1501–3
28 Oborne and Heller, 'The Graces CC, the club which opens up cricket to LGBT people', *Oborne & Heller on Cricket* [podcast], season 1, episode 75 (10 January 2022)
29 https://www.kiaoval.com/prime-minister-announces-cricket-investement-at-kia-oval
30 https://www.telegraph.co.uk/cricket/2025/08/25/labour-rip-up-grassroots-fantasy-plan-schools-rishi-sunak/
31 'Holding Up a Mirror to Cricket', paragraph 4.3.6
32 https://www.theguardian.com/sport/2017/may/26/john-mcguire-the-indigenous-cricketer-who-lost-out-on-playing-for-australia
33 https://www.thecricketmonthly.com/story/1181098/the-ugly-australian--the-evolution-of-a-cricket-species
34 https://www.espncricinfo.com/story/mcgrath-denies-racism-claim-105996
35 https://www.espncricinfo.com/story/dean-jones-sacked-after-terrorist-remark-255892
36 https://www.telegraph.co.uk/cricket/2017/10/09/usman-khawaja-opponents-racial-abuse-kid-made-support-anyone/
37 https://www.sbs.com.au/news/article/usman-khawaja-stopped-by-security-at-hotel-three-times-in-apparent-racial-profiling-gaffe/66olz9hx1

38 https://www.cricbuzz.com/cricket-news/113562/makhaya-ntini-shaun-pollock-graeme-smith-blm-racism-in-cricket-csa-cricket-south-africa-south-african-cricket-cricbuzzcom
39 https://www.espncricinfo.com/story/ashwell-prince-on-black-lives-matter-south-africa-s-system-broken-1226572
40 https://www.espncricinfo.com/story/paul-adams-i-was-nicknamed-brown-s-when-i-was-playing-1270625
41 https://www.bbc.co.uk/sport/africa/59726569
42 https://www.thecricketer.com/Topics/international/mark_boucher_gross_misconduct_charges_dropped_cricket_south_africa_racism.html
43 https://www.espncricinfo.com/story/graeme-smith-denies-thami-tsolekile-s-allegations-of-racial-discrimination-1229447
44 https://www.news24.com/sport/cricket/proteas/report-finds-ab-de-villiers-unfairly-discriminated-against-khaya-zondo-on-racial-grounds-20211215
45 https://www.republicworld.com/sports/cricket/ex-proteas-bowler-reveals-he-got-shocking-response-from-amla-abd-on-pay-disparity-issue
46 https://www.thecricketmonthly.com/story/1131324/the-rainbow-beauty-of-hashim-amla
47 https://www.espncricinfo.com/story/ashwell-prince-on-black-lives-matter-south-africa-s-system-broken-1226572

Chapter 31: Permanent Revolution

1 Chalke, *Summer's Crown*, p. 302
2 Ibid., p. 293
3 Hughes, *And God Created Cricket*, p. 421
4 Ibid., p. 380
5 https://stats.espncricinfo.com/ci/engine/team/2.html?class=1;spanmin1=1+Jan+2000;spanval1=span;template=results;type=team;view=results
6 https://rapidleaks.com/sports/10-most-popular-sports-leagues-in-the-world
7 https://cricket.one/cricket-news/what-is-concussion-substitute-rule-in-cricket/653bdea1499725b358aa27b6
8 https://resources.cricket-australia.pulselive.com/cricket-australia/document/2023/08/07/13d08f1d-fda8-4b04-8d4f-49848fe085b7/Cricket-Australia-RAP-2019-2021-Web-Compressed.pdf
9 https://www.smh.com.au/sport/cricket/cricket-australia-to-make-south-asian-communities-a-massive-priority-20211028-p5942x.html; https://www.theguardian.com/sport/2023/dec/22/south-asian-fans-in-cricket-australias-sights-as-it-strives-to-be-a-sport-for-all
10 https://www.cricketcountry.com/articles/richard-chee-quee-first-of-chinese-origin-to-play-for-new-south-wales-563438/
11 Stefan Syzmanski and Tim Wigmore, *Crickonomics: The Anatomy of Modern Cricket* (Bloomsbury Sport, 2023), pp. 49–52
12 David Tossell, *One Day at a Time: The History of Limited-Overs Cricket in 25 Matches* (Fairfield Books, 2023), p. 296
13 https://cricketarchive.com/Archive/Players/302/302557/302557.html
14 Syzmanski and Wigmore, *Crickonomics*, p. 58

15 https://www.espncricinfo.com/story/west-indies-downward-spiral-in-the-2000s-441065
16 Tossell, *One Day at a Time*, pp. 283–7
17 Syzmanski and Wigmore, *Crickonomics*, pp. 53–71; and Oborne and Heller, 'No longer underdogs but still undervalued . . . New Zealand's world-class cricketers', *Oborne & Heller on Cricket* [podcast], season 1, episode 56 (14 June 2021)
18 Brookes, *An Island's Eleven*, pp. 275–6
19 Syzmanski and Wigmore, *Crickonomics*, pp. 158–61
20 https://emergingcricket.com/insight/thailand-halted-by-crickets-red-tape/#:~:text=It%20would%20be%20difficult%20to,not%20qualify%20because%20of%20their
21 https://www.bbc.co.uk/sport/cricket/27291212
22 https://resources.ecb.co.uk/ecb/document/2025/11/13/82c0fae4-0a76-43fa-9f77-049fd2bbe0d1/State-of-Equity-in-Cricket-Report-2025.pdf, pp. 9–10
23 Nicholson, *Ladies and Lords*, p. 338
24 Ibid., pp. 334–7
25 Ibid., p. 340
26 Ibid., pp. 336–7
27 https://www.wisden.com/cricket-features/crickets-diversity-problem-chasing-the-rainbow
28 https://www.bbc.co.uk/sport/cricket/58149676
29 Tossell, *One Day at a Time*, chapter 24
30 https://indianexpress.com/article/sports/cricket/180-million-people-watched-icc-womens-world-cup-2017-4790820/

Chapter 32: The ICC Expands Cricket Globally

1 https://www.espncricinfo.com/story/a-brief-history-209608
2 Speed, *Sticky Wicket*, pp. 111, 114
3 Oborne, *Wounded Tiger*, pp. 444–7
4 Brookes, *An Island's Eleven*, pp. 214–16
5 Speed, *Sticky Wicket*, pp. 167
6 https://www.espncricinfo.com/story/a-brief-history-209608; and https://www.icc-cricket.com/about/cricket/history-of-cricket/21st-century
7 https://www.nytimes.com/2015/03/05/sports/cricket/after-years-in-shadows-cricket-emerges-in-ireland.html
8 Wigmore, *Test Cricket*, p. 512–14
9 https://stats.espncricinfo.com/ci/engine/team/2234.html?class=10;spanmin1=01+Jan+2000;spanval1=span;template=results;type=team
10 Siggins, *Green Days*, chapter 12
11 Brookes, *An Island's Eleven*, pp. 221–3
12 https://www.theweek.in/theweek/sports/2023/10/07/world-cup-mavericks-dwayne-leverock-the-rotund-jailer.html
13 Brookes, *An Island's Eleven*, pp. 223–7
14 Misbah in conversation with Richard Heller in person

15 Brookes, *An Island's Eleven*, p. 236; https://cricketbhutan.org/ and https://www.espncricinfo.com/records/team/bhutan-112
16 Brookes, *An Island's Eleven*, pp. 226–7, 276–8
17 https://www.espncricinfo.com/story/afghanistan-get-associate-membership-645971
18 Ibid.
19 https://www.thecricketmonthly.com/story/1183566/the-definitive-rashid-khan-story–afghanistan-s-most-famous-export
20 Ibid.
21 https://cricketarchive.com/Archive/Events/26/Afghanistan_in_Zimbabwe_2015-16.html
22 https://www.cricket.com.au/news/3290881/rashids-record-pace-rewarded-with-no1
23 Ibid.
24 https://www.telegraph.co.uk/news/2020/07/19/british-expat-leads-unexpected-rise-cricket-germany-help-afghan/
25 https://www.dailymail.co.uk/news/article-13826149/freddie-flintoffs-ragtag-young-cricket-team-reveal-what-they-did-next-after-the-star-transformed-their-lives-on-field-of-dreams.html
26 Tuba Sangar, 'Afghanistan and the Taliban' in Booth (ed.), *Wisden Cricketers' Almanack 2022*, pp. 54–8; https://www.espncricinfo.com/story/afghanistan-women-request-icc-to-help-set-up-a-refugee-cricket-team-in-australia-1441819; https://www.forbes.com/sites/tristanlavalette/2024/07/23/push-to-fund-afghanistan-womens-cricket-fails-to-materialize/; Doctor Grim, 'Taliban Watch', *Private Eye*, Issue 1632 (13 September 2024), and Richard Heller's letter of reply to this in *Private Eye*, Issue 1633 (27 September 2024)
27 Asian Cricket Council committee for the evaluation of cricket in China, from the private archive of Ehsan Mani; see also Speed, *Sticky Wicket*, p. 168
28 https://www.bbc.co.uk/news/world-asia-pacific-11718145
29 https://cricketarchive.com/Archive/Events/14/Asian_Games_Womens_Cricket_Competition_2010-11.html
30 Brookes, *An Island's Eleven*, pp. 282–3
31 Both quotes in this paragraph taken from Preamble, 'Project USA' feasibility study, 2003, from the private archive of Ehsan Mani
32 https://www.espncricinfo.com/story/icc-slams-us-board-s-poor-administration-145494
33 Speed, *Sticky Wicket*, p. 170
34 Brookes, *An Island's Eleven*, pp. 282–3; and Oborne and Heller, 'The United States: Paradise regained for cricket?', *Oborne & Heller on Cricket* [podcast], season 1, episode 37 (11 January 2021)
35 Speed, *Sticky Wicket*, p. 170
36 Brookes, *An Island's Eleven*, p. 218
37 https://www.espncricinfo.com/story/maurice-odumbe-banned-for-five-years-135253
38 https://www.espncricinfo.com/story/a-brief-history-of-kenyan-cricket-261613
39 Speed, *Sticky Wicket*, pp. 200–1

40 ICC World Cricket Review Discussion Paper, January 2006 (accessed by kind permission of Ehsan Mani)
41 Brookes, *An Island's Eleven*, pp. 289–90
42 Brookes, *An Island's Eleven*, p. 291–4
43 Bose, *Nine Waves*, p. 465
44 Brookes, *An Island's Eleven*, pp. 298–9

Chapter 33: Cricket Comes Full Circle

1 Speed, *Sticky Wicket*, p. 214
2 Tossell, *One Day at a Time*, pp. 236–7
3 Wilde, *England: The Biography*, pp. 475–6
4 'Misbah ul-Haq on the last ball from the World Twenty20 Final in 2007 - I Am Misbah', YouTube, uploaded by likeMEDIA.tv, 20 June 2018, https://www.youtube.com/watch?v=hostWXYAyLE
5 Tossell, *One Day at a Time*, p. 247
6 Speed, *Sticky Wicket*, p. 203
7 Tossell, *One Day at a Time*, pp. 245–9; Bose, *Nine Waves*, pp. 382–3; Syzmanski and Wigmore, *Crickonomics*, p. 20
8 Tossell, *One Day at a Time*, p. 245
9 Tossell, *One Day at a Time*, p. 246; Bose, *Nine Waves*, p. 382
10 Tossell, *One Day at a Time*, p. 246; Hughes, *And God Created Cricket*, p. 413
11 Tossell, *One Day at a Time*, p. 257
12 Ibid., p. 259
13 Bose, *Nine Waves*, p. 390
14 Ibid.
15 Ibid., p. 380
16 Nathan Leamon and Ben Jones, *Hitting Against the Spin* (Constable, 2022), pp. 256–61, 266–8
17 Syzmanski and Wigmore, *Crickonomics*, pp. 22–4
18 Ibid.
19 Ibid., p. 21

Chapter 34: Cricket Reborn

1 https://www.statista.com/outlook/amo/sports/worldwide.
2 https://www.statista.com/outlook/amo/sports/cricket/worldwide
3 https://crickettimes.ca/articles/how-much-profit-does-cricket-generate-around-the-world/
4 https://www.craincurrency.com/sports/cricket-second-most-popular-sport-world-private-equity-wants
5 https://www.brandvm.com/post/top-5-most-profitable-sports-make-money
6 https://www.sportspro.com/news/ipl-2023-bcci-income-expenditure-surplus-wpl/
7 https://www.ecb.co.uk/about/what-we-do/finance#
8 https://www.statista.com/statistics/1458255/cricket-australia-total-revenue/

9 https://www.reddit.com/r/Cricket/comments/1fdgdkz/cricket_south_africa_released_their_202324/
10 Source: annual report of Sri Lanka Cricket Board 2022, of New Zealand Cricket 2024; https://srilankacricket.lk/2023/02/sri-lanka-cricket-earned-a-record-net-profit-of-rs-6-3-billion-in-2022/#:~:text=The%20highest%20annual%20net%20profit,invested%20a%20sum%20of%20Rs; and https://www.sportbusiness.com/2024/08/cricket-west-indies-well-set-to-enter-new-commercial-era/
11 https://propakistani.pk/2024/09/11/psl-no-longer-pcbs-top-revenue-source/
12 Ireland, 2024: https://cricketireland.ie/wp-content/uploads/2025/07/CI-2024-ANNUAL-REPORT.pdf. Afghanistan, 2022: https://api.acb.af/storage/annual-reports/682af23f0cbc8_1747644991.pdf
13 https://www.thecricketpanda.com/richest-cricket-leagues/
14 https://www.espncricinfo.com/story/bcci-set-to-get-nearly-40-of-icc-s-annual-net-earnings-in-new-revenue-distribution-model-1387167
15 https://www.thetimes.com/sport/cricket/article/hundred-sale-is-endorsement-of-english-game-that-will-now-change-for-ever-9vl90fmt2
16 https://www.sportspro.com/news/the-hundred-cricket-franchise-teams-sales-investment-ecb-july-2025/
17 https://www.ecb.co.uk/news/4215323/all-you-need-to-know-about-the-hundred-investment-process-as-it-enters-its-final-stage
18 https://www.thetimes.com/sport/cricket/article/counties-relieved-to-get-hundred-windfall-but-is-it-a-golden-handshake-6l6xh7htk
19 https://www.lords.org/lords/news-stories/the-lord-s-franchise-an-update
20 https://www.thetimes.com/sport/cricket/article/investors-hundred-sale-non-host-counties-gjdtcmqx3
21 https://www.thetimes.com/sport/cricket/article/counties-relieved-to-get-hundred-windfall-but-is-it-a-golden-handshake-6l6xh7htk
22 Booth (ed.), *Wisden Cricketers' Almanack 2024*
23 https://www.espncricinfo.com
24 https://www.espncricinfo.com
25 https://earth.org/cricket-in-peril-can-the-popular-sport-survive-in-the-face-of-a-rapidly-changing-climate/
26 Lawrence Booth (ed.), *Wisden Cricketers' Almanack 2020* (Wisden, 2020), pp. 172–3
27 https://www.theguardian.com/sport/2023/apr/22/a-perfect-vehicle-for-climate-action-why-cricket-is-taking-a-stand
28 https://www.theguardian.com/sport/2023/nov/27/a-great-step-forward-cricket-ecb-signs-up-to-un-climate-framework
29 https://earth.org/cricket-in-peril-can-the-popular-sport-survive-in-the-face-of-a-rapidly-changing-climate/
30 https://contradiction.com.au/articles/pat-cummins-the-climate-conscious-cricketer-with-a-carbon-conundrum/4
31 https://www.theguardian.com/sport/2024/oct/23/cricket-for-climate-pat-cummins-australia-the-spin
32 https://mofa.gov.pk/foreign-office-observes-plant-4-pakistan-day
33 https://www.theguardian.com/sport/blog/2022/oct/18/aramco-cricket-deal-saudi-sport-revenue-t20-world-cup; and https://www.theguardian.com/

sport/2023/apr/22/saudi-arabias-grand-sportswashing-campaign-comes-to-finish-off-crickets-current-order
34 https://www.theguardian.com/law/2015/dec/22/gay-british-man-avoids-extradition-to-dubai; and https://www.lse.ac.uk/research/research-for-the-world/society/peril-and-privilege-gay-expat-nightlife-in-dubai
35 Private conversation in 2018 with the former CEO of the ICC, Dave Richardson
36 https://www.bbc.co.uk/sport/cricket/47212367
37 https://www.bbc.co.uk/news/world-asia-india-59130756
38 See our podcast interviews with Olivier (one in besieged Kyiv where he holed up with his beloved dogs) https://chiswickcalendar.co.uk/episode-96-rebuilding-ukraine-cricket-and-childrens-lives-despite-the-icc/ and https://chiswickcalendar.co.uk/episode-80-waiting-for-the-assault-on-kyiv/; and https://www.espncricinfo.com/story/ukraine-though-torn-by-war-is-making-a-pitch-for-associate-membership-of-the-icc-1314749; and https://www.forbes.com/sites/tristanlavalette/2022/07/26/ukraines-all-important-bid-for-coveted-associate-cricket-membership-deferred-due-to-ongoing-war/
39 https://www.sports.legal/2024/04/afghanistan-cricket-an-icc-conundrum/
40 Lawrence Booth (ed.), *Wisden Cricketers' Almanack 2025* (Wisden, 2025)

Chapter 35: Does Cricket Make Money to Exist or Exist to Make Money?

1 Altham, *A History of Cricket*, p. 8
2 *Observer*, 6 June 1926
3 Altham, *A History of Cricket*, p. 347
4 Ibid., pp. 367–8
5 https://www.espncricinfo.com/story/gideon-haigh-a-taxing-question-for-the-bcci-444442
6 James, *Beyond a Boundary*, pp. 196–9
7 Nick Hoult, 'The Birth of the Hundred' and John Crace, 'The ECB Faces the Politicians' in Booth (ed.), *Wisden Cricketers' Almanack 2020*
8 https://alsamaproject.com/
9 https://www.lordstaverners.org/how-we-help/charitable-programmes/cricket-kit-recycling/case-study-ukraine/; https://chiswickcalendar.co.uk/episode-96-rebuilding-ukraine-cricket-and-childrens-lives-despite-the-icc/
10 https://comptoncricketclub.us/
11 Abraham and Coyne, *Evita Burned Down Our Pavilion*, pp. 392–4
12 Timeri N. Murari, *The Taliban Cricket Club* (Allen & Unwin, 2013), pp. 47–8

INDEX

A
Adams, Paul 315
Adhikari, Hemu 235n, 279
Afghanistan 336–9, 360, 370
Ahmed, Mushtaq 289, 300, 353
Ahmed, Niaz 273, 274
Akram, Wasim 282, 299, 300
Alcock, Charles 49, 55–6, 63, 85
Aldred, Tanya 367–8
Alexander, Gerry 226–8, 229, 236
Ali, Abid 279
Allen, David 212, 231
Allen, Gubby 173, 176, 182–3, 207, 211, 219, 244
Alley, Bill 207, 259
Altham, H. S. xv, xvi, 39, 72, 159, 207, 371–4
Amarnath, Lala 234, 235
amateurs vs professionals 15–16, 29, 34–5, 41–3, 63, 53–5, 68–9, 87, 154–9, 203–5, 222, 263
Ambrose, Curtly 285, 286
Ames, Les 158
Amir, Mohammad 303–5
Amla, Hashim 314
Anglo-Boer War 105–8
apartheid 88, 100n, 107, 108, 178, 185, 239–47, 260, 308–9
Archdale, Betty 50, 162, 164, 195
Argentina 132–3, 134, 135–7
aristocracy and cricket 9, 12–15, 18, 20, 29–30
Arlott, John 239, 243, 247, 261
Armstrong, Warwick 90, 166–7
Arnold, Thomas 31–2
Artillery Ground, Finsbury 13, 15, 46
Ash, Eileen 163
The Ashes 65, 85–6, 185
    1926: 374–5
    1928–29: 167–8
    1932–33: 173–8
    1934–35: 182
    1953–54: 210
    1954–55: 210–11
    1956: 211
    1961: 212–13
    1981: 286
    1985: 287
    1987: 287
    1989: 287
    2021–22: 320–1
    2026: 375–7
Ashley-Cooper, F. S. 109
Asian Cricket Conference 269
Asian Cricket Council 339–40
Asif, Mohammad 303–5
Aslam, Sheikh Mohammad 114, 115
Attlee, Clement 18, 43–4, 194, 203
Auckland 94, 95
Australasian Cricket Council 87, 89
Australia 72, 73, 75–7
    21st century 320–1, 360
    Board of Control 89–91
    Bodyline crisis 165–83
    and climate change 368
    early domestic matches 77–9
    English influence on 78
    and First World War 153
    immigrants to 75–6
    indigenous people 76, 80–3, 178, 214, 321
    interwar years 165–7
    and Kerry Packer 263–4, 266–7
    non-white policies 76
    Pacific Islanders 76
    post-Second World War 211–13
    and racism 308, 314, 321
    residential qualification 259
    and Second World War 192

Australia (continued)
  and television 264
  women in cricket 163–4, 326–7
The Australian Club 77
Australian Cricket Board (ACB) 264, 298, 338
Australian cricket team 211
  1876 first Test match 84–5
  1876–1914: 89–91
  1920s 166–7
  1930s 168–71
  21st century 320–1
  betting & corruption 298
  first-class cricket status 59
  v England 76, 79–80, 84–7, 167–8, 208–10, 212–13, 287, 320–1, 374–5
  v India 280–1
  v New Zealand 95, 278
  v Philadelphia 126–7
  v South Africa 88–9, 240
  v South Africa (1902) 88–9
  v Sri Lanka 271, 297
  v West Indies 221–2, 227–30, 286
  see also Bodyline crisis
  The Ashes
Australian women's cricket team: v England 162, 214–15, 327, 365
  v India 327
Azharuddin, Mohammad 298–9, 300–1

B
Bacher, Ali 277
Bailey, Abe 107, 108, 109
Bailey, Trevor 42, 199, 204, 210, 223
Bairstow, Jonny 368
Baldwin, Stanley 48, 170
balls 7, 8, 17, 49, 161
Baloo, Palwankar 187
Bangladesh 272–6, 342
  see also East Pakistan cricket team
Bangladesh Premier League 276, 351, 361
Bannerman, Charles 80, 84
Bannister, Jack 261
Barbados 118, 119, 219, 220, 223, 369
Barnes, Sydney 64, 66, 152, 156, 278
Barrington, Ken 212, 236
baseball and cricket 124–5
bats 17, 23, 39, 49
batting: defensive 207
  hitting ball to leg 77
  LBW 154

left-handers 47, 77, 154
pad-play 225
and T20: 353
Bavuma, Temba 316
Beckett, Samuel 143
Bedi, Bishan 279, 280
Bedser, Alec 199, 203, 208, 210, 261
Belize 132
Benaud, Richie 207, 211–13, 227–9, 265
Benson & Hedges Cup 254–5, 257
Bergman-Österberg, Martina 50
Bermuda 334
betting & corruption xvi, xviii, 8, 11–15, 46, 27, 28, 253, 258, 295–7, 301
  see also spot-fixing
Bevin, Ernest 194
Bhutan 335
Big Bash League 320, 351
Bindra, I. S. 344
Bird, Dickie 265
Birley, Derek 6, 8, 205
Bishop, Ian 285, 322
Blackham, Jack 85, 87
Blair, Bob 213, 214
Blanckenberg, Jimmy 158
Bligh, Ivo 86, 116
Blythe, Colin 65, 151
Board of Control for Cricket in India (BCCI) 347–8, 349–51, 355–6
Bodyline crisis 165–83
Boland, Scott 83, 320–1
books & cricket 3, 4, 6, 8, 19–20, 28–9, 32, 33, 47, 126n, 135n, 141, 158–9, 371–4, 381–2
  see also Wisden Cricketers' Almanack
Border, Allan 267, 297
Bosanquet, Bernard 66, 106
Botham, Ian 15n, 214, 286, 339
Boucher, Jimmy 144
Boucher, Mark 315
Bowden, Monty 104–5
Bowen, Rowland 4, 5, 6, 8, 16, 17, 68, 117
Bowes, Bill 173, 174, 198, 203
bowling 16–17, 21–2, 353
  doosras 290
  flippers 207
  googlies 39n, 66, 106
  left-arm 65, 66
  leg theory 171–2, 174
  no-ball rule 211–12
  overarm 126
  reverse swing 282

round-arm 16, 21–2, 23
spin 289, 290–1
swerve/swing 67
underarm 16–17
yorkers 127
see also Bodyline crisis
Box, Tom 26
Boxall, Thomas 3, 4, 20
boxes 23
Boycott, Geoffrey 265, 266, 286
Bradman, Don 38, 76, 83, 144, 155, 165, 167–8, 173–8, 182–3, 199, 209–10, 211, 265, 308
Brassey, Lady Marie 48
Brathwaite, Carlos 322
Brazil 131, 132, 133, 134, 136
Brearley, Mike 244, 263, 286
Briggs, Johnny 65, 102, 109
British Dominions xvi, xvii, 72, 73, 180, 195–6
British Empire xvi–xvii, 27–8, 32, 69–70, 72–3, 103, 165, 262, 358
The British Empire Eleven 196
British Guiana *see* Guyana
Broad, Chris 309, 310
Broad, Stuart 348
Broadbridge, James 22
Brooks, Reginald Shirley 85–6
Brown, Freddie 133, 195, 198, 204, 211, 246
Bryant, Mabel 49
Budding, Edwin 23–4
Bukhatir, Sheikh 335, 336n
Burgst, Huibert Nahuys van 99
Burton, Tommy 121
Butt, Ijaz 305
Butt, Salman 304
Buttler, Jos xiv–xv

C

Cadwallader, Harry 101
Caesar, Julius 26
Caffyn, Billy 29, 34, 80
Cahn, Sir Julien 23n, 156, 182
Canada 19, 72, 128–30, 333
Canterbury Cricket Club, NZ 94–5
Carberry, Michael 311
Cardus, Neville 67–8, 159, 179–80, 189, 371
Caribbean Super League 351
Carr, Arthur 151, 158, 172, 173, 182
Carr, Donald 114, 236, 256–7
Central America 131, 132, 137

Ceylon *see* Sri Lanka
Chanderpaul, Shivnarine 286, 322
Chandrasekhar, Bhagwat 279
Channel Islands 197
Chapman, Percy 167, 168, 245
Chee Quee, Richard 321
Chester, Frank 153
Chile 131, 133–4, 336
China 335, 339–40, 343, 361
Cipriani, Arthur 120
Clarke, Alfred 27
Clarke, Bertie 196
Clarke, Giles 345
Clarke, William 25–30
Clean Bowl Racism 287–8
climate change 357, 366–9
Close, Brian 212, 236, 263, 367n
coaching 126, 207, 324, 325, 355
Cocker, John 79
Collins, A. E. J. 152
Collins, Michael 310
commercialisation xiii, 53–5, 252–3, 362–4, 376–8
    17th century 9
    18th century 15, 33, 46, 357
    19th century 26–7, 29–30
    21st century 358–9, 376
    and county cricket xiii–xiv, xvii, 362–3, 376
Compton, Denis 193, 196, 206, 208, 211, 255
Condon, Paul 302–3
Connor, Clare 325
Constantine, Learie 119, 121, 157, 181, 192, 194–5, 200, 372
Constantine, Lebrun 121
Contractor, Nari 112, 230
Conway, John 84
Cornell, John 264
corruption *see* betting & corruption
County Championship 56–60, 66
    21st century 319–20, 376
    decline of 253–4
    impact of commercialisation xiii, xv
    interwar years 154, 156
    and league cricket 60–1
    post-Second World War 203–4, 206
    and professional teams 57
    and Second World War 192
county cricket 66
    19th century 57–9
    21st century 319–20

county cricket (continued)
   aristocratic patrons 59
   future of 378–80
   impact of commercialisation xiii–xiv, 362–3
   impact of The Hundred 362–3
   interwar years 154, 155–6, 158
   long-form cricket xvi–xvii
   loss of best players xiv, 319–20
   overseas recruitment 67, 260–1, 319
   player qualifications 58, 62
   points system 63–4
   post-Second World War 203–7
   salaries 63
Couzens, Johnny and Jimmy (Yellenach and Grougarrong) 82
Cowdrey, Colin 57, 225, 230–1, 273
creag 5
Cricket Council (England) 262, 287
   see also England and Wales Cricket Board
cricket season, expansion of xiii
Cromwell, Oliver 9, 46, 140
Cronje, Hansie 298–9, 300, 302
Cummins, Pat 368
Curran, Sam xiv

D
Daft, Richard 27, 38, 49
Davidson, Alan 212, 227–8
Davis, Joan 163
de Grise, Jehan 4
de Mello, Anthony 233–4, 235n
de Silva, Aravinda 271–2, 297
De Valera, Eamon 142–3
Demerara *see* Guyana
Denmark 197
Derbyshire County Cricket Club 58, 59, 121, 155, 156n
Deutrom, Warren 146, 332
Dev, Kapil 258, 280–1, 301
Dexter, Ted 212, 254
Dhoni, M. S. 348, 351
Dilshan, Tillakaratne 353
disability and cricket 313
discrimination in cricket 312–14, 325–6 *see also* racism and cricket
Disraeli, Benjamin 25, 37, 38, 72
Doggett, Brendan 321
Doig, Chris 323–4
D'Oliveira, Basil 100n, 208, 241–5, 247
D'Oliveira, Lewis 241

Donnelly, Desmond 196
Douglas-Home, Sir Alec 205, 244
Duckworth-Lewis-Stern method 354n
Duggan, Mary 214
Dukes, Penshurst 17
Duleepsinhji, K. S. 144, 155, 189

E
Eade, Andrew 330
East India Company 9, 19, 111
East Pakistan *see* Bangladesh
East Pakistan cricket team 273–4
Ecuador 132
Edgbaston 378–9
Edrich, Geoff 198–9
Egypt 195–6
Emburey, John 309
Engineer, Farokh 260, 279, 280
England xv–xviii
   14th century 4–5
   16th century xv, 5–7, 45
   17th century 7–9, 45–6
   18th century 3, 4, 9, 11–16, 17–20, 45, 46, 357
   19th century xvi–xvii, 3, 20, 25–35, 55, 65–70, 357–8
   20th century xvii, 65–70, 286–8
   21st century 347
   administration 253, 262
   and apartheid 308–9
   discrimination in cricket 312–14, 325–6
   First World War 154–6
   imperial expansion 72–3
   and racism 287–8, 307–8, 309–14
   Sunday cricket 201, 254, 256
   tobacco sponsorship 254–6
   women in cricket 161–3, 288–9, 325–6
   see also Bodyline crisis
England and Wales Cricket Board (ECB) 287–8
England Women's Cricket Federation (EWCF) 163
English Cricket Board: and county cricket 319–20
   and The Hundred 362–4, 376
   and racism 311–12
   response to corruption 301–2
   response to success of IPL 352
   revenue 360
   and women's cricket 326

English cricket team
   and apartheid 243–5, 310
   betting & corruption 301–2
   choice of captain 204–5, 222, 263
   post-Second World War 208–11, 239
   v Argentina 135, 137
   v Australia 79–80, 84–7, 167–8, 208–10, 212–13, 287, 320–1, 374–5
   v East Pakistan 273–4
   v India 112, 278–80, 287
   v Ireland 332
   v New Zealand 95, 213
   v Pakistan 235–6, 309–10
   v Philadelphia 127
   v South Africa 101–4, 106–7, 108–9, 239, 286
   v Sri Lanka 116, 272
   v USA 126
   v West Indies 181, 192, 220–1, 222–3, 225–6, 230–1, 286, 287, 352
   v Zimbabwe 105–6, 343
   see also Bodyline crisis
   The Ashes
English women's cricket team: v Australia 162, 214–15, 327, 365
   v New Zealand 162
entertainment, cricket as xv–xvi, 7–9, 29, 46, 268, 357, 358–9, 374
export of cricket 9, 18–20

F

Faulkner, Aubrey 106
Federation of International Cricketers' Associations (FICA) 354
Fellows, Harvey 21
Fender, Percy 42, 172
Ferslev, Frederick 197
Fiji 96–7, 262
Fingleton, Jack 176, 183
first-class cricket 59–60, 204–5, 251–3, 358, 374, 377, 379, 381
First World War 67, 151–9
Fitzgerald, R. A. 126
Fleming, Stephen 278, 323, 324, 355
Fletcher, Duncan 319
Flintoff, Freddie 337–8, 352, 381
football 55–6, 61, 155
   comparison with cricket 53–5, 252–3, 260, 262

Foreman, Denis 245
Foster, Frank 171–2
Foy, Philip 132–3
franchises *see* private equity & franchises
Free Foresters 34, 59, 60
Fry, C. B. 42, 55, 65, 68
future of cricket 357, 360–1
   climate change 357, 366–9
   county cricket 378–80
   first-class cricket 374, 379
   impact of T20: 365–6
   private equity & franchises 361–4, 377–8, 379

G

Ganteaume, Andy 210n
Gatting, Mike 236, 287, 289, 309–10
Gavaskar, Sunil 258, 279, 280
The Gentlemen 39, 42, 59, 113n, 205
Germany 144, 151, 153, 194, 335, 337
Gibbs, Lance 226, 227, 229
Giffen, George 86
Gilbert, Eddie 83, 178
Gilchrist, Roy 208, 226, 236
Gillette Cup 56, 145, 254
Glamorgan cricket team xiii–xiv, 156, 203, 204
Gloucestershire County Cricket Club 58, 59, 151, 156n
gloves 23
Goddard, John 220, 221–2, 225–6
Gomez, Gerry 220
Gooch, Graham 286, 308–9
Gordon, Sir Home 193
Gower, David 267, 287
Grace, Bessie 49
Grace, E. M. 39, 58, 80
Grace, W. G. 23–4, 37–44, 47, 55, 65, 84, 88, 126, 144, 151, 152, 255
Green, Thomas 24
Greenidge, Gordon 275
Gregory, Jack 167
Gregory, Ned 77
Gregory, Syd 90
Griffith, Charlie 112, 230
Grimston, Robert 24
Gujarati Metropolitan Cricket League (GMCL) 311
Gunasekara, G. H. 116
Gupta, M. K. 298–9
Guyana 118, 120

H

Hadlee, Richard 277–8, 281
Hailsham, Lord 181
Hain, Peter 106, 244, 308
Hall, Wesley 225, 227, 228, 229, 230, 259
Hambledon Club 13, 16–18
Hammond, Walter 38, 105, 155, 167–8, 181, 195, 199, 208, 209
Hampshire County Cricket Club 58, 156n, 319, 363
Haringey Cricket College 210–11
Harlequins 34
Harris, Lord George 57–8, 103–4, 158, 185, 371
Harvey, Neil 199, 212
Hawke, Lord Martin 62, 84–5, 87, 136–7, 152
Hayman, William 81–2
Haynes, Johnny 246n
Hazare, Vijay 193n, 234–5
Headley, George 128, 157, 192, 220, 223
Healy, Alyssa 326, 327
Heine, Peter 240
Heller, Richard 336
helmets 267, 320
Hendren, Patsy 38, 141, 155, 167
Hendricks, William Henry 'Krom' 100–1, 103, 245
Hignell, Andrew 18–19
Hill, Clem 67, 77, 90
Hirst, George 43, 65, 67
Hitler, Adolf 171, 193, 194
Hobbs, Jack 38, 65, 68, 89, 151–2, 155, 167, 255, 375
Holsinger, Alfred 116
Hughes, Phil 320
The Hundred xiii, 320, 326, 351n, 352, 379
  and the ECB 362–4, 376
Hunte, Conrad 208, 226, 227, 228, 229, 230
Hussain, Nasser 308
Hutton, Len 62, 204–5, 208, 210, 222–3, 255
Hyndman, H. M. 18

I

I Zingari 34, 42
Ibadulla, Khalid 235
Illingworth, Ray 261, 263, 367n
Imperial Cricket Conference (ICC) 58n, 59, 107–8, 262
  associate members 1965: 145, 146, 262
  denies membership to South Africa 240
  expansion of test cricket 1926: 185–6
  Intercontinental Cup 146
  see also International Cricket Council
Independent Commission for Equity in Cricket 312–14
India
  20th century 186–8, 278–81
  21st century 347–51, 360–1
  betting & corruption 295–6
  bid for control of ICC 344–6
  caste system 28, 111–12
  and climate change 366, 368–9
  dominance of 360–1
  export of cricket to 9, 19, 72, 73, 111–13
  and First World War 153
  and the ICC 344–6, 366
  impact of TV on 253, 281
  Indian princes build teams 186–7
  indigenous people and cricket 111–12
  Pentangular tournament 188, 193
  post-Second World War 233–5
  Quadrangular tournament 112, 153, 187–8
  Ranji Trophy 188, 193
  and Second World War 193
  and T20 internationals 347–8
  and Test cricket 185–6
  tobacco industry and cricket 257–8
Indian cricket team: betting & corruption 298–9, 300–1
  matches with Pakistan 237
  post-Independence 234–5
  v Australia 280–1
  v England 112, 278–80, 287
  v New Zealand 323
  v Pakistan 237, 279, 348
  v West Indies 220, 230, 279
Indian Premier League (IPL) xiv–xv, 320, 349, 350–2, 354–6, 358–9, 360–2, 364,
Indian women's cricket team v Australia 327
indigenous people and cricket: Australia 76
  India 111–12
  Latin America 132
  New Zealand 93
  Sri Lanka 115–16
  West Indies 117–18
Industrial Revolution 20, 25, 72
Intercontinental Cup 146, 333–4
international cricket
  18th century 15
  bilateral series 283, 329, 332, 342, 344, 345, 347, 355, 366
  and Covid pandemic 355

one-day matches 258–9
post-Second World War 208–11
and the T20: 365–6
see also British Dominions
International Cricket Council (ICC) 262
  21st century 329–36
  absorbs women's cricket 324–5
  Anti-Discrimination Code 369
  ban on gambling advertising 258
  and China 339–40
  financial hierarchy of members 360–1
  global expansion 269–83, 329–36
  income from TV rights 330
  independent review of 344–6
  and India 344–6, 366
  Intercontinental Cup 331, 333
  and Kerry Packer 265–6
  power struggle within 344–6
  response to corruption 296, 302–3, 305
  T20 internationals 347–8
  and the USA 340–1
  women's representation on 325
  youth competitions & development 333
  and Zimbabwe 343
  see also Imperial Cricket Conference
Iqbal, Asif 281, 282, 296
Ireland
  before 1921: 137–43
  1922–1999: 143–5
  21st century 145–7, 360
  emigrants to Australia 76, 141
  emigrants to the USA 141
  export of cricket to 19
  full membership of ICC 331–2
Irish cricket team 139
  20th century 143–5
  21st century 145–7, 331–3
  and the ICC 145, 146
  T20 competitions 147, 332
  Test matches 146–7
  v England 332
  v Pakistan 332
  v West Indies 144
Irish women's cricket team 147, 332–3
Ironmonger, Bert 174, 178
Islamia College 114, 233

J

Jackson, F. S. 34, 55
Jackson, Russell 81
Jamaica 118, 120

James, C. L. R. 119, 120, 121, 226, 242, 379–80
Jardine, Douglas xvii, 34, 167, 169, 172–3, 174–5, 176, 177, 179, 181
Javed, Aaqib 156n
Jayasuriya, Sanath 271, 314
Jayawardene, Mahela 272, 355
Jessop, Gilbert 42, 55, 65, 67
The John Player League 254
Johnston, Brian 134, 309
Jones, Alan 185n
Jones, Dean 314
Joyce, Ed 143, 145, 146, 332
Jupp, Harry 38

K

Kaneria, Danish 303
Kanhai, Rohan 225, 228, 229, 230, 259
Kardar, Abdul Hafeez 115, 281
Kent County Cricket Club 57–8, 59, 156n
Kenya 275, 333–4, 341–2, 343
Khan, Ayub 235, 273–4, 281
Khan, Imran 112, 114, 267, 274, 282–3, 369
Khan, Jahangir 112–3
Khan, Majid 114, 282, 283, 299
Khan, Rashid 337
Khan, Shaharyar 188
Khawaja, Usman 314
King, Bart 67, 127
Kingsley, Charles 32–3
Kline, Lindsay 228, 229
Knight, G. T. 22
knockout competitions 56, 61, 155
Knott, Alan 274, 286
Kohli, Virat 351

L

Laker, Jim 199, 210, 211, 246–7, 265
The Lambert & Butler Cup 257
Lancashire County Cricket Club xiv, 58, 59, 63, 156n, 257, 302
Lancashire League 61, 63, 157
Lang, Andrew 371
Lang, Jack 170
Langford, Brian 254
Lara, Brian 286, 322
Larsen, Gavin 96
Larwood, Harold 167, 170, 172, 173, 174–5, 177, 181–2, 196
Latif, Rashid 297

Latin America 131–3
Laver, Frank 90
Lawrence, Charles 80, 82
Lawrence, John 141–2
Laws of Cricket 3, 7, 14, 16, 17
   1890–1914: 66
   batting 66
   Bodyline crisis 177
   bowling 66
   impact of First World War 154
   impact of Second World War 200–1
   ICC 59
   no-ball rule 211–12
   residential qualification rules 139, 157–8, 207, 259–61
   and round-arm bowling 21, 22
leg before wicket (LBW) 14, 154, 225
Leach, Rev. A. W. 61
league cricket 60–1
   and First World War 152
   interwar years 157–9
   lack of media attention 63–4
   player quality 64
   post-Second World War 207–8
   salaries 63
   women's cricket 163
Lennox, Charles, Duke of Richmond 12, 14, 18, 20
Leverock, Dwayne 334
Lewis, Chris 301–2, 308
LGBTQ+ experience of cricket 313, 326, 369
Lillee, Dennis 265
Lillywhite, Fred 28, 126
Lillywhite, James 34, 84, 95
Lillywhite, John 43
Lillywhite, William 22, 26
Llewellyn, C. B. 67, 88
Lloyd, Clive 260, 285
The London Counties Eleven 196
long-form cricket xvi–xvii, 44
   benefits of 381
   impact of T20: 365–6
   and the media 252, 254, 380
   and sponsorship 256–7
   survival of 358
Lord, David 265
Lord, Thomas 15
Lord's Cricket Ground xiii–xiv, 3, 15n, 24, 26, 86, 192, 241, 262, 269, 327, 329, 378
Lowe, Muriel 163
Lupton, Arthur 158
Lyttelton, R. H. 24

M

MacDonald, Ramsay 170
Maclagan, Myrtle 162, 195
MacLaren, Archie 42, 55, 65, 68, 83, 137, 166
MacLaurin, Lord 287–8
Mahanama, Roshan 314
Mahmood, Fazal 208, 233–4
Major, John 9
Malaysia 334
Malik, Saleem 277n, 297–8, 299
Malinga, Lasith 21
Mani, Ehsan 329–31
Mankad, Vinoo 208, 235n, 237
Marcon, Rev. W. 21
Marquand, David 30, 379
Marsh, Jack 83, 178
Marsh, Rodney 265
Marshall, Alex 305
Martindale, Manny 181
Martin-Jenkins, Christopher 309
Marylebone Cricket Club (MCC) xvi, 14–16
   21st century 378
   and apartheid 244
   Bodyline crisis 175–7
   changing remit of 262
   and county cricket 57, 59
   failed attempt at knockout competition 56
   and Lord Harris 58
   and players 58, 62
   post-Second World War 203, 207
   regulations and laws 17
   and round-arm bowling 22
   and South Africa 240, 241
   and strikes by players 63
   and W. G. Grace 42, 43
   women accepted as members 288–9
Maxwell, Glenn 367–8
May, Peter 204, 211, 212, 213, 225, 246
May, Tim 290, 298
McAlister, Peter 89–90
McCabe, Stan 144, 174
McCullum, Brendon 376–7
McDonald, Ted 78, 157, 167
McGrath, Glenn 290, 314
McGuire, John 314
McKenzie, John 3–4
McMaster, Emile 102, 109, 141
Mead, Phil 38
Meckiff, Ian 211, 212, 228

media and cricket: xiii–xiv, xv, xvii, 63–4, 158, 163, 166, 168, 174, 175–6, 179–83, 251–3, 359
   see also newspapers
Melbourne Cricket Club 78, 82
Merchant, Vijay 112n, 193n
Mexico 131, 132
Miakhel, Adnan 337, 338n
Miandad, Javed 282, 283, 296n
Middlesex County Cricket Club 58, 59, 154, 156n
Miller, Charles 136
Miller, Keith 199, 209, 211
Milton, Arthur 206
Milton, William 100–1
Minor Counties Championship 60
Misbah-ul-Haq 305, 335, 348
Mitchell, Arthur 68
Mitchell, Bruce 189, 195
Mitchell, Tommy 176
Modi, Lalit 349–50
Mohammad, Hanif 236, 274, 286, 353
Mohammad, Mushtaq 119n, 235, 282
Monckton, Walter 222, 246
Morocco 335–6
Mullagh, Johnny (Unaarrimin) 82–3
Muralitharan, Muttiah 271, 272, 278, 289, 290
Murdoch, Billy 85, 87, 95
Murphy, Florence 86
Murray, Deryck 230
Murtagh, Tim 145, 146, 331, 332
Mushtaq, Saqlain 289, 290
Mynn, Alfred 23, 26

N
Nash, Dion 323
National Cricket Association 262
National Cricket League 311
Nawaz, Sarfraz 275n, 282
Nayudu, C. K. 187n, 234
Nelson Cricket Club 157
Nepal 334
Netherlands 164, 197
New Zealand 72, 73, 93–6
   21st century 323–4, 360
   English influence on 93–5
   independent cricket country 95–6
   indigenous people 93, 324
   post-Second World War 213–14
   and Second World War 192–3
   and Test cricket 185–6, 277–8
   women in cricket 164, 288
New Zealand cricket team: v Australia 95, 278
   v England 95, 213
   v India 323
   v South Africa 213–14
   v Sri Lanka 272
   v West Indies 213
New Zealand women's cricket team 162, 164
Newland, Richard 13
newspapers 12, 15, 19, 28, 40, 63–4, 67–8, 79, 166, 174, 299, 301, 304–5, 310
nightwatchman 177n
Noble, Monty 89, 90, 166
Nooyi, Indra 325
North, Marcus 319
Northeast, Sam xiii–xiv
Nottinghamshire County Cricket Club 25, 58, 59, 155, 156n, 158, 260
Nourse, Dave 107
Ntini, Makhaya 315
Nupen, Buster 189
Nurse, Seymour 229
Nyren, John 22
Nyren, Richard 13, 16

O
Oakman, Alan 246–7
O'Brien, Kevin 146, 332
Oldfield, Bert 175
Ollivierre, Charles 121
Olympic Games 339, 340, 366
Oman 335
one-day cricket 157, 200, 252, 254, 256–9, 267, 347
   see also short-form cricket
O'Reilly, Bill 76, 144, 174, 178, 183
The Oval 55–6, 151, 192
Oxbridge universities 57, 59, 60

P
Packer, Kerry 29, 261, 263–8, 269, 324,
pads 23
Paine, Tom 18
Pakistan 28, 188, 275n, 360
   1960s to 1990s 281–3
   1970s player revolt 260
   export of cricket to 113–15
   post-Second World War 233–4
   tobacco industry and cricket 257–8
   Tours by England 273–4

Pakistan cricket team 156n, 277n
	betting & corruption 297–301, 303–5
	post-Independence 235
	post-Second World War 234
	v England 235–6, 309–10
	v India 237, 279, 348
	v Ireland 332
	v West Indies 236
Pakistan Super League 351, 361
Papua New Guinea 97, 195
Parr, George 27, 80, 95
Parsis 111–12
Patterson, Kurtis 210n
Patterson, Patrick 285
Perera, C. E. 116
Phangiso, Aaron 315
Philadelphia cricket team 125–7
Philip, Duke of Edinburgh 207
Pietersen, Kevin 352
pitches
	19th century 22–4, 63
	and climate change 367
	historical development 17, 23–4, 63, 66
	international standards for 262–3
	and the lawn mower 23–4
	'square' roped off 66
players
	18th century 12–13
	19th century 26–7, 29–30, 34–5
	all-round sportsmen 206
	amateurs vs professionals 15–16, 29, 34–5, 41–2, 43, 63
	batters v bowlers 15, 33
	benefits & testimonials 43, 62
	campaigns against overseas recruits 67
	and commercialisation 252–3, 255
	interwar years 157–8
	and Kerry Packer 263–8
	professional xiv–xv, 15–16, 26–7, 29–30, 34–5, 261–2, 354
	recruitment from overseas 157–8, 259–61
	residential qualifications 139, 157–8, 207, 259–61
	salaries xiv, xv, 63, 261–2
	threatened strikes by 63, 87
	underpayment of 260–1
	see also women in cricket
politics and cricket 342–3
	Bodyline crisis 165, 168, 171, 180–1
	and ICC policies 369–70
	India & Pakistan 237
	Ireland 142–3

left-wing supporters 18
Pakistan 272–4, 283
post-Second World War 208–9
Second World War 193–4
South Africa 102–4, 107, 109
West Indies 222
Zimbabwe 104–6, 342–3
see also apartheid
Pollard, Marjorie 50, 161–2, 215
Pollock, Graeme 240, 265, 308n
Pollock, Peter 240, 308n
Ponsford, Bill 166
Poore, Major 'Bertie' 105
Porbandar, Maharaja of 187
postal service and cricket 28
Prabhakar, Manoj 299, 301
Prasanna, Erapalli 279
Priestley, J. B. 68
Prince, Ashwell 315
private equity & franchises 361–4, 376, 377–8, 379
Procter, Mike 240, 260, 309
Professional Cricketers' Association 261, 267
professional players xiv–xv, xviii
	19th century 34–5
	21st century 323, 354
	and amateurs 15–16, 29, 34–5, 41–2, 43, 63
	and commercialisation 252–3
	impact of IPL on 354
	improved conditions 261–2
	interwar years 157–9
	MCC conditions and sanctions 58, 62
	New Zealand 323
	post-Second World War 203
	salaries 261–2
	stigma against 41–2
	tension with amateurs 68, 87
	touring teams in the 19th century 26–9
	West Indies 322
protective gear/clothing 23
public domain and cricket 30
public schools and cricket 31–5, 314, 357–8
	19th century 20, 21, 57
	employed professionals as coaches 34–5
	Eton v Harrow at Lord's 20, 21
	feeds players to county cricket late 19th century 57
	girls public schools 48–9
	marketing value of cricket 33–4
	moral and physical benefits of cricket 32–3, 34
Puritanism 6, 9, 33, 45–6

Q

Qadir, Abdul 282
Quadrangular tournament 112, 153, 187–8
Quaid e Azam League 311

R

racism and cricket 307–9
    Australia 178, 314, 321
    England 236, 287–8, 307–8, 309–14
    ICC 107–8
    Second World War 200
    segregation 73
    South Africa 100–1, 239–47, 276–7, 315–16
    USA 127–8
    West Indies 119, 120–2, 219–20, 222
    women's cricket 326
    see also apartheid
radio and cricket 166, 168, 252
Rae, Allan 285
Rafiq, Azeem 311–12
railways and cricket: in Argentina 136
    in Australia 88
    in Canada 128–30
    in England 25, 27–8, 31, 40
Rajasthan Royals xiv–xv, 350, 351
Ramadhin, Sonny 119, 208, 220–1, 225, 227
Rana, Shakoor 236, 309
Ranatunga, Arjuna 116, 270–1, 297
Ranjitsinhji, K. S. 55, 62, 65, 69–70, 76, 144
Rathore, Kunal Singh xv
Reid, John 129n, 213
religion and cricket 6, 7–8, 9, 32–3, 45–6
Rhodes, Cecil 100–1, 103, 104, 105, 106
Rhodes, Wilfred 38, 61, 65, 167, 375
Rhodesia see Zimbabwe
Rice, Clive 277
Richards, Viv 280, 285, 286
Richardson, Vic 182
Ridsdale, Lucy 48
Roach, Kemar 322
Robertson, Austin 264
Robinson, Robert 23
rollers 24
Root, Fred 153, 159, 172
Root, Joe 369
Roro, Frank 245
Rosenwater, Irving 265
Rumsey, Fred 261
Russia 370

S

Samoa 97–8
Samuels, Marlon 303
Sangakkara, Kumar 272, 301
schools 312–14
    state schools 162, 313, 314
    see also public schools
Schwarz, Reggie 106–7
scoring, historical development 3, 19
Scotland 18, 27, 333
Scullin, James 169, 170
Second World War xvii, 191–201
Sellers, Brian 158
Shackleton, Derek 204, 230
Shah, Jay 370
Shah, Niranjan 347–8
Shaw, Alfred 43, 63, 95
Sheffield Shield (Australia) 78, 79, 88, 166, 192, 230, 259
Sheppard, David 205, 211, 239, 244, 246
short-form cricket xvii, xviii
    20-over competition 347
    effects on play 352–4
    history of 44, 65
    impact of TV on 253
    influence of Kerry Packer 267
    international 258
    T20: xiv–xv, 258n, 347, 349–52
    see also one-day cricket
Shrewsbury, Arthur 43, 63, 66, 95
Shrubsole, Anya 327
Singh, Amar 157
Singh, Bhupinder 114, 187
Singh, Yuvraj 348
Small, John 17
Smith, Aubrey 102, 108
Smith, Collie 208, 225, 236
Smith, George 15, 46
Smith, Graeme 315
Smith, Jamie 375
Smith, M. J. K. 246, 263
Smith, Sydney 121n
Snow, John 274
Snowball, Betty 162
Sobers, Garry 119, 144, 207–8, 223–4, 225, 227, 229, 230, 236, 259, 260, 265, 270, 286, 308n
social class 15–16, 17–18, 25, 29–30, 46, 161, 310–11, 312–14, 321, 326
social media, impact of 253
Solkar, Eknath 279
Solomon, Joe 227, 228, 229n

South Africa
  21st century 360
  Anglo-Boer War 106–8
  apartheid 239–47, 260, 276–7, 308–9
  and Basil D'Oliveira 241–5
  boycotts of 241–5
  cricket exported to 73
  export of cricket to 72, 99–104
  and First World War 153
  founding member of the ICC 107–8
  gold rush 102–3
  impact of Empire on 102–4
  indigenous people and cricket 76
  membership of ICC 188–9
  post-Second World War 239
  racism 99, 100, 102–3, 107, 185, 241, 243n
  and racism 315–16
  and Second World War 192
  Union of South Africa (1910) 99, 100
South African Cricket Association 107
South African cricket team: betting & corruption 298–9
  first-class cricket status 59
  and the googly 39n
  interwar years 189
  post-Second World War 239
  v Australia 88–9, 240
  v Australia 1902: 88–9
  v England 101–4, 106–7, 108–9, 239, 286
  v New Zealand 213–14
South Pacific, export of cricket to 96–8
Speed, Malcolm 329, 330–1, 339, 343
Spencer, Herbert 32–3
Spofforth, Fred 80, 84, 85, 126
Spooner, Reggie 67
spot-fixing 11–12, 295–7
  English cricket team 301–2
  Indian cricket team 298–9, 300–1
  Pakistan cricket team 297–300
  South African cricket team 298–9
Sri Lanka 73, 115–16, 270
  21st century 360
  betting & corruption 297, 301
  indigenous peoples 115–16, 271–2
  joins the ICC 269, 270
  and Second World War 193
  World Cup 1993: 271–2
Sri Lanka cricket team: and Arjuna Ranatunga 270–1
  v Australia 271, 287, 297
  v England 116, 272
  v New Zealand 272

St Lucia 9, 19
Staffordshire County Cricket Club 66
Stanford, Allen 322, 352
Starc, Mitchell xv, 326
Statham, Brian 210, 223
Stephenson, H. H. 34, 79
Stevens, Lumpy 11, 16, 17
Stoddart, A. E. 68, 89
Stokes, Ben 39, 322
Stollmeyer, Jeff 222, 224
Stonyhurst College 6
Strauss, Sir Andrew 377–8
Strudwick, Herbert 375
Suez Canal 83, 84n, 116
Surrey County Cricket Club 55–6, 58, 59, 63, 151–2
Surrey Cup 61
Sussex County Cricket Club 58, 59
Sutcliffe, Herbert 167, 179, 196, 213–14, 375
Swanton, E. W. 179, 372
Swanton, Jim 198

T
T20: xviii, 258n, 347, 352–4, 360–1, 365–6
  Australia 320, 351
  Bangladesh 351
  England 347
  India 349–52
  Pakistan 351
  West Indies 351
  and women's cricket 351
  see also Indian Premier League
Tarapore, Keki 278–9
Tarrant, Frank 67
Tasmania 78
Tate, Maurice 167, 173
Tayfield, Hugh 214, 240
Taylor, Bob 267
Taylor, Claire 325
Taylor, Herbie 189
Taylor, Ross 324
technological developments 295–7, 353–4
  see also radio; television
television xiii, 251–6, 262, 263–4, 267–8, 319, 335
  England 258–9, 267, 288, 319
  global reach of cricket 359
  India 281, 348–51
  one-day cricket 252, 254, 258–9, 267
  Pakistan 282–3

Tennyson, Lionel 158
Test and County Cricket Board (TCCB)
   and first-class cricket 262
   and Kerry Packer 264, 265–6
   and the Professional Cricketers'
      Association 261
   and racism 309–10
   and tobacco sponsorship 256–7
   see also England and Wales Cricket
      Board
Test cricket 62
   expansion of 185–6, 269–83
   first use of the term 79
   ICC definition of 108
   impact of T20: 365–6
   impact of TV on xiii, 252
   one-day matches 289–91
   post-Second World War 208
   women's matches 365
   see also international cricket; The Ashes
Thai women's cricket team 325
Thomas, Faith 214
Thomas, Jimmy 170, 180–1
tobacco industry 254–8
Tolsi, Niren 315–16
Tonga 97
Trent Bridge 25–6
Trevelyan, G. M. 17–18
Triangular Tournament 90, 112, 188
Trinidad 118, 119, 120
Trueman, Fred 210, 212, 234, 235n, 265
Trumper, Victor 66, 67, 83, 89, 90, 95, 178
Tsolekile, Thami 315
Tyson, Frank 210–11

U
Uffenbach, Zacharias von 11
Ukraine 370
umpires 14, 209
United All-England Eleven 29
United Arab Emirates (UAE) 283, 333, 334, 351
Uruguay 133, 134–5
USA 9, 19, 123–8, 340–1
   absence from the ICC 108
   amateur nature of cricket 125
   baseball's rise and cricket's decline 124–5, 127, 141
   English influence on cricket 125
   Philadelphia 125–7

   racism 127–8, 195
   Second World War 195
USA Cricket Association (USACA) 341

V
Valentine, Alf 220–1, 225, 227, 228, 229, 236
Vansittart, Frederick 113
Venkataraghavan, Srinivasaraghavan 279, 280
Verity, Hedley 173, 174, 177, 181, 192, 199, 210
Vettori, Daniel 278, 324
Victoria, Queen 39, 41n, 43, 72, 89
Viswanath, Gundappa 279
Voce, Bill 173, 196, 203
Vorster, John 244, 308

W
Wadekar, Ajit 279
Waite, John 247
Walcott, Clyde 199, 219–20, 225, 269, 329
Wales 18–19, 27, 156
Walker, Tom 16, 17, 21–2
Walsh, Courtney 285, 286, 332
Wanostrocht, Nicholas 23
Warne, Shane 271, 289–90, 298, 350–1
Warner, Aucher 121
Warner, Pelham 'Plum' 68, 83, 86, 89, 100, 106, 121, 132, 137, 154, 159, 171, 173, 176, 180, 181, 192, 193, 194, 200, 371
Warwickshire County Cricket Club 58, 378–9
Washington, George 123
Waugh, Mark 298
Waugh, Thomas 33
Waymark, Thomas 12–13
Weekes, Everton 199, 219–20, 225, 367n
Wellington, Duke of 19, 140
Wellington, NZ 93–4, 95
West Indies 9, 19, 73, 117–22
   21st century 322, 360
   first-class cricket 120
   indigenous people and cricket 117–18
   racism 119, 120–2, 222
   Second World War 192, 193n
   Test cricket 185–6
West Indies cricket team xiii, 285–6, 322
   and apartheid 242
   post-Second World War 219–31
   v Australia 221–2, 227–30, 286

West Indies cricket team (continued)
   v England 181, 192, 220–1, 222–3, 225–6, 230–1, 286, 287, 352
   v India 220, 230, 279
   v Ireland 144
   v New Zealand 213
   v Pakistan 236
   v Philadelphia 126
Westfield, Mervyn 303
Wharton, Alan 246
Whatmore, Dav 275
White, Thomas 17
White Conduit Club 15, 46
White Heather Club 48
wickets 17, 263, 367
Wildblood, Andrew 350
Willes, Christiana 22
Willes, John 22
Willis, Bob 286, 287
Wills, Thomas Wentworth 80–1, 96,
Willsher, Edgar 126
Wilson, Betty 214
Wisden, John 27, 28, 29
Wisden Cricketers' Almanack 28, 109, 141, 152–3, 157, 159, 174, 198, 208, 287, 310, 367–8, 370
women in cricket 4, 45–51, 161–4, 312–14
   18th century 46
   19th century 47–50
   20th century 50–1, 161–4, 214–15, 288–9
   21st century 324–7
   Afghanistan 338–9, 370
   Argentina 135
   attitudes towards 47–8
   Australia 163–4, 320, 326–7
   China 340n
   county cricket 47
   England 161–3, 325–6
   equipment 49, 161
   first recorded matches 45–6
   first-class cricket 60
   girls public schools 48–9, 215
   higher education opportunities 50–1
   impact of T20: 365
   impact of TV 253
   Ireland 147, 332–3
   league cricket 163
   Married v Single Women of Upham 46
   Netherlands 164
   'New Women' of the 19th century 50–1
   New Zealand 164
   obstacles to 161–2
   Oxbridge universities 57
   Second World War 191, 195
   and social class 46, 50–1, 161, 163, 215
   T20: 351
   teacher training opportunities 50
   and television 324–5
   under-represented in administration 325
   workplace teams 163
Women's Cricket Association 161, 162, 288–9
Women's Cricket Southern League 325–6
Woodfull, Bill 174–5, 176, 177–8
Woods, 'Float' 121
Woolf, Lord Harry 344–6
Wooller, Wilf 156, 204
Woolley, Frank 38, 65, 67, 154, 155, 196
Woolmer, Bob 146, 286, 331–2
Worcestershire County Cricket Club 58, 156n, 206, 367
World Cup
   1975: 258, 260, 264
   1983: 295, 349
   1987: 259, 269
   1992: 259, 269
   1993: 271–2
   1996: 269, 275n, 329
   1999: 330
   2003: 275n, 342–3
   2007: 275–6, 331–2, 348
   2011: 146, 348
   2015: 276
World Cup (women's) 327
World Test Championship 147, 316, 323, 346, 355, 365–6
Worrell, Frank 199, 208, 219, 225–31, 242
Wyatt, Bob 173, 176n

Y

Yorkshire County Cricket Club 58, 59, 154, 155, 156n, 158, 192, 261, 311–2, 364
Youth Cricket Association 207

Z

Zimbabwe 104–6, 275, 277n, 298, 337, 342–3, 360
Zondo, Khaya 315